FISHING
THE CANADIAN ROCKIES

an angler's guide to every lake, river and stream

Disclaimer

This book was originally published in 2001. Much has changed in the waters of the Canadian Rockies since this time. Some lakes now have no fish, some lakes have been stocked with new species and provincial and parks fishing regulations have changed dramatically. Please check your local fishing guidelines for current information.

The new and updated 2020 version of this title is also available from HancockHouse.com

JOEY AMBROSI

ISBN-13: 978-0-88839-900-7 [trade paperback]
ISBN-13: 978-0-88839-424-8 [epub]
Copyright © 2001 Joseph Ambrosi

Library and Archives Canada Cataloguing in Publication

Title: Fishing the Canadian Rockies : an angler's guide to every lake, river and stream / Joey Ambrosi.
Names: Ambrosi, Joey, author.
Description: Includes index. | Originally published: Blairmore, Alta. : Assiniboine Productions, ©2001.
Identifiers: Canadiana (print) 20190207124 | Canadiana (ebook) 20190207132 | ISBN 9780888399007 (trade paperback) | ISBN 9780888394248 (epub)
Subjects: LCSH: Fishing—Canadian Rockies (B.C. and Alta.)—Guidebooks. | LCSH: Canadian Rockies (B.C. and Alta.)—Guidebooks. | LCGFT: Guidebooks.
Classification: LCC SH572.A4 A62 2019 | DDC 799.1/109711—dc23

All rights reserved. No part of this publication may be reproduced, stored in a retrieval system or transmitted, in any form or by any means, electronic, mechanical, audio, photocopying, recording, or otherwise (except for copying permitted by Sections 107 and 108 of the U.S. Copyright Law and except for book reviews for the public press), without the prior written permission of Hancock House Publishers. Permissions and licensing contribute to the book industry by helping to support writers and publishers through the purchase of authorized editions and exerpts. Please visit www.accesscopyright.ca.

Illustrations and photographs are copyrighted by the artist or the Publisher.

Originally published by Assiniboine Productions, 2001.

Printed in the United States

Cover Photo by M. Lamont in Waterton Lakes National Park
Inside Cover Photo: Wayne Pierce at Lower Fish Lake (Louise Region/Hector Sub-Region)
Page 11: Author with son, Tyler, at Wall Lake (Flathead Region/Akamina-Kishinena Sub-Region)
Page 231: Author's mother, Eileen Tyler (Ambrosi) at Sunburst Lake (Palliser Region/Assiniboine Sub-Region), 1944

We acknowledge the financial support of the Government of Canada through the Canada Book Fund and the Canada Council for the Arts, and of the Province of British Columbia through the British Columbia Arts Council and the Book Publishing Tax Credit.

Hancock House gratefully acknowledges the Semiahmoo, Kwantlen, Katzie and Lummi First Nations, whose unceded traditional territories our offices reside upon.

Published simultaneously in Canada and the United States by
HANCOCK HOUSE PUBLISHERS LTD.
19313 Zero Avenue, Surrey, B.C. Canada V3Z 9R9
(604) 538-1114   Fax (604) 538-2262
HANCOCK HOUSE PUBLISHERS
#104-4550 Birch Bay-Lynden Rd, Blaine, WA, U.S.A. 98230-9436
(800) 938-1114   Fax (800) 983-2262
www.hancockhouse.com   sales@hancockhouse.com

Table of Contents

Foreword 4
Acknowledgements 5
Dedication 6
Introduction 7
Canadian Rockies Classics 13
Waterton Region 25
    Prince of Wales Sub-Region 25
    Tamarack Sub-Region 28
    Mountain View Sub-Region 32
Flathead Region 36
    Akamina-Kishinena Sub-Region 36
    Upper Flathead Sub-Region 38
Koocanusa Region 42
    Elko Sub-Region 42
    Jaffray Sub-Region 46
    Wardner Sub-Region 49
    Fort Steele Sub-Region 52
West Castle Region 58
    Beaver Mines Sub-Region 58
    Pincher Sub-Region 63
Crowsnest Region 67
    Coleman Sub-Region 67
    Bellevue Sub-Region 70
Fernie Region 73
    Hosmer Sub-Region 73
    Sparwood Sub-Region 74
    Corbin Sub-Region 77
Skookumchuck Region 80
    Wasa Sub-Region 80
    Premier Sub-Region 82
Elkford Region 86
    Fording Sub-Region 86
    Elk Lakes Park Sub-Region 88
Livingstone Region 92
    Oldman Sub-Region 92
    Highwood Sub-Region 94
Foothills Region 99
    Chain Lakes Sub-Region 99
    Lower Elbow Sub-Region 101
    Sibbald Sub-Region 102
Kananaskis Region 105
    Lougheed Park Sub-Region 105
    Upper Elbow Sub-Region 108
    Barrier Sub-Region 110
Canal Flats Region 115
    Whitetail Sub-Region 115
    Whiteswan Sub-Region 119
Palliser Region 122
    Height of the Rockies Sub-Region 122
    Assiniboine Sub-Region 125

Invermere Region 128
    Windermere Sub-Region 128
    Westside Sub-Region 130
Columbia Region 133
    Brisco Sub-Region 133
    Parson Sub-Region 138
Kootenay Park Region 143
    Upper Kootenay Sub-Region 143
    Vermilion Sub-Region 146
Canmore Region 148
    Three Sisters Sub-Region 148
    Smith-Dorrien Sub-Region 151
    Marvel Sub-Region 154
Banff Region 157
    Minnewanka Sub-Region 157
    Cascade Sub-Region 160
    Sunshine Sub-Region 163
    Egypt Sub-Region 166
Louise Region 170
    Castle Junction Sub-Region 170
    Temple Sub-Region 174
    Hector Sub-Region 178
Skoki Region 183
    Baker Sub-Region 183
    Front Ranges Sub-Region 186
Yoho Park Region 190
    O'Hara Sub-Region 190
    Emerald Sub-Region 192
    Kicking Horse Sub-Region 194
North Saskatchewan Region 197
    Mistaya Sub-Region 197
    Saskatchewan Crossing Sub-Region 199
    Abraham Sub-Region 202
Icefields Region 206
    Upper Athabasca Sub-Region 206
    Brazeau Sub-Region 209
    Tonquin Sub-Region 211
Jasper Region 214
    Miette Sub-Region 214
    Skyline Sub-Region 217
    Maligne Sub-Region 221
Robson Region 224
    Yellowhead Sub-Region 224
    North Boundary Sub-Region 227

Index 231
About the Author 239

Foreword

I was born in Invermere, B.C., in the heart of the Canadian Rockies, and, thanks to my parents, have been an avid angler since I could hold a rod. Fly fishing has been a passion since I was ten. Somewhat by chance and somewhat by design, fishing and hiking trips over the years took me to all corners of the Rockies. By 1986, I had amassed enough information to put together *Fly Fishing the Canadian Rockies*, which was published by Rocky Mountain Books in 1987. In the years since the publication of *Fly Fishing the Canadian Rockies*, I have covered a lot of waters new to me, as well as revisiting old favourites. Although fishing "research" never really ends, I felt that I had accumulated enough new information to put together a revised, comprehensive guidebook on the lakes, rivers and streams of the Rocky Mountains. My goal has been to accurately describe as many bodies of waters in the Canadian Rockies as possible, and to include maps to each and every body of water. One of my personal peeves is fishing articles that do not describe, or only vaguely describe, where a "hot spot" is. In this book, no "secret lakes" have been excluded, and every body of water described can be found on a map in the book. A substantial number of photographs have been included in *Fishing the Canadian Rockies*. Being a visual person myself, I have always been intrigued by photos of places I have never been, and I also enjoy reminiscing over photos of places that I have been. *Fishing the Canadian Rockies* was assembled as a labour of love, and it is my sincere hope that this book opens the world of fishing to newcomers, and broadens the horizons of those already "hooked".

Joey Ambrosi

Crowsnest Pass, Alberta
March, 2001

Author's mother, Eileen Ambrosi

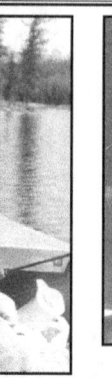

Author's father, Luigi Ambrosi (1926-1992)

Author's son, Tyler Ambrosi

Author's uncle, Graham Tyler (1927-1996)

Don Shandrowsky

Henry Lim (1926-1994)

Kazumasa Suzuki

George Kolibas

Dorgam Hideib

Jody Gilbert

Alfie Tome

Teresa Hemphill and Tyler Ambrosi

Ryan Ponto

Rob Reid and Tyler Ambrosi

Acknowledgements

A project of this magnitude could not have been completed without assistance from others. Jim Rennels of Calgary is extremely resourceful, and gave generously of his time, knowledge and great photographs to improve this book. A very sincere thanks goes to those who searched through their photo archives in order to help with photographs: Laird Seimens and staff at the Kootenay Trout Hatchery at Bull River; Vic Bergman of the Crowsnest Angler in Bellevue; Allan Brice of Alberta Fly Fishing Adventures in Coleman; Janice Strong of Mountain Footsteps in Cranbrook; Mike Furfaro of Fortress Lake Lodge; Robin Campbell and Mike Merilovich at On Line Sports in Jasper; Ward Hughson and Matt Garnett from the warden staff of Jasper National Park; and the Friends of the Frank Slide Centre Society. Others supplied me with photographs of their favourite waters or their big catch. In particular, thanks go to Bryan and Nathan Bond, Lorenda Jahoda, Mas Kimoto, Armando Morotoli, Yutaka Awamura, Kazuhiko Fukawa and Ken Mason. Many of the aforementioned also provided me with updated fishing information on waters. Thank you to Sheila Juhlin for proof reading the manuscript.

To me, spending time with friends is what fishing is all about, and I would like to acknowledge all of those who I have spent time with in the outdoors. Special mention goes to regular fishing partners of recent years: Don Shandrowsky, Ryan Ponto, Rob Reid, Dorgam Hideib, Jody Gilbert, Teresa Hemphill, George Kolibas and Alfie Tome (my personal Kitimat guide). My work as an Outdoor Education instructor at the Nippon Institute of Technology Inter-Cultural Campus in Blairmore, Alberta, has afforded me the wonderful opportunity to take Japanese students into the world of the Rocky Mountains. Their love of the mountains and of fishing continually rekindles my spirit. Many of the students matured into excellent anglers, most notably Kazumasa Suzuki, but also including Daisuke Negishi, Mashi Ikeda, and Sohei Yamane.

Most notably, I could not have completed this project without the loving support of my family: my wife, Valerie; and my #1 fishing buddy: my son, Tyler.

This book is dedicated to my mother, **Eileen Ambrosi**.
Through her own fondness of nature, she taught me to appreciate and
respect the outdoors. I will always be grateful for her support and love.

This book is also dedicated to the memory of **Elizabeth Drury**:
friend and fellow lover of the Canadian Rockies.

May your eternal hike be to the accompaniment of wildflowers and waterfalls.

INTRODUCTION

Fishing the Canadian Rockies is a comprehensive guidebook to the lakes, rivers and streams of the Rocky Mountains that straddle the British Columbia-Alberta border. This extends from the U.S. border in the south, through Mt. Robson Provincial Park and Jasper National Park in the north. Virtually every lake or stream of any consequence in the Canadian Rockies is described within this book.

Regions

The area covered by *Fishing the Canadian Rockies* is divided into 25 geographical Regions. Each chapter in the book covers one of the 25 Regions. All Regions have been further subdivided into geographical Sub-Regions.

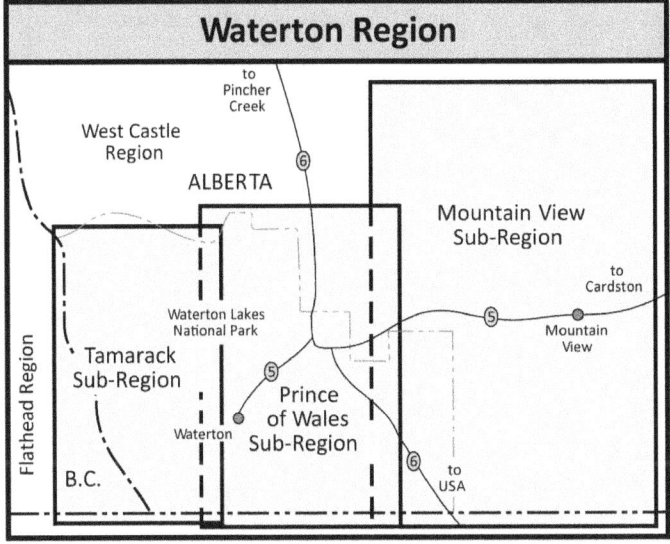

Maps

Each Region and Sub-Region has a map, and every body of water described in the text can be found on a map. The Region maps identify the location of the corresponding Sub-Regions. The Sub-Region maps are more detailed, but are for general orientation only, and it is strongly recommended that topographic maps be used for any backcountry use. Topographic maps in a variety of scales can be purchased at many sporting goods stores or retail book outlets.

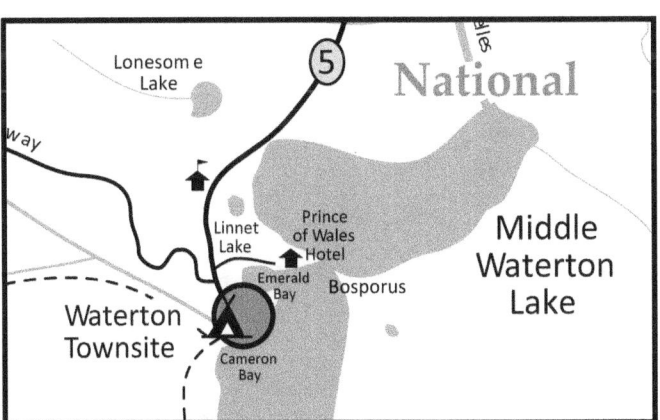

Names

The official name, or most common name, for a body of water is given, plus any alternate or local name.

Norbury (Garbutts) Lake

Fishing Licenses

Three separate jurisdictions cover the waters described in *Fishing the Canadian Rockies*. These are the Province of British Columbia (BC); the Province of Alberta (AB); and the Government of Canada in the National Parks (NP). Each jurisdiction requires a separate license, and each jurisdiction has a different set of angling regulations. In the text, following the name of the body of water, the abbreviation for the appropriate jurisdiction is given (BC, AB or NP). Individual anglers must be aware of the regulations in effect on the body of water in which they are fishing. *Regulations change each year*, and anglers must be aware of the changes. **This book is not a substitute for the regulations! Check the regulations before you go fishing!**

Fish

Fishing the Canadian Rockies identifies the game fish that inhabit a particular body of water. The size and weight given for each species is for larger specimens that one would expect to catch in that body of water. The average size of individuals caught will be less than the stated sizes. *Species recognition by anglers is essential. All angling regulations are based in some manner on species identification.* The Regulation Synopses provided by all three jurisdictions provide good descriptions and/or illustrations of game fish species. *Fishing the Canadian Rockies* provides an accurate description of fish species present in specific bodies of water at the time of publication. Winter kill, new plantings and fish migration will undoubtedly change the status of many bodies of water over time.

FISHING THE CANADIAN ROCKIES: Introduction

Status
For bodies of water with unique characteristics, there are three status levels. Locations that have been **closed to angling** for a number of years are listed as such in the text. Check the appropriate regulations each year to see if they continue to be closed, and to see if new locations have been closed to angling. **Doubtful** status indicates that fish were present in the body of water at some point in the past. However, recent survey of these lakes indicates that it is unlikely that any fish are still present. Annual restocking programs can change the status of these locations. **Unknown** status indicates that there is no up-to-date information available on a particular body of water.

Description
Each body of water is given a general description in the text, including access and physical characteristics. The expectations in terms of fish species, quantity and size are given, and general angling tactics are provided where applicable.

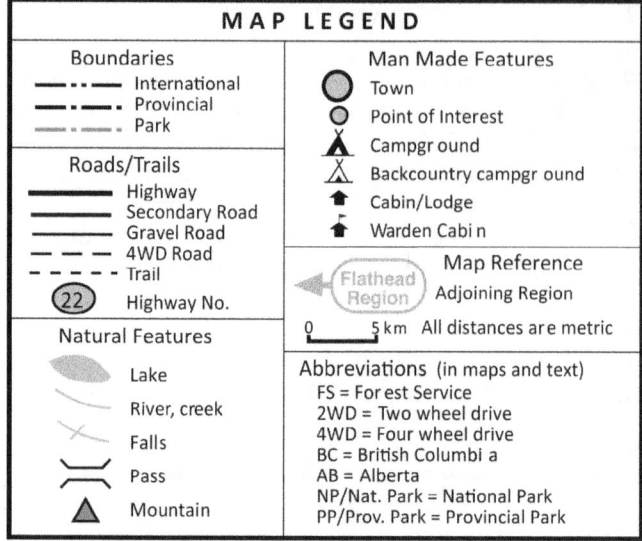

Photographs
Photographs of selected bodies of waters are provided. Photographs of fish caught in selected bodies of water are also provided. The selection of colour photographs entitled *Canadian Rockies Classics* represent a cross-section of some of the more popular or scenic angling destinations in the

Elizabeth Lake (Palliser Region)

Rockies.

Index
The index at the back of *Fishing the Canadian Rockies* lists alphabetically every body of water in the text. Alternate names for bodies of waters are also listed. For locations with similar names, the Region and Sub-Region are identified for clarification.

FISHING THE CANADIAN ROCKIES: Introduction

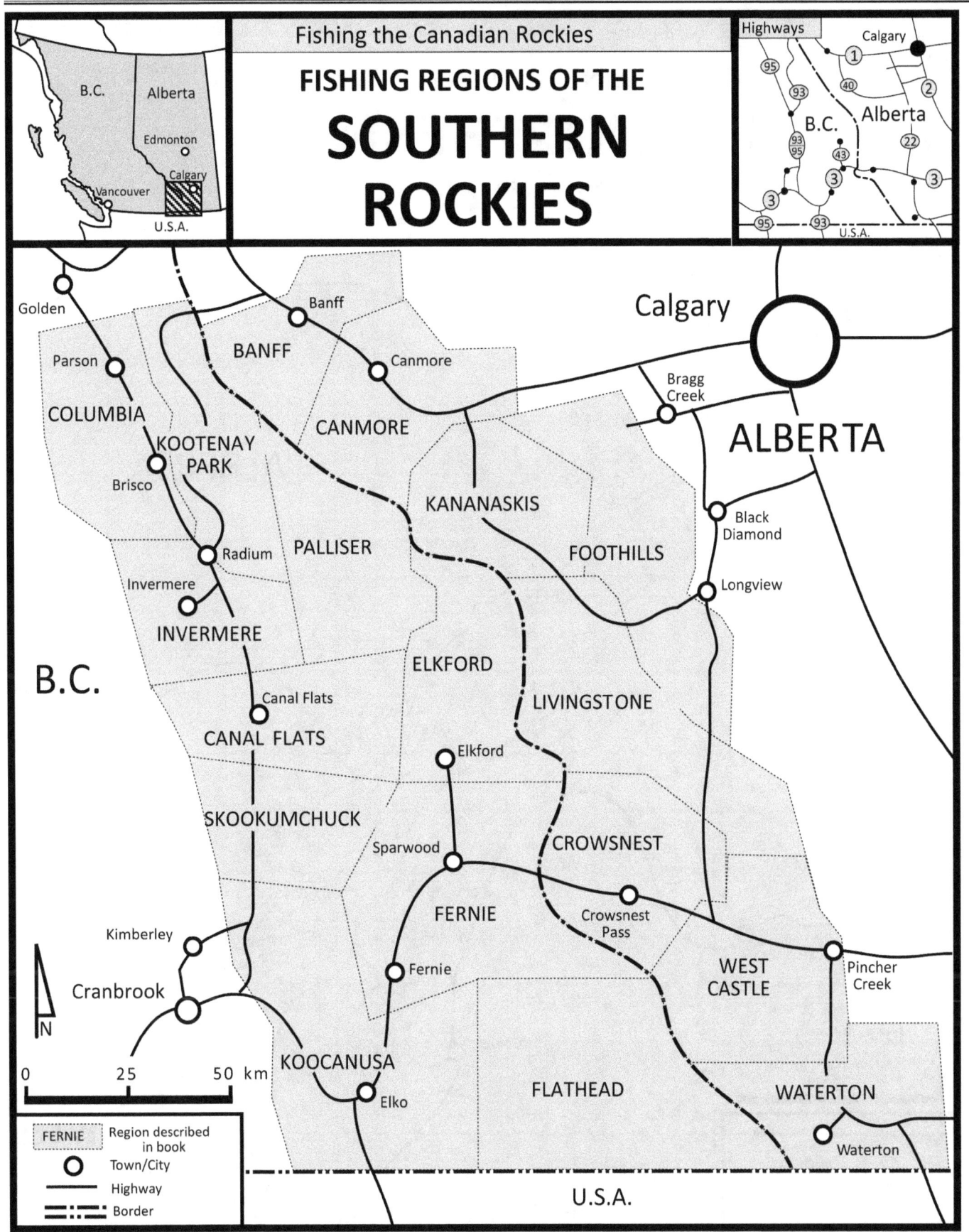

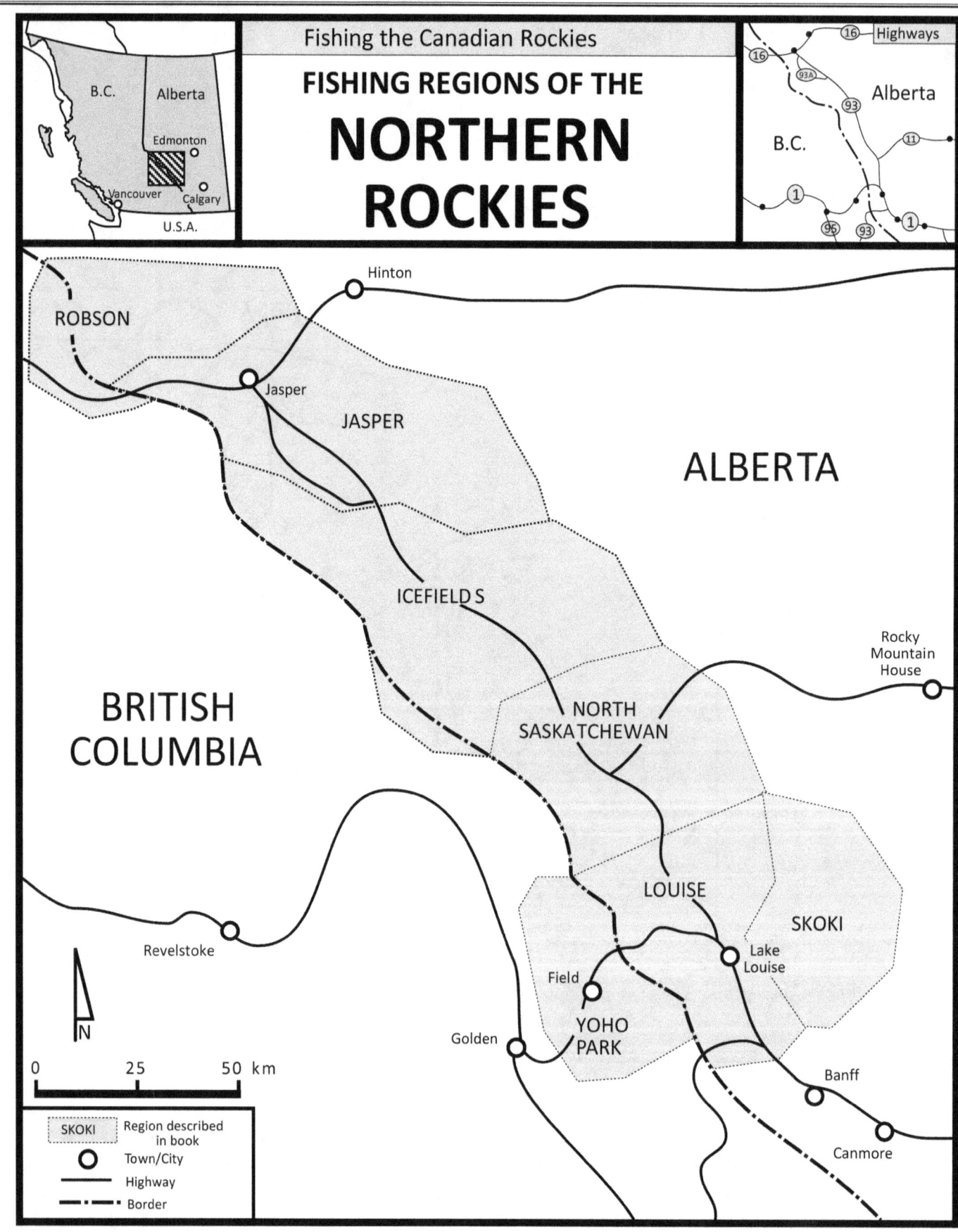

FISHING
The Canadian Rockies

an angler's guide to every lake, river and stream

Give a person a fish, and you feed them for a day.

Teach a person to fish, and you get rid of them every weekend!

FISHING THE CANADIAN ROCKIES: Canadian Rockies Classics

Canadian Rockies Classics

Crypt Lake
(Waterton Region/Prince of Wales Sub-Region)

Payne Lake
(Waterton Region/Mountain View Sub-Region)

Upper Waterton Lake
(Waterton Region/Prince of Wales Sub-Region)

Burl (Middlepass) Lakes
(Flathead Region/Upper Flathead Sub-Region)

Lineham Lakes
(Waterton Region/Tamarack Sub-Region)

Police Outpost Lake
(Waterton Region/Mountain View Sub-Region)

Cherry Lake
(Koocanusa Region/Wardner Sub-Region)

Lund Lake
(Koocanusa Region/Wardner Sub-Region)

Castle River
(Westcastle Region/
Beaver Mines Sub-Region)

Wall Lake
(Flathead Region/Akamina-Kishinena Sub-Region)

Bull River
(Koocanusa Region/Ft. Steele Sub-Region)

FISHING THE CANADIAN ROCKIES: Canadian Rockies Classics

Summer Lake
(Koocanusa Region/Fort Steele Sub-Region)

Procter Lake
(Flathead Region/Upper Flathead Sub-Region)

Bathing Lake
(Westcastle Region/Pincher Sub-Region)

Grizzly Lake
(Westcastle Region/Beaver Mines Sub-Region)

Brook trout
(Grizzly Lake/Westcastle Region)

Rainy Ridge Lake
(Westcastle Region/Beaver Mines Sub-Region)

Bovin Lake
(Westcastle Region/Pincher Sub-Region)

Frozen Lake
(Flathead Region/Upper Flathead Sub-Region)

Upper Southfork Lake
(Westcastle Region/Beaver Mines Sub-Region)

Golden trout
(Rainy Ridge Lake/Westcastle Region)

Southfork Lakes
(Westcastle Region/Beaver Mines Sub-Region)

Silver Spring Lake
(Koocanusa Region/Elko Sub-Region)

Suzanne (Manistee) Lake
(Koocanusa Region/Jaffray Sub-Region)

FISHING THE CANADIAN ROCKIES: Canadian Rockies Classics

Window Mountain Lake
(Crowsnest Region/Coleman Sub-Region)

Crowsnest River
(Crowsnest Region/Bellevue Sub-Region)

Rainbow trout
(Crowsnest River/Crowsnest Region)

Grave Lake
(Fernie Region/Sparwood Sub-Region)

Lee Lake
(Crowsnest Region/Bellevue Sub-Region)

Barnes Lake
(Fernie Region/Corbin Sub-Region)

Norbury (Garbutts) Lake
(Koocanusa Region/Fort Steele Sub-Region)

Yankee Lake
(Skookumchuck Region/Premier Sub-Region)

Cutthroat trout
(Summit Lake/Fernie Region)

Quartz Lake
(Skookumchuck Region/Premier Sub-Region)

Phillipps Lake
(Crowsnest Region/Coleman Sub-Region)

Harriet Lake
(Fernie Region/Sparwood Sub-Region)

FISHING THE CANADIAN ROCKIES: Canadian Rockies Classics

Fish Lake
(Canal Flats Region/Whiteswan Sub-Region)

Engstrom Pond
(Canal Flats Region/Whitetail Sub-Region)

Elk River
(Elkford Region/Elk Lakes Park Sub-Region)

Whitetail Lake
(Canal Flats Region/Whitetail Sub-Region)

Hartley Lake
(Fernie Region/Hosmer Sub-Region)

Cutthroat trout
(Elk River/Elkford Region)

Abruzzi Lake
(Elkford Region/Elk Lakes Park Sub-Region)

Lazy Lake
(Skookumchuck Region/Wasa Sub-Region)

Kaufmann Lake
(Canal Flats Region/Whiteswan Sub-Region)

Cutthroat trout
(Abruzzi Lake/Elkford Region)

Sibbald Lake
(Foothills Region/Sibbald Sub-Region)

Lower Galatea Lake
(Kananaskis Region/Barrier Sub-Region)

Carnarvon Lake
(Livingstone Region/Highwood Sub-Region)

Frozen Lake
(Elkford Region/Elk Lakes Park Sub-Region)

FISHING THE CANADIAN ROCKIES: Canadian Rockies Classics

Upper Elk Lake
(Elkford Region/Elk Lakes Park Sub-Region)

Cutthroat trout
(Picklejar Lakes/Livingstone Region)

Chain Lakes Reservoir
(Foothills Region/Chain Lakes Sub-Region)

Picklejar Lake #4
(Livingstone Region/Highwood Sub-Region)

Spurr Lake
(Canal Flats Region/Whitetail Sub-Region)

Fenwick Lake
(Palliser Region/Height of the Rockies Sub-Region)

Lake of the Horns
(Livingstone Region/Highwood Sub-Region)

Running Rain Lake
(Livingstone Region/Highwood Sub-Region)

Elbow Lake
(Kananaskis Region/Upper Elbow Sub-Region)

Sunburst Lake
(Palliser Region/Assiniboine Sub-Region)

Big Iron Lake
(Foothills Region/Chain Lakes Sub-Region)

Memorial Lakes
(Kananaskis Region/Barrier Sub-Region)

Jim Rennels photo

17

FISHING THE CANADIAN ROCKIES: Canadian Rockies Classics

Rock Lake
(Palliser Region/Assiniboine Sub-Region)

Arctic grayling
(Bear Pond/Foothills Region)

Allen Bill Pond
(Foothills Region/Lower Elbow Sub-Region)

Talus Lake
(Kananaskis Region/Upper Elbow Sub-Region)

Ralph Lake
(Palliser Region/Height of the Rockies Sub-Region)

Diana Lake
(Kootenay Park Region/Upper Kootenay Sub-Region)

Jade Lake
(Columbia Region/Brisco Sub-Region)

Dainard Lake
(Kootenay Park Region/Upper Kootenay Sub-Region)

Lower Connor Lake
(Palliser Region/Height of the Rockies Sub-Region)

Rawson Lake
(Kananaskis Region/Lougheed Park Sub-Region)

Jim Rennels photo

Twin Lakes
(Invermere Region/Windermere Sub-Region)

Magog Lake
(Palliser Region/Assiniboine Sub-Region)

Cutthroat trout
(Og Lake/Palliser Region)

FISHING THE CANADIAN ROCKIES: Canadian Rockies Classics

Mitten Lake
(Columbia Region/Parson Sub-Region)

Sam's Folly Lake
(Invermere Region/Westside Sub-Region)

Lillian Lake
(Invermere Region/Westside Sub-Region)

Dog Lake
(Kootenay Park Region/Upper Kootenay Sub-Region)

Grassi Lakes
(Canmore Region/Three Sisters Sub-Region)

Gloria Lake
(Canmore Region/Marvel Sub-Region)

Upper Halgrave Lake
(Columbia Region/Brisco Sub-Region)

Rocky Point Lake
(Columbia Region/Parson Sub-Region)

Rainbow trout
(Wilbur Lake/Columbia Sub-Region)

Twin Lakes
(Columbia Region/Brisco Sub-Region)

Dunbar Lake
(Columbia Region/Brisco Sub-Region)

Bourgeau Lake
(Banff Region/Sunshine Sub-Region)

Lead Queen Lake
(Columbia Region/Brisco Sub-Region)

Floe Lake
(Kootenay Park Region/Vermilion Sub-Region)

19

FISHING THE CANADIAN ROCKIES: Canadian Rockies Classics

Chief Hector Lake
(Canmore Region/Three Sisters Sub-Region)

Leman Lake
(Canmore Region/Marvel Sub-Region)

Egypt Lake
(Banff Region/Egypt Sub-Region)

Cuthead Lake
(Banff Region/Cascade Sub-Region)

Marvel Lake
(Canmore Region/Marvel Sub-Region)

Elk Lake
(Banff Region/Cascade Sub-Region)

Loon Lake
(Columbia Region/Parson Sub-Region)

Luellen Lake
(Louise Region/Castle Junction Sub-Region)

Scarab Lake
(Banff Region/Egypt Sub-Region)

Smith Lake
(Louise Region/Castle Junction Sub-Region)

Rainbow trout
(Chief Hector Lake/Canmore Region)

Moose Lake
(Louise Region/Hector Sub-Region)

FISHING THE CANADIAN ROCKIES: Canadian Rockies Classics

Healy Lakes
(Banff Region/Egypt Sub-Region)

Rummel Lake
(Canmore Region/Smith-Dorrien Sub-Region)

Rockbound Lake
(Louise Region/Castle Junction Sub-Region)

Jim Rennels photo
Natalko Lake
(Banff Region/Egypt Sub-Region)

Rock Isle Lake
(Banff Region/Sunshine Sub-Region)

Kingfisher Lake
(Louise Region/Temple Sub-Region)

Smuts Creek
(Canmore Region/Smith-Dorrien Sub-Region)

Sawback Lake
(Banff Region/Cascade Sub-Region)

Cutthroat trout
(O'Brien Lake/Louise Region)

Little Herbert Lake
(Louise Region/Temple Sub-Region)

Lake Minnewanka
(Banff Region/Minnewanka Sub-Region)

Moraine Lake
(Louise Region/Temple Sub-Region)

FISHING THE CANADIAN ROCKIES: Canadian Rockies Classics

Taylor Lake
(Louise Region/Castle Junction Sub-Region)

Upper Fish Lake
(Louise Region/Hector Sub-Region)

Merlin Lake
(Skoki Region/Baker Sub-Region)
Jim Rennels photo

Chephren Lake
(North Saskatchewan Region/Mistaya Sub-Region)

Amiskwi River
(Yoho Park Region/Emerald Sub-Region)

Bighorn River
(N. Saskatchewan Region/Abraham Sub-Region)

Emerald Lake photo below:

Baker Lake
(Skoki Region/Baker Sub-Region)

Ptarmigan Lake
(Skoki Region/Baker Sub-Region)

Pinto Lake
(N. Saskatchewan Region/Sask. Crossing Sub-Region)

Linda Lake
(Yoho Park Region/O'Hara Sub-Region)

Brown trout
(Bow River/Canmore Sub-Region)
Alberta Fly Fishing Adventures photo

Emerald Lake
(Yoho Park Region/Emerald Sub-Region)

FISHING THE CANADIAN ROCKIES: Canadian Rockies Classics

Abraham Lake
(North Saskatchewan Region/Abraham Sub-Region)

Helen Lake
(Louise Region/Hector Sub-Region)

Landslide Lake
(North Saskatchewan Region/Abraham Sub-Region)

Margaret and Hector Lakes
(Louise Region/Hector Sub-Region)

Red Deer Lakes
(Skoki Region/Baker Sub-Region)

Lake of the Falls
(North Saskatchewan Region/Abraham Sub-Region)

Isabella Lake
(Louise Region/Hector Sub-Region)

Brazeau Lake
(Icefields Region/Brazeau Sub-Region)

Lower Waterfowl Lake
(North Saskatchewan Region/Mistaya Sub-Region)

Amethyst Lakes
(Icefields Region/Tonquin Sub-Region)

Brazeau River
(Icefields Region/Brazeau Sub-Region)

23

FISHING THE CANADIAN ROCKIES: Canadian Rockies Classics

Berg Lake
(Robson Region/Yellowhead Sub-Region)

Moab Lake
(Icefields Region/Upper Athabasca Sub-Region)

Cavell Lake
(Icefields Region/Tonquin Sub-Region)

Princess Lake
(Robson Region/North Boundary Sub-Region)

Medicine Lake
(Jasper Region/Maligne Sub-Region)

Amethyst Lakes
(Icefields Region/Tonquin Sub-Region)

Medicine Lake
(Jasper Region/Maligne Sub-Region)

Saturday Night Lake
(Jasper Region/Miette Sub-Region)

Moose River
(Robson Region/Yellowhead Sub-Region)

Rainbow trout
(Maligne Lake/Jasper Region)

Robin Campbell photo

Adolphus Lake
(Robson Region/Yellowhead Sub-Region)

Astoria River
(Icefields Region/Tonquin Sub-Region)

Pyramid Lake
(Jasper Region/Skyline Sub-Region)

WATERTON REGION

Each year hundreds of thousands of tourists flock to Waterton Lakes National Park to take in the magnificent scenery. In addition to its scenery, the area in and around the park offers excellent fishing opportunities, with the Waterton Lakes and Waterton Townsite serving as the focal point of the Region. The park itself can be reached from Pincher Creek via Highway 6, from Cardston via Highway 5, and from the United States via the Chief Mountain Highway (Highway 6). The Townsite has a major campground, as well as motels, restaurants, gas stations and a variety of tourist-related stores, including stores selling fishing tackle and offering current fishing information. The Parks Canada Information Centre (opposite the Prince of Wales Hotel turnoff) and the warden office (in the park compound) are located just east of the Townsite on Highway 5. The Region nicely divides into three Sub-Regions, with the Waterton Lakes being the focal point of the central Prince of Wales Sub-Region. The backcountry surrounding the Tamarack Trail is the westernmost Sub-Region. The rolling hills and grasslands around the small community of Mountain View outside the National Park forms the eastern Sub-Region

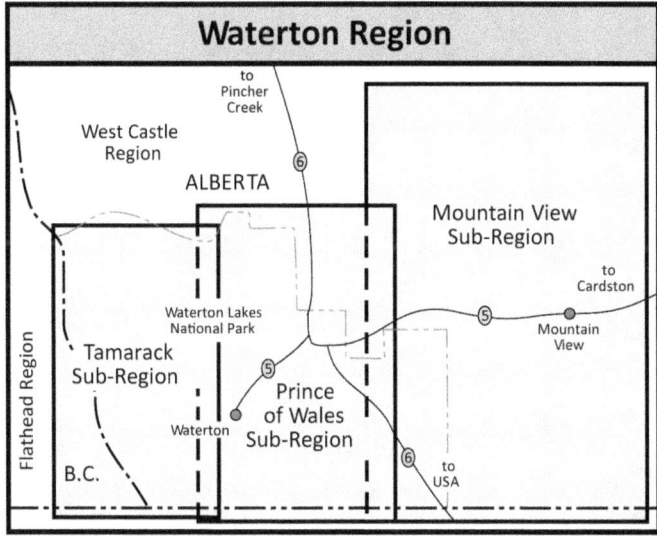

Prince of Wales Sub-Region

All three Waterton Lakes are readily accessible, and are very popular with anglers. Daily boat tours take sightseers down the entire length of Upper Waterton Lake and arrangements can be made with the operators for drop-offs and pick-ups at the Crypt Lake trailhead. From the Townsite, trails branch to Bertha Lake, and to Alderson and Carthew Lakes via the Carthew Trail. Crandell Lake is located at the midway point, by trail, between the Akamina Highway and the Red Rock Canyon Road. The Belly River is noted for its fine stream fishing, and is located in the extreme southeast corner of the park alongside Highway 6.

Waterton Lakes [Upper and Middle] (NP)
Lake trout to 1.2 m (12.0 kg)
Rainbow trout to 65 cm (3.0 kg)
Cutthroat trout to 55 cm (1.5 kg)
Brook trout to 60 cm (2.5 kg)
Bull trout to 75 cm (5.0 kg)
Whitefish to 50 cm (1.5 kg)

The Waterton Lakes are world-renowned for their spectacular beauty, and offer some superb angling for a wide variety of fish. Although the sheer size of the lakes dictate that fishing from a boat will be the most effective method, fishing from shore can be productive from many locations. Areas around the numerous inlet creeks are generally the best waters, with Bertha Bay and Boundary Bay particularly noted for their good fishing. Large lake trout are the main quarry, and they can be caught in sizes upwards of 10 kg. Lake trout are generally caught in the deep waters, by anglers using bait or lures. Whether casting from shore or trolling, rainbow, cutthroat, and brook trout can all be taken from Waterton Lakes. Bull trout, suckers, chub, burbot and the odd northern pike are also taken from the Waterton Lakes. In the fall, whitefish can be taken in good numbers from the Bosporus, the narrow channel that separates the Upper and Middle Waterton Lakes. Boat rentals are available in Waterton Townsite. Be aware that the Waterton Lakes are known for their strong winds that will keep most small craft off the lakes, and will foil any attempts at fly fishing. Boaters and canoeists should pay particular attention to changing weather conditions, as storms can arrive very quickly.

Upper Waterton Lake

Lower Waterton (Knight's) Lake (NP)
Rainbow trout to 45 cm
Cutthroat trout to 45 cm
Brook trout to 45 cm
Whitefish to 50 cm (1.5 kg)
Bull trout to 60 cm (4.0 kg)
Lake trout to 80 cm (6.0 kg)
Northern pike to 70 cm (5.0 kg)

Located two kilometres downstream from the outlet of Middle Waterton Lake, Lower Waterton Lake holds virtually the same variety of fish as the upper two lakes. However, since Lower Waterton Lake is much shallower than either Middle or Upper Waterton Lake, very few lake trout are present, while northern pike are more abundant. The inlet and outlet areas have the best potential for anyone fishing from shore.

WATERTON REGION: Prince of Wales Sub-Region

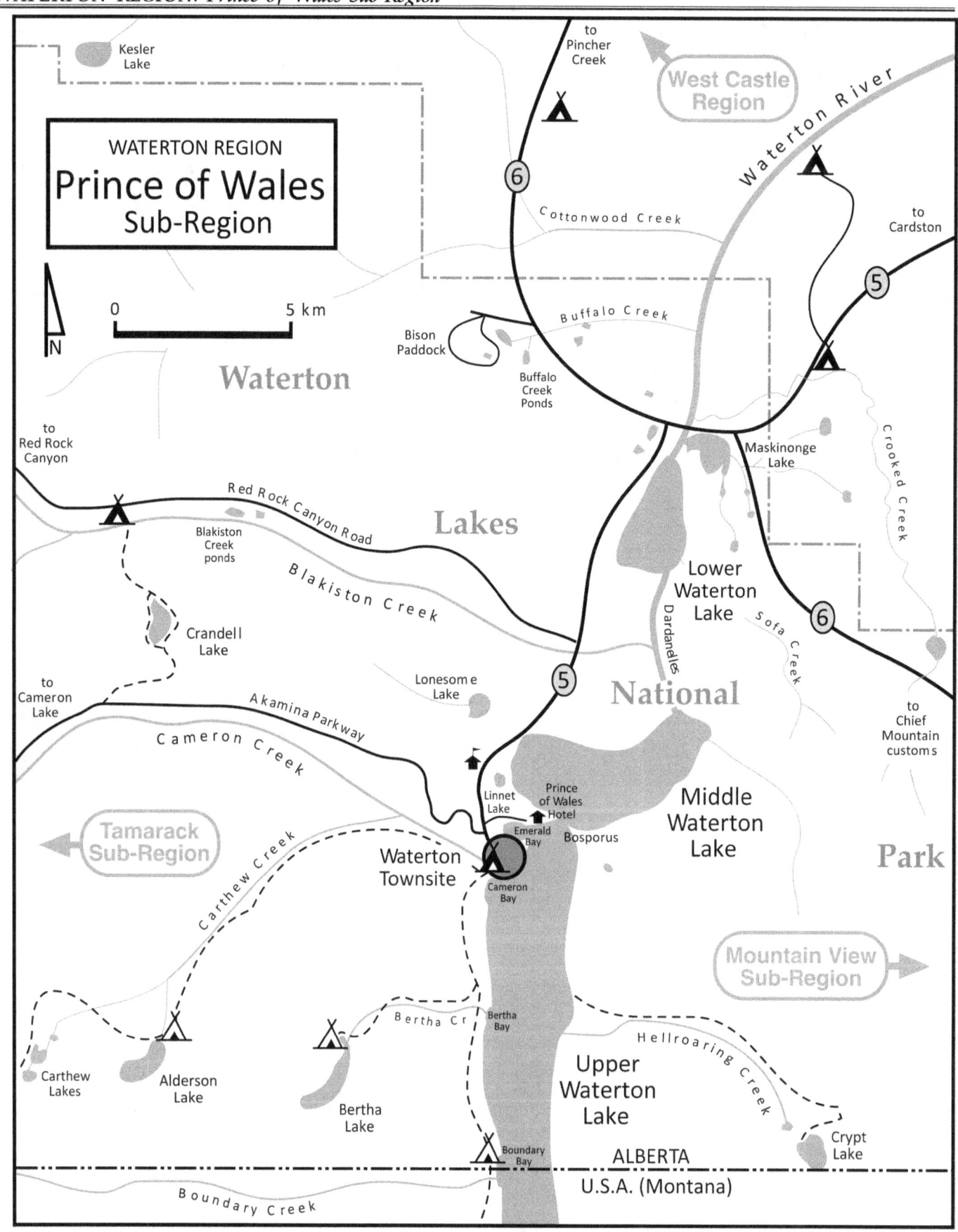

WATERTON REGION: Prince of Wales Sub-Region

Maskinonge Lake (NP)
Northern pike to 80 cm (6.0 kg)
Little more than a large slough, the shallow waters of Maskinonge Lake are seldom more than 1 m deep and hold only northern pike. Pike fishing is best in the early season, and fly fishing for pike has become very popular in recent years. Those with a boat will have an advantage over shore-bound anglers due to the extensive reeds around the lake.

Waterton River (NP)
(Waterton Lakes to National Park boundary)
Rainbow trout to 45 cm
Cutthroat trout to 45 cm
Bull trout to 75 cm (5.0 kg)
Whitefish to 35 cm
The Waterton River offers some fine stretches of fishable water as it flows for a short distance between Middle and Lower Waterton Lakes, and then, further downstream, out of Lower Waterton Lake,. Particularly good for cutthroat and rainbow trout is the two kilometre section between Middle and Lower Waterton Lakes, called the Dardanelles. The odd pike is taken in the river near Maskinonge Lake. In the fall, whitefish are taken regularly from all stretches of the river.

Crypt Lake (NP)
Cutthroat trout to 60 cm (2.5 kg)
A unique 9 km access trail, which includes a boat crossing of Waterton Lake and a crawl through a 20 m long tunnel, leads to a rocky amphitheatre containing Crypt Lake. The lake's emerald green waters hold large numbers of wary cutthroat trout averaging 30-40 cm in length. If the water is not too choppy from wind, fish can be sighted from most locations around the lake. Due to the clarity of the water, however, the fish are spooked easily. Anglers with a little patience are generally rewarded in Crypt. Simply find a promising-looking location and have a seat. Within minutes a school of trout will cruise by. Fly fishing is the most effective tactic, and backcasting space is available along most of the shoreline. Due to its sheltered position, Crypt usually remains frozen into early July, and ice floes dot the lake for the entire summer.

Crypt Lake

(cutthroat trout)

Bertha Lake (NP)
Rainbow trout to 50 cm (1.5 kg)
Nestled in a hanging valley, 6 km from Waterton Townsite by trail, Bertha Lake is very popular with hikers and anglers. Be forewarned that although the length of the trail is not long, it is very steep over the final few kilometres. Bertha's blue waters hold a fair number of rainbow trout, most averaging 25-30 cm in length. Although fly fishing is usually productive, most of Bertha's shoreline has heavy brush, and those spin casting will be able to fish from more locations. The waters around the logjam at the outlet creek invariably hold fish, regardless of the time of year or time of day.

Bertha Lake

Alderson Lake (NP)
Cutthroat trout to 55 cm (2.0 kg)
Alderson Lake sits in a spectacular basin, 8 km from Waterton Townsite along the Carthew Trail. Most hikers bypass Alderson Lake near the end of a long day on their way from Cameron Lake to Waterton Townsite. For those who do make the effort to fish in the beautiful blue waters of Alderson Lake, cutthroat trout averaging 25-35 cm will be the reward. For those fly fishing, roll casting will be necessary from much of the shore, particularly in the deep waters along the scree slopes which form the northwest corner of the lake.

Alderson Lake

Carthew Lakes (NP)
Cutthroat to 50 cm (1.5 kg)
Situated two kilometres beyond and almost 400 vertical metres above Alderson Lake on the Carthew Trail, a windswept alpine basin holds the Carthew Lakes which are comprised of the Upper and Lower Carthew Lakes, plus the diminutive Carthew Pond. Although all three lakes hold cutthroat trout ranging from 20-35 cm., the upper lake at one time contained a few rainbow trout, most of which have now been absorbed into the cutthroat population. The Middle Lake holds the best angling

WATERTON REGION: Prince of Wales Sub-Region

possibilities, particularly in the bay near the outlet stream, and brightly coloured cutthroat trout can be taken from most locations. The alpine surroundings ensure reasonable fly casting room from most locations, although the strong winds that are very common will hamper fly fishing. Due to their lofty elevation, the lakes are usually frozen and access trails are snowbound into early July.

Carthew Lakes

Crandell Lake (NP)
Rainbow trout to 35 cm
Brook trout to 35 cm
Accessible by short hiking trails from both the Akamina Highway and the Red Rock Canyon Road, Crandell Lake's crystal clear waters are a favourite of local anglers, especially in the early season. Both rainbow trout, which predominate, and brook trout are caught from Crandell Lake, most averaging 20-25 cm in length. The open slabs of rock along the northeast shore are the most popular location for angling, although fish can be taken from most locations around the lake.

Crandell Lake

Lonesome Lake (NP)
Status: Devoid of fish
Lonesome Lake is located near the Waterton Golf Course, and at one time contained both rainbow and brook trout, but both species failed to reproduce.

Linnet Lake (NP)
Status: Devoid of fish
Linnet Lake is situated just north of the Waterton Townsite, and was stocked in the past with rainbow, cutthroat and brook trout, all of which failed to take hold. On occasion, when spring flood waters are high enough to connect Linnet Lake and Middle Waterton Lake, a few fish inevitably swim into Linnet and are trapped there when the high water recedes.

Buffalo Creek ponds (NP)
Rainbow trout to 25 cm
Brook trout to 25 cm
This series of beaver dams west of the park gates along Highway 6 contain small rainbow and brook trout. As with most beaver ponds, heavy brush dominates the shoreline and wet feet are a certainty if you want to get a clear cast.

Kesler Lake (NP)
Rainbow trout to 25 cm
Kesler Lake is located along the northern boundary of Waterton Lakes National Park on a tributary of Dungarvan Creek. The shortest access is by ill-defined trail from Yarrow Creek. Seldom fished, Kesler Lake holds rainbow trout in smaller sizes.

Tamarack Sub-Region

This Sub-Region encompasses the western half of Waterton Lakes National Park, and is centred on the 36-km long Tamarack Trail, which leads hikers through some spectacular country from the Akamina Highway to Red Rock Canyon. In addition to the promise of outstanding scenery, the trail passes close to several fine lakes, including Rowe, Lineham, Lone, Twin, and Goat. The Lineham Lakes basin can also be reached via a difficult and dangerous route from the Akamina Highway that includes a 100 m-high cliff. Red Rock Canyon is the northern terminus of the Tamarack Trail, as well as the Blakiston Creek access to Twin Lakes. Cameron Lake, at the western end of the Akamina Highway, is popular with anglers throughout the summer and serves as a starting point for short hikes to Akamina and Summit Lakes. After crossing Akamina Pass into British Columbia, prospective anglers can hike to Wall or Forum Lake in the Flathead Region.

Cameron Lake (NP)
Rainbow trout to 50 cm (1.5 kg)
Brook trout to 50 cm (1.5 kg)
Cameron Lake is set in a large subalpine basin, 15 km from Waterton Townsite along the Akamina Highway, and is one of the more popular fishing spots in Waterton Park. Both rainbow and brook trout are caught regularly, with most fish averaging 25-35 cm in length. Fishing from shore is usually not overly productive due to the size of the lake, although areas around the larger outlet creek and the many small inlet creeks hold fish. Fortunately for the perpetually shore-bound anglers, boat rentals are available. Trolling a fly or lure slowly behind a rowboat generally works well, and requires little skill on the part of the angler. Take note that even though the fishing season at Cameron Lake technically opens on the long weekend in May, the lake itself is often ice-bound well into June.

Cameron Lake

WATERTON REGION: Tamarack Sub-Region

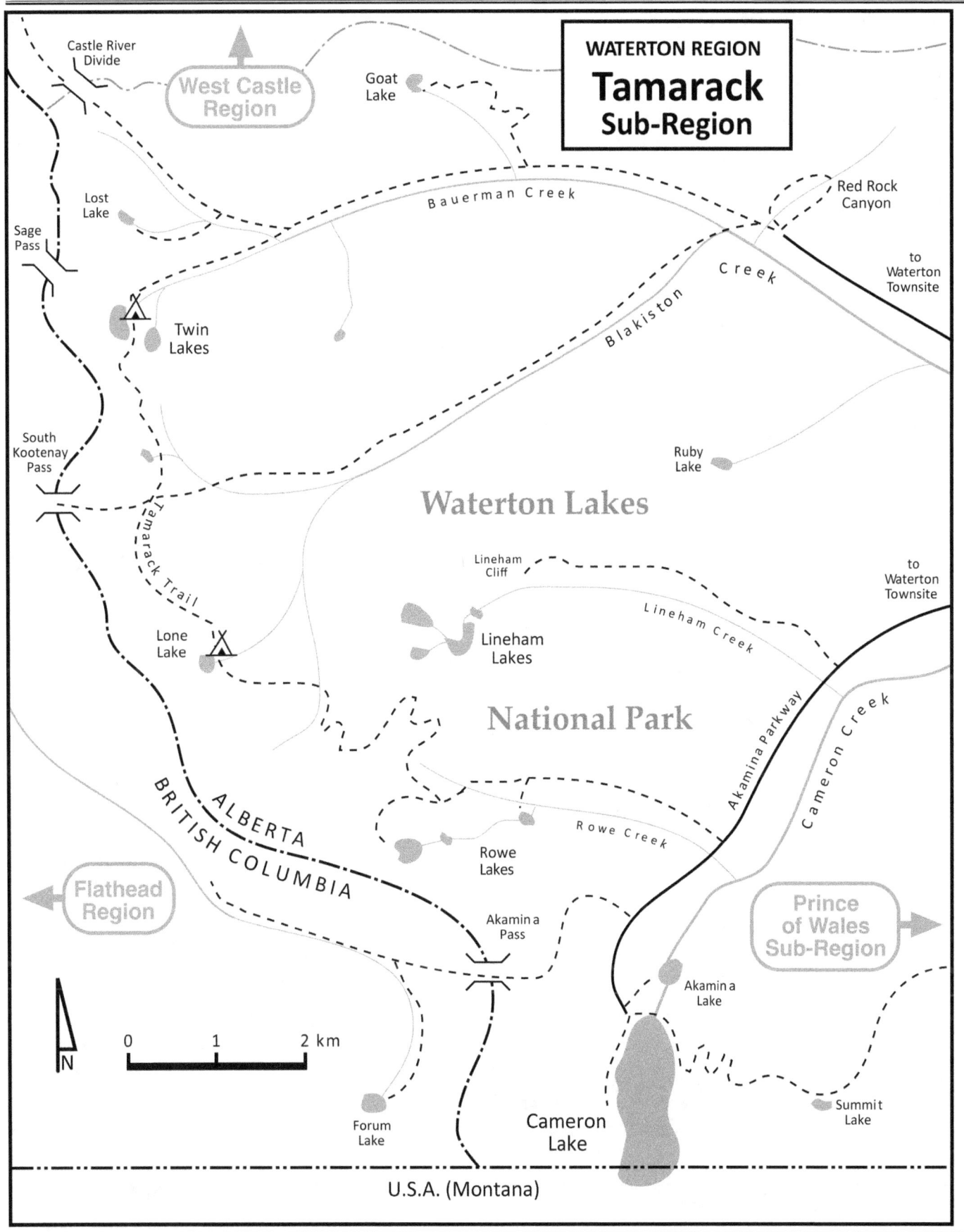

29

WATERTON REGION: Tamarack Sub-Region

Akamina Lake [Little Cameron Lake] (NP)
Rainbow trout to 30 cm
Brook trout to 30 cm

Pretty Akamina Lake sits in a marshy opening in the midst of heavy forest half a kilometre downstream from Cameron Lake. The lake can be reached by a half kilometre trail that begins in the Cameron Lake parking area. Fishing of any kind is difficult in Akamina Lake, as Cameron Creek, which forms both the inlet and outlet stream, must be forded in order to reach fish-holding waters. From the edge of the lake, shallows extend far out from shore, making long casts a necessity.

Akamina Lake

Cameron Creek (NP)
Rainbow trout to 25 cm
Brook trout to 25 cm

Cameron Creek, which parallels the Akamina Highway, flows for approximately 16 km from the outlet of Cameron Lake to Waterton Lake. Accessible from the highway, the many pools along Cameron Creek's tumbling route hold small rainbow and brook trout. Take extreme caution if you are planning to fish any of Cameron Creek's canyons.

Cameron Falls

Summit Lake (NP)
Status: Devoid of fish

Tiny Summit Lake, situated 4 km by trail from Cameron Lake on the Carthew Trail, was at one time stocked with cutthroat trout. However, the trout failed to take hold, likely due to winter kill.

Summit Lake

Rowe Lakes (NP)
Brook trout to 30 cm (Lower Lake only)

These three small lakes nestled on the flank of Mt. Rowe all contained populations of brook trout at one time. However, reports indicate that the two Upper Lakes are devoid of fish, and the Lower Lake may contain a very limited population of small brook trout. Lower Rowe Lake, 4 km by trail from the Akamina Highway, has sparse vegetation around its shoreline. The Upper Rowe Lakes are set in an alpine basin reached via a steep 1 km spur trail from the Rowe Meadow, a total distance of 6.5 km from the trailhead.

Lone Lake (NP)
Cutthroat trout to 35 cm

Diminutive Lone Lake is situated close to the midway point on the Tamarack Trail. It holds plenty of small cutthroat trout in its emerald green waters. Most of the fish average 25-30 cm in length, and are generally very eager to take a fly. Except for a break around the area of the outlet stream, the lake is encircled by forest and requires reasonable roll-casting abilities from those fly fishing.

Lone Lake

Lineham Lakes (NP)
(Known individually as Lineham North, Lineham South, Lineham; also known individually as Water Cugel, Hourglass, Ptarmigan, Channel, Larch)
Cutthroat trout to 50 cm (1.5 kg)

Access to the magnificent Lineham Basin, which holds the three Lineham Lakes, is extremely hazardous, at one point requiring the hiker to negotiate a narrow ledge across the top of a 100 m-high cliff. Anglers using this route must register out with the warden service. For those unwilling to risk their life on the cliff, an alternate route exists which leads from Lineham Ridge on the Tamarack Trail down a steep, ill-defined trail into Lineham Basin. This route is very arduous, and also requires registering with the warden service. Those who do make it to Lineham Lakes are blessed with some of the best backcountry fishing in Waterton Park, with all of the lakes holding plenty of cutthroat trout in the 25-35 cm range. Adequate fly casting room is available around all of the lakes. Due to their high elevation and sheltered location, the Lineham Lakes are seldom ice-free until mid-July. Accordingly, spawning often occurs into late-July.

Lineham Lake

WATERTON REGION: Tamarack Sub-Region

Twin Lakes (NP)
Brook trout to 35 cm
Rainbow trout to 40 cm (Upper Lake only)
These two small lakes, situated 11 km from the Red Rock Canyon trailhead, are a very popular destination for backpackers. Both lakes contain brook trout, with the Upper Lake also holding a few rainbow trout. Lower Twin Lake serves as an ideal training ground for novice fly fishers, as it has plenty of small (15-25 cm) brook trout eager to bite. Fly casting room is available around much of the shore and short casts of only 5-10 m are usually all that are required to reach the fish. The fish in Upper Twin Lake are somewhat larger and are usually a little more difficult to catch. Fly and lure will both work effectively in either lake.

Upper Twin Lake

Lost Lake (NP)
Status: Doubtful
Tiny Lost Lake is located 2 km by trail from the Snowshoe Fire Road (10 km from Red Rock Canyon). It has been stocked in the past with cutthroat, brook and rainbow trout, all of which, according to Park records, failed to reproduce. For those eternal optimists wishing to test the waters of Lost Lake, be forewarned that fishing will be a difficult proposition as the lake is completely surrounded by heavy brush.

Goat Lake (NP)
Cutthroat trout to 35 cm
Set in a splendid hanging valley, 7 km by trail from Red Rock Canyon, the beautiful green waters of Goat Lake hold hordes of small cutthroat trout in the 25 cm range. The crystal-clear waters will allow the angler to see fish far out in the lake, particularly near the outlet. Casting ahead of cruising fish with a lure or fly is your best bet. If the fish are beyond your casting range, try the little pond just below Goat Lake's outlet. It usually holds a few fish, although they tend to spook easily.

Goat Lake

Ruby Lake (NP)
Status: Doubtful
Ruby Lake is nestled high in a basin beneath the east face of Mt. Blakiston, and is seldom visited and seldom fished. A topographic map is recommended, as only ill-defined game trails lead steeply for 5 km up the north side of Ruby Creek to Ruby Lake. Although stocked in the past with rainbow trout, recent reports indicate that few, if any, trout exist today.

Ruby Lake

Blakiston Creek (NP)
Cutthroat trout to 25 cm
Rainbow trout to 25 cm
Brook trout to 25 cm
Bull trout to 30 cm
Whitefish to 25 cm
Despite its variety of fish, Blakiston Creek holds few in number and is generally regarded as below average stream fishing. It is accessible from the Red Rock Canyon Road, and the best potential lies in the lower half of the creek, between Crandell Mountain Campsite and the Waterton River. Note, however, that torrential flooding each spring rearranges the main channel on an annual basis, and good holes may disappear or move from one year to the next.

Blakiston Falls

Blakiston Creek ponds (NP)
Brook trout to 25 cm
A number of small beaver ponds in the lower Blakiston Creek valley can be accessed from the Red Rock Canyon Road. The ponds are generally guarded by a nearly impenetrable tangle of brush. For those brave (or foolish) enough to fish these waters, small brook trout averaging 15-20 cm can be taken.

WATERTON REGION: Mountain View Sub-Region

Mountain View Sub-Region

This Sub-Region literally sits in the shadow of the Rocky Mountains, and dramatic vistas are present at every turn. From Waterton Lakes National Park, the primary access to fishable waters is via Highway 6 (to Pincher Creek and Chief Mountain Customs), Highway 5 (to Cardston) and Highway 800 (to Hill Spring). There are a number of excellent rainbow trout lakes in the sub-region, including Police Outpost, Payne and Dipping Vat Lakes. For those boating, be aware of strong west winds that regularly whip across the open prairie. The Belly and Waterton Rivers also provide fine angling opportunities, particularly in the fall.

Belly River (NP-AB)
Rainbow trout to 40 cm
Whitefish to 40 cm
Cutthroat trout to 40 cm
Brown trout to 40 cm
Bull trout to 75 cm (5.0 kg)

The Belly River enters the extreme southwest corner of Waterton Lakes National Park and flows north and east, eventually joining the Waterton River. The Belly River offers some excellent stream fishing in deep pools holding a variety of trout. Within the national park, the Belly River is accessible at the point where it parallels Highway 6 for several kilometres. It can also be reached by following the Belly River Wagon Road, a 3 km-long trail that begins at the Belly River campground, and eventually crosses the International Boundary. To the north, and outside the National Park boundary, the river can be accessed from Highways 5 and 800. Historically, the Belly River, and its tributary, the North Fork of the Belly River, provided outstanding angling for huge bull trout. The over harvesting of bull trout eventually took its toll, and their numbers began a dramatic decline. In recent years, with the legislated protection of the bull trout, numbers have begun to improve significantly. The river holds a variety of trout, with rainbow trout or whitefish in the 20-35 cm range the most likely catch. However, don't be surprised if you hook into a big bull in one of the deeper pools. As one fishes further downstream, the likelihood of catching brown trout increases, with a few pike in the river as well.

Belly River

Giant's Mirror (NP)
Status: Doubtful

The Giant's Mirror is a small pond located a short distance north of Highway 6 as it re-enters Waterton Lakes National Park from the Blood Indian Reserve. The outlet dam has been breached and the Giant's Mirror has dried up to the point of no longer being able to hold fish. The few small ponds between the Belly River and the Giant's Mirror site may hold a few rainbow or brook trout.

Police Outpost (Police, Outpost) Lake (AB)
Rainbow trout to 55 cm (2.0 kg)
Brook trout to 45 cm

Police Outpost Lake and its lovely campground are located in a Provincial Park approximately 18 km southeast of Mountain View. The lake is very shallow and is prone to winter kill on occasion. Weed growth is rampant in the lake by mid-summer, and it is only the centre of the lake that is free of weeds. Although it is possible to fish from shore from numerous locations, a boat will significantly increase the angling quality. Bait, lures and flies are all effective at Police Outpost Lake. Rainbow trout ranging from 20-30 cm in length will be the normal catch. The fish grow rapidly due to the abundant feed, and if they survive a winter or two, they can easily top the 2 kg mark.

Yolanda Reimer and Dorgam Hideib with Police Outpost rainbow trout

Police Outpost Lake

Lee Creek (AB)
Rainbow trout to 35 cm
Cutthroat trout to 35 cm
Whitefish to 35 cm

Lee Creek is a tributary of the St. Mary River, and is accessible from a number of gravel roads southeast of Mountain View. The creek holds rainbow and cutthroat trout in small sizes, with few larger than 30 cm in length.

Tough Creek (AB)
Rainbow trout to 35 cm
Cutthroat trout to 35 cm
Whitefish to 35 cm

Tough Creek is a tributary of Lee Creek, is of similar character and holds the same variety of fish as Lee. Access is from gravel roads southeast of Mountain View.

Boundary Creek (AB)
Northern pike to 60 cm (3.0 kg)

Boundary Creek crosses into Alberta from Montana in Police Outpost Provincial Park, then does a short 15 km loop before recrossing the border back into Montana. Fishing in Boundary Creek is marginal, with northern pike found in some of the slower sections.

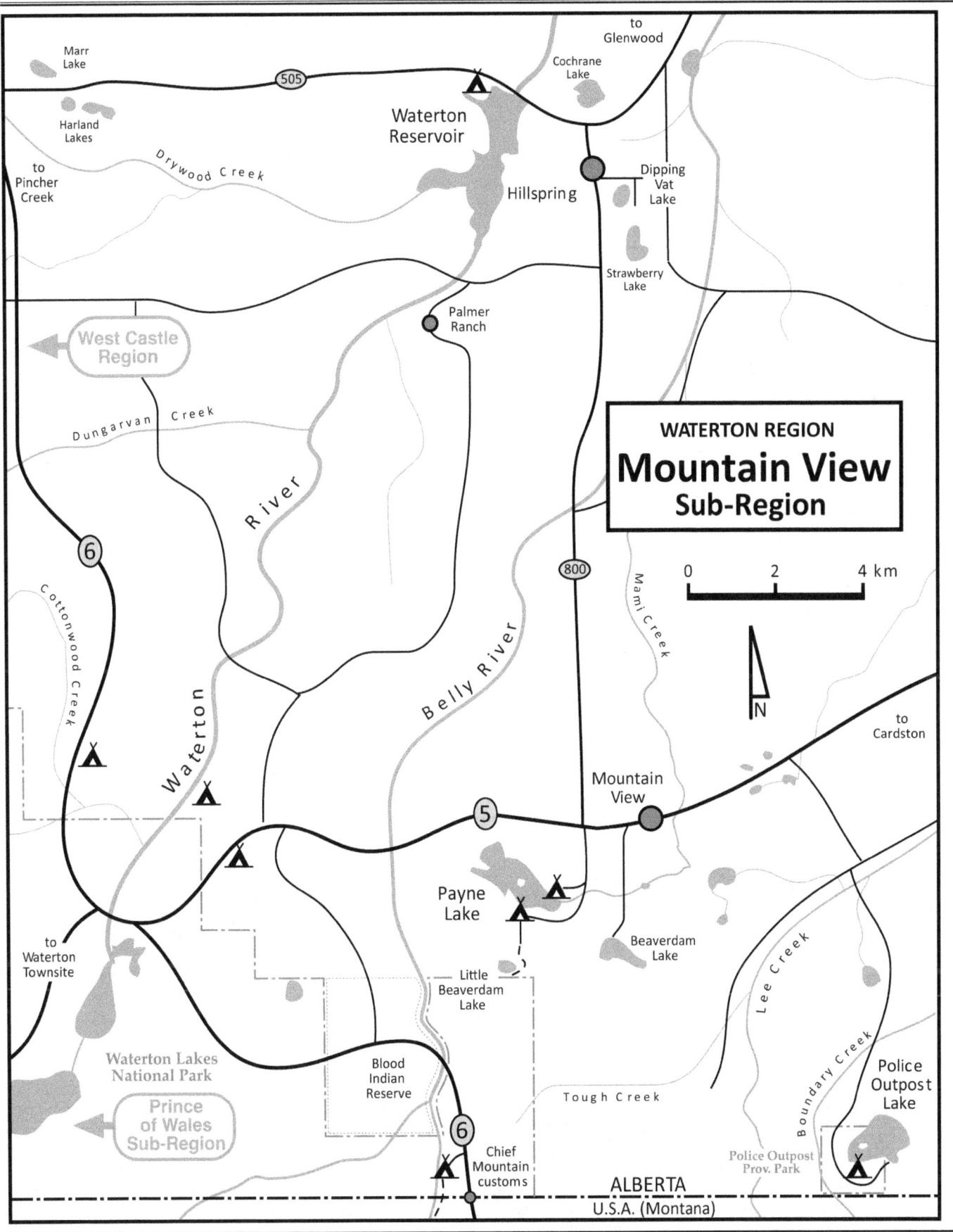

WATERTON REGION: Mountain View Sub-Region

Payne (Paine, Mami) Lake (AB)
Rainbow trout to 55 cm (2.0 kg)

This large reservoir is the most popular fishing spot in the Mountain View area. The two campgrounds at the lake are active during spring, summer and fall. Payne Lake is very shallow and has lots of feed, making for ideal trout growing conditions. Rainbow trout are stocked annually in large numbers, and despite the heaving fishing pressure, fish are still plentiful in the fall. In 1999, water was drawn down in the lake to allow repair work on the dam, and fish stocks suffered. Rainbow trout caught in Payne Lake will average 20-35 cm in length. Bait fishing from shore is very popular and is generally successful. Fishing from a boat and simply trolling a lure or fly is also very effective at Payne Lake.

Payne Lake

Little Beaverdam Lake (AB)
Brook trout to 40 cm

Little Beaverdam Lake is located approximately 2 km due south of the main campground at Payne Lake. A dirt road leads to within a half kilometre of Little Beaverdam Lake. Although a road does lead up a steep hill to the lake, it has been closed to motorized vehicles to prevent further erosion. Little Beaverdam Lake is man-made, not beaver-made, and serves as a watering hole for range cattle. There is a reproducing population of brook trout in the lake, and most brookies caught will be in the 20-30 cm range. There are numerous locations to fish from around the entire lake.

Little Beaverdam Lake

Nathan Bond with brook trout from Little Beaverdam Lake

Beaverdam Lake (AB)
Brook trout to 35 cm

Beaverdam Lake is a large, shallow reservoir situated 5 km south of Mountain View. Access to much of the shoreline is limited by private property. Fishing is generally poor, although there are some brook trout in the lake.

Beaverdam Lake

Waterton River (AB)
(Downstream from National Park boundary)
Rainbow trout to 55 cm (1.5 kg)
Brown trout to 55 cm (1.5 kg)
Cutthroat trout to 50 cm
Whitefish to 45 cm
Bull trout to 75 cm (6.0 kg)
Northern pike to 80 cm (6.0 kg)

After leaving Waterton Lakes National Park, the Waterton River flows northeast to Waterton Reservoir, and beyond that, joins the Belly River. Between the National Park boundary and the reservoir, the Waterton River offers good fishing for a variety of trout. Rainbow trout predominate, although brown trout are also found in good numbers. Trout caught in the river will average 25-35 cm in length. Downstream from the reservoir, pike can also be taken from the Waterton River. The river is crossed by Highway 5/6 at the park boundary, and by a number of secondary roads farther downstream. The fall, when water levels are at their lowest, is the most popular time of year to fish the river.

Alan Brice with Waterton River brown trout

Cottonwood Creek (AB)
Brown trout to 35 cm
Rainbow trout to 35 cm

This small tributary of the Waterton River flows south from the foothills, joining the main river near the park boundary. Cottonwood Creek is crossed by Highway 5 approximately 4 km north of the park boundary. Much of the creek flows through private property, although there are a few places where it can be accessed. Small brown and rainbow trout in the 15-25 cm range are the average catch.

WATERTON REGION: Mountain View Sub-Region

Waterton Reservoir (AB)
Brown trout to 55 cm (1.5 kg)
Rainbow trout to 55 cm (1.5 kg)
Lake trout to 65 cm (3.0 kg)
Whitefish to 45 cm
Northern pike to 80 cm (6.0 kg)

The Waterton Reservoir, located 5 km northwest of Hill Spring, is very much an irrigation reservoir. Water levels are dictated by agricultural water needs. As such, water levels in the reservoir fluctuate wildly during the year, making it very unstable as a fishery. There are fish in the reservoir, but the quality of fishing is not particularly good. Depending on the time of year, brown, rainbow or even the odd lake trout can be taken from the reservoir. Pike and whitefish are also present.

Waterton Reservoir

Dipping Vat Lake (AB)
Rainbow trout to 65 cm (4.0 kg)

Dipping Vat Lake is located just a half kilometre southeast of the small community of Hill Spring. Large rainbow trout are the order of the day at Dipping Vat. The water level in the lake is maintained by irrigation runoff, and levels are usually fairly stable during the year. There is a tremendous amount of feed in the lake and the annually stocked rainbows grow big very quickly. Although the lake is relatively small and fishing from shore can be effective, a boat is an asset when fishing at Dipping Vat Lake. By mid-summer, weeds are choking much of the shallow waters near the shoreline. The centre of the lake is not much deeper, but it tends to have fewer weeds, which will then at least permit some casting. Rainbow trout in the lake average 35-45 cm in length, with whoppers in excess of 3.0 kg taken each year.

Dipping Vat Lake

(rainbow trout)

Strawberry Lake (AB)
Status: Devoid of fish

Strawberry Lake is situated half a kilometre south of Dipping Vat Lake. Strawberry Lake dries up to the point of being incapable of holding fish.

Cochrane Lake (AB)
Northern pike to 70 cm (5.0 kg)

Cochrane Lake is a large irrigation reservoir located 2 km north of Hill Spring. Due to the shallow nature of the lake and likelihood of winter kill, northern pike are the only fish that are present in any substantial numbers.

Marr Lake, Harland Lakes (AB)
Status: Devoid of fish

These small ponds alongside Highway 565 do not hold any fish.

Palmer Ranch (Fee required to fish)
Rainbow trout to 60 cm (3.0 kg)
Brown trout to 60 cm (3.0 kg)
Northern pike to 70 cm (5.0 kg)

The Palmer Ranch is located southwest of Hill Spring, and directly south of the Waterton Reservoir. The ranch has private fishing on a small stream that's loaded with big fish. Rainbows in the 40-50 cm range are average catches. Large brown trout and monster northern pike can also be taken.

Palmer Ranch rainbow trout

FLATHEAD REGION

The mighty Flathead River flows south from headwaters in the upper Flathead Valley in British Columbia to Flathead Lake in Montana. All of the fishing opportunities in this Region are part of the Flathead River watershed. The main access to the Region is via logging roads from Highway 3 in British Columbia. River and stream fishing attract most anglers' attention, although there are some fine alpine lakes in the Region. However, the Region is much more suited to explorers and those who want to get away from civilization, as many of the lakes have little or no defined trails. Akamina-Kishinena Provincial Park, in the southeast corner of the Region and bordering on Waterton Lakes National Park, merits description on its own. The rest of the waters are spread throughout the Upper Flathead River Valley proper.

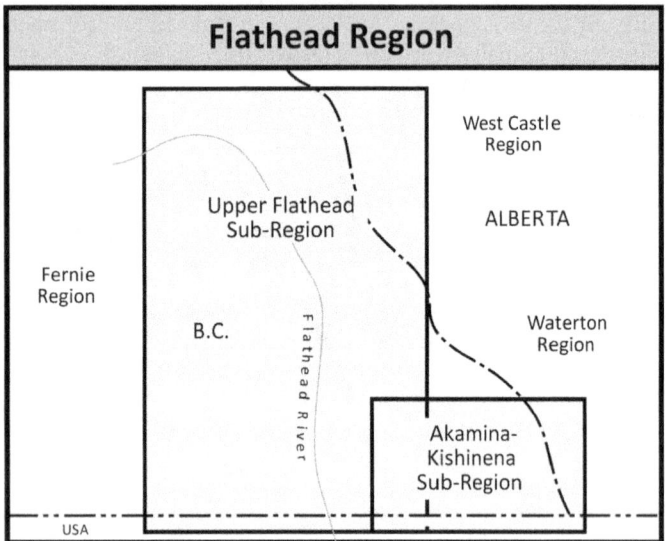

Akamina-Kishinena Sub-Region

This Sub-Region's boundaries conform to those of the recently created Akamina-Kishinena Provincial Park in the extreme southeastern corner of British Columbia. Much of the park is beyond the reach of unmotivated anglers, requiring a long (120+ km) drive on rough gravel and dirt roads from Morrissey on Highway 3 just to reach the park. Even after reaching the park by vehicle, lakes including Polar and Ledge are protected by some very difficult terrain and an absence of trails. Wall and Forum Lake are the park's most visited locations, as access is over shorter trails from paved roads in neighbouring Waterton Lakes National Park.

Wall Lake (BC)
Cutthroat trout to 45 cm
Wall Lake is situated on the south side of the Akamina Valley beneath a spectacular headwall. It offers some fine cutthroat trout fishing, and is a popular destination for anglers from nearby Waterton Park. Fish can be can be taken from shoreline locations all around the lake, with the area near the main inlet creek on the western side always being productive. Most fish taken from Wall Lake will average 25-30 cm in length. A well-maintained 5 km trail leads to Wall Lake from the Akamina Pass trailhead on the Akamina Parkway in Waterton Lakes National Park.

Wall Lake (cutthroat trout)

Forum Lake (BC)
Cutthroat trout to 50 cm (1.5 kg)
Forum Lake is set in a rocky amphitheatre at the head of Akamina Creek, and is overlooked by most hikers intent on Wall Lake, despite the promise of good cutthroat trout fishing. Access is via a steep 4 km trail that begins at the Akamina Pass trailhead in Waterton Park, the same trailhead as Wall Lake. Hard-fighting cutthroat trout averaging 30-40 cm can be taken from Forum, with the late season (August and September) much more productive than the early season. Ice-out is slow on Forum due to its sheltered location, and ice floes are on the lake well into summer. The lake level fluctuates during the year, continually dropping to a low point in the late fall.

Forum Lake

Akamina Creek (BC)
Cutthroat trout to 35 cm
Bull trout to 50 cm (1.5 kg)
Akamina Creek flows west from Akamina Pass at the Alberta-B.C. border, eventually joining Kishinena Creek as a major tributary. Small cutthroat trout are plentiful in the creek's pools, with a few bull trout present as well. An abandoned road leads from Akamina Pass and parallels Akamina Creek downstream for its entire length.

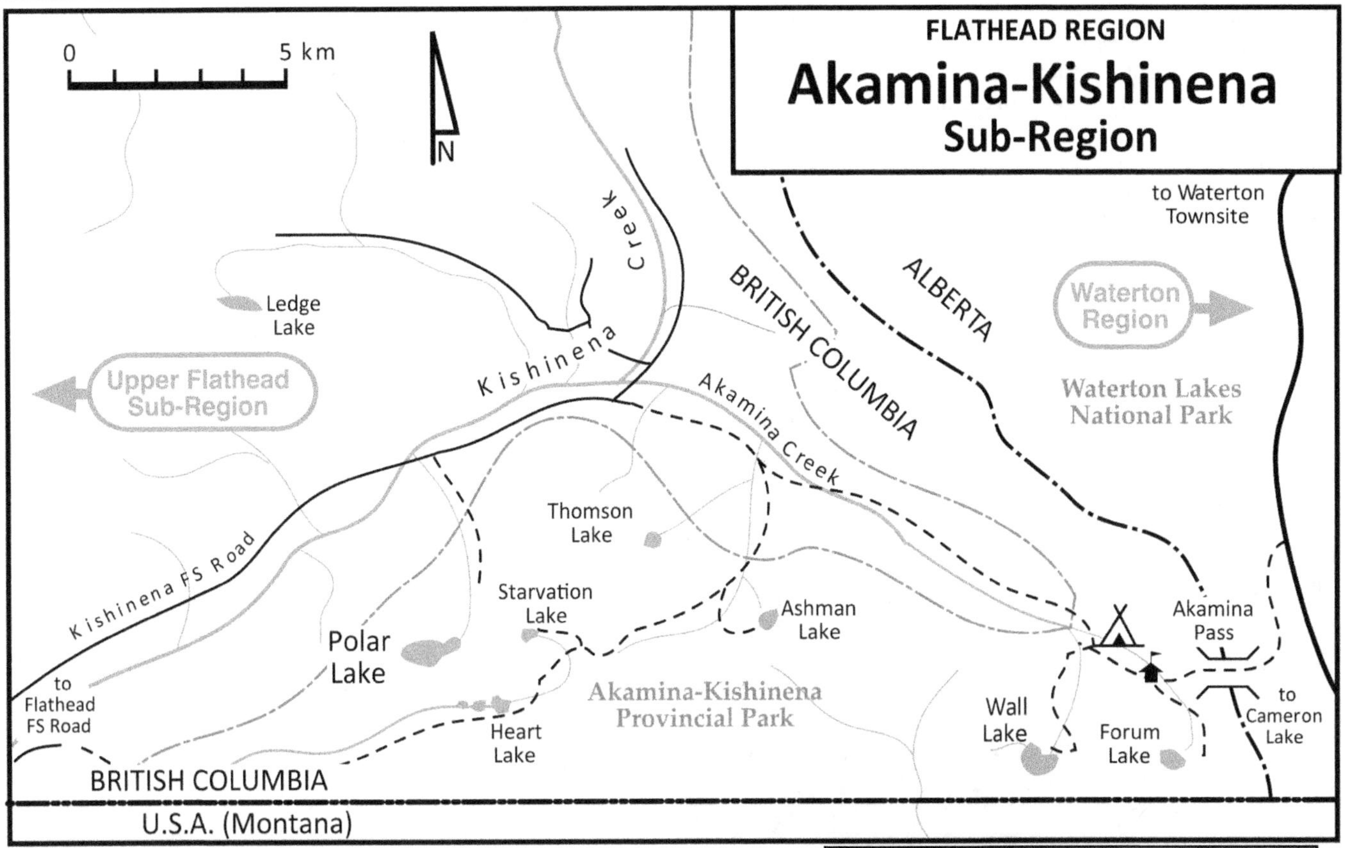

FLATHEAD REGION
Akamina-Kishinena Sub-Region

Kishinena Creek (BC)
Cutthroat trout to 50 cm (1.5 kg)
Bull trout to 90 cm (8.0 kg)
Whitefish to 35 cm

A tributary to the Flathead River, Kishinena Creek receives some enormous bull trout each year during spawning season. Many of these monsters have made it all the way from Flathead Lake in Montana. In years past, the large bull trout were fished unmercifully, especially below waterfalls where they congregated, and their numbers subsequently declined dramatically. New regulations on the Flathead River and its tributaries were put in place to protect the bull trout. Nice cutthroat trout in the 25-35 cm range can be taken throughout the summer from Kishinena Creek's numerous pools and whitefish become plentiful in the fall.

Ashman Lake (BC)
Cutthroat trout to 30 cm

Set in the heart of prime grizzly bear habitat, just off appropriately named Grizzly Gulch, tiny Ashman Lake receives few visitors each year. An 8 km hike leads to Ashman from logging roads at the confluence of Akamina and Kishinena Creeks. Ashman Lake holds plenty of cutthroat trout, but most are stunted, with large heads and small bodies, due to the large number of fish and limited food supply. A large cutthroat from Ashman will seldom exceed 25 cm. Fly casting room is available around most of the lake. Be sure to keep an eye on the surrounding terrain for four-legged visitors.

Ashman Lake

Thomson Lake (BC)
Status: Unknown

Tiny Thomson Lake, at the head of See Creek, has no access trails and is strictly for explorers. The lake has never been stocked, although cutthroat trout may have made their way in from See Creek. Have a look if you have the time and Band-Aids to spare.

Starvation Lake (BC)
Cutthroat trout to 35 cm

This tiny tarn at the head of Starvation Creek is reached by a 15 km trail from Akamina Creek through Grizzly Gulch and over an unnamed pass. Other than hunting parties that work this area in the fall, few humans make their way into Starvation Lake. The lake holds cutthroat trout in the 20-30 cm range. Like Grizzly Gulch, its companion valley to the east, the Starvation Creek valley holds a healthy population of grizzly bears. Obviously, they're not the ones starving.

Heart Lake (BC)
Cutthroat trout to 35 cm
Situated on Starvation Creek, petite Heart Lake and its two accompanying ponds hold small cutthroat trout. Access is very long and difficult, either from the west via a trail along Starvation Creek from logging roads on lower Kishinena Creek, or from the east via the Grizzly Gulch trail. In either case, expect plenty of solitude. Winter avalanches occasionally rumble down onto Heart Lake, prolonging ice-out into the early summer.

Polar (Beavertail) Lake (BC)
Cutthroat trout to 40 cm
Polar Lake is set high on a ledge on Kishinena Ridge, and is accessible to only the most determined hikers. No formal trails lead into Polar Lake, and the final two kilometres are guarded by a very steep headwall. The lake was stocked in the past with cutthroat trout, but recent reports indicate poor fishing.

Polar Lake

Ledge Lake (BC)
Cutthroat trout to 45 cm
In a location similar, but even more dramatic than Polar Lake, Ledge Lake is virtually inaccessible to anglers. A sheer cliff protects Ledge Lake from the most direct line of ascent, and any would-be visitors will have to do an inordinate amount of bushwhacking and scrambling to reach this remote lake. As would be expected, fishing reports on Ledge Lake are non-existent. Stocked with cutthroat trout, this lake is for explorers only.

Ledge Lake

Upper Flathead Sub-Region

Good cutthroat and bull trout fishing typify the Flathead River and its tributary streams. Individual lakes are scattered at tributary headwaters along the entire length of the valley, and few if any, have maintained access trails. Procter Lake and Frozen Lake are two of the few lakes that are accessible to vehicles. Most anglers confine themselves to the Flathead River and the more easily reached streams. Intrepid hikers and horse parties are the only ones who frequent the Flathead's pristine backcountry. All visitors should note that the Flathead Valley is prime grizzly bear habitat and they should take the appropriate precautions.

Flathead River (BC)
Cutthroat trout to 50 cm (1.5 kg)
Bull trout to 1 m (10.0 kg)
Whitefish to 40 cm
The Flathead River flows for 65 km in British Columbia before crossing the border into neighbouring Montana. For virtually all of its length in B.C., the Flathead is close to logging access roads. Typical of mountain rivers of the Rockies, the Flathead experiences major runoff in mid-June, followed by a gradual clearing of the waters. By mid-summer, the Flathead is usually crystal clear, and fishing picks up and continues to improve into the fall. The river is characterized by long stretches of fast water with the occasional nice pool. Cutthroat trout in the 25-35 cm range are the normal catch in the river, although big bull trout are making a comeback, thanks to protective legislation. At many locations in the valley, beaver dam complexes are connected to the main river, and most hold a few trout.

Flathead River

Flathead ponds

Sage Creek (BC)
Cutthroat trout to 40 cm
Bull trout to 75 cm (6.0 kg)
Whitefish to 35 cm
Sage Creek is one of the major tributaries of the upper Flathead River, beginning high in the Clark Range and flowing south to join the Flathead just south of the Canada-U.S. boundary.

FLATHEAD REGION: Upper Flathead Sub-Region

Logging roads allow for reasonable access to most of Sage Creek, although a bit of bushwhacking may be required to reach the actual streambed. The campsite at the Kishinena Forest Service Road bridge over Sage Creek is popular, and fishing pressure is accordingly high, especially downstream from the campground, where the creek widens out. Small cutthroat trout are plentiful for those who get away from the most accessible points.

Sage Creek

Harvey Creek, Squaw Creek, McLatchie Creek, St. Eloi Brook, Packhorse Creek, Middlepass Creek, Commerce Creek, Howell Creek, Cabin Creek, Couldrey Creek (BC)
Cutthroat trout to 30 cm
Bull trout to 60 cm (2.0 kg)
Whitefish to 30 cm

These tributaries of the Flathead River generally hold cutthroat trout in small sizes. Most of the creeks are in valleys that have been logged in the past or are currently being logged, and are at least in some manner accessible. Reaching the fishable waters will require some walking. The confluence of the smaller creeks with the Flathead River is usually a good fish-holding spot, especially when the tributaries are clearer than the main river.

Procter Lake (BC)
Cutthroat trout to 45 cm

Procter Lake is located on a flat, forested bench above Sage Creek, two kilometres south of the Kishinena Forest Service Road crossing of Sage Creek. A rough half kilometre 4WD road leads off the main road into a primitive campsite at the north end of Procter Lake. The lake is very shallow and reeds circle the entire lake, making fishing from shore a difficult proposition. For those with a boat, the best fishing can be found around the island on the south side of the lake. The lake's few deep holes are in the vicinity of the island, and cutthroat trout in the 25-35 cm can be caught, although the numbers are somewhat limited. Patient anglers will be able to take cruising fish from the shallower waters as well.

Procter Lake

Marl Lake, Beryl Lake (BC)
Status: Devoid of fish

These two shallow lakes are approximately one kilometre west of the junction of the Flathead and Kishinena Forest Service Roads. The have never been stocked and contain no fish.

Three Mile Lake (BC)
Cutthroat trout to 40 cm

Located, appropriately enough, approximately three miles from the B.C.-Montana border crossing at Flathead, shallow Three Mile Lake has been stocked in the past with cutthroat trout. Fishing where Calder Creek enters and exits Three Mile Lake can be productive, although the extensive shallows found near the inlet may pose a problem. The lake is reached via a short one kilometre bushwhack from the Calder Creek road. It is best to follow Calder Creek upstream from the road to Three Mile Lake.

Frozen Lake (BC)
Cutthroat trout to 55 cm (1.5 kg)
Bull trout to 65 cm (3.0 kg)

A long, long drive of well over 100 km on gravel and dirt roads leads to Frozen Lake, which straddles the Canada-U.S. border. Despite the long access, rumours of large cutthroat trout in Frozen Lake attract anglers from both Canada and the U.S. (the U.S. access requires a short hike to reach the lake). Although cutthroat trout upwards of 50 cm in length are present, you are more likely to hook into one of the lake's plentiful bull trout, which average 40-50 cm in length. The lake is long and narrow and forest-bound. Angling from shore is productive from many locations for those using lures or bait.

Frozen Lake

Hunger Lake (BC)
Status: Unknown

This isolated lake, set in the Leslie Creek drainage, receives few visitors each season, as there are no formal access trails. Hunger Lake is the catchment basin for Leslie Creek and has no outlet. As such, there are major fluctuations in the lake level during the year. The lake likely drains underground, as Leslie Creek reappears a kilometre below the lake. The lake has not been stocked, and it is doubtful if it contains any trout.

FLATHEAD REGION: Upper Flathead Sub-Region

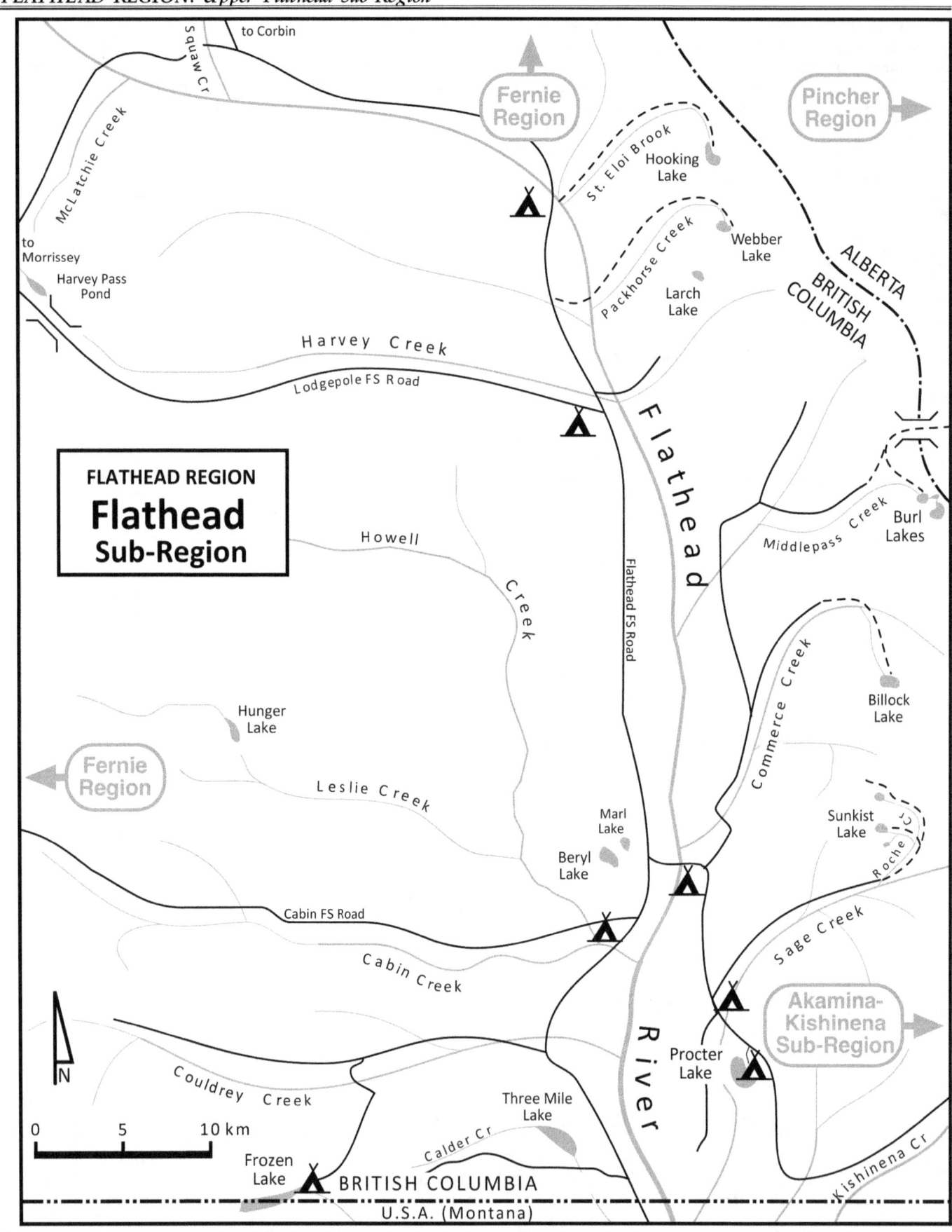

FLATHEAD REGION: Upper Flathead Sub-Region

Sunkist Lake (BC)
Cutthroat trout to 30 cm
This tiny lake is located beneath Sunkist Mountain, at the head of a tributary of Roche Creek. Access is via a poor 8 km trail that begins from the Sage Creek Forest Service Road and ascends the Roche Creek drainage. How far you can travel up the Sage Creek FSR by vehicle can change from year to year, potentially making this hike an even longer one than anticipated. Water levels in Sunkist Lake are highest after spring run-off is complete, and then drop throughout the summer and fall. Cutthroat trout in the lake are small but plentiful, most in the 20-25 cm range. A forest fire from years past has denuded half the tree cover that surrounds the lake.

Sunkist Lake

Burl (Middlepass) Lakes (BC)
Cutthroat trout to 40 cm
The three Burl Lakes are situated in a stunning alpine basin below Rainy Ridge and the Continental Divide. Access is via an ill-defined 3 km route from Middle Kootenay Pass. Middle Kootenay Pass can be reached by 4WD from the West Castle River Road in Alberta. Many anglers bypass the Burl Lakes on their way to the "golden" waters of Rainy Ridge Lake, back over the border in Alberta. All three Burl Lakes hold stunted cutthroat trout in the 20-30 cm range, which can be taken from shore with ease. Fly fishing is the preferred method, although spin casting will also be effective. The upper lake is the largest and offers the most angling opportunities. The small, shallow middle lake holds a few trout that are easily spooked, while the rockbound lower lake allows for some fine sight fishing. A few informal backcountry campsites can be found in the stands of larch along the upper lake's west shore.

Billock Lake (BC)
Cutthroat trout to 50 cm (1.5 kg)
Billock Lake is set in a scenic amphitheatre below massive Commerce Peak at the headwaters of Commerce Creek. Trail access begins on the Commerce Creek Forest Service Road. The trail is used by hunting parties annually and is decent in the lower valley, deteriorating as one begins the climb into Billock Lake basin. Fishing is excellent for cutthroat trout in the 30-40 cm range.

Webber Lake (BC)
Cutthroat trout to 45 cm
Webber Lake is the larger of the two lakes in the upper Packhorse Creek watershed. Webber, and nearby Larch Lake, can be reached on trails that begin at a major ford on the Flathead River, approximately four kilometres below the bridged crossing of the river above St. Eloi Brook. The rockbound basin and dramatic cliff face along Webber's south side make for an unforgettable setting. The cutthroat trout that inhabit Webber average 30-35 cm in length, although larger ones are definitely present.

Larch Lake (BC)
Cutthroat trout to 35 cm
Located in a splendid larch-filled subalpine valley just south of the basin holding Webber Lake, tiny Larch Lake is stocked with cutthroat trout. Trout in the lake are not large, with most in the 20-25 cm range.

Hooking Lake (BC)
Cutthroat trout to 45 cm
Hooking Lake is set in a forest fire ravaged basin near the headwaters of St. Eloi Brook. Access is via abandoned seismic roads and horse trails from the Flathead River Forest Service Road, a distance of 10 km. The final pitch up into the lake is very steep. The lake itself has two deep, connected holes and fish can be taken from the area separating the shallower waters from the deep. Fish feed in the shallows, but are easily frightened. Cutthroat trout in Hooking Lake average 30-40 cm in length and are plentiful. Scree slopes make up the majority of the lakeshore, with a few stands of forest cover.

Hooking Lake

Upper Burl Lake

(cutthroat trout)

KOOCANUSA REGION

The Koocanusa Region is one of the most unique in all of the Canadian Rockies. Spring comes very early to this Region, as it is at the southern end of the Rockies and it is very low in elevation. Snow is generally gone by March, and many of the lakes will be free of ice by late-March or early-April. The fish species available to the Region are also unique. Kokanee are found in great numbers in Lake Koocanusa and largemouth bass can be caught in many lakes. The Region's focal point is Lake Koocanusa and its source, the Kootenay River. Highway 3 provides east-west access and Highway 93 provides north-south access. The Region divides into four distinct Sub-Regions, all centred on small communities: Elko to the south and east; Jaffray in the middle; Wardner to the west; and Fort Steele to the north.

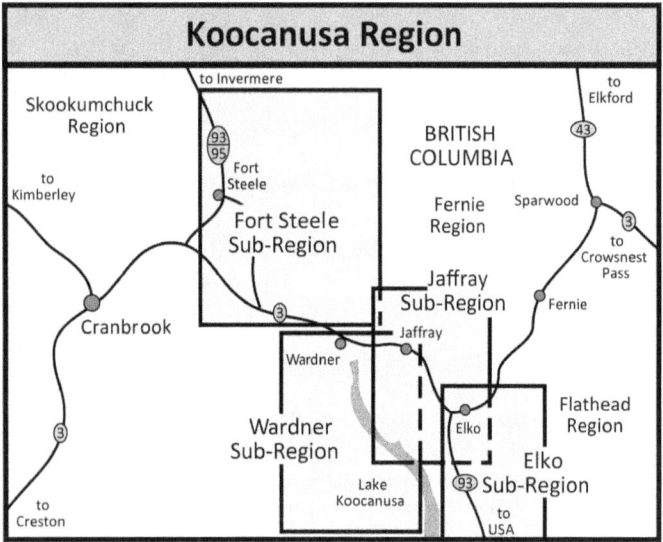

climb down into the canyon. For those who do make it down to the Elk River, the fishing is excellent, as there is little or no fishing pressure. Cutthroat trout from 30-40 cm are the regular catch. Bull trout and whitefish can also be caught, and there may be the odd rainbow or brook trout as well. The canyon finally opens up as it nears the Highway 93 bridge, and it is a little more accessible, although it will still require walking upstream along the river amid heavy forest cover and a lot of high-water debris. Less than a kilometre below the Highway 93 bridge, the Elk River flows into Lake Koocanusa. Fishing can be good where the river enters the lake, but the lake level fluctuates massively during the year, and this will affect the quality of fishing. Fishing at the lake can be hit-and-miss - plenty of fish one day, and none a week later. Boating on Lake Koocanusa where the Elk River enters can be very dangerous due to floating and submerged debris.

Elk River

Phillipps Canyon

Elko Sub-Region

The small logging community of Elko on Highway 3 is the hub of this Sub-Region, which extends south along Highway 93 to Grasmere and the United States border. The Elk River, flowing west to Koocanusa Lake, is fishable above and below major canyons around Elko. The Wigwam River, a major tributary to the Elk, is an outstanding catch-and-release cutthroat and bull trout fishery. Closer to Elko, Silver Spring Lakes provide some great fishing for large rainbow trout, and Burton Lake holds some fine brook trout. Near the small community of Grasmere, chunky rainbow trout thrive in both Loon and Edwards Lakes.

Elk River (BC) *(Elko to Lake Koocanusa)*
Cutthroat trout to 55 cm (1.5 kg)
Bull trout to 1 m (8.0 kg)
Whitefish to 40 cm
Downstream from Elko, the Elk River drops into a steep canyon that is impenetrable to all but hard-core anglers. Whitewater raft companies regularly pass through Phillipps Canyon in summertime with tour groups, but seldom stop to fish. Road access above the canyon is limited, and anglers will have to make a significant trek, even before attempting the dangerous

Silver Spring Lakes (BC)
Rainbow trout to 55 cm (2.0 kg)
The Silver Spring Lakes are a series of lakes and ponds of various sizes that stretch for approximately 5 km down a narrow, cliff-walled side valley above the Elk River. A short, but steep, 0.5 km hike leads from the Elko-Morrissey Road to the first and largest Silver Spring Lake, a stunning blue-green body of water. The rainbow trout in the first lake grow to good sizes, with the average being 30-40 cm in length. Fishing is productive off of the scree slopes along the east shore, and at the shallows at the south end of the lake. The shallows can be especially tantalizing during low-light periods, when many of the larger fish move in to feed. A well-worn trail continues past the end of the first lake to the second and third Silver Spring Lakes. The second lake, half a kilometre beyond the first, is a shallow pond that does not hold any trout. Fifteen minutes of hiking past the second lake brings one to the third lake, a dark body of water backed by high cliffs. Forest cover and extended shallows make shore fishing difficult. One of the better options is to fish off of the 5 m high rock bluffs, where you can at least cast to fish-holding waters. The difficulty arises when you hook a big one and have to figure out how to land it. There are other ponds beyond the third lake, but none have been stocked.

KOOCANUSA REGION: Elko Sub-Region

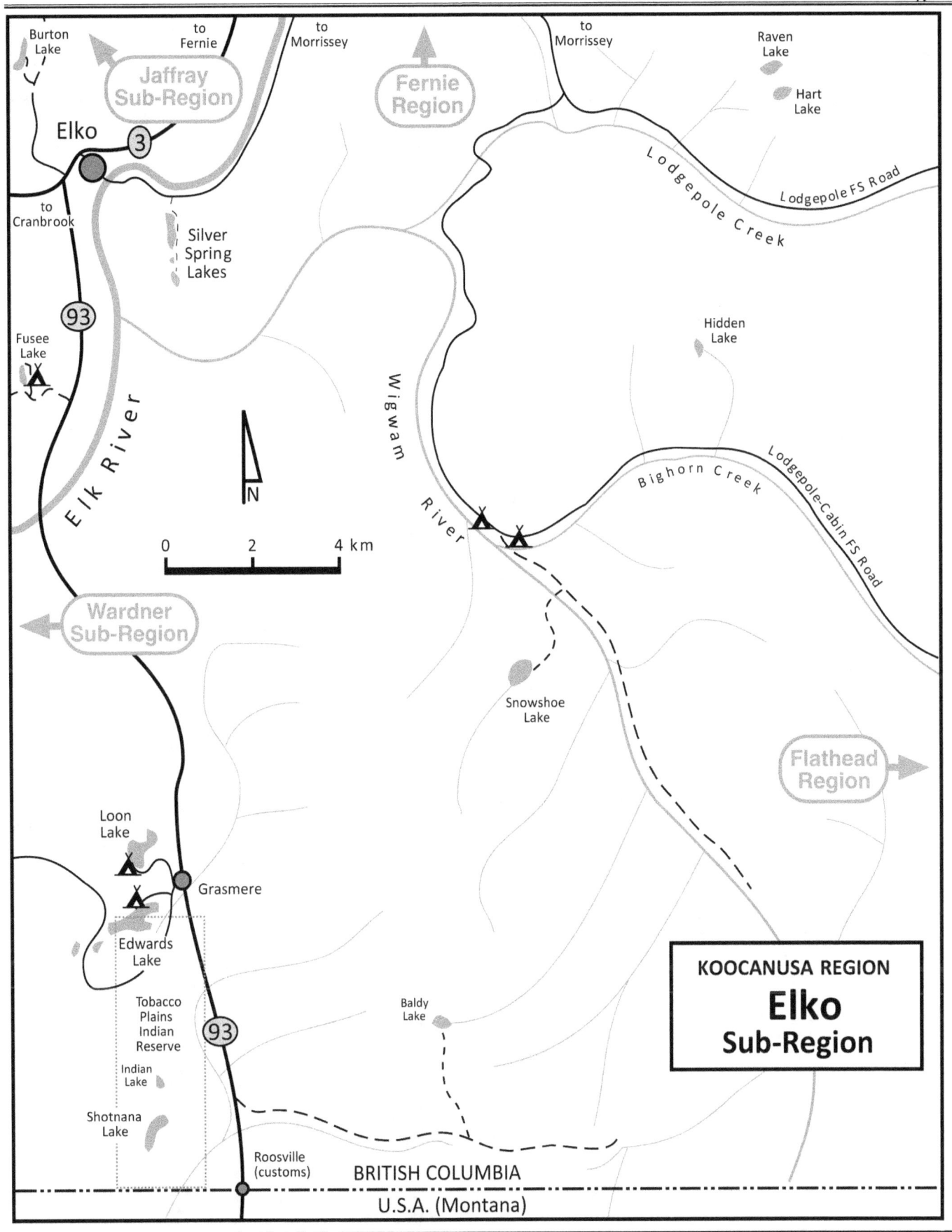

Silver Spring Lakes (first lake)

(third lake)

Wigwam River

Alan Brice with Wigwam River bull trout

Burton Lake (BC)
Brook trout to 45 cm

Burton Lake is located just west of Elko, and is accessed by a gravel road off Highway 3. From the parking area, it's a steep walk down to the lakeshore. Casting room is at a premium due to forest cover and a series of cliffs. Burton Lake's cheerful green waters are home to a population of colourful brook trout, most of which run in the 25-35 cm range. Although rare, a few rainbow trout from previous plantings may still be in the lake. Lures and spinners are very effective at Burton Lake.

Burton Lake

Wigwam River (BC)
Cutthroat trout to 50 cm (1.5 kg)
Bull trout to 1 m (8.0 kg)
Whitefish to 40 cm

The Wigwam River is a major tributary to the lower Elk River and was one of the East Kootenay's first experiments with catch-and-release fishing. Catch-and-release has been an unqualified success on the Wigwam, with fish stocks as healthy as anywhere in the Rockies. The primary access to the Wigwam River is over logging roads from Morrissey. The upper reaches of the Wigwam Forest Service Road tend to waver between rough 2WD and 4WD. Cutthroat trout in the Wigwam River are plentiful and generally range from 25-35 cm in length. Virtually every likely looking spot will have a trout lurking about. Large bull trout also make their way up the Wigwam River in early summer from the Elk River to spawn, and many anglers plan fishing expeditions around their annual return.

Snowshoe Lake (BC)
Cutthroat trout to 50 cm (1.5 kg)

Snowshoe Lake is hidden in a side valley off of the Wigwam River. Finding Snowshoe Lake is usually an angler's first problem. To reach the lake, one first must ford the Wigwam River, approximately 4 km above its confluence with Bighorn Creek. Once across the Wigwam, it's a matter of finding a rough trail that leads up to the lake. Normally, the outlet creek of a lake would be a good landmark, but Snowshoe's outlet flows underground and is of no help. One kilometre up from the Wigwam River, Snowshoe Lake is found amid its pleasant forest and meadow surroundings. The lake fills up after run-off in late spring, and then gradually drops in level over the summer to a low point in the fall. The active cutthroat trout in Snowshoe Lake average 25-35 cm in length, and can be taken from most locations along the shore.

Snowshoe Lake

Baldy (Thomas, Ted's) Lake (BC)
Cutthroat trout to 35 cm

This tiny pond is located high in the Galton Range, at the head of an unnamed tributary of the Wigwam River. Although the lake is in the Wigwam River watershed, it is reached by a 5 km trail from roads in the Phillipps Creek drainage. Baldy Lake has been stocked in the past with cutthroat trout, which are still present in small sizes and limited numbers.

Baldy Lake

KOOCANUSA REGION: Elko Sub-Region

Lodgepole Creek, Bighorn (Ram) Creek (BC)
Cutthroat trout to 40 cm
Bull trout to 60 cm (3.0 kg)
Whitefish to 35 cm
These two main tributaries to the Wigwam River are easily accessed from Forest Service Roads that parallel the creeks for their entire length. Small cutthroat trout, in the 20-30 cm size range, are the normal catch.

Harvey Pass pond (BC)
Cutthroat trout to 25 cm
This small lake, which drains westward into Lodgepole Creek, is located alongside the logging just west of Harvey Pass (the pass between Lodgepole and Harvey Creeks). Heavy brush surrounds the lake, and just finding an opening to make a cast is very difficult. The lake holds small cutthroat trout, few larger than 20 cm in length.

Harvey Pass pond

Hidden Lake (BC)
Cutthroat trout to 40 cm
Located north of Bighorn Creek at the head of a steep, narrow valley below Overfold Mountain, Hidden Lake does not attract many anglers due to its very difficult access. The lake contains cutthroat trout that are small (20-30 cm) and easy to catch. There is heavy forest cover and lots of deadfall around the shoreline at Hidden Lake.

Raven Lake, Hart Lake (BC)
Cutthroat trout to 35 cm
These two tiny lakes, located less than kilometre from each other, are found in the Lodgepole Creek watershed. Both lakes are on a bench at the top of Flathead Ridge, and can be reached by hiking reclaimed mining roads that traverse the length of the ridge. Cutthroat trout have been stocked in both lakes, with the size of most trout caught being in the 20-30 cm range.

Hart Lake

Fusee Lake (BC)
Brook trout to 50 cm (1.5 kg)
Fusee Lake is a small, shallow lake off of Highway 93 that holds good numbers of brook trout. Reed growth and a few large trees make casting difficult in many spots, although there is still enough room for shore bound anglers to toss a line out. The brook trout in this small lake are surprisingly large, with the average fish being 30-35 cm in length. Spin casting is generally productive at Fusee Lake.

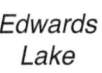

Fusee Lake brook trout

Loon Lake (BC)
Rainbow trout to 60 cm (2.5 kg)
Loon Lake is located on a wooded bench, approximately 2 km west of Highway 93 and the small community of Grasmere. A large forestry campground is at the lake. A boat is recommended for fishing, as the lake is fairly large, and the trout tend to stay in the deeper waters, other than late in the evening. The rainbow trout in Loon Lake are Blackwater Lake stock, which tend to do well when there is baitfish around. Loon Lake has red-sided shiners and the rainbow trout feed on them and grow rapidly. Trolling is the most popular technique on Loon Lake, although fly fishers who use a sinking line and a streamer will also do well. Loon Lake and its nearby counterpart, Edwards Lake, are generally ice free by late-March, which is much sooner than most lakes in the Rockies.

Loon Lake
(rainbow trout)

Edwards Lake (BC)
Rainbow trout to 65 cm (4.0 kg)
Edwards Lake is located south of Loon Lake, approximately 2 km west of Grasmere. Fishing from shore is possible at Edwards, particularly at the eastern end, where the lake narrows significantly. The Blackwater strain of rainbow trout in Edwards Lake grow quickly on the abundant feed, and trout caught from the lake average 25-40 cm in length, with some big, fat lunkers in the 2-3 kg weight class taken regularly. The lake is not very deep and is susceptible to winter kill on occasion. Fly fishing is great at Edwards, whether tossing a dry fly to rising trout or trolling a nymph through the deeper waters.

Edwards Lake

Shotnana Lake, Indian Lake *(on First Nations Reserve)*
Brook trout to 45 cm
The two lakes on the Tobacco Plains Reserve were stocked in the past with brook trout. Permission is required to fish either lake.

KOOCANUSA REGION: Jaffray Sub-Region

Jaffray Sub-Region

The town of Jaffray, situated just south of Highway 3, is the main centre of human activity for this Sub-Region, which stretches east from the shores of Lake Koocanusa. Lake Koocanusa is the dominant physical feature of the area, and has been increasing exponentially in terms of angling attention in recent years due to the popularity of its kokanee fishery. Many of the Sub-Region's lakes, including Surveyors, Baynes, Suzanne, Tie and Rosen, are unique in that they contain largemouth bass. Virtually all of the Sub-Region's lakes can be reached by vehicle on paved or gravel roads.

Lake Koocanusa (BC)
Kokanee to 40 cm
Bull trout to 80 cm (6.0 kg)
Cutthroat trout to 55 cm (2.0 kg)
Rainbow trout to 65 cm (3.0 kg)
Whitefish to 45 cm

Lake Koocanusa is the large reservoir that extends for 150 km, from the Libby Dam on the Kootenai (Kootenay) River in Montana to Wardner, B.C. and Highway 3. The name Koocanusa is derived from "Koo" for Kootenay River, "can" for Canada, and "usa" for United States of America. The reservoir is subject to massive draw downs, and by springtime the upper 10 km of the lake is no more than the Kootenay River meandering through mud flats. In June, runoff waters from snow melt fill the reservoir and the lake level rises, in some years as much as 20 m. Lake Koocanusa's popularity with anglers is derived from its dynamic kokanee population. These landlocked sockeye salmon were stocked following the reservoir's creation, and they have flourished. Kokanee live for four years in the lake before heading upstream to spawn and die. In the lake, these beautiful silver salmon range from 25-35 cm in length, and are most effectively caught using trolling gear. Gang trolls followed by a bright pink flatfish or lure are the standard rig for kokanee. Bull trout in the lake feed on the kokanee and grow to very large sizes. Cutthroat and rainbow trout have also been stocked in Koocanusa, but are not present in numbers anything close to the kokanee population. Cutthroat and rainbow trout taken from Koocanusa average 30-35 cm in length. The rainbow trout in the lake are Gerrard-strain, which have grown to enormous sizes in other lakes with bountiful kokanee stocks. The best fishing on Lake Koocanusa tends to be close to where tributary streams enter the lake. Anglers working from shore can have success in these areas as well.

Kootenay River (BC) *(Fort Steele to Lake Koocanusa)*
Cutthroat trout to 55 cm (1.5 kg)
Bull trout to 80 cm (6.0 kg)
Rainbow trout to 55 cm (1.5 kg)
Whitefish to 45 cm

The section of the Kootenay River upstream from Lake Koocanusa to Fort Steele has never gained a good reputation among anglers. In contrast, nearby Lake Koocanusa is swamped with anglers during the summer. The river remains murky for much of the summer, seldom clearing until well into the fall. Although some of the river's reputation as mediocre fishing is deserved, those who take the time to work the river may be pleasantly surprised. Cutthroat trout in the 25-35 cm size range are the normal catch, with a few rainbow and bull trout present as well.

Kootenay River

Baynes Lake (BC)
Rainbow trout to 60 cm (2.5 kg)
Largemouth bass to 50 cm (2.0 kg)

Baynes Lake is located just south of Kikomun Creek Provincial Park and west of Highway 93. The lake is a popular destination in the summer, and many people have built recreational and permanent homes on its shore. Largemouth bass are present in good numbers and can be taken throughout the summer. Spin casting with a jig or worms, or fly fishing with a big deer hair mouse will bring the bass a runnin'. Largemouth in Baynes Lake average 20-30 cm in length, with big 2 kg+ whoppers caught on occasion. Rainbow trout are also stocked in Baynes Lake, and they grow quickly because of the plentiful food supply in the lake. Rainbow trout in the lake average 30-40 cm in length, but are normally caught in lesser numbers than largemouth bass, other than in the springtime. Fishing off a dock is a popular way to fish at Baynes (assuming you have a dock to fish off). Bass can be taken from shore at many locations, but if you are after the lake's rainbow trout, a boat is strongly recommended.

Lake Koocanusa (kokanee)

Baynes Lake

Tyler Ambrosi with Baynes Lake rainbow trout

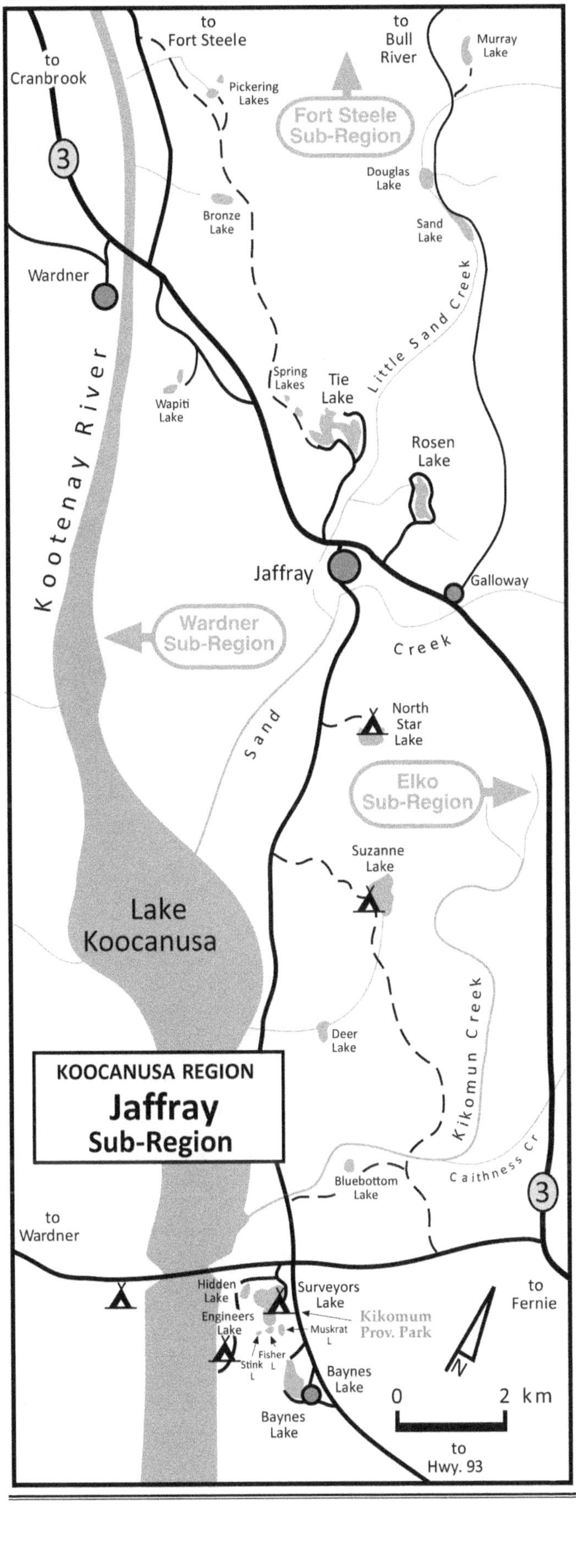

KOOCANUSA REGION: Jaffray Sub-Region

Surveyors Lake (BC)
Brook trout to 60 cm (2.5 kg)
Largemouth bass to 50 cm (2.0 kg)
Rainbow trout to 50 cm (1.5 kg)

Surveyors Lake is the crown jewel of Kikomun Creek Provincial Park, located 15 km south of Jaffray. The campground at Surveyors Lake is extremely popular and is filled to the brim throughout the summer. Two sandy beaches on the lake attract hordes on sunny days. The beach bunch always far outnumbers anglers at Surveyors Lake, even though the lake does hold some very nice fish. Brook trout and largemouth bass predominate, although there may be a few rainbow trout around as well. The brook trout grow to large sizes, with many specimens exceeding the 1 kg weight class. Normally, trout are caught in the deeper waters and the bass are caught in the shallows. The largemouth bass like to hide under lily pads, deadfall, or overhanging tree branches - just about anything your hook is likely to get caught on. Most of the bass are in the 20-25 cm range, but there are always bigger ones around. Sight fishing is very effective as long as you can get your lure in a position to attract the bass that you can see. Take a rod and make a circuit of the lake on the fine hiking trail. As you are walking along, keep a sharp eye on the water - you will undoubtedly see some bass.

Surveyors Lake

Engineers Lake (BC)
Largemouth bass to 50 cm (2.0 kg)
Brook trout to 45 cm

Engineers Lake is a small lake attached directly to Surveyors Lake by a narrow channel. Although there may be the odd brook trout present, largemouth bass tend to prefer the shallow, warm waters of Engineers Lake. A tangle of brush surrounds the lake and makes casting difficult.

Engineers Lake

(largemouth bass)

KOOCANUSA REGION: Jaffray Sub-Region

Muskrat Lake, Fisher Lake, Stink Lake (BC)
Largemouth bass to 40 cm
These three small lakes are located north of Engineers Lake. Largemouth bass may be present in the lakes in limited numbers.

Hidden Lake (BC)
Largemouth bass to 40 cm
Hidden Lake is located in a small basin alongside the paved road that leads from Surveyors Lake campground to the Lake Koocanusa boat launch. Hidden Lake's population of turtles likely exceeds any bass that may be present.

Deer Lake (BC)
Rainbow trout to 40 cm
This small lake is located just east of the Jaffray-Baynes Lake Road on Suzanne Creek. The lake's rainbow trout, which average 20-30 cm in length, are best fished in the springtime.

Bluebottom Lake (BC)
Brook trout to 40 cm
Bluebottom Lake is located approximately 3 km north of the entrance to Kikomun Creek Provincial Park, and is reached on rough roads that lead east from the Jaffray-Baynes Lake Road. Bluebottom Lake has been stocked with brook trout, which average 25-35 cm in length. Fishing is generally difficult due to heavy brush around the lake and extended shallows.

Bluebottom Lake

North Star Lake (BC)
Rainbow trout to 55 cm (2.5 kg)
This popular lake and campground is located approximately 5 km south of Jaffray, west of the Jaffray-Baynes Lake Road. The lake contains Blackwater-strain rainbow trout, which prey on the red-sided shiners in the lake. Rainbow trout in North Star average 30-40 cm in length, and large trout over 50 cm are caught often. Trolling the deeper water works well at North Star, although patient fly fishers will be very successful.

North Star Lake

Suzanne (Manistee) Lake (BC)
Rainbow trout to 60 cm (3.0 kg)
Largemouth bass to 55 cm (2.5 kg)
Suzanne Lake can be reached on good dirt roads west from the Jaffray-Baynes Lake Road. A nice campground is located at the lake. Suzanne has a substantial bass population, and there have been problems in the past with the bass eating the stocked rainbow fingerlings. To alleviate the problem, two-year-old Gerrard-strain rainbow trout have been stocked in Suzanne. The hope is that the rainbows will not be eaten by the bass, and will be able to grow to large sizes. The lake itself is big and requires a boat for any quality fishing opportunities. The rainbow trout in the lake average 30-40 cm in length and are generally taken from the deeper water. Largemouth bass can be taken from the shallows wherever there is sufficient cover for the bass to hide.

Suzanne Lake

Kylie Butler with Suzanne Lake rainbow trout

Wapiti (Warm) Lake (BC)
Rainbow trout to 50 cm (1.5 kg)
Brook trout to 50 cm (1.5 kg)
Wapiti Lake is located on a bench east of Lake Koocanusa, approximately 5 km west of Jaffray. Wapiti is actually two small, interconnected lakes. The lakes are very shallow and tend to winter kill regularly. Fish are stocked annually and grow very quickly due to the massive amount of food available in this productive pond. Catchable-size rainbow trout have been stocked in recent years, with brook trout also stocked on occasion. Trout in the lake average 30-40 cm by mid-summer and many will reach 50 cm by late fall. There is little forest cover around the lake and fishing from shore can be productive, although a boat will enhance angling opportunities.

Sand Creek, Kikomun Creek, Caithness Creek (BC)
Rainbow trout to 35 cm
Cutthroat trout to 35 cm
These three creeks in the Jaffray region are easily accessed from good gravel roads. Fishing is decent for small rainbow and cutthroat trout, which average 20-25 cm in length.

KOOCANUSA REGION: *Wardner Sub-Region*

Douglas Lake, Sand Lake (BC)
Rainbow trout to 40 cm
Douglas and Sand Lakes are located north of Jaffray and can be reached from the Galloway-Bull River road. Fishing for rainbow trout has been reported as poor in these lakes. Cutthroat trout may also be present in Sand Lake.

Murray (Mirror) Lake (BC)
Rainbow trout to 40cm
This small lake is located 2 km southwest of the northern junction of the Bull River-Galloway road. Murray Lake is stocked regularly with rainbow trout. Trout in the lake average 25-35 cm in length. Access to the lake requires permission from private landowners.

Rosen (McBaines) Lake (BC)
Largemouth bass to 55 cm (2.0 kg)
Rainbow trout to 55 cm (2.0 kg)
Rosen Lake is situated just northeast of Jaffray and can be reached on roads from Highway 3. A boat is essential at Rosen, as shore fishing is restricted by private property that surrounds virtually the entire lake. Largemouth bass and rainbow trout both inhabit Rosen's waters, but the fishing is fair at best. The lake warms up significantly in the summer and the rainbow seem to disappear into the deeper, cooler waters. In the springtime, however, fishing for the lake's rainbow trout is good, and trout in the 30-40 cm range are the regular catch. Bass averaging 25-35 cm in length can be caught in the shallower waters throughout the season.

Rosen Lake

Tie Lake (BC)
Largemouth bass to 55 cm (2.0 kg)
Rainbow trout to 60 cm (2.5 kg)
Located directly north of Jaffray and accessible by paved road, Tie Lake has much in common with nearby Rosen Lake. Private property also encircles much of Tie Lake, cutting the shoreline off from prospective anglers. A boat is the only reasonable alternative for fishing on Tie Lake unless you own lakeshore property. As with Rosen Lake, largemouth bass and rainbow trout will be the catch of the day. The rainbows in Tie Lake grow quickly, with trout 30-40 cm in length being the average size. Largemouth bass tend to be a bit smaller than the rainbow trout, averaging 20-35 cm in length, but are more plentiful than the rainbow trout. Tie Lake has winter killed on occasion in the past.

Tie Lake

Spring Lakes (BC)
Brook trout to 55 cm (2.0 kg)
The Spring Lakes can be reached via rough 2WD drive roads that lead north off Highway 3 just west of the Highway 93 junction to the U.S. The lakes are fed by springs and hold brook trout in good numbers. Trout taken from the lake will average 30-40 cm in length.

Wardner Sub-Region

The Wardner Sub-Region extends south and west from the small community of Wardner along the western side of Lake Koocanusa. To the immediate west of Wardner, along the Ha Ha Creek Road, are the cluster of lakes that include Lund, Ha Ha, Bednorski and Edith. To the south of Wardner in the Caven Creek drainage, Cherry Lake is the most popular of the mountain lakes.

Lund Lake (BC)
Brook trout to 45 cm
Rainbow trout to 45 cm
Lund Lake is situated less than two kilometres west of Wardner on the Ha Ha Creek Road. This small lake is beside the road and is easily accessed. Lund Lake has been stocked with rainbow and brook trout, and may even hold a few bass. Using a boat or float tube and venturing out into the middle of the lake will enhance angling results. Flies and lures are both effective at Lund Lake.

Lund Lake

Ha Ha (Rothwell) Lake (BC)
Brook trout to 55 cm (1.5 kg)
Ha Ha Lake is a shallow lake alongside Ha Ha Creek Road, a few kilometres west of Lund Lake. Waterfowl seems more at home at Ha Ha Lake than do trout. The lake is stocked regularly, and does hold brook trout averaging 20-30 cm in length. A boat or float tube is essential for fishing this lake, as reed growth and very shallow water will inhibit shore bound anglers.

Ha Ha Lake

KOOCANUSA REGION: Wardner Sub-Region

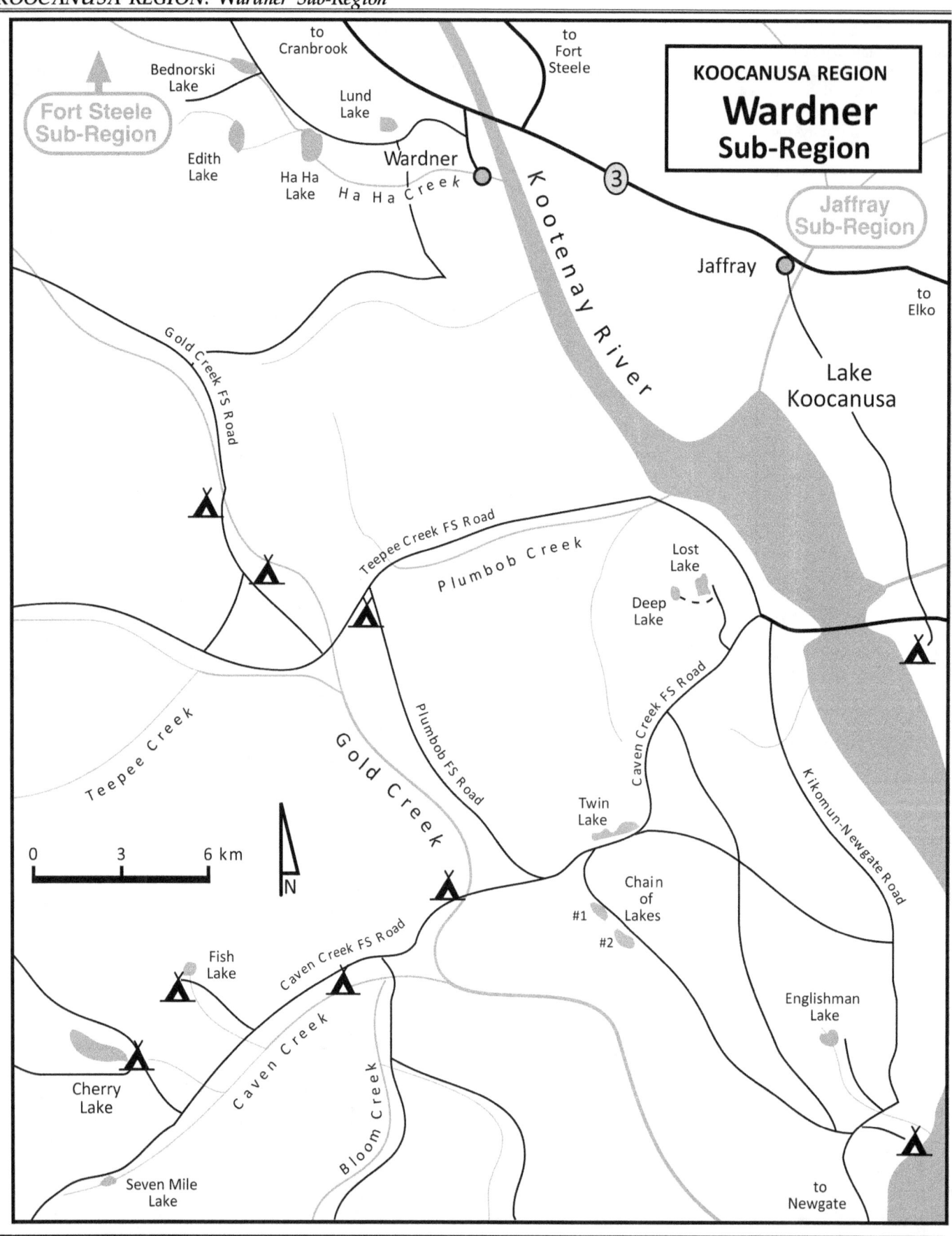

KOOCANUSA REGION: Wardner Sub-Region

Bednorski (Simon's) Lake (BC)
Brook trout to 55 cm (1.5 kg)
Bednorski Lake is similar in character to nearby Ha Ha Lake. Bednorski Lake is very shallow and is ringed by substantial reed growth. Fishing from shore is generally unproductive. Although most of the lake is surrounded by private property, there is a small public boat launch area on the south side of the lake. The brook trout in Bednorski Lake average 25-35 cm in length, although there are larger fish present.

Bednorski Lake

Edith Lake (BC)
Brook trout to 45 cm
Edith Lake is reached by branching west off the Ha Ha Creek Road onto a side road at Bednorski Lake. Although Edith Lake is visible from the access road, private property must be crossed to reach the lakeshore. Be sure to gain permission before crossing any private property. Edith Lake holds a limited number of brook trout in the 25-35 cm range.

Edith Lake

Ha Ha Creek (BC)
Brook trout to 30 cm
Ha Ha Creek flows through both Bednorski Lake and Ha Ha Lake before passing through Wardner and emptying into the Kootenay River. Small brook trout can be taken from the upper reaches of the creek.

Cherry Lake (BC)
Rainbow trout to 55 cm (1.5 kg)
Cherry Lake is situated amid heavy forest cover in the upper Caven Creek watershed, and is reached from the Caven Creek Forest Service Road. There is a Forest Service Recreation Site at the lake. The lake sits in a sunken basin, and although there is forest all around the lake, the shoreline has receded to the point that there is generally a 20-30 m wide swath around the lake that is free of vegetation. Water levels at Cherry Lake rise in the spring and early summer with the runoff, and then continue to decline during the late summer and fall. Fishing from shore is possible around the entire lake, with some deep holes visible in the clear water. If fishing from shore, watch for rising fish, and make your way to that location. A boat will be very helpful at Cherry Lake, as it seems that the fish tend to keep to that point just beyond your longest cast from shore. The rainbow trout in Cherry Lake are plentiful, and most will average 25-35 cm in length. There may also be the odd cutthroat trout present from previous plantings.

Cherry Lake

Fish Lake (BC)
Cutthroat trout to 40 cm
Fish Lake is located in the small valley just to the west of Cherry Lake, and is also accessed from the Caven Creek Forest Service Road. The most prominent access road into Fish Lake leads to private property. The Forest Service Recreation Site is only a few hundred metres down the lakeshore on a rough road. Although Fish Lake is relatively small, it has extensive shallows, and long casts will be required to reach the fish holding waters. The best fishing for the lake's small cutthroat trout is along the deeper waters on the opposite side of the lake from the Recreation Site. Dry flies work very well in Fish Lake.

Fish Lake

Seven Mile Lake (BC)
Cutthroat trout to 40 cm
Seven Mile Lake is found at the headwaters of Caven Creek. There is a Recreation Site at this small lake. Seven Mile Lake is stocked regularly, and holds plenty of cutthroat trout in the 20-30 cm range. Flies and lures are equally effective in Seven Mile Lake.

Chain of Lakes (Twin Lakes) (BC)
Brook trout to 50 cm (1.5 kg)
Chain of Lakes are two lakes that are located south of the intersection of the Caven Creek and Plumbob Creek Forest Service Roads. Access is on a rough 2WD road. Although both lakes have been stocked with brook trout, the southern lake

KOOCANUSA REGION: Wardner Sub-Region

(#2) holds better angling opportunities. Deadfall in both lakes affords good fish habitat. Brook trout in the lakes average 25-35 cm in length, and can be taken with lures from shore.

Chain of Lakes #2 (brook trout)

Twin Lake (BC)
Status: Doubtful
Twin Lake is a large, shallow, two-headed pond that is located alongside the Caven Creek Forest Service Road, approximately 10 km west of Lake Koocanusa. Brook trout were stocked in the past, but it is likely they all succumbed to winter kill.

Englishman Lake (BC)
Rainbow trout to 45 cm
This small lake is situated at the head of Englishman Creek, and is accessed from the Kikomun-Newgate Road. Englishman Lake is stocked regularly with rainbow trout, and anglers will catch trout averaging 25-35 cm in length in good numbers.

Lost Lake (BC)
Brook trout to 40 cm
Lost Lake is reached by taking a short, but very nasty, 4WD road north off of the Caven Creek Forest Service Road. Although Lost Lake is relatively shallow, there are a number of deeper pools that can be accessed by intrepid anglers who fight there way around the underbrush to far side of the lake. Brook trout in Lost Lake average 20-30 cm in length and are very limited in number. Although unlikely, there may be a few rainbow trout present in the lake, remnants of past plantings.

Lost Lake

Deep Lake (BC)
Rainbow trout to 55 cm (1.5 kg)
To reach Deep Lake, one must first take the bad road into Lost Lake. From Lost Lake, a rough trail around the northwest side of Lost Lake leads in 20 minutes to Deep Lake, a small, but not surprisingly, deep body of water. Rainbow trout are stocked regularly, and they seem to do well in Deep Lake, likely due to the general absence of fishing pressure. Expect to catch rainbow trout averaging 25-35 cm in length, with larger ones present in decent numbers.

Gold Creek, Caven Creek, Plumbob Creek, Teepee Creek, Bloom Creek (BC)
Cutthroat trout to 35 cm
All of the major creeks to the west of Lake Koocanusa hold cutthroat trout in good numbers in their upper reaches. Forest Service roads ascend most of the drainages. Rainbow trout, bull trout, brook trout, whitefish and kokanee may also be present in the lower sections of Gold and Plumbob Creeks at various times of the year.

Fort Steele Sub-Region

This Sub-Region is concentrated around Fort Steele Heritage Town, a popular tourist attraction on Highway 93/95. The paved Fort Steele-Wardner Road branches off Highway 93/95 at Fort Steele, and leads to several fine lakes in and near Norbury Lake Provincial Park. Logging roads up the Bull River drainage allow access to some excellent stream fishing, as well as to secluded mountain lakes. The Kootenay Trout Hatchery at Bull River provides an interesting perspective on fish management and angling in southeastern B.C. and is well worth a visit.

Kootenay Trout Hatchery

Kootenay River (BC) (Wasa to Fort Steele)
Cutthroat trout to 55 cm (1.5 kg)
Bull trout to 80 cm (6.0 kg)
Whitefish to 45 cm
The Kootenay River flows south from Wasa to Fort Steele, en route to Lake Koocanusa. This section of the river receives light fishing pressure for its cutthroat and bull trout populations. The water remains mud-coloured for most of the year, clearing only in the fall. Although fishing is fair at best, cutthroat trout averaging 25-35 cm in length can be taken from most stretches of the river. Bull trout and whitefish, as well as the occasional rainbow trout can also be caught.

Wild Horse Creek (BC)
Cutthroat trout to 35 cm
Wild Horse Creek was the scene of a frantic gold rush in the 1860's, and the streambed was utterly destroyed in the search for gold. With over 100 years to recuperate, the stream now looks normal in most respects. The flow is generally turbulent, although there are small pools along the length of Wild Horse Creek. Small cutthroat trout can be taken from the creek, with most fish averaging 15-25 cm in length.

KOOCANUSA REGION: Fort Steele Sub-Region

Bull River (BC)
Cutthroat trout to 50 cm
Bull trout to 70 cm (5.0 kg)
Whitefish to 45 cm

The Bull River is the major tributary to this segment of the Kootenay River. The Bull River experiences very high stream flow during runoff in June and early July, but then clears quickly. Logging roads extend to the upper reaches of the Bull River drainage, offering good access to the river. Cutthroat trout fishing is excellent in the Bull River's many fine pools. The cutthroat trout are plentiful in the Bull River, and average 20-35 cm in length. Big bull trout in the 3-4 kg range can also be found in the deeper pools. The Bull River has a significant whitefish run each fall. Fall also brings spawning kokanee salmon into the lower river in great numbers.

Bull River

(whitefish)

Galbraith Creek, Summer Creek, Tanglefoot Creek, Quinn Creek (BC)
Cutthroat trout to 40 cm

These tributaries of the Bull River are all noted for their good stream fishing for cutthroat trout. Logging roads have been built up each watershed, allowing anglers relatively easy access. The cutthroat trout tend to be small, in the 20-30 cm range, but are plentiful. Bull trout and whitefish may also be present in the fall.

Norbury and Little Bull Creeks (BC)
Rainbow trout to 35 cm
Cutthroat trout to 35 cm

Norbury Creek, which flows beside the Kootenay Trout Hatchery at Bull River, is formed by the joining of Norbury and Little Bull Creeks a kilometre above the hatchery. Hatchery staff at one time regularly released surplus trout into the creek near the hatchery, a practice that is no longer continued. Rainbow and cutthroat are the most likely species to be caught, but there could be a few brook trout as well. These creeks have an age restriction on them, so be sure to check your fishing regulations.

Summer Lake (BC)
Cutthroat trout to 55 cm (1.5 kg)

Summer Lake is reached via taking a series of Forestry Service Roads up the Bull River, Galbraith Creek and Summer Creek, respectively. Camping sites are available along the lake at several locations. The lake itself is a blue-green gem, set in a crown of fine peaks. Water levels rise with the melting of the snow into early summer, and then recede for the rest of the year. Hard-fighting cutthroat trout are plentiful in the lake, and average 30-40 cm in length. Fishing from shore is possible from almost any location once the lake level begins to recede, but shore bound anglers should keep to areas around inlet creeks and near drop-offs. If the lake is calm, watch for rising fish. Many times, they will be close enough to cast to. If fishing from a boat, you can either troll a lure through the deeper water, or anchor and try fly fishing in the shallows where feisty cutthroat cruise back and forth.

Summer Lake

Ruault Lake (BC)
Cutthroat trout to 35 cm

This tiny lake is located approximately 4 km west of Summer Lake and is accessed by a steep trail. Cutthroat trout were present at one time in the lake, but their status is precarious at best. Expect little more than small trout in the 15-25 cm range.

Ruault Lake

Bear Lake (BC)
Cutthroat trout to 35 cm

Bear Lake is located in a basin above Wild Horse Creek and can only be reached by trail. One 4 km trail climbs up the valley of the outlet stream from the Wild Horse Creek Forest Service Road. A second, less-formal route crosses the ridge above Ruault Lake before descending to Bear Lake. Bear Lake holds cutthroat trout in small sizes, few growing larger than 30 cm in length.

Bear Lake

KOOCANUSA REGION: Fort Steele Sub-Region

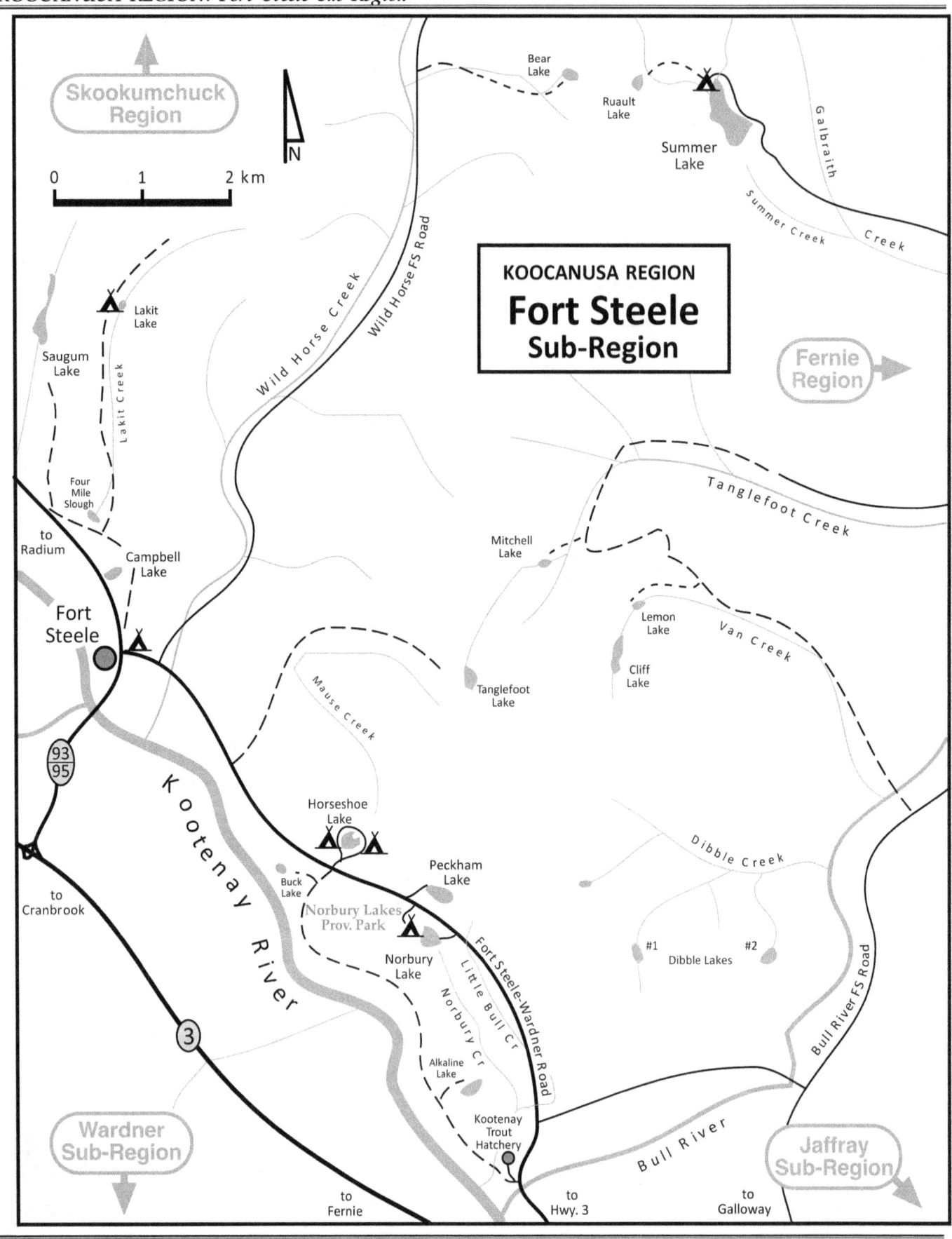

KOOCANUSA REGION: Fort Steele Sub-Region

Lemon Lake (BC)
Cutthroat trout to 35 cm

Lemon Lake is the first of two lakes reached by trail at the head of the Van Creek Valley. Vehicle access to the trailhead is off the Bull-Van Forest Service Road. A mix of forest, meadow and rock around Lemon Lake affords adequate casting room. Cutthroat trout in the lake are small, most being 20-25 cm in length.

Cliff (Blue) Lake (BC)
Cutthroat trout to 40 cm

A steep and rocky headwall protects Cliff Lake from most intruders who venture beyond Lemon Lake. Cliff Lake lies a little over 2 km and 400 vertical metres above Lemon Lake. For those who do reach the cobalt blue waters of Cliff Lake, cutthroat trout can be taken from most locations along its rocky shoreline. The cutthroat trout in the lake average 25-35 cm in length.

Cliff Lake

Mitchell Lake (BC)
Cutthroat trout to 35 cm

This small forest-bound lake can be reached by taking a 1 km trail up Tanglefoot Creek from the Tanglefoot Forest Service Road. Casting room is at a premium due to the dense forest cover. Cutthroat trout in the lake are plentiful but small, with the average being under 30 cm.

Mitchell Lake

Dibble Lakes (BC)
Cutthroat trout to 40 cm

The two Dibble Lakes are situated in pretty basins to the south of Dibble Creek. Access to Dibble #1 (the more westerly one) is on abandoned logging roads and rough trail. Access to Dibble #2 is more difficult, following a poor trail up from Dibble Creek. Both lakes hold plenty of cutthroat trout that average 20-30 cm in length. Fly fishing with a sinking line and nymph is normally very productive.

Dibble Lake #2

Norbury (Garbutts) Lake (BC)
Rainbow trout to 60 cm (2.5 kg)

Located alongside the Fort Steele-Wardner Road, Norbury Lake is located within namesake Norbury Lake Provincial Park. A large campground is located just north of the lake. Shore fishing is restricted by private land, but those with boats or float tubes will have no problems. Rainbow trout in the lake grow quickly, with the average trout caught being in excess of 30 cm. There may be a few cutthroat trout in the lake as well. The water is very clear, and sight fishing in the extensive shallows is possible. During most of the day, the larger trout are in the deeper water, and a lure or sinking fly line will be needed in order to drum up any action.

Norbury Lake

Peckham's Lake (BC)
Rainbow trout to 50 cm (1.5 kg)
Brook trout to 50 cm (1.5 kg)

Peckham's Lake is found along the Fort Steele-Wardner Road in Norbury Lake Provincial Park. A nice picnic area covers much of the lake's east shore. Fishing is especially productive in the springtime at Peckham's Lake, and throngs of anglers show up for the first few weeks of the season. Even though the lake is relatively small and a good cast will reach well out into the lake, many anglers prefer watercraft when fishing Peckham's. Those on shore using a bubble and mealie worm rig will catch fish. Rainbow and brook trout are stocked regularly, and they have plenty of food to get fat on. Trout caught in the lake average 30-35 cm in length, with larger fish caught often.

Peckam's Lake

Tyler Ambrosi with Peckhams Lake rainbow trout

KOOCANUSA REGION: Fort Steele Sub-Region

Horseshoe Lake (BC)
Rainbow trout to 60 cm (2.5 kg)

Horseshoe Lake is located less than a kilometre north of the Fort Steele-Wardner Road in an open Ponderosa pine forest. A popular forestry campground encircles the entire lake. Tree cover does not extend down to the lakeshore, so fishing from shore is possible. Horseshoe Lake is relatively shallow and has extensive weed beds, which produce plenty of food for the lake's fat rainbow trout. Trout taken from Horseshoe Lake tend to be on the chunky side and average 30-40 cm in length. Trolling a fly slowly over the weed beds will produce well on most occasions. Fishing tends to slow significantly in the summer months, but picks up well again in the fall.

Horseshoe Lake

Pickering (Crowsnest) Lakes (BC)
Brook trout to 45 cm

Pickering Lakes can be reached via rough 2WD drive roads that that lead southeast from the Bull River bridge on the Fort Steele-Wardner Road. The two tiny Pickering Lakes are completely encircled by reeds, making fishing from shore rather troublesome. Brook trout in good numbers live out beyond the reeds for those who reach them with a good cast. The brookies in Pickering average 25-35 cm in length, with some larger, fatter models available as well.

Pickering Lake

(brook trout)

Bronze (Weatherhead) Lake (BC)
Brook trout to 50 cm (1.5 kg)

This small lake can be reached by driving on a rough 2WD road for approximately 3 km southeast from the Bull River bridge. Casting room is available around the entire lake. Stumps and deadfall in the lake will undoubtedly claim a few lures. Bronze Lake contains stocked brook trout, which thrive in the nutrient rich environment. Brook trout in the lake average 25-40 cm in length, and can be taken with equal effectiveness by lure or fly. If fishing is poor, sit back and watch the numerous turtles that like to sun themselves on logs along the lakeshore.

Bronze Lake

Alkaline Lake (BC)
Brook trout to 40 cm

Alkaline Lake is a shallow body of water located southwest of Norbury Lake Provincial Park. Brook trout have been stocked in the past, but problems with the lake's water level and its alkalinity have affected productivity. Although trout likely still inhabit Alkaline Lake, their numbers are very limited.

Buck Lake (BC)
Status: Doubtful

Located northwest of Norbury Lake Provincial Park, tiny Buck Lake has never been stocked and probably holds no fish.

Campbell (Campbell Meyer) Lake (BC)
Brook trout to 45 cm
Rainbow trout to 45 cm

Campbell Lake is conveniently located at a Rest Area north of Fort Steele on Highway 93/95. The lake is prone to winter kill, and it is a rarity that fish will survive the winter. However, Campbell Lake is stocked each spring with catchable-size brook or rainbow trout, which grow rapidly during the year. By the fall, most of the fish are close to 40 cm in length. The lake is relatively small and fishing from shore is usually productive, although a boat will allow you to fish the deeper waters in the middle of the lake.

Campbell Lake

Four Mile Slough (BC)
Brook trout to 40 cm
Four Mile Slough is a series of beaver ponds on Lakit Creek. Access is on dirt roads off of Highway 93/95. The ponds hold small brook trout, most in the 15-25 cm range.

Lakit Lake (BC)
Brook trout to 35 cm
This petite pond on Lakit Creek is located east of Highway 93/95. The bottom of the lake is completely covered with deadfall and logs, which makes for good habitat for fish. Brook trout are present in small sizes, with few larger than 30 cm in length.

Lakit Lake

Saugum Lake (BC)
Brook trout to 60 cm (2.5 kg)
Saugum Lake is located on Saugum Creek, east of Highway 93/95, and due west of Lakit Lake. Access is either via a rough dirt road and a short hike or through private property. This shallow lake is stocked regularly with brook trout that grow to large sizes. Trout caught in Saugum Lake average 30-40 cm in length, and lunkers of 2 kg and more are taken from Saugum Lake on occasion.

Saugum Lake

(brook trout)

WEST CASTLE REGION

This Region encompasses the foothills and mountain valleys between Waterton Lakes National Park and the Crowsnest Pass. Variety is foremost, with excellent stream and river fishing opportunities, as well as heavily fished foothill lakes and pristine alpine tarns. The western, mountainous Beaver Mines Sub-Region centres on the Castle and West Castle River drainages south of the hamlet of Beaver Mines. Further to the east, the mountains give way to rolling foothills of the Pincher Sub-Region.

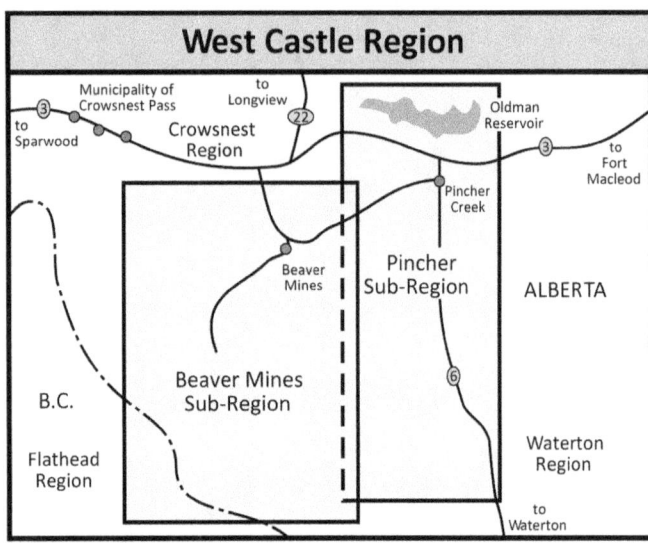

Beaver Mines Sub-Region

Outstanding stream fishing and secluded mountain lakes typify the Beaver Mines Sub-Region. The Castle and West Castle Rivers, both noted for their fine angling for cutthroat trout, flow from south to north through the heart of the area. Vehicle access is from either Pincher Creek, or Highway 3 at Burmis, and then through the small community of Beaver Mines and along Highway 774 to the Castle Mountain Resort ski area. Abandoned logging roads extend up both the Castle and West Castle River valleys, although the enormous destruction of the floods of 1995 is still evident and vehicular access is limited. Beaver Mines Lake, accessible by a good gravel road, has a provincial campground, and receives heavy fishing pressure throughout the year. The Southfork Lakes and Rainy Ridge Lake contain stocked populations of golden trout, the only lakes in the southern Canadian Rockies where this rare species has been successfully planted. Grizzly, Lys and South Scarpe Lakes, all backpacking adventures, are highly regarded fishing destinations.

Beaver Mines (Beaver) Lake (AB)
Rainbow trout to 55 cm (2.0 kg)
Bull trout to 65 cm (4.0 kg)

Beaver Mines Lake is situated beneath the impressive form of Table Mountain, two kilometres west of the Castle River Ranger Station on Highway 774, and is busy with anglers all summer long. The accompanying provincial campground is always crowded with tents and RVs. The lake's popularity arises from its abundance of hard-fighting rainbow trout that average 25-35 cm in length. A few large bull trout are also present in Beaver Mines Lake. Trolling is the usual method of fishing at Beaver Mines, although both spin casting and fly fishing can be productive. Weed growth chokes many parts of the lake by mid-summer, making trolling difficult for those who aren't familiar with the lake. For those without a boat, try alongside the access road near the outlet. Trout can be taken very close to shore in this area. Beaver Mines Lake is well-known for its ravenous insect population, and extra repellent is strongly advised. Camp Impeesa, a Boy Scout camp at the western end of the lake, is busy throughout the summer, and there will invariably be swimmers and canoes near the camp. As one would expect, fishing is not as good in this part of the lake, unless you are planning to catch a Boy Scout.

Beaver Mines Lake

Chase and Tia Morotoli with Beaver Mines Lake rainbow trout

Castle (South Castle) River (AB)
Cutthroat trout to 55 cm (1.5 kg)
Rainbow trout to 55 cm (1.5 kg)
Bull trout to 60 cm (3.0 kg)
Whitefish to 35 cm

The Castle River is renowned locally for excellent fishing, and receives the attention of many anglers each season. Flowing gently along the valley floor, the Castle's pools and riffles provide long stretches of fishable water. The lower Castle River, downstream from the confluence of the Castle and West Castle Rivers, is crossed at several locations by highways and secondary roads. Reaching the better pools will often require a hike along the bank from the main access points. The upper Castle River is known locally as the South Castle River. It can be reached by following a rough dirt road that branches south off of the Beaver Mines Lake road. The upper Castle River road was severely damaged by flooding in 1995, and the distance open to vehicular traffic changes from year to year. The road, however, is completely washed out beyond Scarpe Creek, approximately 20 km south of the Castle River bridge. Cutthroat trout in the 20-30 cm range predominate in the Castle River, with individual specimens in excess of 3.0 kg taken on occasion, including the current Alberta record. Rainbow and bull trout, as well as whitefish, are also taken regularly. Spring run-off is usually complete by early July, and as water levels on the Castle River subside, fishing picks up tremendously. The upper reaches of the river tend to have smaller, but more numerous trout. The stretch of river near Castle Falls holds plenty of trout, but is fished to its limits during the summer. The lower river has some real beauties in its big holes, notably in the area around the old Canyon Bridge site, off Highway 507.

Castle River

Susan Douglas Murray with Castle River cutthroat trout

West Castle River

Yutaka Awamura with bull trout

West Castle (Westcastle) River (AB)
Cutthroat trout to 45 cm
Rainbow trout to 45 cm
Bull trout to 60 cm (3.0 kg)
Whitefish to 35 cm

The West Castle River is very similar in character to the upper (South) Castle River, and provides many kilometres of superb stream fishing. The West Castle River is paralleled by Highway 774 from its confluence with the Castle River upstream to Castle Mountain Resort (ski hill). Beyond the ski area, access is via a rough 4WD road, which follows the valley bottom and is seldom far from the river. As with the upper Castle River, fine cutthroat and bull trout can be caught in the West Castle, with rainbow trout and whitefish taken on occasion as well. After spring run-off is complete, the West Castle can easily be forded, and anglers who do a little searching away from the main access points will be rewarded with lots of beautiful cutthroat trout in the 25-35 cm range. West Castle River Falls, at the upper end of the valley - beyond the reach of vehicles - is particularly outstanding.

Mill Creek, Gladstone Creek, Beaver Mines Creek, Screwdriver Creek (AB)
Rainbow trout to 30 cm
Cutthroat trout to 30 cm

These tributaries of the lower Castle River contain a variety of game fish, but are dominated by cutthroat and rainbow trout in small sizes. However, don't be surprised if you catch a bull or brook trout or a whitefish. These are typical foothill creeks, with nice pools and long stretches of fishable water. All of these creeks are accessible from Highway 507, or from a gravel secondary road.

Grizzly Creek, Scarpe Creek, Font Creek, Jutland Brook, Syncline Brook, Suicide Creek, Gravenstafel Brook (AB)
Cutthroat trout to 25 cm

Located in the headwaters region of the upper Castle and West Castle Rivers, these tributaries do not offer the of quality angling that is available in the lower Castle tributaries. These creeks generally have a much steeper gradient and fish are unable to make it far beyond the confluence with the Castle. An exception is Grizzly Creek, where the better fishing is in the kilometre or so below Grizzly Lake, and small brook trout can be taken. When the Castle River is still murky with run-off, cutthroat trout can often be taken where the tributary joins the main river.

Jutland Creek

WEST CASTLE REGION: Beaver Mines Sub-Region

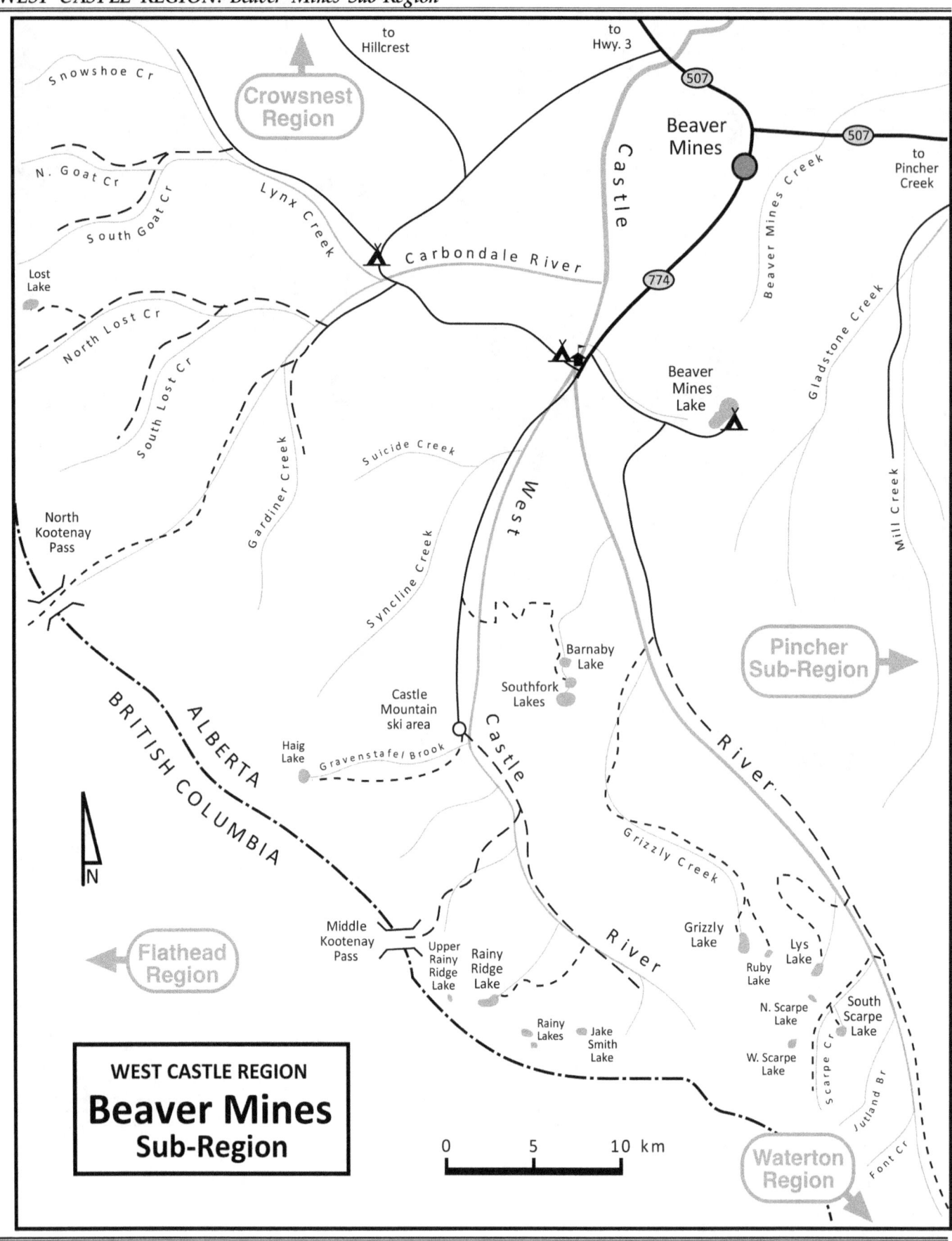

WEST CASTLE REGION: Beaver Mines Sub-Region

Rainy Ridge Lake (AB)
Golden trout to 55 cm (1.5 kg)
Set against the backdrop of the Continental Divide, delightful Rainy Ridge Lake offers much for the prospective angler. The lake contains beautifully coloured golden trout, originally stocked in the late-1950's, and now able to maintain their population through natural reproduction. Most golden trout taken from Rainy Ridge are in the 25-35 cm range, although much larger ones are taken on occasion. Fly fishing is the most successful method of fishing, and casting room is available around most of the lake with the area along the scree slopes on the south shore generally the most productive. Patient anglers can work the shallows near the outlet with success. Two different routes lead into Rainy Ridge. A rough 4 km trail, with a difficult to locate trailhead, begins along the West Castle River and climbs steeply up into Rainy Ridge Lake basin. A second, somewhat longer route, begins at Middle Kootenay Pass at the end of a rough 4WD road that climbs up from the West Castle River. This ill-defined 6 km route passes Burl Lakes, before climbing to a pass and dropping down to Rainy Ridge Lake. Despite the difficult access, expect company at Rainy Ridge Lake.

Rainy Ridge Lake (golden trout)

Upper Rainy Ridge Lake (AB)
Status: Devoid of fish
This small pond is located approximately 1 km above Rainy Ridge, and is tucked in a forested basin below Rainy Ridge. The lake is visible to those who cross the ridge above Burl Lakes, and is often mistaken for Rainy Ridge Lake. There are no fish in Upper Rainy Ridge Lake.

Rainy Lakes (AB)
Status: devoid of fish
Set in a fine subalpine basin below Three Lakes Ridge, these two tarns have never been stocked and contain no fish.

Jake Smith Lake (AB)
Status: devoid of fish
Located on a ridge east of Scarpe Mountain, Jake Smith Lake has never been stocked and contains no fish.

Haig Lake (AB)
Status: Devoid of fish
Haig Lake lies nestled in a cirque immediately below the foreboding east face of Mt. Haig. The lake is four kilometres by trail above Castle Mountain Ski Resort. Haig Lake has never been stocked, and it is impossible for fish to enter the lake from Gravenstafel Brook, as Haig Lake drains underground.

Haig Lake

South (East) Scarpe Lake (AB)
Rainbow trout to 50 cm (1.5 kg)
Set in a large cirque high on the flank of Jutland Mountain, South Scarpe Lake attracts many anglers each summer despite its remote location. Reaching the trailhead requires a substantial effort. Vehicular access beyond the Beaver Mines Lake road changes annually, and can turn the walk-in from a 3 km day hike to a 15 km overnighter. The formal trail begins just downstream from the confluence of Scarpe Creek and the Castle River on an abandoned seismic road. Two kilometres from the Castle River, a steep, less-defined side trail heads up into the forest along South Scarpe Lake's outlet creek. One heart-pounding kilometre later, a primitive campsite and the outlet of the lake are reached. South Scarpe Lake and its basin are a verdant delight, with the emerald green waters of the lake blending with the grass-covered slopes and dark forest. Other than at the outlet, where shallows and a major logjam are present, the steep sides of the basin continue down into the lake. Fishing deep with a fly or lure is generally successful. South Scarpe Lake's once fine reputation has been tarnished somewhat in recent years due to over harvest, although rainbow trout are still found in good numbers, and most average 30-40 cm in length. Many of the fish in the lake appear to be rainbow-cutthroat hybrids, with general rainbow characteristics but having a bright red throat slash.

South Scarpe Lake

Ryan Ponto with South Scarpe Lake rainbow trout

WEST CASTLE REGION: Beaver Mines Sub-Region

West Scarpe Lake (AB)
Rainbow trout to 45 cm

West Scarpe Lake is situated on the southern end of Lys Ridge two kilometres above Scarpe Creek. Stocked a number of years ago with golden trout which apparently failed to reproduce, West Scarpe was long though to be incapable of sustaining fish. However, plantings of rainbow trout have apparently been successful, and rainbows are now present in fair numbers. As access from Scarpe Creek is difficult because of a lack of defined trails over the final 2 km, this lake can only be recommended to the most adventuresome.

North Scarpe Lake (AB)
Status: Devoid of fish

This small tarn is situated in the middle of a high, rocky basin above Scarpe Creek and below Lys Ridge. Access is by bushwhacking up from Scarpe Creek or over Lys Ridge from Lys Lake. North Scarpe Lake is incapable of holding trout.

North Scarpe Lake

Lys Lake (AB)
Rainbow trout to 45 cm

Set in a narrow basin off the southeastern end of Lys Ridge, Lys Lake receives relatively little fishing pressure due to its isolated location. Outfitter parties use the area regularly, but few hikers make the effort to climb up into the pretty, larch-filled valley. Lys Lake holds rainbow trout in the 30-35 cm range in good numbers. Fish can be taken from most locations around the lake with lures being notably successful. Access is on an 8 km horse trail up the outlet creek from the South Castle River road.

Lys Lake

Grizzly Lake (AB)
Brook trout to 50 cm (1.5 kg)

A tiring 13 km hike up Grizzly Creek valley from the Castle River leads to Grizzly Lake, situated at the south end of Barnaby Ridge. A shorter but more difficult access is up Barnaby Ridge from the West Castle River. The lake is popular with anglers despite its lengthy access, and Grizzly's striking green waters provides some of the Southern Rockies' finest brook trout fishing, with many trout in the 40 cm+ range. Fly fishers will enjoy sight fishing in the shallows near the outlet. Other areas, particularly along the scree slopes in the lake's southwest corner, are also very productive.

Grizzly Lake

(brook trout)

Ruby Lake (AB)
Status: Devoid of fish

Set in a basin near tree line one kilometre above Grizzly Lake, the lovely waters of Ruby Lake have never been stocked and contain no fish.

Barnaby Lake, Upper and Lower Southfork Lakes (Barnaby Ridge Lakes) (AB)
Golden trout to 50 cm (1.5 km)

Set in an exquisite subalpine basin immediately beneath Southfork Mountain, these three lakes stand out collectively as the gem of the entire Region in terms of natural beauty. Along with nearby Rainy Ridge Lake, these lakes are the only lakes in the Southern Rockies where golden trout have been successfully planted. Access is by a steep 5 km trail, which leads up from the West Castle River. Barnaby Lake, the first one encountered as one approaches by trail, is at a substantially lower elevation than the other two lakes. Fishing is generally poor in Barnaby, although there definitely are fish present. Half a kilometre by trail above Barnaby Lake is Lower Southfork Lake, the smallest of the three lakes. It is circular in shape and has shallows that extend out for 10-15 m all the way around the lake. These shallows make fly fishing from shore a difficult proposition, as the trout tend to keep to the deeper waters. Upper Southfork Lake is the largest of the three and holds the most trout. Golden trout in all three lakes range from 20-35 cm in length, with larger specimens present. As golden trout are generally spooky by nature, and the water is extremely clear in all three lakes, anglers must be very cautious when approaching the lakes. Although reduced catch limits are in place for Barnaby and the Southfork Lakes, catch and release is strongly recommended in order to maintain fish stocks.

WEST CASTLE REGION: Pincher Sub-Region

Barnaby Lake

Lower Southfork Lake

Upper Southfork Lake

(golden trout)

Carbondale River (AB)
Cutthroat trout to 35 cm
Bull trout to 55 cm (1.5 kg)
Rainbow trout to 35 cm
Whitefish to 35 cm
The Carbondale River is the major tributary of the Castle River, and begins in meadows below North Kootenay Pass along the Continental Divide. Turbulent in its upper reaches, the river provides excellent stream fishing below its confluence with Gardiner and Lynx Creeks, all the way to its junction with the Castle River. Cutthroat trout are the dominant species, most averaging 15-25 cm in length. The occasional bull or rainbow trout or whitefish are also taken. The Carbondale River road is the major route into the Carbondale drainage, and it is accessible from Hillcrest in the Crowsnest Pass via the Adanac Road, or from Highway 507.

Lynx Creek, Gardiner Creek, Macdonald Creek, Lost Creek, Goat Creek, Snowshoe Creek (AB)
Cutthroat trout to 30 cm
These tributaries of the Carbondale River and/or Lynx Creek all contain small cutthroat trout in good numbers. Gardiner and Lynx Creeks, in particular, offer excellent stream fishing.

Lost Lake (AB)
Status: Devoid of fish
This promising looking body of water in the North Lost Creek drainage has never been stocked and contains no fish.

Lost Lake

Pincher Sub-Region

This Sub-Region encompasses the sweeping foothill country around the community of Pincher Creek. Access is west from Pincher Creek off of Highway 507, or south from Pincher Creek off of Highway 6. Beauvais Lake Provincial Park and the Oldman Reservoir are the main attractions for visitors, both in terms of scenery and angling. Despite the ongoing controversy over the merits of the damming of the Oldman River, the Oldman Reservoir has been steadily gaining respect among anglers. Further south, the triumvirate of Butcher and Bathing Lakes and the Shell Waterton Pond are man-made lakes that offer easily accessible fishing opportunities. Bovin Lake is the Sub-Region's sole backcountry angling destination.

Beauvais Lake (AB)
Rainbow trout to 50 cm (1.5 kg)
Brown trout to 55 (2.0 kg)
Lovely Beauvais Lake is set in the foothills west of Pincher Creek, and can be reached by taking Highway 775 eight kilometres south from Highway 507. In addition to the summer cottages that line the lake's east shore, a large campground and an excellent picnic area within the park attract many families each summer. Seldom is there any time of the day when there aren't at least a few boats out on Beauvais Lake. Landlubber anglers should not be deterred, however, as there are many places where fish can be taken in close proximity to the shore. Rainbow trout are stocked annually in large numbers, and over a typical summer, are caught in much greater numbers from Beauvais than brown trout. Most rainbow trout taken from Beauvais Lake average 20-35 cm in length. The browns tend to be larger, but are more difficult to catch. If you're after a big brown, try a dry fly in the late, late evening. Trolling seems to be the preferred method of angling on Beauvais, but fly fishing and spin casting will work very well also. If boating on Beauvais, take note of signs restricting access to the section of the lake where waterfowl nest in the spring.

Beauvais Lake (brown trout)

Marna Lake (AB)
Status: Doubtful
This shallow lake just off the Highway 775 access road to Beauvais Lake Provincial Park has never been stocked and would unlikely be able to sustain fish over the winter.

WEST CASTLE REGION: Pincher Sub-Region

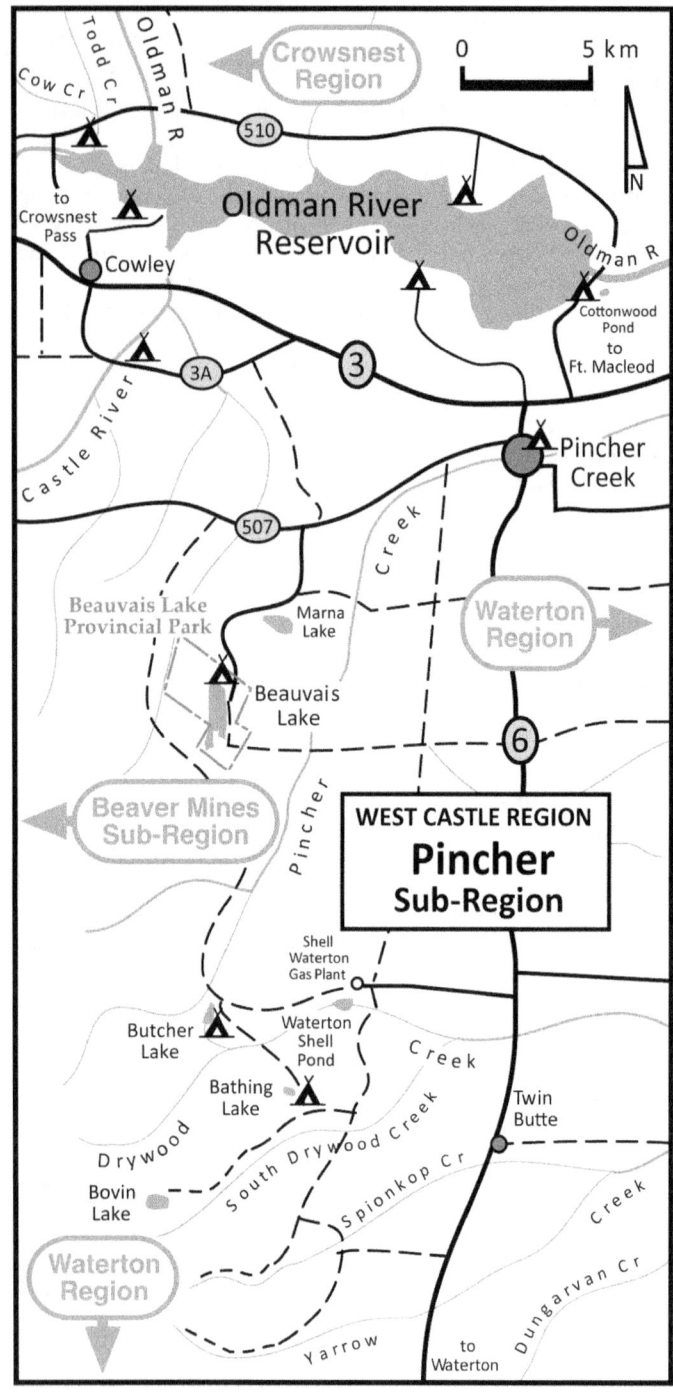

Pincher Creek (AB)
Rainbow trout to 35 cm
Cutthroat trout to 35 cm
Bull trout to 45 cm
Whitefish to 30 cm

Pincher Creek has maintained a good reputation among anglers in Southern Alberta for many years. Even though the massive flooding in 1995 damaged the stream severely, and angling quality declined for a few years, Pincher Creek still ranks among the better foothill streams. Over its entire course, from headwaters between Pincher Ridge and Mount Victoria, to its confluence with the Oldman River near Brocket, Pincher Creek offers excellent creek fishing for small rainbow and cutthroat trout.

Waterton Shell Pond (AB)
Brook trout to 35 cm
Rainbow trout to 35 cm

The Waterton Shell Pond is situated on Drywood Creek immediately below the Waterton Shell Gas Plant, approximately eight kilometres east of Highway 6. This man-made lake, at first glance, appears to be some sort of water storage facility for the gas plant. However, closer inspection will generally reveal trout rising in good numbers. Small brook trout in the 20-30 cm range are the normal catch, although rainbow trout and the occasional cutthroat are present as well. A good cast from the parking area can reach most corners of the lake, so there is no need to walk too far to fish. Due to the ponds close proximity to the gas plant, there may be problems with water quality, so it would be prudent to release all the fish you catch.

Wateton Shell Pond

Butcher (Prairie Bluff) Lake (AB)
Brook trout to 35 cm

Man-made Butcher Lake is located alongside the road, approximately 5 km west of the Waterton Shell Gas Plant, on a small tributary of Drywood Creek. The outflow of the small creek was dammed, forming the small lake. Brook trout have been stocked in Butcher, and most fish from the lake will be 25-30 cm in length, although there are undoubtedly a few larger specimens as well. Fish can be taken from virtually any location around the lake, although most anglers tend to congregate along the lakeshore below the road.

Butcher Lake (brook trout)

WEST CASTLE REGION: Pincher Sub-Region

Bathing Lake (AB)
Rainbow trout to 35 cm

Bathing Lake is located west of South Drywood Creek, and is reached by taking the gravel road that connects South Drywood Creek and Drywood Creek. A small picnic area is at the lake. The lake is very tiny and it is stocked regularly with rainbow trout. The trout in the lake are generally very active, and the surface is usually dimpled with rising trout. Fly fishing room is plentiful around the entire lake. Most rainbow trout taken from Bathing Lake will be in the 15-30 cm range.

Bathing Lake

Bovin Lake (AB)
Brook trout to 40 cm

Bovin Lake is fished less frequently in recent years due to restrictions on vehicular access, but still only provides mediocre angling for those reaching its shores. The lake is reached by a 5 km road walk from gas well maintenance roads in the South Drywood Creek drainage. Bovin Lake contains plenty of small brook trout, few stretching beyond the 30 cm mark. The lake itself is a large, circular sink hole, with no permanent inlet or outlet creek. The water level in the lakes fluctuates during the year, reaching its high point after run-off is complete, and dropping throughout the summer and fall. The changing water levels wreak havoc on the lake's littoral zone, where the fish should be getting most of their food. Fishing is usually the most productive at the far end of the lake, where the scree slopes reach the shoreline and there is deep water within casting distance.

Bovin Lake

Drywood Creek, South Drywood Creek, Spionkop Creek, Yarrow Creek, Dungarvon Creek (AB)
Rainbow trout to 35 cm
Cutthroat trout to 35 cm
Brook trout to 35 cm
Bull trout to 40 cm

All of these foothill tributary streams of the Waterton River hold trout in good numbers. Fishing pressure on these creeks is light, with most angling attention near the most accessible locations. Small rainbow trout are the normal catch, although brook, cutthroat and bull trout are all present as well.

Oldman Reservoir (AB)
Rainbow trout to 60 cm (2.5 kg)
Bull trout to 70 cm (4.0 kg)
Cutthroat trout to 55 cm (2.0 kg)
Brown trout to 60 cm (2.5 kg)
Whitefish to 45 cm

The Oldman Reservoir is the backwater created by the construction of the Oldman Dam. There is paved access from Highway 3 at Cowley and Pincher Creek, and several nice campgrounds around the reservoir. The dam flooded the junction and several kilometres of the Oldman, Castle and Crowsnest Rivers. In its first few years of existence, the dam was not very productive in terms of fish habitat. However, rainbow trout seem to have taken hold, in large part due to regular stocking programs. Having a boat on the Oldman Reservoir is a priority. Trolling is the preferred technique among most anglers on the reservoir, although bait fishers working the shoreline are often successful. The area around the inlets of the major feeder streams and rivers are the best place for those on shore to try. Rainbow trout in the 35-45 cm range are the normal catch, even though there is a mixed bag of fish in the lake. Be aware that the lake is very prone to extremely strong winds that will make boating impossible.

Oldman Reservoir

Cottonwood (Oldman River Campground) Pond (AB)
Rainbow trout to 35 cm
Brown trout to 35 cm

There is a small pond within the Oldman River Campground, which is located below the dam. Cottonwood Pond is stocked on occasion, and will contain whatever has been stocked. It is doubtful if fish could over winter in the pond.

WEST CASTLE REGION: Pincher Sub-Region

Todd Creek, Cow Creek (AB)
Rainbow trout to 45 cm
Cutthroat trout to 45 cm
Brown trout to 45 cm
These two creeks enter the Oldman Reservoir at its western end. Although both creeks tend to be murky during much of the year, they hold trout in reasonable numbers. Seldom will there be a day when you don't see trout rising. Trout in the lower portions of the creeks, near the reservoir, will average 25-35 cm in length, with rainbow trout being the most likely catch.

Oldman River (AB) *(downstream from Oldman Reservoir)*
Brown trout to 60 cm (2.5 kg)
Rainbow trout to 55 cm (2.0 kg)
Bull trout to 80 cm (5.0 kg)
Whitefish to 45 cm
Northern Pike to 60 cm (2.5 kg)
Below the Oldman Dam, the Oldman River flows eastward towards its confluence with the Bow River. In the tailwaters below the dam, and for a few kilometres downstream, fishing is generally very good. Brown trout are in the vast majority, and can generally be taken in the 25-35 cm size range. There is also a small population of bull trout that annually congregate below the dam in a fruitless effort to try to make it to their former spawning beds far upstream.

Oldman Dam spillway

(brown trout)

CROWSNEST REGION

The Crowsnest River and Crowsnest Mountain lend their name to this area which centres on the Municipality of Crowsnest Pass (an amalgamation of the towns of Blairmore, Coleman, Bellevue, Frank and Hillcrest). Highway 3 cuts through the middle of the Region, leading east to Fort Macleod, and west to Sparwood in British Columbia. The Crowsnest River, which begins near the Alberta-B.C. boundary and parallels Highway 3 as it flows east to the Oldman Reservoir, is regarded by many as one of the premier fly fishing streams in Western Canada. The numerous minor tributaries of the Crowsnest hold trout, and are sought out by creek fishing enthusiasts. There are also a large number of well-stocked lakes, making the Crowsnest Region a Mecca for anglers. The region is split geographically east-west, with the town of Blairmore being the dividing line: the Coleman Sub-Region to the west; and the Bellevue Sub-Region to the east.

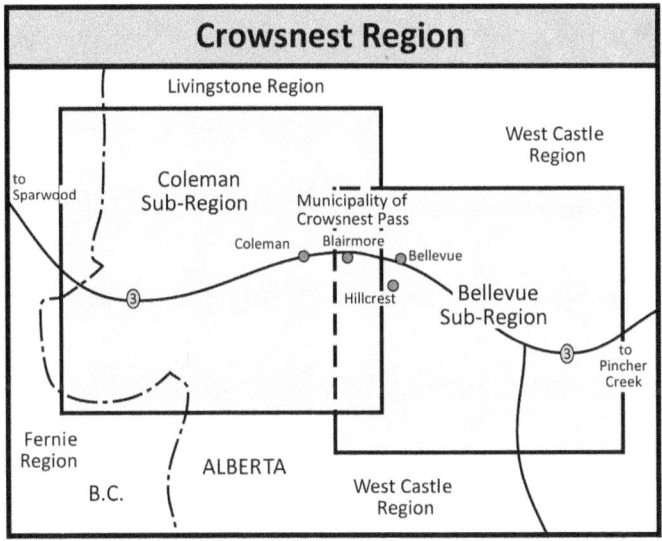

Coleman Sub-Region

The western half of the Crowsnest Region extends from the B.C.-Alberta boundary west to the communities of Coleman of Blairmore. Crowsnest Lake, Island Lake and Emerald Lake at the head of the Crowsnest River are popular with local anglers. Chinook Lake, located just off the Allison Creek Road, has a large forestry campground, which is very busy during the summer. Window Mountain Lake is a short hike off the upper Allison Creek Road, and provides one of the Region's few backcountry fishing opportunities

Crowsnest River (AB) *(Crowsnest Lake to Blairmore)*
Rainbow trout to 50 cm (1.5 kg)
Cutthroat trout to 45 cm
Bull trout to 60 cm (3.0 kg)
Whitefish to 35 cm
Renowned as one of the finest fly fishing streams anywhere in the Rockies, the Crowsnest River flows passively eastward from headwaters in the Crowsnest Pass. Easily accessible from nearby Highway 3 (Crowsnest Highway), which accompanies the river for its entire length, the lower portion of the river receives very heavy angling pressure throughout the summer and fall Crowsnest (see Bellevue Sub-Region). The upper section of the river, between Crowsnest Lake and Blairmore receives much less fishing pressure than the lower river. The upper Crowsnest River is a very slow, meandering river, and is typified by gentle riffles and wide sweeping corners with undercut banks. Reaching the river bank is often difficult due to adjoining swampland and willow thickets. Not as nutrient rich as the lower river, the upper Crowsnest contains less fish in generally smaller sizes. Rainbow trout averaging 20-25 cm in length predominate, and are generally very susceptible to the fly.

Crowsnest River

Island Lake (AB)
Brook trout to 50 cm (1.5 kg)
Rainbow trout to 50 cm (1.5 kg)
Constituting the headwaters of the Crowsnest River, Island Lake is located just east of the B.C.-Alberta boundary, and is divided in half by Highway 3. Stocked regularly, Island Lake contains a good population of brook trout, most averaging 25-35 cm in length, as well as a few rainbows and perhaps the odd cutthroat. Angling is much better in the waters on the north side of the highway, and a boat is suggested, although fish can be taken from shore. Monster trout from the Allison Creek Brood Station, which have outlived their usefulness for the brood stock program, are on occasion put into (north) Island Lake, giving fortunate anglers who hook one a 4 kg, line-screaming thrill ride.

Island Lake

CROWSNEST REGION: Coleman Sub-Region

Crowsnest Lake (AB)
Rainbow trout to 55 cm (1.5 kg)
Lake trout to 70 cm (6.0 kg)
Bull trout to 60 cm (4.0 kg)
Whitefish to 45 cm

With the Crowsnest River as its outlet, Crowsnest Lake is situated one kilometre east of Island Lake, and is the largest lake in the Region. Its deep, dark waters hold lake trout ranging from 35-50 cm in length, with some brutes reaching over 60 cm in length and 5 kg in weight. The lake also holds rainbow trout that measure 25-40 cm in length. The best time of year for lake trout is very early or very late in the season, immediately after ice-out in April, or near freeze-up in November. Bait fishers who patiently work the shoreline are usually productive. Trolling can also work well on Crowsnest Lake, but boaters should be aware that howling winds usually sweep down the lake.

Crowsnest Lake

Emerald (Hart) Lake (AB)
Cutthroat trout to 50 cm (1.5 kg)
Lake trout to 60 cm (4.0 kg)

The pretty green waters of Emerald Lake are situated on the south side of Highway 3 opposite Crowsnest Lake, approximately 8 km west of Coleman. Despite its relatively small surface area, Emerald Lake has been identified as the Region's deepest lake, surprisingly surpassing even nearby Crowsnest Lake in depth. Cutthroat trout are the predominant species in Emerald Lake, most being in the 25-35 cm range. Emerald also holds some decent lake trout, which attract local anglers. The odd rainbow or brook trout may even be present in the lake. As with neighbouring lakes, winds can present a major problem at Emerald Lake.

Emerald Lake

Allison Creek, McGillivray Creek, Nez Perce Creek, Blairmore Creek, Crowsnest Creek, Star Creek, York Creek, Lyons Creek (AB)
Rainbow trout to 30 cm
Cutthroat trout to 30 cm

All minor tributaries of the Crowsnest River, these creeks hold small trout in fair numbers. Rainbows generally predominate in the lower portions of the creeks and cutthroat in the upper. Catching a cutthroat or rainbow longer than 25 cm would be very much of a surprise. Despite the small size of the trout, these tributaries of the Crowsnest remain very popular, especially with local youngsters. Active and abandoned industrial roads extend up the valleys drained by most of these creeks and provide access for anglers. (Note: Lyons Creek generally dries up completely by mid-summer in its lower reaches within the town of Blairmore.)

Tent Mountain Lake (AB)
Cutthroat trout to 30 cm

Tent Mountain Lake is a small brush-fringed lake set at the head of Crowsnest Creek, immediately below Tent Mountain Pass. The lake is accessible from the Tent Mountain Collieries road, which branches south from Highway 3 between Island and Crowsnest Lakes. Although this shallow lake holds a few small cutthroat trout, it is likely that you will see more moose than trout. For keeners, fight through the underbrush and try the area close to the outlet creek.

Tent Mountain Lake

Phillipps Lake (AB or BC)
Cutthroat trout to 35 cm

Phillipps Lake is a small, circular sinkhole lake located at the summit of Phillipps Pass, one kilometre due north of Crowsnest Lake. The lake itself sits on the provincial boundary, and either a B.C. or Alberta license will do. (Regulations regarding catch limits in Phillipps Lake are the same for both jurisdictions) A rocky 3 km road leads to Phillipps Pass from Crowsnest Provincial Park, just west of the B.C.-Alberta boundary. Alternatively, a steep 3 km hike on a gated road can be taken from the eastern end of Crowsnest Lake. Phillipps Lake holds plenty of nice cutthroat trout averaging 20-30 cm in length. Both kokanee and rainbow trout were at one time stocked in the lake, but failed to reproduce. Fish holding waters can be reached from virtually any location around the lake.

Tyler Ambrosi with Phillipps Lake cutthroat *Phillipps Lake*

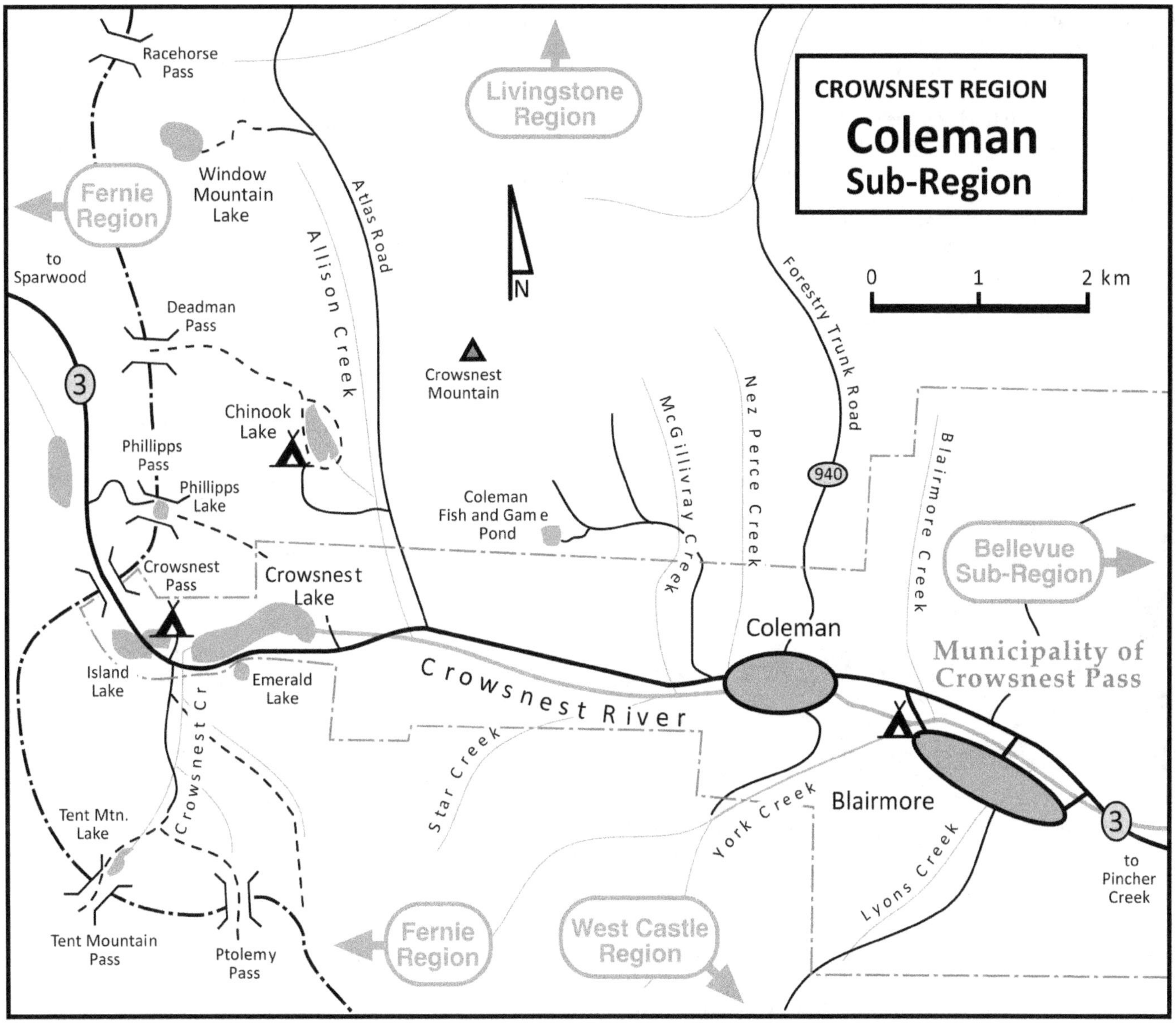

CROWSNEST REGION: Coleman Sub-Region

Chinook Lake (Allison Reservoir) (AB)
Rainbow trout to 55 cm (1.5 kg)
Brook trout to 45 cm

This popular fishing spot is situated west of Coleman and north of Highway 3, and is accessed by a good gravel road. Chinook Lake and its nearby campground are busy all summer long. Extensive flooding caused by the dam at the south end of the lake has left an abundance of sunken deadfall around the entire shoreline. Rainbow trout are stocked regularly, although their numbers diminish significantly by fall. Brook trout are also present, but the rainbow trout tend to be more numerous. Fish caught from Chinook Lake will average 25-40 cm in length. Fly fishing from a boat or float tube is very effective on Chinook Lake, particularly in the evening. Patient anglers who work the shoreline all around the lake will also do well. One section of shoreline (near the access road) serves as a beach for locals in the summertime. Don't expect a lot of solitude at Chinook Lake.

Chinook Lake and Crowsnest Mountain

CROWSNEST REGION: Coleman Sub-Region

Window Mountain Lake (AB)
Rainbow trout to 45 cm
Window Mountain is an exquisite body of water tucked into the side of Mt. Ward, and stands out as one of the Region's hidden treasures. To reach the lake, one must drive 15 km north on the Allison Creek Road and then follow a rough side road for another 2 km to the trailhead. A short but steep 2 km hike leads to the lakeshore. The beautifully coloured waters of Window Mountain Lake contain plenty of rainbow trout, most averaging 25-35 cm in length. Although fly fishing is the most effective method of angling at Window Mountain, casting a fly is difficult from most locations around the lake. If a hatch is not on at Window Mountain Lake, fishing a lure or wet fly deep generally produces. And no, you cannot see the "window" in Window Mountain from the lake.

Window Mountain Lake (rainbow trout)

Coleman Fish and Game Pond (Hidden Lake) (AB)
Rainbow trout to 50 cm (1.5 kg)
This small man-made pond is located northwest of Coleman and it offers very good fishing for those who can find it. From the western end of Coleman, take the (signed) road that leads north to the gun range (bypassing the McGillivray Youth Camp). Opposite the entrance to the gun range, a rough half kilometre long road leads down to the Coleman Fish and Game Pond. Insect life is prolific in the pond, and the fish grow rapidly, with most in the 30-35 cm range. Although many people fish from shore and are successful, a boat or float tube will dramatically increase your fish catching. Fly fishing and spin casting are both effective techniques on the Coleman Fish and Game Pond.

Coleman Fish and Game Pond

Bellevue Sub-Region

The Bellevue Sub-Region extends east from Blairmore, through the Frank Slide and past the communities of Bellevue and Hillcrest, and out to the neighbouring foothills. The Crowsnest River is the primary attraction, and is revered by many fly fishing enthusiasts. Lee Lake is the most significant still water in the Sub-Region, and is very popular with local anglers.

Crowsnest River (AB) *(Blairmore to Oldman Reservoir)*
Rainbow trout to 60 cm (2.5 kg)
Bull trout to 75 cm (4.0 kg)
Brown trout to 75 cm (4.0 kg)
Cutthroat trout to 45 cm
Whitefish to 40 cm
The lower Crowsnest River, from Blairmore downstream to the Oldman River, is an excellent trout stream. Special regulations apply to season, limits and sizes to the Crowsnest River. Be sure to read the Sportfishing Regulations before heading out. Treated sewage effluent from the communities of the Crowsnest Pass enters the river downstream of Bellevue, enriching the waters. Plant, insect, and in turn, trout life, flourishes. In recent years, the Crowsnest River has received, and is deserved of, worldwide attention. As such, fishing pressure is increasing annually, and there are few stretches of water where you won't run into other anglers. Reel-screaming rainbow trout are plentiful in the river, with most fish averaging 25-35 cm, while beauties over 50 cm in length are caught regularly. Above Lundbreck Falls, cutthroat and bull trout can also be caught. Below the falls there are brown trout, some of which reach gigantic proportions (75+ cm), as well as big bulls. The Crowsnest River has excellent hatches of mayflies and caddis flies as well as big stoneflies, and the fly fishing can be spectacular at times. Highway 3 parallels the river for much of its course, although it often means a bit of a walk to actually reach the river. The waters downstream from Lundbreck Falls, particularly those near the base of the falls, are usually busy due to the proximity of the Forestry campground.

Crowsnest River (rainbow trout)

Note: Hatches and action on the Crowsnest River varies considerably from week to week. Visit the Crowsnest Angler Fly Shop and Guide Service in Bellevue for current information and to pick up appropriate tackle.

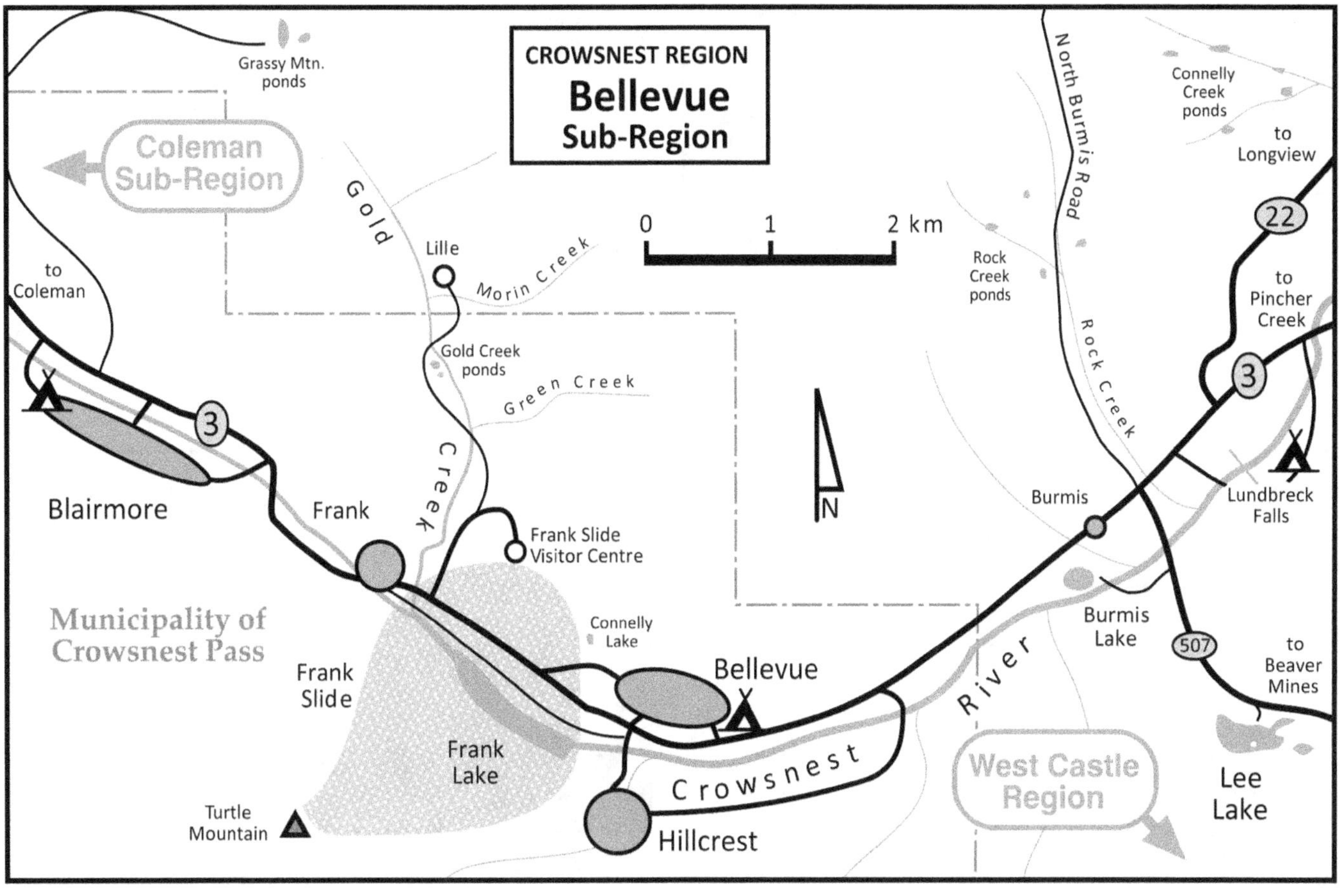

Frank Lake (AB)
Rainbow trout to 55 cm (2.0 kg)
Bull trout to 70 cm (4.0 kg)
Cutthroat trout to 45 cm
Whitefish to 40 cm

Frank Lake is little more than a widening of the Crowsnest River, caused by the multitude of boulders of the 1903 Frank Slide. Stream flow is slowed somewhat, and this stretch of the river does take on some lake-like characteristics. The downstream side of the enormous boulders that are strewn about form potential hiding spots for fish. Mud flats are a problem, as they extend far out from the shore in many places, leaving the fish-holding waters beyond the reach of a cast. Rainbow trout average 20-30 cm in length, with larger ones taken regularly. Plenty of whitefish can be caught in the fall. Techniques that are effective on the Crowsnest River proper are equally effective in Frank Lake.

Gold Creek (AB)
Cutthroat trout to 35 cm
Rainbow trout to 35 cm
Brook trout to 35 cm

Gold Creek is a major tributary of the Crowsnest River, joining at the town of Frank. Gold Creek is an idyllic trout stream, with wonderful pools and riffles over its entire length. The section immediately above the town of Frank is the least accessible, as Gold Creek has carved a deep canyon. Above the canyon, a rough 2WD road crosses Gold Creek twice, and is passable as far as the former townsite of Lille. Cutthroat trout are in the majority in Gold Creek, although both brook and rainbow trout can also be caught. There's plenty of fish, but few whoppers. For those who have had their fill of the Crowsnest River crowds, Gold Creek is a great getaway.

Morin Creek, Green Creek (AB)
Rainbow trout to 25 cm
Cutthroat trout to 25 cm

Green and Morin Creeks are both tributaries of Gold Creek. They contain small cutthroat and rainbow trout in their lower sections, within a few hundred metres of their confluence with Gold Creek.

Frank Lake

CROWSNEST REGION: Bellevue Sub-Region

Gold Creek ponds (AB)
Brook trout to 30 cm

These hard-to-find ponds are located downstream from the second crossing of Gold Creek on the Lille road. The main pond is shallow and the fish can be seen easily. The very small population of brook trout is self-perpetuating, and cannot even stand up to a minimal harvest. Please release all of the trout you catch.

Gold Creek pond

Grassy Mountain (Rainbow) Ponds (AB)
Status: Doubtful

Located at the base of the former Grassy Mountain coal mine on Scurry Rainbow property are several large quarry pits that have filled with water over time. Trout were secretly stocked by locals in the past and grew to large sizes, but failed to reproduce. The waters look very tempting, but recent observations indicate that there are no trout left in any of the ponds.

Grassy Mountain Pond

Connelly Lake (AB)
Status: Devoid of fish

This small pond is located just west of Bellevue on the edge of the Frank Slide. It has never been stocked and contains no fish.

Burmis Lake (AB)
Rainbow trout to 35 cm

This small lake is located between Highway 3 and the Crowsnest River just west of Burmis, and is reached by following a dirt road that leads east from Highway 507 just before the Crowsnest River bridge. Burmis Lake is very shallow, and such is susceptible to winter kill. Food is plentiful in the lake and the fish grow rapidly. Rainbow fingerlings stocked in the spring can easily reach 30 cm by the fall. Fish that manage to over winter can be very respectable in size in their second year. The lake itself is so small that spin casters can generally fling a lure from one side of the lake to the other.

Burmis Lake

Lee (Lees) Lake (AB)
Rainbow trout to 50 cm (1.5 kg)

Lee Lake is located alongside Highway 507, approximately three kilometres south of Highway 3. Formerly enclosed by private property, Lee Lake has had public access for several years now. The lake is very popular with locals, and it is a rare sight not to see anglers at Lee Lake. Bait fishers tend to keep to the shore, while fly fishers take to the water. Lee Lake is stocked annually with rainbow trout. The trout grow quickly in the lake, and most fish caught will be in the 20-30 cm range. In general, the lake is shallow, but it does have a few deep holes accessible to those with a boat. The boundary areas between the shallow and deep water are always productive. Fish also feed in the shallower waters, especially in the evenings, where major mayfly hatches can inspire nightly feeding frenzies.

Lee Lake (rainbow trout)

Connelly Creek ponds, Rock Creek ponds (AB)
Cutthroat trout to 35 cm

Both Connelly Creek and Rock Creek can be accessed from the North Burmis Road, which leads north from Highway 3 at the Highway 507 junction at Burmis. Both creeks have numerous beaver dam complexes, and many hold small cutthroat trout. In the right pond, a 40 cm beast is not out of the question. Access to many of the ponds requires permission from private landowners.

Rock Creek pond (cutthroat trout)

FERNIE REGION

The Elk River is the focal point of the Fernie Region in terms of geography and angling. Changes in the 1990's to fishing regulations on the Elk River transformed it into a world-class cutthroat fishery. The quality fishing opportunities on the Elk River far exceed all other waters in the Region. Grave Lake, near Sparwood, is the only lake of major size. Small backcountry lakes dot the Region and do provide alternate angling experiences. The Fernie Region is split into three Sub-Regions: Hosmer, which includes the city of Fernie; Sparwood and vicinity; and a third Sub-Region, around the former townsite of Corbin at the head of Michel Creek.

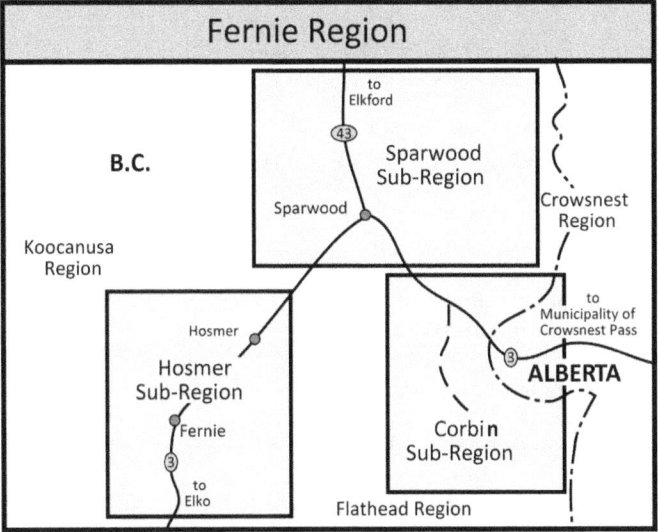

Hosmer Sub-Region

Highway 3 runs lengthwise through the Hosmer Sub-Region, affording access from east and west. The Hosmer area is very Spartan in terms of fishing opportunities. Other than the Elk River, which is outstanding, only two small lakes - Island and Hartley - will even attract the eye of potential anglers.

Elk River (BC) *(Hosmer to Elko)*
Cutthroat trout to 60 cm (2.0 kg)
Bull trout to 80 cm (6.0 kg)
Whitefish to 40 cm

The Elk River flows south down the Elk Valley on its way to Lake Koocanusa. The section between the hamlet of Hosmer and the city of Fernie has become very popular for fly fishers in drift boats. Hosmer is located at a bridged highway crossing of the Elk River and has a good put-in site. Similarly, Highway 3 crosses the Elk River again at Fernie, where there are good take-out sites. The river is wide and strong, with long stretches of riffles and deep pools. Run-off occurs in late spring and continues into early summer, muddying the river significantly. By mid summer, the river clears magnificently, and fishing is at its prime. Cutthroat trout are plentiful, and are of particular delight to dry fly enthusiasts. Cutthroat average 30-40 cm in length, with beauties of 50 cm and over available in good numbers. Bull trout and whitefish are also present in the river. Read your fishing regulations and be aware of all of the special restrictions in force on the river, including which sections of the river are catch-and-release only.

Elk River

(cutthroat trout)

Coal Creek, Fairy Creek, Lizard Creek, Hartley Creek, Hosmer Creek (BC)
Cutthroat trout to 35 cm

The Elk Valley in this Sub-Region is very deep and steep-sided. As a result, minor tributaries to the Elk River tend to be very turbulent much beyond their confluence with the Elk River. Cutthroat trout in the 20-30 cm range can be taken from these creeks. Of more significance, fishing is generally very good where these creeks empty into the Elk River, particularly when the tributaries are clear and the main river is dirty. (Note: Special age restrictions apply to part of Coal Creek. Check regulations.)

Island Lake (BC)
Cutthroat trout to 40 cm

Island Lake is located west of Fernie, and can be reached by taking the dirt road that continues past the Mt. Fernie Provincial Park campground. Signs on the access road indicate that it is private, and accessible only to those staying at Island Lake Lodge. Best to check with the lodge before travelling on the road. Island Lake itself is very pretty, with many bays and tree-studded islands. Below the lodge, a point of land juts out into the lake and most anglers can cast to fish from the peninsula. However, a boat or canoe will allow you to explore the lake more thoroughly. Cutthroat trout have been stocked in Island Lake, and the average trout taken will be in the 25-35 cm range.

Island Lake

FERNIE REGION: Hosmer Sub-Region

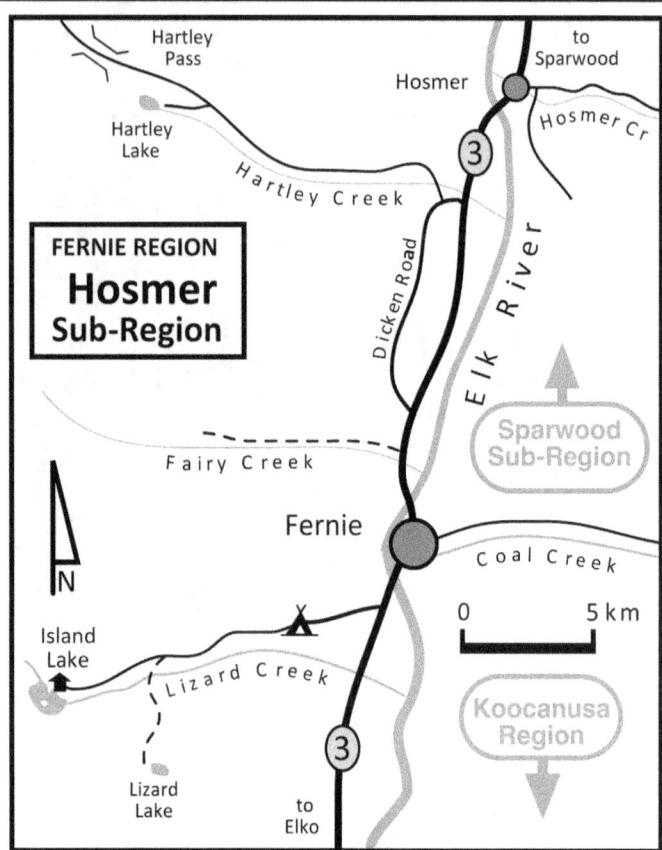

Hartley Lake

Sparwood Sub-Region

The Sparwood Sub-Region has the Elk River as its core, as it flows south to Fernie. Highway 3 is the major transportation link east and west. Highway 43 branches north from Sparwood to connect with Elkford, and provides access to a number of lakes. Grave Lake, northeast of Sparwood, is accessible by vehicle and is popular with locals. Most of the rest of the fishing opportunities in this Sub-Region are secluded alpine lakes, including Harriet and Wilimena.

Elk River (BC) *(Line Creek to Hosmer)*
Cutthroat trout to 60 cm (2.0 kg)
Bull trout to 80 cm (6.0 kg)
Whitefish to 40 cm

This section of the Elk River, which flows south from its confluence with Line Creek to the small community of Hosmer, offers superb angling for cutthroat trout. Line Creek represents the northernmost point to put in watercraft and be able to drift without problems. Upstream on the Elk above Line Creek, the river is very shallow in spots and sweepers can extend far out into the river causing navigation problems. Below Line Creek, the river is generally wide and deep enough to permit a good drift. Access to the put-in point below Line Creek is on the paved road that leads to Line Creek coal mine. The river is paralleled by Highway 3 below Sparwood and Highway 43 above. This allows for good access for those fishing from shore, although a rough walk through a tangle of forest is often required. Cutthroat trout in the 30-40 cm range are found in every good hole along the river. Dry fly fishing is preferred by many anglers, although a nymph fished deep can be dynamite. Be aware that the Elk River is subject to special angling regulations.

Lizard Lake (BC)
Status: Devoid of fish

Lizard Lake is a teeny-tiny, snow-bound, avalanche-swept pond high up on Lizard Ridge that is free of ice for only a few brief weeks each year. It has never been stocked and contains no fish.

Lizard Lake

Hartley Lake (BC)
Cutthroat trout to 35 cm

Diminutive Hartley Lake is located approximately 8 km west of Highway 3 on the Hartley Pass road. The lake is very shallow and is strewn with deadfall, much of it old logs from a former logging operation in the area. Heavy brush surrounds much of the lake, making it difficult to cast to the better fish-holding waters. Cutthroat trout in Hartley Lake are plentiful, but are small, with most being in the 20-25 cm range. Fly fishing is very limited for those on shore. Spin casting is much more likely to get positive results.

Elk River (bull trout)

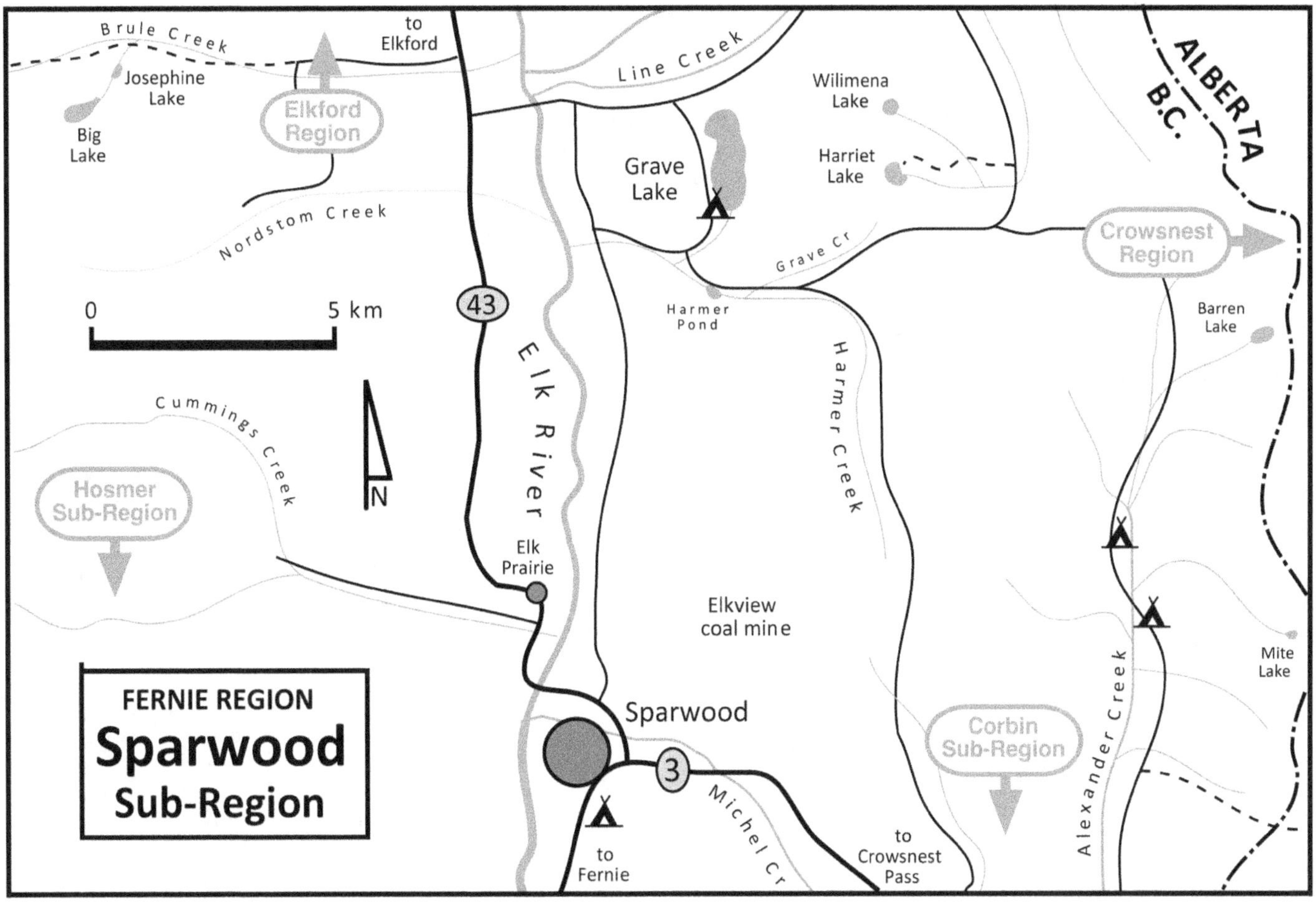

FERNIE REGION: Sparwood Sub-Region

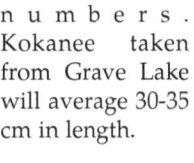

Line Creek (BC)
Status: Closed to angling
Line Creek, one of the major tributaries to this segment of the Elk River, is closed to fishing.

Brule Creek, Cummings Creek, Harmer Creek, Nordstrum Creek (BC)
Cutthroat trout to 35 cm
These tributaries of the Elk River generally hold small cutthroat trout. The best fishing is in the lower sections of the creeks, close to their confluence with the Elk. Trout tend to be small, with most in the 15-25 cm range.

Grave (Emerald) Lake (BC)
Rainbow trout to 60 cm (2.5 kg)
Kokanee to 40 cm
Brook trout to 60 cm (2.5 kg)
Grave Lake is located on the eastern side of the Elk River, approximately 15 km north of Sparwood. Access to the lake is over gravel roads from Highway 43 at Line Creek, or from the LowerElk Valley Road. A campground maintained by the Sparwood Fish and Game Association is situated at the south end of the lake. Private property and recreational homes are found along much of the lake's western shore. Grave Lake is a lovely green body of water almost three kilometres in length, with a dramatic mountain background on its eastern side. A boat is essential for angling on Grave Lake, and trolling is the most effective tactic. Fly fishing is usually restricted to the extensive shallows at the south end. The lake's fish population is made up of rainbow and brook trout, as well as kokanee. Rainbow trout are in the majority and average 25-40 cm in length. Large brook trout are caught on occasion. Kokanee were stocked in the past, and are still in the lake in significant numbers. Kokanee taken from Grave Lake will average 30-35 cm in length.

Grave Lake

Harmer Pond (BC)
Cutthroat trout to 50 cm (1.5 kg)
This small man-made pond on Harmer Creek is located approximately 4 km by road southeast of Grave Lake. Cutthroat trout inhabit the lake, but their numbers are very limited. Size, however, is not a limitation, as most fish taken are in excess of 40 cm. Flashy lures worked from the shore tend to attract trout. Due to the limited population of fish, it is recommended that anglers practice catch-and-release at Harmer Pond.

Tyler Ambrosi with Harmer Pond cutthroat trout
Harmer Pond

Harriet Lake (BC)
Cutthroat trout to 45 cm
This stunning lake is set in a picturesque subalpine basin of the eastern side of Sheep Mountain, due west of Grave Lake. Access to the lake requires driving a rough 2WD road and then a hike on a short but steep 3 km trail. The trail climbs to the crest of a rocky ridge, before dropping down to the shores of Harriet Lake. Several primitive campsites are found along the lakeshore. Harriet Lake holds plenty of cutthroat trout in its emerald waters, with most trout taken ranging from 25-35 cm in length. Heavy forest cover clings to half of the shoreline. The remainder is scree- and grass-covered slopes that offer ample casting room. Fly fishers using a wet line and a nymph will do well. Dry fly fishing tends to improve in the evening. Although many anglers will be frustrated with fish jumping just beyond the reach of their longest cast, those who are patient at Harriet Lake will be successful.

Harriet Lake

Wilimena Lake (BC)
Cutthroat trout to 35 cm
Wilimena Lake is situated in the basin immediately north of its neighbour, Harriet Lake. The trailhead for Wilimena Lake is the same as Harriet, although the trail into Wilimena is much less defined. Be prepared for a little scrambling and stumbling before you reach the shore at Wilimena. Cutthroat trout are bountiful in Wilimena Lake, but their size is not impressive. Most trout caught will be in the 15-25 cm range. The best fishing is off of the open slopes on the lake's south side.

Wilimena Lake

Big Lake, Josephine Lake (BC)
Cutthroat trout to 40 cm
These two remote, subalpine lakes are located high in a secluded basin off upper Brule Creek near Hornaday Pass. A well-defined trail leads up Brule Creek and over Hornaday Pass, but the route into Big and Josephine Lake is a little more rugged. Josephine is the smaller of the two lakes and is set lower in the basin. Both Big and Josephine Lakes have stocked populations of cutthroat trout. Trout in the two lakes average 20-30 cm in length.

Barren Lake (BC)
Cutthroat trout to 40 cm
"Barren" aptly describes this tiny lake and the desolate, rockbound basin in which it is set. Barren Lake is located at the head of a tributary of upper Alexander Creek, and can be reached on a combination of 2WD, 4WD roads, seismic cut lines and poor trails. The lake contains cutthroat trout that average 20-30 cm in length. The lack of vegetation around the lake allows plenty of backcasting room for fly fishers.

Barren Lake
Kootenay Trout Hatchery photo

Mite Lake (BC)
Cutthroat trout to 40 cm
Pint-size Mite Lake is situated in a stark basin beneath the peaks of the Continental Divide, due west of Mt. Ward. Mite's outlet creek is a tributary of Alexander Creek. Some route finding will be required to reach the lake from logging roads along Alexander Creek. Cutthroat trout are present in Mite Lake, with the average fish being 20-30 cm in length. It's doubtful that you will meet up with other anglers at Mite.

FERNIE REGION: Corbin Sub-Region

Corbin Sub-Region

Set amid the rugged peaks on the western side of the Continental Divide gap at Crowsnest Pass, this Sub-Region offers some good stream and lake fishing for cutthroat trout. The main east-west transportation connection is Highway 3. The Coal Mountain Mine road and the Flathead River Forest Service Road offer vehicular access north from Highway 3 to the upper Michel Creek environs. The former mining community of Corbin and the existing Coal Mountain mining operations are the geographical centre of the Sub-Region. Summit Lake, alongside Highway 3 just west of the B.C.-Alberta boundary, is a popular angling location. Michel Creek and its tributaries are great cutthroat trout waters once the spring runoff has passed.

Summit Lake (BC)
Cutthroat trout to 60 cm (2.5 kg)
Summit Lake is situated in a narrow valley below Highway 3 on the B.C. side of Crowsnest Pass. Fine rainbow trout in Summit Lake were a big attraction until a severe winter kill in the mid-1990's. Cutthroat trout were planted in the lake and have flourished, although winter kill is still an ever-present threat. Hard-fighting cutthroat trout in the 30-40 cm range are the normal catch in Summit Lake. In early season, the fish tend to congregate at the western end of the lake. Once the weather warms, and the lake temperature rises, the fish spread throughout the lake. Fishing from shore is practical at Summit, and fish can be taken from most places along the railway tracks. Those with a boat or float tube will have access to more fish holding waters, and will likely have slightly more success. Very heavy weed growth in the summer months will inhibit some tactics such as trolling. Due to the amount of pollutants that have seeped into the lake over time from the C.P.R. operations, it is strongly suggested that you return your catch to the water and not take any home for supper.

Summit Lake

(cutthroat trout)

Summit Creek (BC)
Cutthroat trout to 35 cm
From the outlet at Summit Lake to its confluence with Alexander Creek, Summit Creek holds cutthroat trout and a possibly a few rainbow trout. The waters immediately below Summit Lake that include some overgrown ponds hold the best potential.

Michel Creek (BC)
Cutthroat trout to 35 cm
Bull trout to 50 cm (1.5 kg)
Whitefish to 30 cm
Michel Creek boasts some excellent waters as it flows from headwaters near Flathead Pass to its confluence with the Elk River at Sparwood. Cutthroat trout in the 20-30 cm range can be taken from virtually every pool on the creek. Some of the best waters are below the confluence of Alexander Creek with Michel Creek.

Michel Creek

Alexander Creek (BC)
Cutthroat trout to 30 cm
A major tributary of Michel Creek, Alexander Creek is accessed from the weigh scales, 3 km west of the B.C.-Alberta boundary. Alexander Creek holds plenty of small cutthroat trout along its entire length.

Leach Creek, Wheeler Creek, Carbon Creek, Andy Good Creek (BC)
Cutthroat trout to 25 cm
These tributaries of Michel Creek all hold small cutthroat trout.

Michel Creek Ponds (BC)
Brook trout to 35 cm
This series of very small interconnected ponds alongside the Coal Mountain road hold a population of skittish brook trout. The trout can easily be seen in the ponds, but tend to flee at the slightest hint of shadow or movement. Sometimes frustrating, but a lot of fun. Catch-and-release is the only option to maintain this fragile population.

Barnes Lake (BC)
Cutthroat trout to 35 cm
Barnes Lake is reached via a 6 km hike on old roads from the Flathead Forest Service Road. Hunters in the fall and snowmobilers in the winter will visit this area a lot more than anglers will in the summer. A primitive campsite is located along the shore. Barnes Lake is surrounded by forest and is set in a steep-walled basin. Avalanche paths sweep down onto the lake at several locations. The thick forest cover will restrict most attempts at fly fishing. Cutthroat trout are present in Barnes Lake, with the average being 20-30 cm in length.

Barnes Lake

FERNIE REGION: Corbin Sub-Region

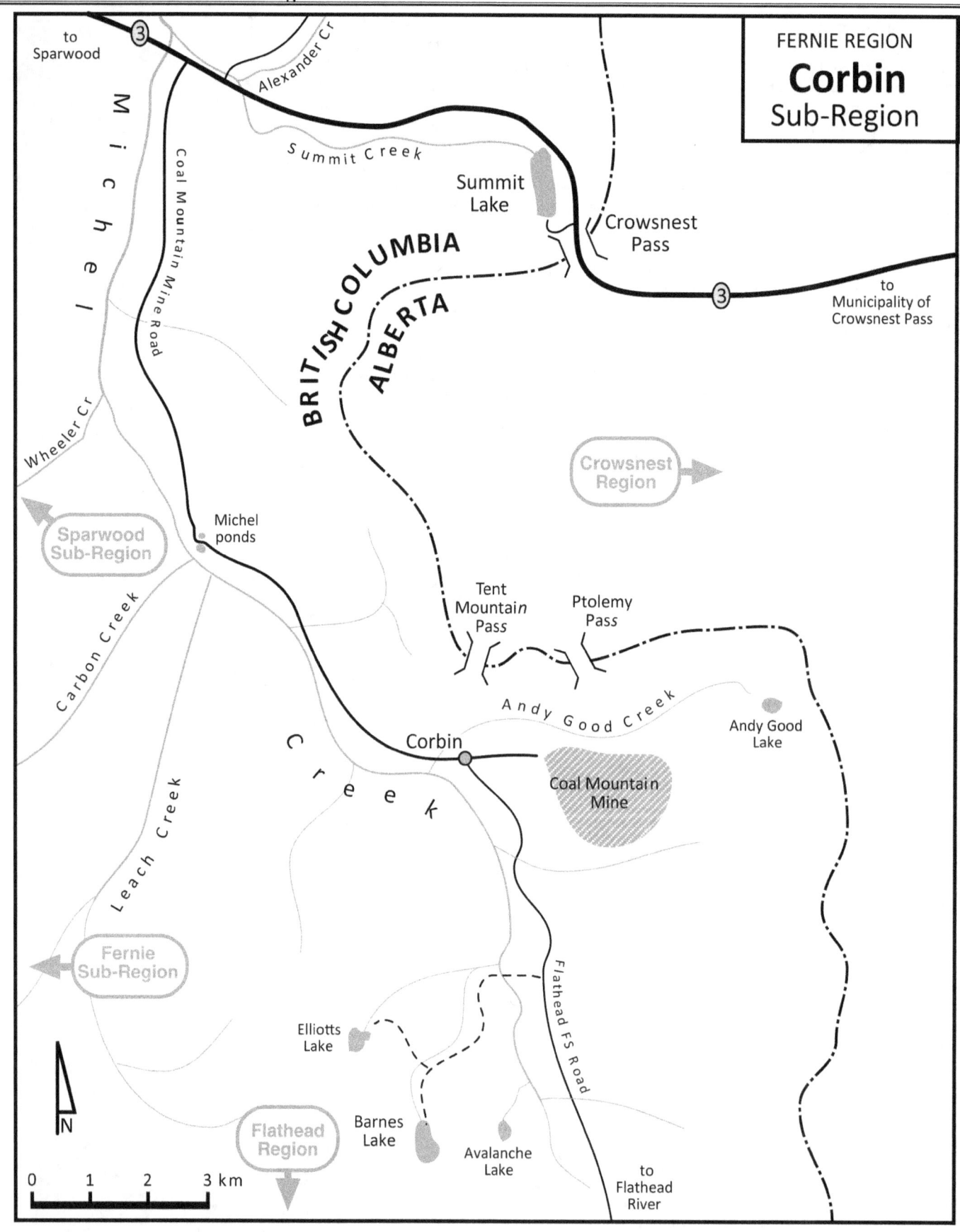

Elliotts Lake (BC)
Status: Doubtful
This beautiful lake is located in a subalpine basin approximately 3 km south of Barnes Lake. An abandoned mining road leads to within 400 m of the lake. Simply following the outlet stream up from the road will lead to the lakeshore. The lake looks as though it has the potential to hold trout, but it has never been stocked. Even though you won't catch any fish, the scenery at the lake makes a trip worthwhile.

Elliotts Lake

Avalanche Lake (BC)
Status: Doubtful
To reach Avalanche Lake requires a wicked 3 km bushwhack from the Flathead Forest Service Road. There are no trails here. The lake is at the base of a major avalanche path and each winter the lake is buried by snow slides. This means ice-out is much later than would normally happen and winter kill is likely. Although the lake has been stocked several times with cutthroat trout, recent examination indicates that there are few or none remaining.

Avalanche Lake

Andy Good Lake
Status: Devoid of fish
Diminutive Andy Good Lake at the head of Andy Good Creek was determined to be incapable of supporting a permanent trout population. As such, it was never been stocked and holds no fish.

SKOOKUMCHUCK REGION

Fine lake fishing for rainbow trout is the attraction of the Skookumchuck Region, which divides into two Sub-Regions. The main access is along Highway 93/95, running north-south through the Region. The southern Sub-Region extends south of the tiny community of Skookumchuck, and includes the popular summer resort of Wasa Lake. The northern Sub-Region includes Skookumchuck, and centres on Premier Lake Provincial Park.

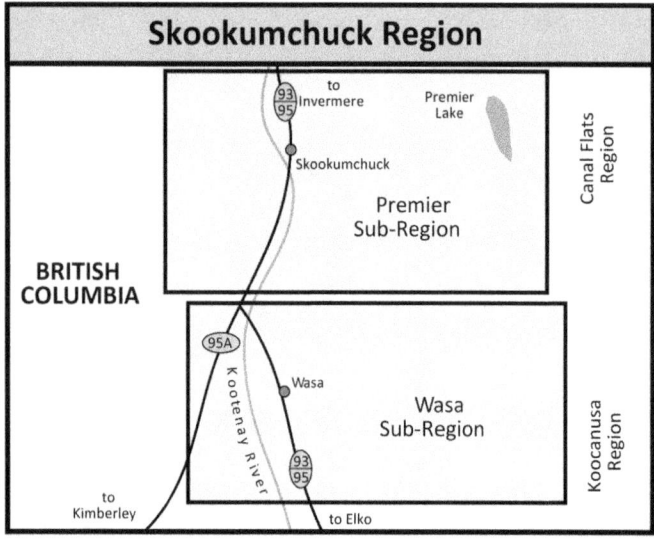

Wasa Sub-Region

The Kootenay River and Wasa Lake are the major water features of this Sub-Region, but they are not the major angling attractions. Several lakes in the Sub-Region, including Lazy, Sowerby and Ha Has contain large rainbow trout, and are undoubtedly the area's prime destinations.

Kootenay River (BC) *(Skookumchuck to Wasa)*
Cutthroat trout to 55 cm (1.5 kg)
Bull trout to 80 cm (6.0 kg)
Whitefish to 45 cm
This section of the Kootenay River flows from Skookumchuck to Wasa, paralleling Highway 93/95. Fishing can be good after spring runoff, although anglers tend to prefer local lakes to the Kootenay River. Cutthroat trout predominate in the river, with specimens regularly exceeding 45 cm in length. As the river is murky much of the fishing season, anglers using bright lures often have the best success.

Kootenay River

Wasa Lake (BC)
Largemouth bass to 60 cm (2.5 kg)
Yellow perch to 35 cm
Wasa Lake is much more popular with the beach crowd than it is with anglers. Wasa is promoted as the "Warmest Lake in the Kootenays" for good reason. The nearby Provincial Park is packed each summer with families who partake in sun, sand and water fun. Fishing at Wasa Lake is focussed on the lake's population of largemouth bass and yellow perch. A variety of lures, spinners and buzz baits will attract the attention of the bass, most of which will average 25-35 cm in length. The perch are smaller, but more numerous, and are fun to catch. A bubble and worm or fly will drum up some perch action.

Wasa Lake

Lewis Slough (BC)
Largemouth bass to 55 cm (2.0 kg)
Yellow perch to 30 cm
This large slough extends south from Wasa Lake and contains largemouth bass and yellow perch. It is seldom fished, as it is difficult to reach the fish-holding waters due to the swampy nature of the shoreline.

Lazy (Rock, Stevens) Lake (BC)
Rainbow trout to 60 cm (2.5 kg)
This pretty lake is located approximately 15 km east of Wasa Lake in the upper Lewis Creek valley. Access is via a good gravel road that begins on the south side of Wasa Lake. Lazy Lake is hemmed in large part by significant cliff formations and is very deep. Fishing from a boat is the only viable option at Lazy Lake. Rainbow trout caught in Lazy Lake will average 30-40 cm in length, although much larger trout are caught regularly. Gang trolls and flatfish are the standard angling technique at Lazy Lake.

Lazy Lake

SKOOKUMCHUCK REGION: Wasa Sub-Region

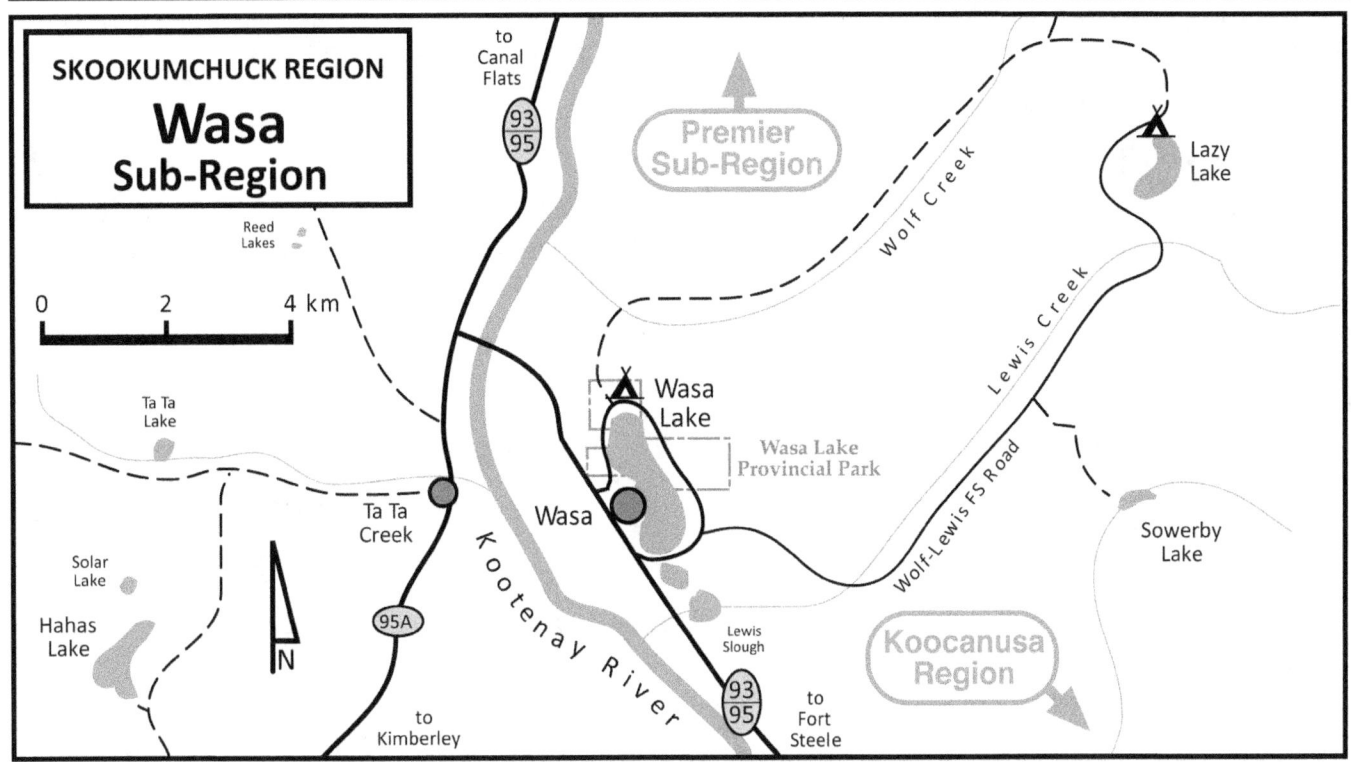

Sowerby (Grundy) Lake (BC)
Rainbow trout to 55 cm (2.0 kg)

Sowerby Lake is located south of the Wasa-Lazy Lake Road, and is protected by a 1 km section of ugly, potholed 4WD road. Fishing is best in the deeper waters at the far end of the lake, opposite the access road. The lake can be fished from shore, but a boat, canoe or float tube is much preferable. Most fish taken will be in the 25-40 cm range. Fly fishing is generally excellent at Sowerby. If the fish are rising, use a dry line. If all seems quiet on the surface, a wet line and nymph will bring on some action.

Sowerby Lake (rainbow trout)

Wolf Creek (BC)
Rainbow trout to 35 cm
Cutthroat trout to 35 cm

Wolf Creek flows west to the Kootenay River and is accessed by a good gravel road that leads northeast from Wasa Lake. Wolf Creek has many good sections as it flows through open meadows and farmland. Rainbow and cutthroat in small sizes predominate, and a few brook trout may be present as well. Be sure to gain permission before accessing private land.

Ha Has (Stony) Lake (BC)
Rainbow trout to 60 cm (3.0 kg)

Ha Has Lake is located southwest of the hamlet of Ta Ta Creek, and is accessible from Lost Dog Creek Forest Service Road. The lake has had problems with alkalinity in the past, particularly when water levels have been low. With normal or high water levels, the fertility of the lake is outstanding, and the rainbow trout grow very quickly. An average trout from Ha Has Lake will generally be in the 40 cm + range. Large trout, weighing 2-3 kg, are caught regularly. The lake is very shallow, with extensive weed beds. Fishing a shrimp pattern over the weed beds is usually effective. Dry fly enthusiasts will enjoy the evening hatches at Ha Has.

Ha Has Lake

Solar (Little Ha Has, Stony Pothole) Lake (BC)
Rainbow trout to 55 cm (2.5 kg)

Tiny Solar Lake is located less than a kilometre north of Ha Has Lake, and is accessed by a rough 4WD road. Solar Lake has experienced the same alkalinity problems as nearby Ha Has.

SKOOKUMCHUCK REGION: Wasa Sub-Region

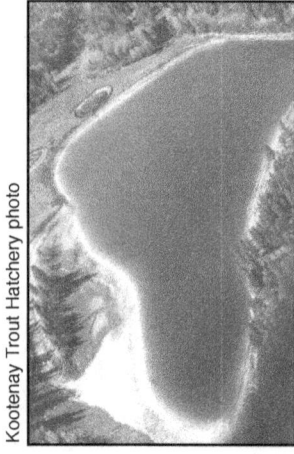

Lake during times of low water. The rainbow trout in Solar Lake also grow large on the abundant feed. Expect fat rainbows in the 30-40 cm range.

Solar Lake

Ta Ta Lake (BC)
Brook trout to 45 cm
Ta Ta Lake is situated on Ta Ta Creek, approximately 4 km by gravel road west of Highway 95A. On first appearance, Ta Ta Lake seems little more than a large marsh with a few patches of open water. Casting to the open water is difficult from shore due to the vast reed growth around the lake. The lake holds brook trout that average 25-35 cm in length.

Reed Lakes (BC)
Status: Devoid of fish
The two tiny Reed Lakes can be accessed from Ta Ta Lake on very rough roads. Reed Lakes have never been stocked and hold no fish.

Premier Sub-Region

Premier Lake Provincial Park is the focal point for this Sub-Region. The park can be accessed by a paved and gravel road that leads west from Highway 93/95 just north of the community of Skookumchuck. Premier Lake is renowned, along with Whitetail and Whiteswan Lakes, as one of the East Kootenay's trophy rainbow lakes. Much of the Sub-Region's fishing pressure is directed at Premier Lake. Quartz, Johnson, Larchwood and Tamarack Lakes are also accessible to vehicles, and receive steady business during the summer and fall. Skookumchuck Creek, a tributary of the Kootenay River, is highly regarded as an excellent cutthroat trout stream.

Premier Lake (BC)
Rainbow trout to 70 cm (4.0 kg)
Brook trout to 60 cm (3.0 kg)
If you're after huge rainbow trout, then Premier Lake stands out as, indeed, one of the "premier" fishing lakes in the East Kootenays. This fact is attested to by the large number of anglers who annually make their way to this beautiful body of water set in wooded hills 15 km east of Highway 93/95 at Skookumchuck. A major campground with boat launch facilities is located at the south end of the lake in Premier Lake Provincial Park. Rainbow trout in excess of 15 kg have been taken from Premier in the past, although average catches today tend to be in the 35-45 cm range, with trout in the 2-3 kg category taken frequently. A few chunky brook trout also inhabit Premier. A boat is essential for fishing on Premier and trolling is a most effective technique. Although gang trolls and flatfish predominate among fishing gear on Premier, anglers slowly trolling a wet fly behind a boat can expect good results. A productive area is along the rock bluff approximately half way down the lake. Dry fly fishing can be excellent in the evenings in the shallows at either end of the lake.

Premier Lake (rainbow trout)

Quartz (Rockbluff) Lake (BC)
Rainbow trout to 55 cm (2.0 kg)
Quartz Lake is located less that 3 km south of Premier Lake. Access is by road from either Premier Lake Provincial Park, or up Wolf Creek from Wasa Lake. Taking the road south from Premier Lake affords a wonderful cliff top view of Quartz's elongated form and stunning green waters. The cliff top road eventually works its way down to Quartz's south end and a campground and boat launch. Quartz holds hard-fighting rainbow trout in the 30-40 cm range, with larger ones taken in good numbers. Tactics for Premier Lake apply equally well to Rockbluff. The area around the island in the middle of Quartz Lake has some excellent shallows that usually hold trout. The drop-off between the shallow and deep water is highly visible in Quartz Lake and should not be overlooked by anglers.

Quartz Lake

Cat's Eye (Bear Paw) Lake (BC)
Rainbow trout to 35 cm
Cat's Eye Lake is the first of a series of lakes that can be reached via an excellent hiking trail from the campground at the south

SKOOKUMCHUCK REGION: Premier Sub-Region

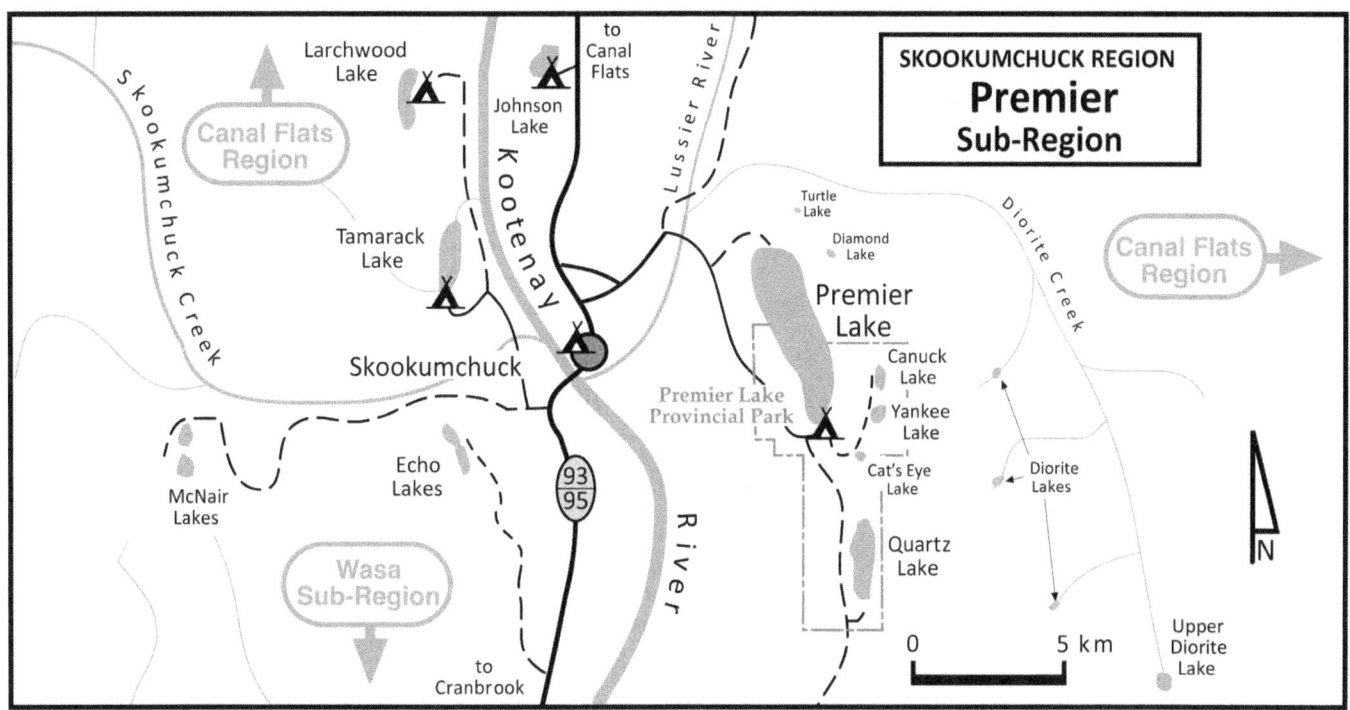

Cat's Eye Lake

end of Premier Lake. Cat's Eye is small and shallow and although the water is clear, it has a distinctive green-yellow hue. Rainbow trout taken from the lake will average 25-35 cm in length. Spin casters will have a distinct advantage over fly fishers due to the heavy forest and brush cover around the lake

Yankee (Twin) Lake (BC)
Rainbow trout to 55 cm (1.5 kg)
Yankee Lake is the next stop on the hiking trail from the Premier Lake campground. Yankee's pretty green waters hold plenty of rainbow trout that are not subject to heavy fishing pressure. As such, fishing tends to be very good at Yankee for trout that average 30-40 cm in length. Fishing from shore is practical from many locations, although an energetic soul who brings a float tube to the lake will be rewarded handsomely. If fly fishing from shore, expect to put your roll casting technique to good use.

Yankee Lake

Canuck (Twin) Lake (BC)
Rainbow trout to 55 cm (1.5 kg)
Canuck Lake is located a short distance by trail beyond Yankee Lake, and is similar in size and character, hence the name Twin Lakes is used by some people to describe the two. The rainbow trout in Canuck Lake tend to be similar in size to those in Yankee Lake, mostly in the 30-40 cm range, with a few exceeding 45 cm in length. Lily pads and shallows are a bit more of a problem at Canuck, but a short search along the shoreline will access good casting spots. Lures and flies will both be effective at Canuck Lake.

Canuck Lake

Diamond Lake (BC)
Rainbow trout to 40 cm
Diamond Lake is the last of the fishable waters along the trail around the eastern side of Premier Lake. Being at the end of the chain, Diamond receives the least fishing pressure of the four lakes. Rainbow trout inhabit the lake in good numbers, and average 25-35 cm in length.

Turtle Lake (BC)
Status: Doubtful
Tiny Turtle Lake, at the northeastern end of Premier Lake, is home to plenty of western painted turtles, but nothing in the way of game fish.

SKOOKUMCHUCK REGION: Premier Sub-Region

Echo (Echoes) Lakes (BC)
Brook trout to 55 cm (1.5 kg)

The Echo Lakes are set on a pleasant forest and meadow bench west of Skookumchuck. Access is on rough roads that lead northwest from Ta Ta Creek. The lakes are very shallow and have substantial reed growth. However, there are numerous places along the lakeshore from which to fish. Lures will be the most effective in catching the lakes' brook trout. Trout from Echo Lakes average 25-35 cm in length. Early fall is normally the best time of year to take trout from Echo Lakes.

South Echo Lake

McNair Lakes (BC)
Cutthroat trout to 45 cm

The McNair Lakes are located in heavy forest at the height of land between the Skookumchuck River and Lost Dog Creek, approximately 15 km west of Highway 93/95 at Skookumchuck. Logging roads from Skookumchuck pass by the lakes. The level of water in the lakes fluctuates significantly from season to season, and during most of the fishing season there is a wide gravel beach surrounding the lakes. The two largest lakes (North and South McNair Lakes) are stocked regularly with cutthroat trout. Trout close to shore are spooked easily, making long casts or patience necessary to take fish. Cutthroat trout from the lakes will average 25-35 cm in length.

North McNair Lake

Skookumchuck Creek (BC)
Cutthroat trout to 50 cm (1.5 kg)
Bull trout to 70 cm (5.0 kg)
Whitefish to 45 cm

Skookumchuck Creek is a major tributary of the Kootenay River in this Sub-Region. Upper Skookumchuck Creek offers outstanding cutthroat trout fishing. Access to the upper river is not from roads leading west from near the confluence of Skookumchuck Creek and the Kootenay River as one would expect, but is from the Findlay Creek Road, northwest of Canal Flats. Skookumchuck Creek has innumerable fine holes that are home to beautifully coloured cutthroat trout that average 25-35 cm in length, and fly fishing is great for beginner and expert alike.

Tamarack Lake (BC)
Rainbow trout to 60 cm (2.5 kg)

Tamarack Lake sits amid forested surroundings 5 km by gravel road west of the Skookumchuck pulp mill. Rainbows averaging 30-40 cm in length are the average catch from Tamarack. Fish taken from Tamarack Lake tend to be larger but less plentiful than at nearby Larchwood Lake. A boat or float tube is strongly suggested at Tamarack, as fish tend to keep to the deeper waters for most of the day. Slowly trolling a wet fly behind the boat will produce positive results.

Tamarack Lake

Larchwood Lake (BC)
Rainbow trout to 55 cm (2.0 kg)

Larchwood Lake was rehabilitated in the early 1990's, and has proven to be an excellent lake since the restocking program began. Rainbow trout are plentiful in the lake, with most trout in the 25-40 cm range. Fly fishers do well in Larchwood and there always seems to be insects on the surface. Trolling is also popular at Larchwood Lake. The lake is long and narrow and fishing from shore is possible from many locations. The campground at Larchwood Lake is very popular throughout the summer months.

Larchwood Lake

SKOOKUMCHUCK REGION: Premier Sub-Region

Johnson Lake (BC)
Rainbow trout to 50 cm (1.5 kg)
Johnson Lake is set in a wooded hollow west of Highway 93/95, approximately 4 km north of Skookumchuck. Access is good on a gravel road from the highway to one of the two recreation sites at the lake. Johnson Lake itself is fairly shallow and nutrient rich. Stocked rainbow trout grow well in this habitat, and most fish caught will be in the 30-40 cm range. There are a number of spots to fish from shore, but long casts will be required to get out past the shallow water. A boat or float tube is recommended.

Johnson Lake

Lussier River (BC) *(Diorite Creek to Kootenay River)*
Cutthroat trout to 45 cm
Bull trout to 70 cm (4.0 kg)
Whitefish to 40 cm
The lower section of the Lussier River, from the Diorite Creek junction to the Lussier's confluence with the Kootenay River, is a good cutthroat trout fishery. Private land and the lack of access to the creek are the main problems. The main access points outside the private lands (near bridges, etc.) tend to be over fished. For those who receive permission from landowners to fish the river, cutthroat trout in the 25-35 cm range will be in good supply.

Lussier River: confluence with Kootenay River

Diorite Creek (BC)
Cutthroat trout to 40 cm
The sparkling waters of Diorite Creek constitute a major tributary of the lower Lussier River. There has been little or no human activity in much of the Diorite Creek valley, and access is generally difficult. The creek holds small cutthroat trout that are very willing to rise to a fly.

Diorite Lakes #, #, # (BC)
Cutthroat trout to 45 cm
All of the larger lakes in the Diorite Creek drainage have been stocked in the past with cutthroat trout, which now reproduce naturally. The valley is for explorers only, as there are few trails of any significance. For those who have the energy and willpower to search out the Diorite Lakes, the prize will be feisty cutthroat trout in the 25-35 cm range.

Diorite Lake #2

Upper Diorite Lake (BC)
Cutthroat trout to 50 cm
Upper Diorite Lake is situated in a pristine basin at the head of Diorite Creek. Reaching the lake will be very difficult, with a good option being a continuation of the Mt. Fisher hike down into upper Diorite Creek valley. Take note that this area is for explorers only. The Upper Diorite Lake population of stocked cutthroat trout has done well, and are in the lake in good numbers. Expect an average trout to be 30-40 cm in length. Due to the general absence of anglers, virtually any technique will be successful at Upper Diorite Lake.

ELKFORD REGION

The Elkford Region covers the upper Elk River Valley, from the town of Elkford north to, and including, Elk Lakes Provincial Park. Highway 43 connects Elkford south to Sparwood and Highway 3. The Elk River Forest Service Road extends north for 70 km from Elkford to Elk Lakes Provincial Park. Most fishing opportunities in the Region are of the backcountry nature, with many fine cutthroat trout lakes. The area around the town of Elkford constitutes the Fording Sub-Region, with the glacier-mantled peaks and high country of Elk Lakes Provincial Park serving as a second Sub-Region.

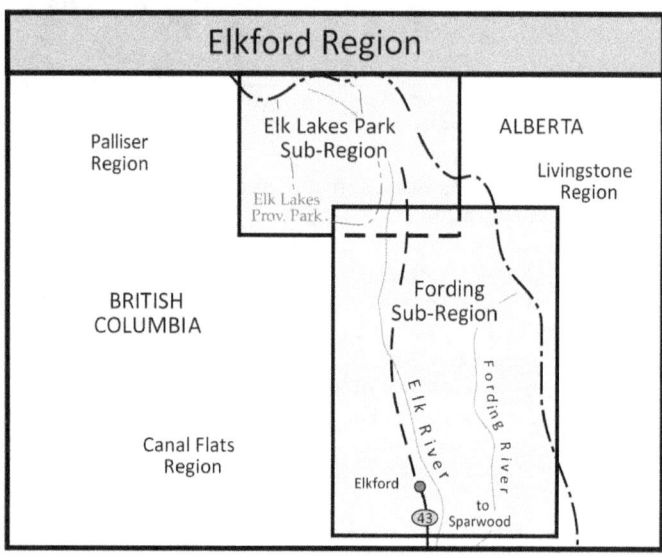

Fording Sub-Region

The coal-mining community of Elkford is the self-proclaimed "Wilderness Capital of B.C". Unarguably the most isolated town in the Rockies, Elkford is indeed the gateway to the rugged tracts of land of the upper Elk River Valley. The rise in prominence of the Elk River and its cutthroat fishery have raised the profile of Elkford in recent years, but there are many who have enjoyed the upper Elk Valley for many years, whether for fishing, hunting or camping. The Elk River dominates angling opportunities in and around Elkford. Other fishing locales are rather limited, with Lost Lake being one of the few bright spots.

Elk River (Weary Creek to Line Creek) (BC)
Cutthroat trout to 60 cm (2.0 kg)
Bull trout to 80 cm (6.0 kg)
Whitefish to 45 cm
The Elk River passes through the town of Elkford on its journey from Weary Creek downstream to Line Creek. This section of the river is an outstanding cutthroat trout fishery. Although it is technically possible to take a canoe on the Elk River below Elkford to Line Creek, it would strongly be suggested that your have superior canoeing skills, as there are numerous obstacles. The Elk River Forest Service Road parallels the river above Elkford, although it will always require some nasty bushwhacking to actually reach the river. Below Elkford, Highway 43 serves as a general access, with bushwhacking also required here. Once the river clears up in mid-summer, fly fishing for cutthroat trout is excellent. Many people consider the Elk River to be the best cutthroat trout stream in the Rockies. Cutthroat trout taken are normally 30-40 cm in length, as well as being very fat and healthy. Larger trout in the 50 cm range are not uncommon. Bull trout and whitefish can also be taken from the river, and most large pools will have its resident bull trout.

Elk River

(bull trout)

Fording River, Boivin Creek, Crossing Creek, Bingay Creek, Forsyth Creek, Aldridge Creek, Bleasdell Creek (BC)
Cutthroat trout to 40 cm
Bull trout to 65 cm (3.0 kg)
All of the major tributaries of this segment of the Elk River hold cutthroat trout in good numbers. Active and abandoned logging and mining roads lead up most tributary valleys, allowing some form of access. Trout in these creeks will tend to average 15-30 cm in length. Special restrictions apply to the sections of Fording River above and below Josephine Falls. The 3 km section of Forsyth Creek below Connor Lakes is permanently closed to angling.

Fording River

Lost Lake (BC)
Rainbow trout to 45 cm
Brook trout to 45 cm
Lost Lake is one of the primary destinations for hikers on Elkford's popular Forest, Falls and Lakes Interpretive Hiking Trails. The trail to Lost Lake is a pleasant 2.5 km walk from the trailhead on the Greenhills Mine Road. An alternate access involves driving rough roads from the Line Creek bridge over the Elk River, followed by a short 1 km hike. Heavy forest cover that makes casting quite difficult in places surrounds Lost Lake. Two wooden docks have been built at the lake, and

ELKFORD REGION: Fording Sub-Region

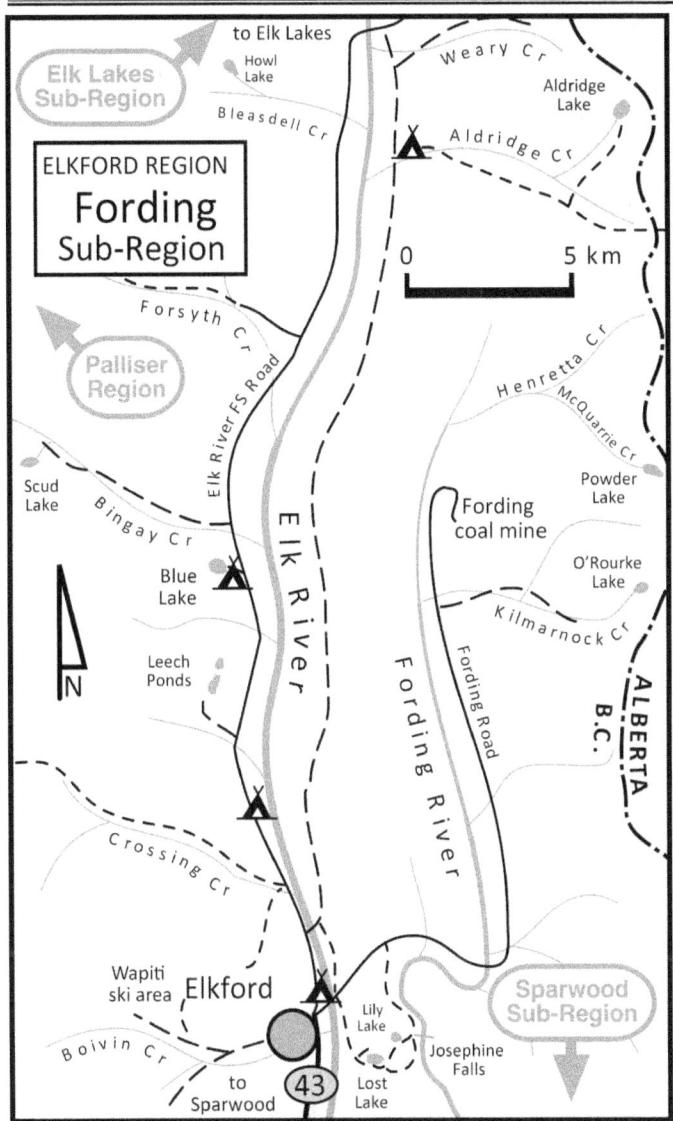

Lily Lake (BC)
Status: Devoid of fish

Diminutive Lily Lake is located 1 km beyond Lost Lake on the Forest, Falls and Lakes circuit. There's no fish in Lily Lake, but there's plenty of waterfowl if you're into bird watching.

Lily Lake

Blue Lake (BC)
Status: Doubtful

Blue Lake and its campground are located just west of the Elk River Forest Service Road approximately 20 km north of Elkford. The lake was stocked in the past, and fish populations were dependent on regular stockings. Likely not much in the lake today.

Blue Lake

Leech Ponds (BC)
Brook trout to 40 cm

These small ponds are located a few hundred metres west of the Elk River Forest Service Road. Heavy reed growth and extensive shallows make shore fishing difficult. The ponds have been stocked with brook trout, which average 25-35 cm in length.

Leech Ponds

Scud Lake (BC)
Cutthroat trout to 45 cm

Scud Lake is a tiny body of water situated in the upper Bingay Creek watershed. Rough roads lead up the Bingay Creek valley from the Elk River Forest Service Road, and an even rougher trail leads into the basin holding Scud Lake. The lake is seldom visited, and reports indicate that there still are cutthroat trout present. Expect trout in the 25-35 cm range.

anglers are usually present from these preferred locations. The lake contains both rainbow and brook trout, which are stocked regularly. Fish in the lake average 25-35 cm in length. Spin casting with lures is usually very effective at Lost Lake.

Lost Lake

ELKFORD REGION: Elk Lakes Park Sub-Region

O'Rourke Lake (BC)
Cutthroat trout to 45 cm
O'Rourke Lake is located in a stark basin at the head of Kilmarnock Creek. An abandoned road leads up Kilmarnock Creek from the Greenhills Mine Road, but the final few kilometres to the lake are for route finders only. O'Rourke Lake was stocked in the past with cutthroat trout, but few reliable reports are available as to their current status.

Powder Lake (BC)
Cutthroat trout to 45 cm
Abandoned logging and seismic roads lead from the Elk River into the Henretta Creek valley and eventually to McQuarrie Creek and Powder Lake. The lake is in a high, alpine basin that sees few humans. Cutthroat trout have been stocked in Powder Lake in the past, but their reproductive success is unknown. Trout in other lakes of similar character tend to be 25-35 cm in length.

Aldridge Lakes (BC)
Cutthroat trout to 35 cm
There are several fine lakes located at the source of Aldridge Creek in the rocky basin northwest of Fording River Pass. They reportedly hold cutthroat trout in the 20-30 cm size range. The lakes are worth a look, scenically at least, if you are in the Fording River Pass environs.

Aldridge Lakes

Howl Lake (BC)
Cutthroat trout to 40 cm
Howl Lake is secluded high up in the Bleasdell Creek drainage, west of the Elk River. Access is for explorers only. Howl Lake was stocked in the past with cutthroat trout, which are still present in good numbers and average 25-35 cm in length.

Elk Lakes Park Sub-Region

The rugged beauty of Elk Lakes Provincial Park attracts numerous hikers each summer despite the lengthy 70 km drive on gravel and dirt roads from Elkford to reach the core area of the park. An alternate route of access along a 10 km long hiking trail leads to the Elk Lakes from Peter Lougheed Provincial Park in Alberta. Both the Upper and Lower Elk Lakes are of interest to anglers, as are Cadorna, Abruzzi and Wolverine Lakes in the Cadorna Creek watershed.

Elk Lakes (Upper and Lower) (BC)
Cutthroat trout to 50 cm (1.5 kg)
Bull trout to 60 cm (2.5 kg)
Whitefish to 40 cm
The Elk Lakes are set amid the spectacular glaciated peaks of the French Military Group and are an increasingly popular destination for hikers. The Elk River Forest Service Road is a 70 km long road that is usually in decent shape and leads to the parking area below Lower Elk Lake. From the trailhead, it is an easy 2 km hike to Lower Elk Lake. Upper Elk Lake is another kilometre above the lower lake. Fishing is slow much of the summer in both the larger Upper and smaller Lower Elk Lakes due to heavy silting. In the late summer, as the lakes begin to clear, the fishing generally picks up, and cutthroat trout averaging 25-35 cm in length can be taken in fair numbers. Bull trout and whitefish can also be caught. The Upper Lake has a massive log jam in which the trout tend to hide and is definitely worth a look. The outlet of the Lower Lake is very productive in the fall.

Lower Elk Lake

Upper Elk Lake

Don Shandrowsky with Lower Elk Lake cutthroat trout

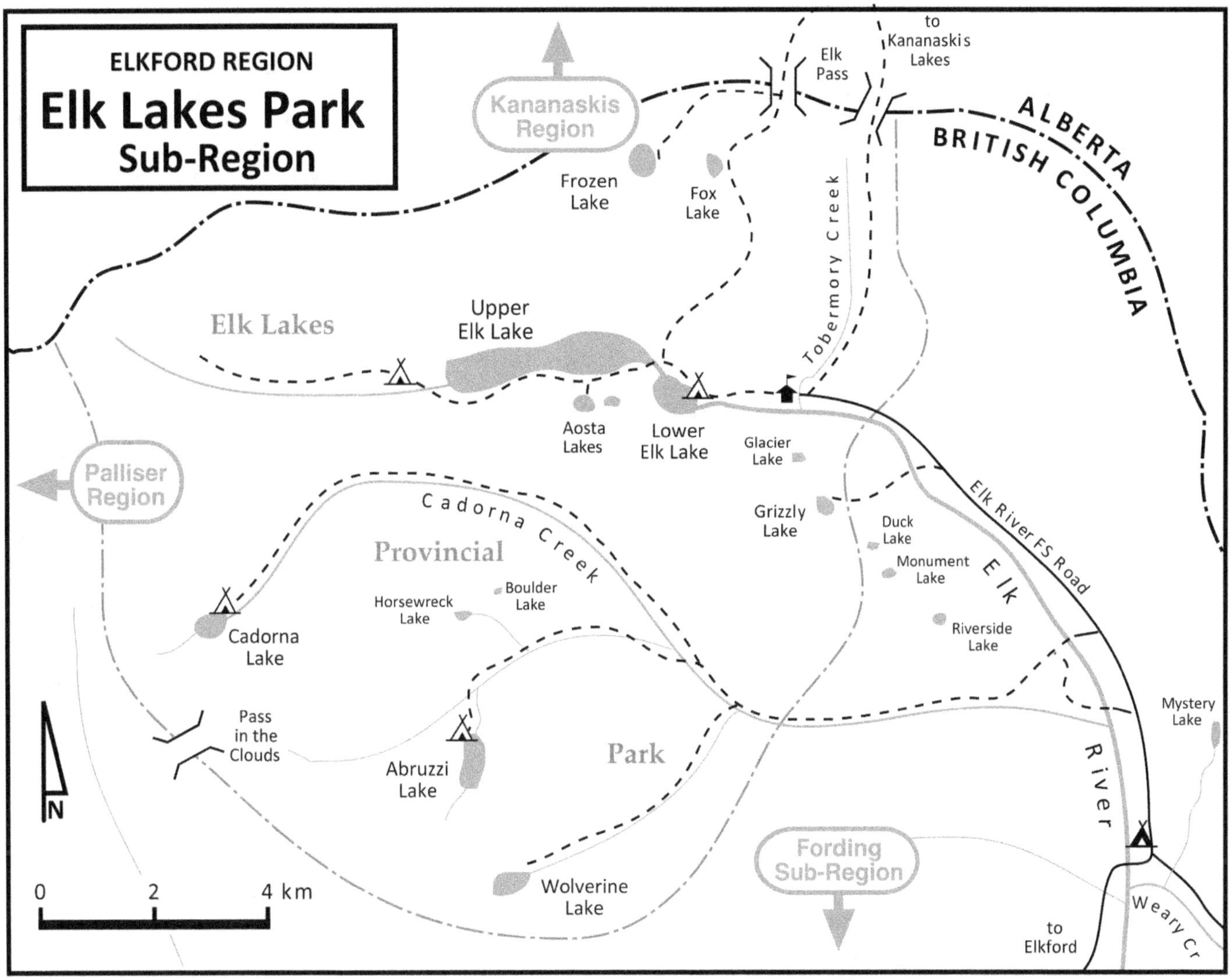

ELKFORD REGION: Elk Lakes Park Sub-Region

Aosta Lakes (Upper and Lower) (BC)
Cutthroat trout to 40 cm

The Aosta Lakes are set on a low bench just above the southern shoreline of Upper Elk Lakes. Upper Aosta can be reached via a short but steep 200 m trail from the Upper Elk Lake shoreline trail. Both Upper and Lower Aosta Lakes hold fish, but the Upper Lake offers better angling opportunities. Cutthroat trout are present in both lakes, with the Upper Lake holding a more substantial population, both in numbers and size. Trout from the Lower Lake average 15-25 cm in length and are rather stunted in appearance with their large heads and small bodies. The cutthroat trout in the Upper Lake are a little larger, with most in the 20-30 cm range.

Lower Aosta Lake

Frozen Lake (BC)
Cutthroat trout to 45 cm

Frozen Lake is a particularly stunning lake set precariously on a lip high on Mount Fox. It is popular among day hikers from both the Elk Lakes and Peter Lougheed Provincial Parks. The final approach to the lake is most easily accomplished by following the provincial boundary, where the semblance of a trail exists. As its name suggests, Frozen Lake is very sheltered and generally remains icebound well into July. The lake holds plenty of cutthroat trout, with most in the 30-40 cm range. The lake's crystal clear waters allow for sight fishing. A nymph on a wet line will definitely attract some attention.

Frozen Lake

ELKFORD REGION: Elk Lakes Park Sub-Region

Fox Lake (BC)
Status: Devoid of fish
Fox Lake is a small lake located less than a kilometre west of Elk Pass and 3 km above Upper Elk Lake. Fox Lake was stocked in the past with cutthroat trout. However, this planting was unsuccessful, as Fox Lake annually dries up to the point of being incapable of holding fish.

Fox Lake

Elk River (BC) *(Elk Lakes to Weary Creek)*
Cutthroat trout to 50 cm (1.5 kg)
Bull trout to 80 cm (5.0 kg)
Whitefish to 45 cm
The Elk River, which eventually flows into Lake Koocanusa, some 200 km distant, has its humble beginnings in the glaciers of Elk Lakes Provincial Park. The Elk River Forest Service Road, north of Elkford, follows the course of the river and provides vehicle access. A tough bushwhack through thick forest will often be required to reach the water. As it drains Lower Elk Lake, the Elk River flows at a gentle gradient, with plenty of wide sweeping corners and undercut banks. Fishing quality in this section of the river, extending for 25 km below Elk Lakes, is limited due to the high amount of silt carried by the river. Cutthroat trout are in the river, but their size and numbers are not as bountiful as in the lower Elk River. Trout caught between Elk Lakes and Weary Creek will average 25-35 cm in length. As the Elk River picks up tributary streams and begins to increase in size, the quality of fishing increases.

Elk River

Nathan Bond with Elk River cutthroat trout

Glacier Lake (BC)
Cutthroat trout to 45 cm
Glacier Lake is the northern most of a series of lakes in a line of hanging valleys on the eastern side of the Elk River Valley that begins approximately 5 km south of Lower Elk Lake. A rough trail leads up to Glacier Lake from the valley bottom. The cutthroat trout in Glacier Lake have done well, with the average fish being 30-40 cm in length.

Grizzly Lake (BC)
Cutthroat trout to 50 cm (1.5 kg)
Grizzly Lake is the largest of the small lakes on the eastern side of the upper Elk River Valley. A well-defined trail with a difficult to find trailhead leads steeply up for 4 km into the secluded valley holding Grizzly Lake. Cutthroat trout, which average 30-40 cm length, are plentiful in the lake.

Grizzly Lake

Duck Lake, Monument Lake (BC)
Cutthroat trout to 40 cm
These two lakes are found in consecutive valleys extending south from Grizzly Lake. They are similar in character, in that they are high, subalpine lakes in small basins at a substantial elevation above the Elk River Valley. Trails in some manner lead to each of the lakes, although the going will generally be very rough. Both Duck and Monument Lakes have been stocked with cutthroat trout. The trout tend to be plentiful, but small, with the average size being 20-30 cm in length.

Monument Lake

Cadorna Creek, Weary Creek, Tobermory Creek (BC)
Cutthroat trout to 45 cm
These tributaries of the upper Elk River all offer good fishing for cutthroat trout. All three creeks are accessed by trail and are fished lightly. Cutthroat trout caught from these creeks average 20-35 cm in length. Larger trout are regularly caught in the meadow section of Cadorna Creek, along the Abruzzi and Cadorna Lake trails.
and Boulder Lakes both contain cutthroat trout, which average

ELKFORD REGION: Elk Lakes Park Sub-Region

Cadorna Creek

Mystery Lake (BC)
Cutthroat trout to 50 cm (1.5 kg)
Mystery Lake sits beneath the peaks of the Continental Divide, at the head of the northernmost tributary of Weary Creek. Access is difficult, and good route finding skills will be required to reach the lake. Mystery Lake holds plenty of cutthroat trout in the 30-40 cm range.

Cadorna Lake (BC)
Cutthroat trout to 50 cm (1.5 kg)
Lovely Cadorna Lake is situated in a grand basin at the head of Cadorna Creek. The 15 km access trail makes this hike an overnighter. The lake holds plenty of cutthroat trout averaging 25-35 cm in length. Fish can be taken from most locations around the lake, although the outlet and its accompanying log jam provide the best opportunities. Take note that all of the lakes in the Cadorna Creek drainage (Cadorna, Abruzzi, Wolverine) are in prime grizzly bear habitat.

Cadorna Lake

Abruzzi Lake (BC)
Cutthroat trout to 55 cm (2.0 kg)
Abruzzi Lake is reached by following a well defined, 11 km long horse trail up from the Elk River. Abruzzi Lake is a stunningly beautiful body of water, and the quality of angling equals its scenic splendour. The lake holds plenty of cutthroat trout, with fish in the 30-45 cm range being the normal catch. The area around the log jam at the outlet invariably holds trout, but anglers shouldn't confine their efforts to the outlet. Fish can be caught from almost anywhere around the lake. Watch for fish cruising slowly along the shoreline, often within a few metres of shore. A well-placed Royal Coachman in front of a cruising trout will bring on some frantic action.

Abruzzi Lake

(cutthroat trout)

Wolverine Lake (BC)
Cutthroat trout to 50 cm (1.5 kg)
Wolverine is the most southerly of the three lakes that make up the Cadorna Creek trio, Abruzzi and Cadorna Lakes being the northern counterparts. Wolverine is reached by a 9 km trail from the Elk River. Wolverine holds cutthroat trout in good numbers, with an average catch being 25-35 cm in length.

Horsewreck Lake, Boulder Lake (BC)
Cutthroat trout to 35 cm
These two small tarns are located in a rocky basin north of Abruzzi Creek, opposite the Abruzzi Lake outlet creek. Access is by bushwhacking up from the valley bottom. Horsewreck and Boulder Lakes both contain cutthroat trout, which average 25-35 cm in length. Horsewreck generally offers better angling than Boulder.

Riverside Lake (BC)
Cutthroat trout to 40 cm
This small lake is located in a hidden valley north of Cadorna Creek on the east face of Riverside Mountain. It was stocked in the past with cutthroat trout, and it is likely that they are present in small numbers. Expect to catch trout in the 25-35 cm range.

LIVINGSTONE REGION

The Livingstone Region consists of two major river basin watersheds - the Oldman and the Highwood. Vehicle access is via Highways 3, 22, and 541 and the Forestry Trunk Road. The Region divides naturally on geographical boundaries into the Oldman and the Highwood Sub-Regions. Fishing opportunities in the south are generally stream oriented. In the Highwood Valley to the north, backcountry lakes are the primary destination for anglers.

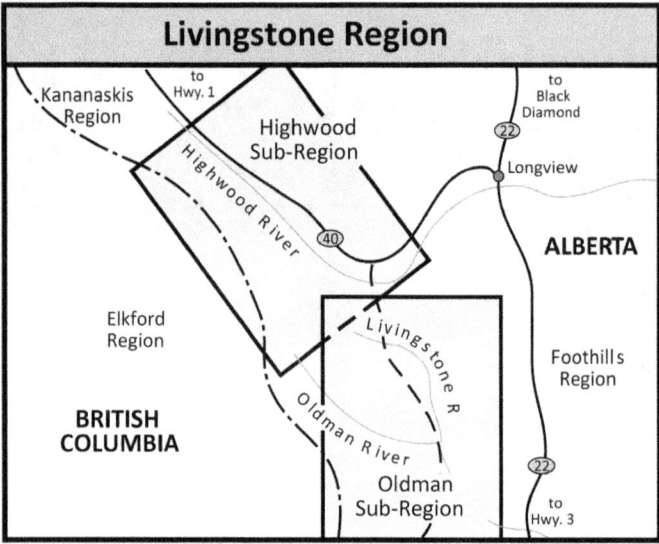

Oldman Sub-Region

The Oldman Sub-Region extends from the headwaters of the Oldman River, high among the peaks of the Continental Divide, to the Oldman Reservoir. Above the reservoir, the Oldman River is regarded as an outstanding trout stream, particularly in its more inaccessible spots. The Livingstone River, a major tributary of the Oldman, has been protected for several years by catch-and-release regulations, and affords excellent angling. The upper Oldman River basin is the source for many tributary streams, including Dutch and Racehorse Creeks, which have fine cutthroat trout fisheries.

Oldman River (AB) *(Oldman Falls to Oldman Reservoir)*
Rainbow trout to 55 cm (2.0 kg)
Cutthroat trout to 55 cm (2.0 kg)
Bull trout to 70 cm (4.0 kg)
Brown trout to 55 cm (2.0 kg)
Whitefish to 40 cm
This section of the Oldman River flows from Oldman Falls into the Oldman Reservoir north of Cowley. Primary vehicular access is via Highways 22 and 517, and the Forestry Trunk Road. This section of the river has many kilometres of fishable water, including the canyon, known as The Gap, which cuts through the Livingstone Range. From The Gap downstream to the reservoir, you are more likely to catch a rainbow trout, although cutthroat trout and even a few brown trout are present. Much of this section is catch-and-release. Above The Gap cutthroat trout predominate, with rainbow still present. Most fish taken from this stretch of river will be in the 25-35 cm range. Anglers should note that the Oldman is usually very turbulent and dirty until late July when run-off is complete.

Oldman River at The Gap

(cutthroat trout)

Oldman River (AB) *(Upstream from Oldman Falls)*
Cutthroat trout to 40 cm
Bull trout to 60 cm (3.0 kg)
The extreme upper reaches of the Oldman River, above splendid Oldman Falls, are reached from logging roads that branch west of the Forestry Trunk Road. The falls serve as a natural barrier, preventing stocked fish from the lower river from travelling upstream. Above the falls, there are only native cutthroat and bull trout. Most of the cutthroat trout in the river are small, with a 15-25 cm long trout being the average.

Upper Oldman River

Jim Rennels photo

Gap Pond (AB)
Cutthroat trout to 40 cm
This small pond is located west of the Forestry Trunk Road at the Livingstone Ranger Station. Gap Pond is stocked regularly with cutthroat trout. Trout in the pond average 20-30 cm in length.

Racehorse Creek (AB)
Cutthroat trout to 35 cm
Bull trout to 55 cm (1.5 kg)
Racehorse Creek, including both North and South Racehorse Creeks, is a major tributary of the Oldman River, connecting just west of The Gap. Lower Racehorse Creek is accessible from the Forestry Trunk Road and from trails that lead west from the Racehorse Creek campground. The upper sections of North

LIVINGSTONE REGION: Oldman Sub-Region

and South Racehorse Creeks can be reached from the Atlas (Allison Creek) Road, which joins Highway 3 west of Coleman. Virtually the entire Racehorse watershed is fishable, with cutthroat trout in the 20-30 cm range being the normal fare.

Tyler Ambrosi at Racehorse Creek

Vicary Creek, Daisy Creek (AB)
Cutthroat trout to 35 cm
Vicary and Daisy Creeks are both tributaries of Racehorse Creek, and abandoned logging roads up both creeks offer easy access to anglers. They have been favourites of local anglers for many years, particularly the lower section of Daisy Creek. Both creeks contain healthy populations of small cutthroat trout averaging 15-25 cm in length.

Daisy Creek

Fly Creek, Station Creek (AB)
Cutthroat trout to 25 cm
These two minor tributaries of the Oldman River join the big river just north of The Gap. Station and Fly Creek hold cutthroat trout in small sizes, few exceeding 20 cm in length. Both creeks have rough trails that lead up from the Forestry Trunk Road.

Station Creek

Dutch Creek (AB)
Cutthroat trout to 35 cm
Bull trout to 45 cm
Whitefish to 35 cm
Dutch Creek is a major tributary of the Oldman River, and offers excellent stream fishing for small cutthroat trout over its entire length. Lower Dutch Creek can be reached from logging roads branching west from the Forestry Trunk Road, while upper Dutch Creek can be accessed from logging roads on Racehorse Creek. Cutthroat trout averaging 20-30 cm in length are the norm in Dutch Creek. Walking up or downstream from any of the main access points will increase fishing potential.

Oyster Creek, Pasque Creek, Slacker Creek, Honeymoon Creek, Hidden Creek (AB)
Cutthroat trout to 30 cm
Bull trout to 35 cm
These tributaries of the upper Oldman River are seldom fished, but contain small cutthroat trout in good numbers. All can be accessed from roads radiating out from major logging roads in the upper Oldman River watershed. Trout in the creeks are numerous but small, most in the 15-25 cm range.

Livingstone River (AB)
Cutthroat trout to 50 cm (1.5 kg)
Bull trout to 60 cm (2.5 kg)
Whitefish to 40 cm
The Livingstone River is a major tributary of the Oldman River, and flows south from its headwaters on Plateau Mountain to its junction with the Oldman River north of The Gap. The

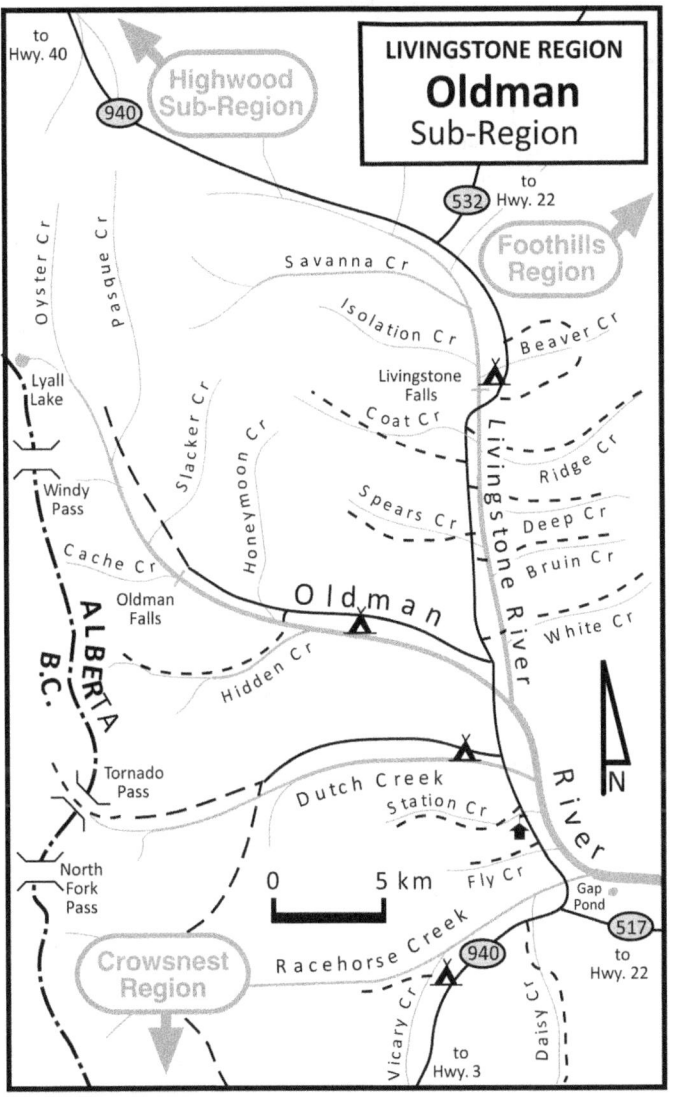

LIVINGSTONE REGION: *Highwood Sub-Region*

Livingstone River is paralleled for much of its length by the Forestry Trunk Road, which offers ready access to anglers. The cutthroat trout fishery in the Livingstone has boomed since the institution of catch-and-release regulations on the river. Cutthroat trout taken from the river average 25-35 cm in length. Bull trout are present in limited numbers, and there are large runs of whitefish in the Livingstone each fall. Cutthroat trout can be taken almost anywhere along the river, although the stretch around Livingstone Falls is particularly promising. Expect company if fishing anywhere near Livingstone Falls, due to the proximity of the large forestry campground.

Livingstone Falls

(cutthroat trout)

Savanna Creek, Isolation Creek, Coat Creek, Spears Creek, Beaver Creek, Ridge Creek, White Creek, Deep Creek, Bruin Creek (AB)
Cutthroat trout to 30 cm
Bull trout to 40 cm

All of the tributaries of the Livingstone River contain populations of small cutthroat trout. Although the trout are small, with few specimens larger than 30 cm in length, they are plentiful, and even the most inexperienced angler should catch fish. The best waters are those nearest the Livingstone River, especially when the tributaries are clearer than the main river.

Savanna Creek
(bull trout)

Highwood Sub-Region

The Highwood River serves as the backbone of this Sub-Region, which is situated directly north of the Oldman River watershed. The area's main thoroughfare is Highway 40 (Kananaskis Trail), which runs north-south between Peter Lougheed Provincial Park and Highwood Junction. Highway 541 is the continuation of Highway 40 east to Longview. The Forestry Trunk Road connects Highway 541 with the Oldman River and eventually the Crowsnest Pass. A gas station, with a selection of fishing supplies, is located at Highwood Junction, at the merger of Highways 40 and 541 and the Forestry Trunk Road. The Highwood River is popular with anglers, but it is the Highwood's backcountry lakes that are the real magnets. The majority of the Sub-Region's fine lakes, including Carnarvon, Loomis, Running Rain and Lake of the Horns, are located high among the peaks of the Continental Divide and require substantial effort by foot to reach.

Note: Highway 40 is closed from December through mid-June each year to protect sensitive wildlife habitat.

Highwood River (AB)
Rainbow trout to 50 cm (1.5 kg)
Brook trout to 45 cm
Cutthroat trout to 45 cm
Bull trout to 70 cm (3.5 kg)
Whitefish to 40 cm

The Highwood River begins as a tiny stream below Highwood Pass, and then flows south and east, eventually joining the Bow River as a major tributary east of Calgary. The upper Highwood, bracketed by the Elk Range to the west and the Highwood Range to the east, is readily accessible to anglers from Highways 40 and 541, which parallel the river. Rainbow trout are in the majority in the Highwood River, with trout mostly averaging 25-35 cm in length. The river has a repetitive sequence of pools and riffles over its course, and the fishing is generally good after the river clears in mid-summer.

Highwood River

LIVINGSTONE REGION: Highwood Sub-Region

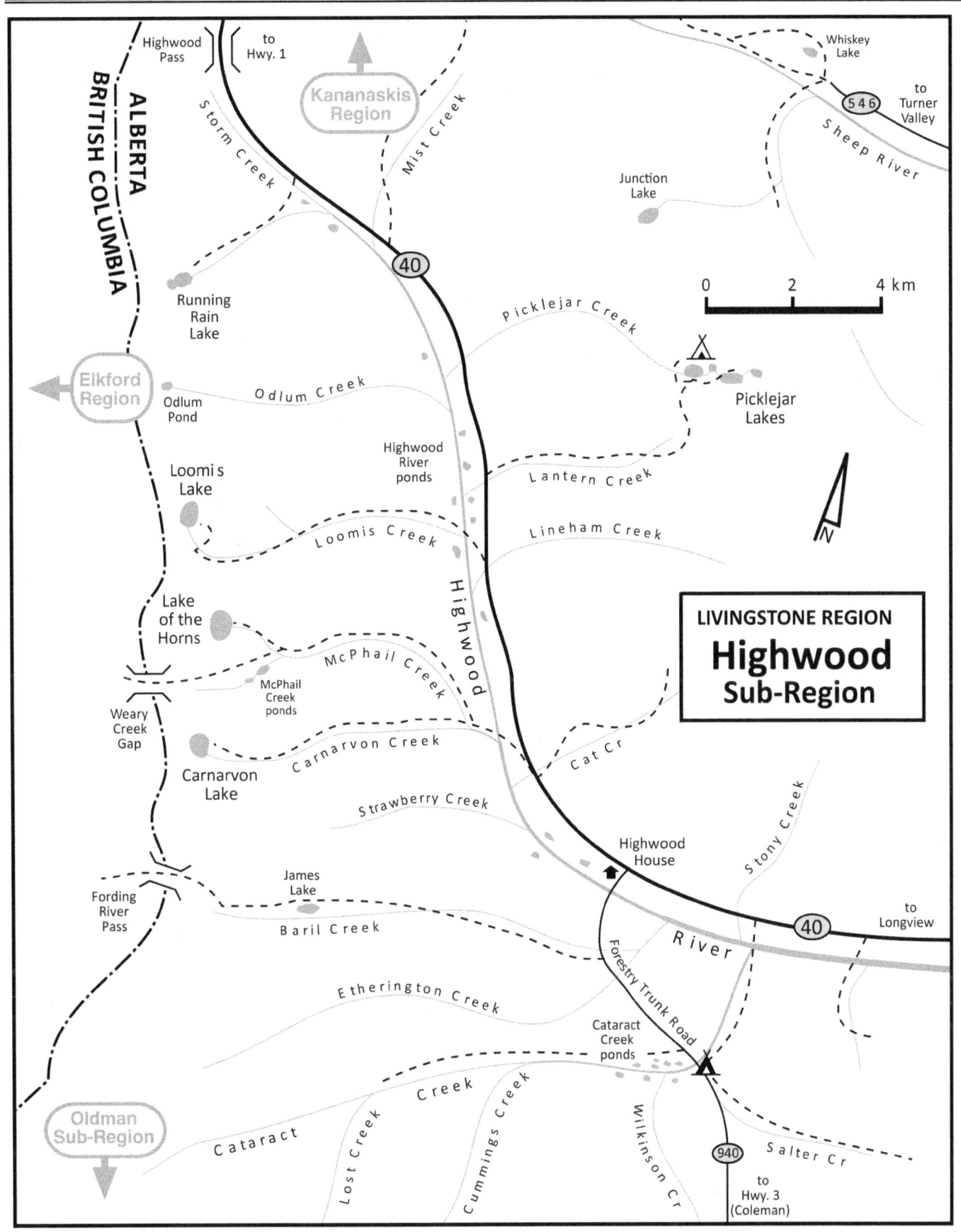

LIVINGSTONE REGION: Highwood Sub-Region

Highwood River ponds (AB)
Rainbow trout to 40 cm
Brook trout to 35 cm

The wide, forested Highwood River valley provides excellent habitat for the local beaver population, a fact attested to by the area's seemingly endless chain of beaver ponds. Many of the ponds contain rainbow or brook trout. Some of the ponds are subject to winter kill and only personal inspection will determine which ponds hold trout and which don't. Two of the better systems are the ponds immediately west of Highwood Junction, and those at the Trout Ponds Day Use Site, just south of the confluence of Picklejar Creek and the Highwood River. Trout taken from the ponds will average 20-30 cm in length.

Highwood River ponds

Mist Creek, Odlum Creek, Loomis Creek, McPhail Creek, Carnarvon Creek, Picklejar Creek, Lantern Creek, Stony Creek, Cat Creek, Strawberry Creek, Baril Creek, Etherington Creek (AB)
Rainbow trout to 35 cm
Cutthroat trout to 35 cm
Brook trout to 35 cm

These tributaries of the upper Highwood River contain small trout. The lower portions of the creeks, near their junction with the Highwood, usually hold rainbow and brook trout, while the upper reaches are more likely to hold cutthroat. Regardless of species, don't expect many trout larger than 30 cm in length.

Storm Creek (AB)
Status: Closed to angling

Storm Creek, which joins with Mist Creek to form the Highwood River, is closed to angling.

Picklejar Lakes (AB)
Cutthroat trout to 40 cm

The chain of four Picklejar Lakes is set in a spectacular subalpine basin. The lakes are very popular with anglers in the summer, so expect a little company. Picklejar Lakes can be reached by a 4 km trail from Highway 40 at Lineham Creek (not Picklejar Creek, as one would normally expect). Each of the four Picklejar Lakes is unique in its setting and quality of angling. The upper (first) lake holds the least potential, although a few trout do make it in each summer via the outlet creek. The second lake is the deepest of the four lakes, and its shoreline is largely made up of scree slopes. The best location for fishing in the third lake is near the inlet stream. The third lake is very shallow, but always seems to have a few schools of skittish, but slightly larger, trout cruising about. The lowest (fourth) lake is generally regarded as the best fishing. Fish can be taken from almost any location around the lake, although the area near the outlet is invariably full of fish ("like catching fish from a pickle jar"). Fly fishers will have a heyday at the fourth lake. Cutthroat trout in the lakes are plentiful, but are not large. Most fish caught will be in the 20-30 cm range. It's interesting to note that the Picklejar Lakes have never been stocked, and maintain their population through natural propagation.

Picklejar Lake #4

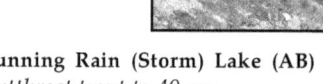

Picklejar Lake #2

Running Rain (Storm) Lake (AB)
Cutthroat trout to 40 cm

Tiny Running Rain Lake, nestled in a small basin immediately beneath the Continental Divide, is seldom visited by anglers. From Highway 40, a rough 3 km trail leads up the north side of the outlet creek to the lake. Running Rain Lake has two distinct components: extensive shallows above the outlet, and a small deep bay at the far end of the lake. Cutthroat trout are present in very limited numbers in the lake. An average trout will be 20-30 cm in length. Running Rain Lake is very susceptible to over harvest, and catch-and-release is strongly recommended.

Running Rain Lake

LIVINGSTONE REGION: Highwood Sub-Region

Loomis Lake (AB)
Cutthroat trout to 55 cm (2.0 kg)

Access to the pleasing blue waters of Loomis Lake is difficult, and includes a 12 km hike, a ford of the Highwood River and a steep headwall. Despite its lengthy and problematic access, Loomis is popular with backcountry anglers due to the number and size of its cutthroat trout. Trout caught from Loomis will average 35-45 cm in length. Much of the lake has a scree-covered shoreline, and the bottom drops away quickly. Lures or flies fished deep tend to produce results.

Loomis Lake

Odlum Pond (AB
Cutthroat trout to 30 cm

Odlum Pond is the small tarn at the head of Odlum Creek, and is reached by a 12 km trail, which includes a ford of the Highwood River. Cutthroat trout in Odlum Pond are small, averaging 15-25 cm in length.

Odlum Pond

Lake of the Horns (McPhail Lake) (AB)
Cutthroat trout to 55cm (2.0 kg)

Lake of the Horns is nestled in a rocky amphitheatre high on the flank of Mt. McPhail. Superb cutthroat trout fishing is the reward for those completing the 12 km trek to reach its shores. A ford of the Highwood River and a tricky ascent of a cliff band loom as major hazards on this hike. The lake itself is above tree line, and there is plenty of casting room, although wind will likely be a significant factor. The cutthroat trout in Lake of the Horns average 30-40 cm in length, with fish exceeding 50 cm taken on occasion. As it is a very deep lake, and the bottom drops off quickly, a wet fly line fished deep is generally a successful technique.

Lake of the Horns

McPhail Creek Ponds (AB)
Cutthroat trout to 35 cm

The interconnected series of beaver ponds on McPhail Creek directly below the Lake of the Horns hold small cutthroat trout. The trout in the ponds and creek tend to be wary and challenging to catch. Cutthroat trout caught in the ponds will average 20-30 cm in length.

McPhail Creek Ponds

Carnarvon Lake (AB)
Cutthroat trout to 55 cm (2.0 kg)

Carnarvon Lake is similar in character to other lakes in the region. It is located in an enclosed basin high on Mt. Strachan, immediately east of the Continental Divide. Reaching the lake requires a ford of the Highwood River, and later, a short climb up exposed rock that is very dangerous in foul weather. Despite its protective barriers, Carnarvon Lake is popular with hikers and anglers. Set amid stark, rocky surroundings, Carnarvon's exquisite blue water holds plenty of cutthroat trout, most of which will be in the 30-40 cm range. The lake drops off quickly around most of the shore, but a shelf exists on the western end of the lake near the primitive campsite. Hungry trout continually cruise the shallows, and if the wind conditions are tolerable, sight fishing is possible. A dry fly in the shallows is sure to attract attention. If fishing in the deep water, a wet fly line and nymph or a lure fished deep are the best options.

LIVINGSTONE REGION: Highwood Sub-Region

Carnarvon Lake

(cutthroat trout)

Cataract Creek ponds

James Lake (AB)
Status: Doubtful
This picturesque lake is located along the Fording River Pass trail in the Baril Creek drainage. It has never been stocked, and likely does not hold any fish.

Cataract Creek (AB)
Brook trout to 40 cm
Cutthroat trout to 40 cm
Rainbow trout to 40 cm
Bull trout to 60 cm (3.0 kg)
Whitefish to 35 cm
Cataract Creek, as its name suggests, contains many splendid waterfalls along its length. Joining the Highwood just east of the junction of the Forestry Trunk Road, Highway 40 and Highway 541, Cataract Creek possesses several stretches of fine fishing with numerous falls and deep pools in the lower section. However, a difficult ford of the Highwood River is required to reach lower Cataract Creek. Above the Cataract Creek Forest Service campground, there are numerous beaver ponds where the creek flows through a wide, flat valley. Fishing in the creek and the beaver ponds is excellent for small brook trout. Most of the trout taken will be in the 15-25 cm range, but they are very plentiful. In the upper reaches of Cataract Creek, more cutthroat trout will be present.

Lost Creek, Cummings Creek, Wilkinson Creek (AB)
Brook trout to 30 cm
Cutthroat trout to 30 cm
Lost, Cummings and Wilkinson Creek are tributaries of Cataract Creek and they all contain small brook or cutthroat trout. Trout caught from these creeks will be small, with the average in the 15-25 cm range. The Forestry Trunk Road parallels Wilkinson Creek and provides easy access. Cummings and Lost Creek are reached by logging roads that branch off the Forestry Trunk Road.

Whiskey Lake (AB)
Status: Devoid of fish
This small lake is located just west of the Bluerock Campground at the terminus of the Sheep River Trail (Highway 546). Whiskey Lake has never been stocked and likely does not contain any fish.

Junction Lake (AB)
Status: Devoid of fish
Junction Lake is located in a high basin at the head of a tributary of Junction Creek. Nine kilometres of hiking are required to reach the lake. There is no record of fish plantings in Junction Lake, and the lake dries up each fall to the point of being unable to hold fish.

Cataract Creek

FOOTHILLS REGION

This scenic Region stretches west and south of Calgary amid the foothills of the spectacular Rocky Mountains. Highway 22 is the main north-south transportation route and passes through the Chain Lakes Sub-Region. Highways 66 and 68 provide direct links to the Lower Elbow and Sibbald Sub-Regions, respectively. The area is popular with Calgarians, due to the proximity to the city. Most of the lakes are man-made, including Chain Lakes Reservoir, the Region's largest body of water. The majority of the lakes hold rainbow trout in smaller sizes. Angling on the many small streams in the Region is very popular, with the Elbow River and its tributaries being prime objectives.

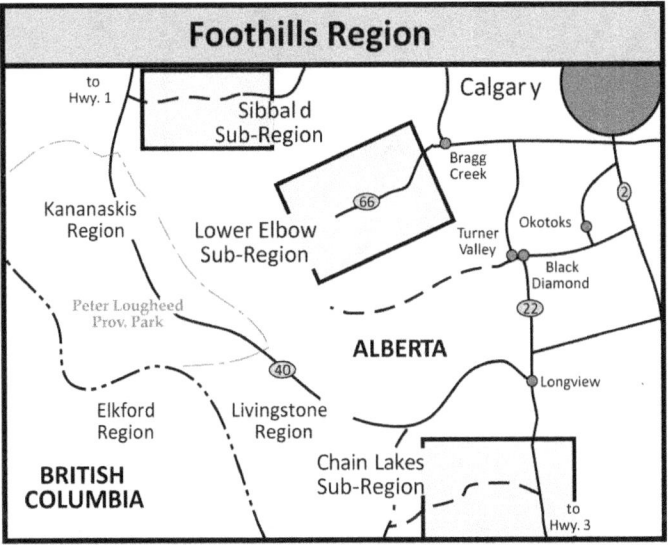

Chain Lakes Sub-Region

Chain Lakes Reservoir is the focal point of the Sub-Region, and is located alongside Highway 22, approximately 25 km south of Longview. Highway 22 is the main transportation link north and south, with Secondary Roads 532 and 533 offering alternate access. Chain Lakes Reservoir provides good fishing for rainbow trout throughout the summer. West of Chain Lakes, along Secondary Road 532, Bear Pond and Big Iron Lake are unique in having arctic grayling populations, and have become very popular angling destinations. The rest of the Sub-Region's fishing opportunities are found in the many small streams that flow west and hold a variety of trout.

Chain Lakes Reservoir (AB)
Rainbow trout to 60 cm (2.5 kg)
Bull trout to 60 cm (2.5 kg)
The elongated form of Chain Lakes Reservoir sits between two long, low hills on the western side of Highway 22 between the junctions of Highways 532 and 533, approximately 25 km south of Longview. A major provincial campground is located at the south end of the lake. Rainbow trout can be taken in good numbers throughout the season, most averaging 25-35 cm in length, with larger ones taken regularly. Bull trout have recently been stocked in the lake, but it will likely be a few years before their numbers or size become significant factors in the fishing equation at Chain Lakes. Bait fishing from shore is the most popular technique for catching rainbow trout, but not necessarily the most productive technique. Bait fishers tend to catch a lot of suckers as well as rainbows. Fly fishing or trolling from a boat tends to reduce the number of suckers caught.

Chain Lakes Reservoir

Chain Lakes Reservoir Spillway Pond (AB)
Rainbow trout to 35 cm
The section of Willow Creek that flows below the Chain Lakes Reservoir spillway generally holds trout that have been swept over the dam. This stretch is worthwhile if there is water flowing over the spillway. Rainbow trout can be very plentiful at times, and will average 20-30 cm in length.

Chain Lakes spillway pond

Willow Creek (AB)
Rainbow trout to 25 cm
Brook trout to 25 cm
Bull trout to 35 cm
The upper reaches of Willow Creek, which can be accessed from Highway 532 west of Chain Lakes, hold rainbow, bull and brook trout in small sizes, with few larger than 25 cm. The odd cutthroat or whitefish may be present as well. Some of the best waters can be in the vicinity of Indian Graves campground on Highway 532, where Willow Creek is characterized by long stretches of fishable pools.

Rice Creek (AB)
Rainbow trout to 25 cm
Rice Creek is a tributary of Willow Creek, and joins downstream from the outlet at Chain Lakes Reservoir. Rice Creek holds small rainbows in fair numbers.

Timber Creek, Johnson Creek (AB)
Rainbow trout to 20 cm
Brook trout to 20 cm
Timber and Johnson Creeks are the two major tributaries of upper Willow Creek. Both creeks hold rainbow and brook trout in small sizes, as well as the odd cutthroat and bull trout. Johnson Creek runs alongside Highway 532, while Timber Creek can be reach via a rough track downstream from Willow Creek at Indian Graves campground.

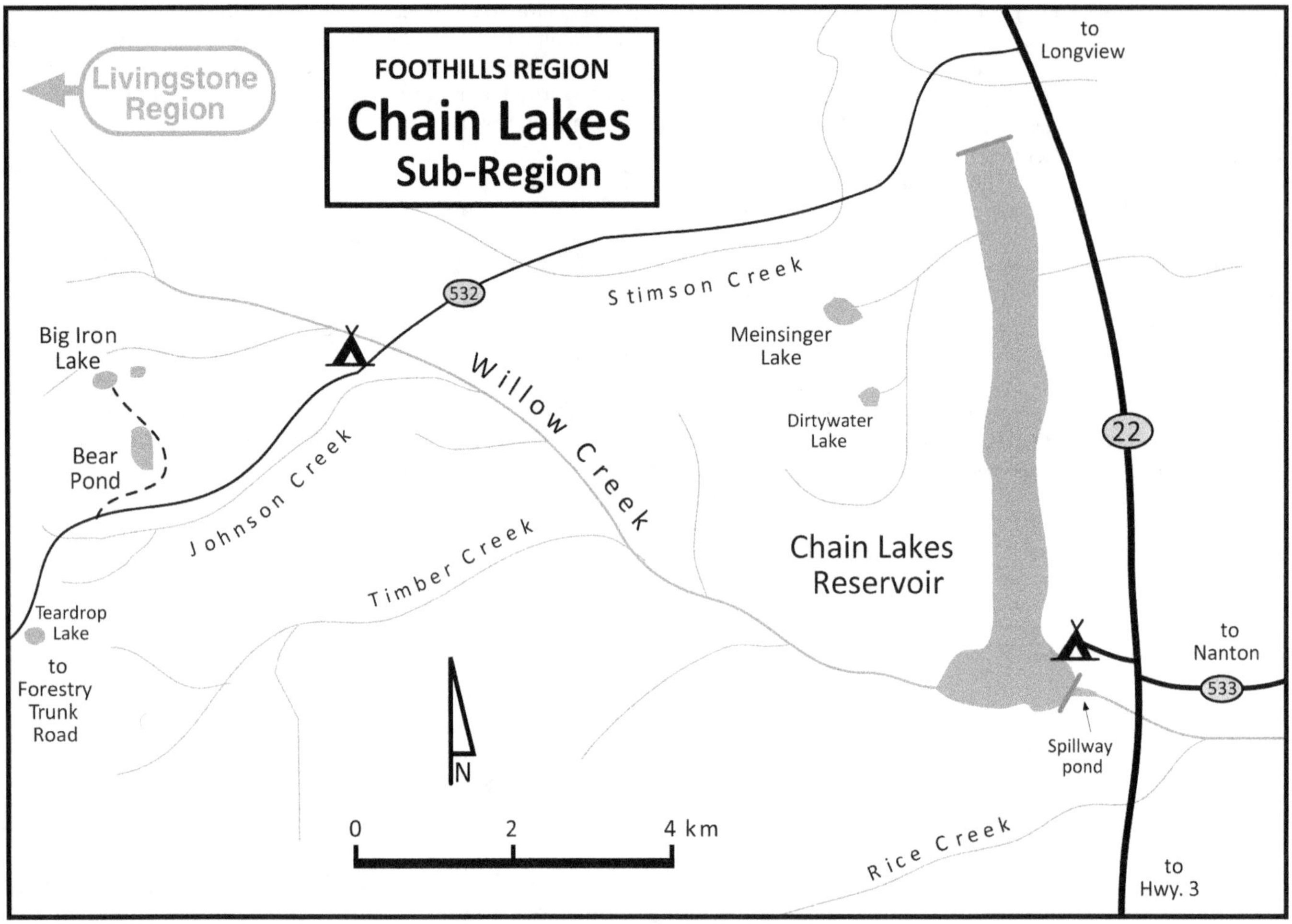

FOOTHILLS REGION: Chain Lakes Sub-Region

Bear Pond (AB)
Arctic grayling to 45 cm

The trail to Bear Pond begins at a signed parking area on Secondary Road 532, approximately 18 west of Highway 22. From the trailhead, a short but steep 1 km hike leads to the shore of Bear Pond, a small, dark body of water. Bear Pond holds plenty of arctic grayling, most in the 20-30 cm range. Grayling, with their large dorsal fin and unique colouration, are very beautiful fish, and are particularly susceptible to fly fishing. They can be taken very close to shore, making Bear Pond an excellent lake for beginners, even though heavy forest cover in spots may cause a few problems. Special regulations are in place to maintain present stocks. Winter kill has been a problem in the past at both Bear Pond and Big Iron Lake.

Bear Pond

Big Iron Lake (AB)
Arctic grayling to 45 cm

Big Iron Lake is a small reed-fringed pond that is located 2 km by trail north of Bear Pond. The trail to Big Iron Lake leads directly north from the north end of Bear Pond. As with nearby Bear Pond, Big Iron Lake offers angling for arctic grayling in the 20-30 cm range. Flies are most effective, and although fly casting room is available around the entire lake, fish-holding water may be beyond the reach of novice fly casters. One of the more popular locations for anglers is the beaver house at the western end of the lake. Those with waders or float tubes will have a distinct advantage over their shore bound counterparts.

Big Iron Lake
(arctic grayling)

FOOTHILLS REGION: *Lower Elbow Sub-Region*

Teardrop Lake (AB)
Status: Devoid of fish
Teardrop Lake is a small, circular pond located alongside Secondary Road 532, west of the Bear Pond parking area. The lake holds no fish.

Tear Drop Lake

Meinsinger Lake, Dirtywater Lake (AB)
Status: Doubtful
These two shallow bodies of water, located south of Highway 532 and west of Chain Lakes Reservoir, have never been stocked and are likely devoid of fish.

Stimson Creek (AB)
Rainbow trout to 20 cm
Brook trout to 20 cm
The upper reaches of Stimson Creek, which is paralleled by Highway 532 west of Chain Lakes Reservoir, hold limited numbers of small rainbow and brook trout.

Lower Elbow Sub-Region

The Lower Elbow Sub-Region is centered on the Elbow River and Elbow Falls Trail (Highway 66) in Kananaskis Country, west of Bragg Creek. This Sub-Region has good brook and rainbow trout fishing at several man-made lakes and beaver ponds. Allen Bill, McLean and Forgetmenot Ponds and their accompanying picnic areas are busy spring through fall. When stocked, all three ponds are excellent for novices, and are accessible to handicapped persons. The Elbow River and its tributaries provide decent stream fishing.

Elbow River (AB)
(Downstream from junction with Little Elbow River)
Brown trout to 55 cm (2.0 kg)
Brook trout to 35 cm
Rainbow trout to 40 cm
Cutthroat trout to 35 cm
Bull trout to 50 cm (1.5 kg)
Whitefish to 30 cm
The Elbow River, paralleled by Highway 66 (Elbow Falls Trail) offers good fishing for brown, rainbow and brook trout averaging 20-30 cm in length. Bull and cutthroat can also be taken from the Elbow, with good angling for whitefish in the fall. The river's numerous pools are never more than a short stroll from the highway. Cobble Flats has gained renown as one the Elbow's better stretches of fishable water. Walking a short distance upstream or downstream from one of the region's many day-use sites along the river will generally bring an angler to an undisturbed hole. Check your regulations, as the section between Elbow Falls and Canyon Creek is currently closed to angling.

Allen Bill Pond (AB)
Rainbow trout to 35 cm
Brook trout to 30 cm
Allen Bill Pond is a small man-made lake located on the south side of Elbow River Trail 1 km west of the Elbow River Ranger Station. Allen Bill Pond is stocked annually, but heavy fishing pressure throughout the summer usually reduces the pond's trout population to near zero by autumn. Lures and bait work very well here. Fly casting room is available around the entire pond, and the pond's shape allows even beginners to reach fish-holding waters. Don't expect solitude, or trout larger than 25 cm, at Allen Bill Pond.

Allen Bill Pond

Elbow River Ponds (AB)
Brook trout to 30 cm
This series of small beaver ponds are accessible from Elbow Falls Trail at Beaver Flat campground and Beaverlodge picnic area. The ponds situated between the highway and the Elbow River contain plenty of brook trout in the 15-25 cm range. As with most beaver ponds, the fish are generally very spooky, and fly casting room is inhibited by thick brush.

Elbow River Ponds

Ford Creek Ponds (AB)
Brook trout to 30 cm
Rainbow trout to 30 cm
This beaver pond complex is located at the junction of Elbow Falls Trail and Powderface Trail, where Ford Creek joins the Elbow River. The Ford Creek ponds hold brook trout in small sizes, generally less than 25 cm in length. A few rainbow trout, as well as the odd cutthroat or bull trout, may also be present. Fly casting room is limited at the ponds.

Ford Creek Ponds

FOOTHILLS REGION: Lower Elbow Sub-Region

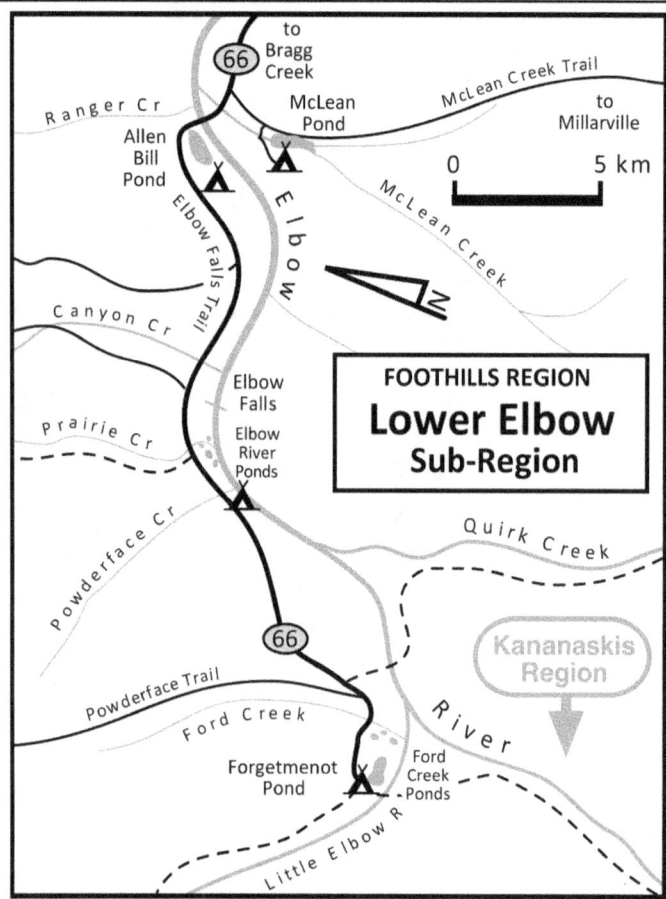

McLean Pond

Forgetmenot Pond (AB)
Status: Devoid of fish
Man-made Forgetmenot Pond is situated at Little Elbow campground and picnic area. This pretty blue body of water was stocked regularly at one time, and held rainbow and brook trout in small sizes. However, it is no longer stocked, and contains no fish. Future plantings would change its status.

Forgetmenot Pond

McLean Pond (AB)
Rainbow trout to 35 cm
Brook trout to 35 cm
McLean Pond was formed by damming McLean Creek, and is located just over 1 km south of Elbow Falls Trail on McLean Creek Trail. Readily accessible from McLean Creek campground, the usually murky waters of McLean Pond hold good numbers of small brook and rainbow trout in the 15-25 cm range, and may hold a few cutthroat and bull trout as well as the odd whitefish. Much of the shoreline is covered with heavy brush, making fly casting difficult. Lures, bait and flies are all effective at McLean Pond. Although it is stocked regularly, McLean Pond suffers from the annual early season rush of anglers.

Little Elbow River (AB)
Brook trout to 30 cm
Bull trout to 35 cm
Cutthroat trout to 30 cm
Rainbow trout to 30 cm
Whitefish to 25 cm
The Little Elbow River is reached via hiking and equestrian trails from Little Elbow campground. The Little Elbow River offers good fishing for small brook trout in the 15-25 cm range, although a wide variety of fish can be taken. The quality of fishing generally improves as one travels upstream.

Quirk Creek, Ranger Creek, Canyon Creek, Prairie Creek, Ford Creek (AB)
Brook trout to 25 cm
Bull trout to 25 cm
Cutthroat trout to 25 cm
These tributaries of the Elbow River contain brook trout throughout, with some cutthroat and bull trout in their upper reaches. Roads or trails branching off Elbow Falls Trail provide access to the creeks.

Sibbald Sub-Region

The Sibbald Sub-Region is located in the extreme northeast corner of Kananaskis Country, and is centered on Highway 68 (Sibbald Creek Trail), which connects the Trans-Canada Highway to Highway 40. Angling opportunities are characterized by stream and beaver pond fishing for small brook and rainbow trout. Sibbald Lake and its campground, located 0.5 km east of the junction of Highway 68 and Powderface Trail, is the Sub-Region's most popular attraction. Jumpingpound and Sibbald Creeks and their accompanying beaver pond complexes also attract anglers each season.

Sibbald Lake (AB)
Rainbow trout to 35 cm
Brook trout to 35 cm
Although Sibbald Lake is the largest body of water in the region, it rates as little more than an overgrown pond. Only 5 m deep at its deepest, Sibbald Lake is subject to regular winter kill. Fish populations are maintained by plantings, and both rainbow and brook trout have been stocked in the past. Due to recent plantings, rainbow trout predominate and average 15-25

FOOTHILLS REGION: Sibbald Sub-Region

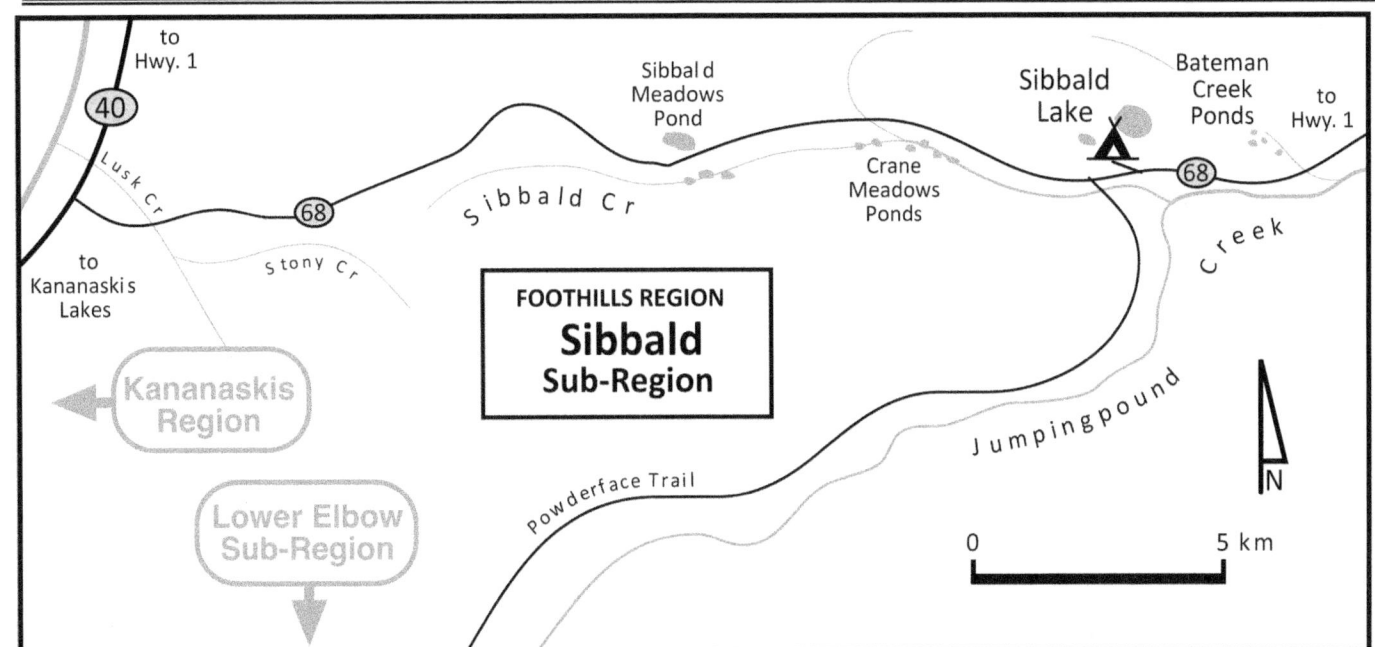

cm in length. Water levels in the lake fluctuate during the season, to a low point in the late fall. Bait fishing is the preferred method at Sibbald Lake. However, fly casting room is adequate, although the better fish-holding waters may be beyond the reach of novices. With a nice campground located at Sibbald Lake, anglers are present in force throughout the fishing season.

Sibbald Lake

Jumpingpound Creek (AB)
Rainbow trout to 25 cm
Brook trout to 25 cm
Cutthroat trout to 25 cm
Bull trout to 25 cm

Jumpingpound Creek is the region's main waterway, and in its upper reaches is accessed from Powderface Trail, off Highway 68. Jumpingpound Creek has long been noted for its good fishing, but it has succumbed in recent years to heavy fishing pressure. Small rainbows in the 15-20 cm range are in the majority, although cutthroat, brook and bull trout can all be taken. Jumpingpound Creek has virtually an unending series of fine pools, and prospective anglers are advised to keep moving either up or downstream, continually testing new holes.

Sibbald Creek (AB)
Rainbow trout to 25 cm
Brook trout to 25 cm

Sibbald Creek cuts through the heart of the Sub-Region, and is the major tributary of Jumpingpound Creek. Sibbald Creek is paralleled by Highway 68 for much of its length. The numerous beaver ponds found along the course of Sibbald Creek generally hold more trout than the free-flowing waters. Rainbow and brook trout in small sizes can be taken, with small cutthroat and bull trout caught on occasion. Although casting distance is not usually a major factor when fishing on Sibbald Creek, wet feet are a certainty and heavy brush cover will deter many anglers.

Sibbald Meadows Pond (AB)
Brook trout to 35 cm
Rainbow trout to 35 cm

This small pond is located on the north side of Highway 68 approximately 7 km west of the junction with Powderface Trail. Sibbald Meadows Pond is a popular destination as trout are stocked regularly. Both rainbow and brook trout in the 15-25 cm range can be taken from locations all around the lake. Fly casting room is available from many spots. Expect lots of company, as the picnic area at the pond is busy with families throughout the summer.

Sibbald Meadows Pond

FOOTHILLS REGION: Sibbald Sub-Region

Crane Meadows Ponds (AB)
Rainbow trout to 25 cm
Brook trout to 25 cm
This series of interconnected beaver ponds is found on Sibbald Creek, on the south side of Highway 68 at Crane Meadows, 6 km west of Sibbald Lake. The ponds hold rainbow and brook trout in small sizes. The ponds are heavily overgrown with bush and fly casting is a virtual impossibility. Reaching some of the better ponds will require a good amount of dexterity and patience, or will result in wet feet.

Bateman Creek Ponds (AB)
Rainbow trout to 25 cm
Brook trout to 25 cm
Bateman Creek is crossed by Highway 68 just east of Sibbald Lake. There is an extensive set of beaver ponds that hold rainbow and brook trout in the 15-20 cm range. The odd cutthroat or bull trout can be taken on occasion. Upstream from Highway 68, prospective anglers can work successive ponds, with better fishing the further upstream one goes.

Stony Creek, Lusk Creek (AB)
Cutthroat trout to 30 cm
Bull trout to 35 cm
Rainbow trout to 30 cm
Lusk Creek is a minor tributary of the Kananaskis River, and Stony Creek is a tributary of Lusk Creek. They can be accessed from Highway 40 or Highway 68. A variety of small trout can be taken from both creeks.

KANANASKIS REGION

Kananaskis is touted as Calgary's playground, and offers virtually every kind of outdoor experience. Peter Lougheed Provincial Park is at the core of the Region. The main access to the Region is on Highway 40, which branches south from the Trans-Canada Highway. Anglers have a wide variety of streams and lakes to choose from. Accessible roadside lakes and hidden backcountry gems abound. The Region divides into three Sub-Regions: the Lougheed Park Sub-Region around the Kananaskis Lakes; the upper Elbow River Sub-Region; and the Barrier Sub-Region along the lower Kananaskis River, extending from Fortress Junction to Barrier Lake.

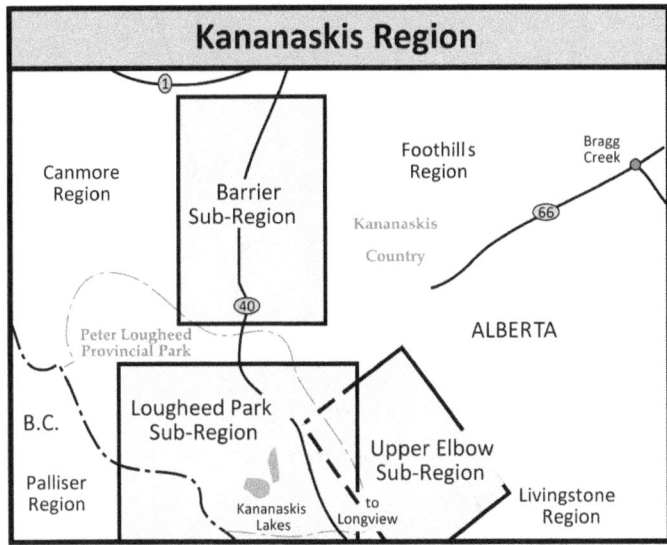

Lougheed Park Sub-Region

The magnificent Kananaskis Lakes are the centrepiece of the immensely popular Peter Lougheed Provincial Park. The lakes are accessed from Highway 40 and the Smith-Dorrien Spray Lakes Trail, and there are several major campgrounds in the immediate vicinity of the lakes. From Upper Kananaskis Lake a series of trails radiate out into the surrounding backcountry. Anglers can make their way to numerous excellent high country cutthroat trout lakes, including Rawson, Aster, Three Isle and Maude.

Upper Kananaskis Lake (AB)
Rainbow trout to 65 cm (2.5 kg)
The Kananaskis Lakes, with their impressive mountain background to the west, attract hordes of anglers and sightseers alike each summer. On the Upper Lake, the mouth of the Upper Kananaskis River is usually productive, as are the waters around the lake's several islands. Shore bound anglers tend to congregate along the numerous bays on the easily accessible northeast side, and although this area often produces well, other less-fished areas of the Upper Lake are definitely worth a look. The Upper Lake has never fulfilled its potential as a trophy lake because of the annual fluctuations in water levels due to the use of the hydroelectric dam on the lake. The upper lake is stocked regularly with large numbers of rainbow trout. Due to the size of the lake, trolling is the popular fishing technique. Plans are in the works to stock Upper Kananaskis Lake with both bull and cutthroat trout.

Upper Kananaskis Lake

Lower Kananaskis Lake (AB)
Bull trout to 80 cm (6.0 kg)
Cutthroat trout to 65 cm (2.5 kg)
Rainbow trout to 65 cm (2.5 kg)
Lower Kananaskis Lake has a history of producing very large bull and cutthroat trout, but as with the Upper Lake, fluctuations in water levels due to the power dam has prevented the creation of a true trophy fishery. In recent years, bull trout stocks in the Lower Lake have stabilized, in large part due to protection in the regulations. Bull trout in the 40-70 cm range are caught regularly. Cutthroat and rainbow trout averaging 30-40 cm in length are also present in decent numbers. On long, narrow Lower Kananaskis Lake, anglers tend to have the most success at the south end in the area around the penstock, and at the far north end in the bay by Canyon Dam. Trolling lures, flies or flatfish is very effective on Lower Kananaskis Lake.

Lower Kananaskis Lake

Hidden Lake (AB)
Status: Devoid of fish
Hidden Lake is a silted body of water situated in heavy forest on the western side of Upper Kananaskis Lake. Hidden Lake dries up each fall to the point of being incapable of holding fish. Attempts in the past to stock the lake have always failed.

Hidden Lake

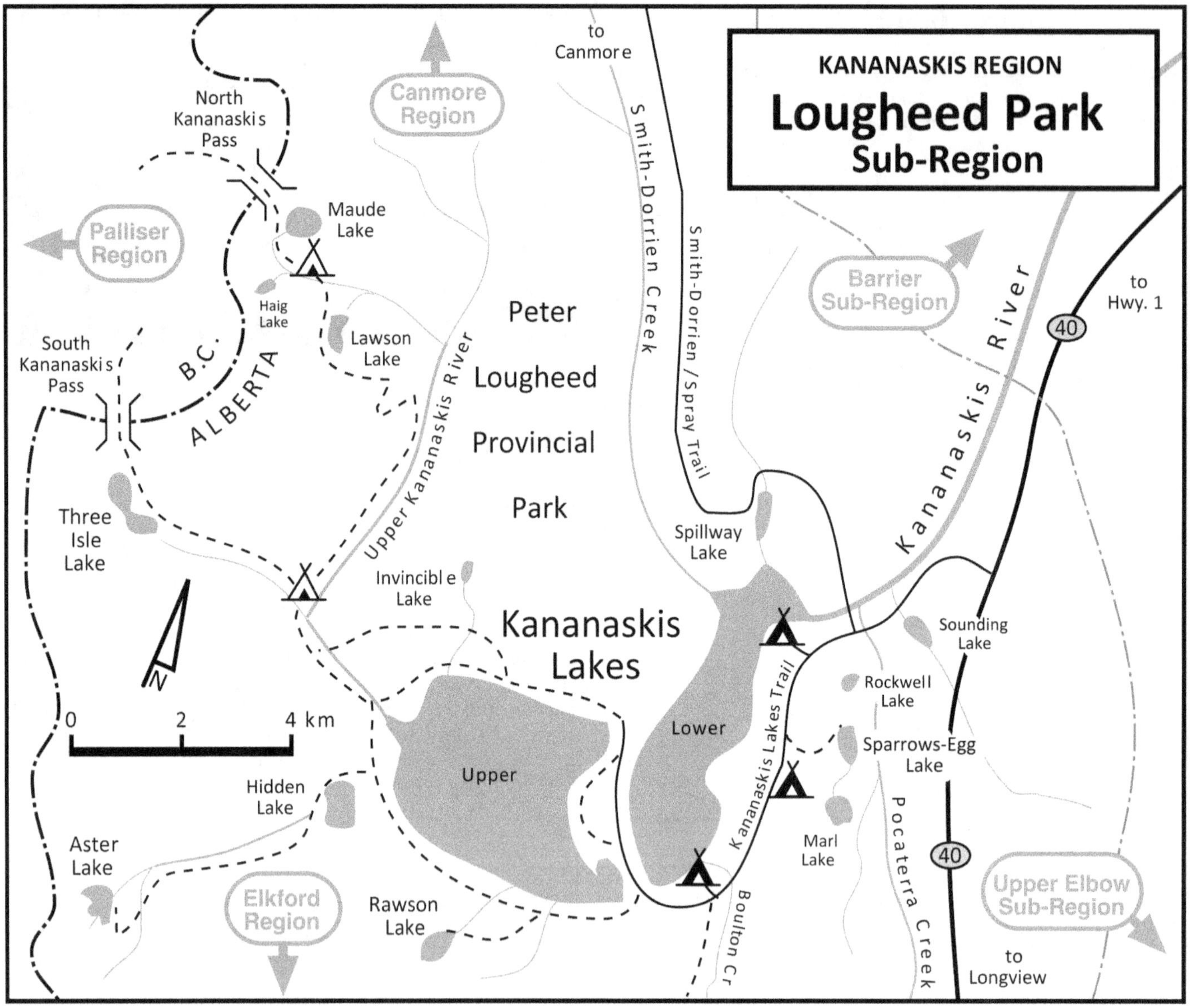

KANANASKIS REGION: Lougheed Park Sub-Region

Aster Lake (AB)
Cutthroat trout to 35 cm

Aster Lake is an oversized glacial tarn in a hidden valley, 10 km by trail above Upper Kananaskis Lake. Aster Lake has been stocked with cutthroat trout that now reproduce naturally. Cutthroat trout caught in Aster will average 20-30 cm in length. Flies work well, and fly casting room is available around the entire lake, due to its distinct alpine setting.

Rawson Lake
Cutthroat trout to 55 cm (2.0 kg)

Rawson Lake is tucked away in a wooded valley south of Upper Kananaskis Lake. Rawson was closed to angling for several years, and the lake's healthy cutthroat trout population was used as brood stock by Alberta Fish and Wildlife. Today, Rawson Lake's cutthroat trout attract plenty of anglers, although the productivity of the first years after the reopening has declined significantly due to heavy fishing pressure. Trout taken from Rawson average 25-35 cm in length, with much larger trout taken regularly.

Aster Lake

Don Shandrowsky at Rawson Lake

KANANASKIS REGION: Lougheed Park Sub-Region

Marl Lake, Rockwall Lake, Sounding Lake (AB)
Status: Devoid of fish
This series of shallow ponds and interconnecting beaver dams in the lower Pocaterra Creek drainage, have held fish at various times in the past, but it is unlikely that any remain. Would-be anglers will be deterred by the marshy access.

Pocaterra Creek (AB)
Cutthroat trout to 30 cm
Rainbow trout to 40 cm
Bull trout to 40 cm
Pocaterra Creek holds cutthroat and bull trout in small sizes and is more productive than the nearby lakes.

Sparrows-Egg Lake (AB)
Rainbow trout to 60 cm (2.5 kg)
Cutthroat trout to 55 cm (2.0 kg)
Sparrows-Egg Lake is located in the marshy valley bottom, 2 km by trail from Elkwood Campground or from Peter Lougheed Visitor Centre. Rainbow and cutthroat trout have both been stocked in Sparrows-Egg with great success. The fertility of the lake allows the trout to grow very quickly. The hard-fighting trout caught from the lake will average 40-50 cm in length. Fishing from shore is possible from many locations, but most anglers prefer to haul their belly boats into the lake. The downside to Sparrows-Egg is that the fish do not reproduce, and the lake is prone to winter kill. Special regulations apply at Sparrows-Egg Lake.

Sparrows-Egg Lake

(rainbow trout)

Boulton Creek
Rainbow trout to 35 cm
Boulton Creek flows into the southern end of Lower Kananaskis Lake. There is a large campground on Boulton Creek. Fishing is generally poor to fair for small rainbow trout.

Spillway Lake (AB)
Rainbow trout to 35 cm
Cutthroat trout to 35 cm
Spillway Lake is located alongside the Smith-Dorrien/Spray Trail at the north end of Lower Kananaskis Lake. Its shallow waters generally hold a few schools of rainbow or cutthroat trout that have made their way in from Lower Kananaskis Lake and are unable to return. Spillway's trout are highly visible and are very wary and difficult to catch. Watch for cars on your back cast if you're fly fishing.

Three Isle Lake (AB)
Cutthroat trout to 45 cm
Three Isle Lake is a beautifully coloured body of water set less than a kilometer below South Kananaskis Pass. Three Isle Lake is a favourite of backcountry anglers who take the 12 km hike up from Upper Kananaskis Lake. Cutthroat trout averaging 25-35 cm are present in good numbers and can be taken from most locations around the lake. Flies and lures will both work well at Three Isle Lake. Water levels in the lake fluctuate dramatically from spring to autumn, continuing to drop as the year progresses. Initial starting levels in the spring are largely determined by winter snowfalls and springtime precipitation.

Three Isle Lake

Lawson Lake (AB)
Status: Devoid of fish
Lawson Lake is a picturesque tarn on the North Kananaskis Pass trail. Lawson was stocked in the early 1970's, but the trout failed to reproduce. At present there are no fish in Lawson.

Lawson Lake

Maude Lake (AB)
Cutthroat trout to 45 cm
Maude Lake is set in the distinctly alpine environs of North Kananaskis Pass, and offers anglers the twin jewels of superb scenery and excellent fishing. A tiring 17 km hike-in from Upper Kananaskis Lake is required to reach Maude Lake. Plenty of cutthroat trout the 25-35 cm range inhabit the lake's clear waters, and they can be caught from most locations around the shoreline. Larger fish tend to keep to the deeper waters off the north and west corners of the lake where steep terrain will generally limit fly casting. On calm evenings with insects hatching, a dry fly can be particularly effective.

KANANASKIS REGION: Lougheed Park Sub-Region

Maude Lake (cutthroat trout)

Haig Lake (AB)
Status: Devoid of fish
Haig Lake is the small tarn located less than a kilometre south of Maude Lake. Haig Lake has never been stocked, and contains no fish.

Invincible Lake (AB)
Cutthroat trout to 40 cm
This small pond high on the west flank of Mt. Invincible holds a few stocked cutthroat trout. Trails are sketchy at best, leading from the north side of Upper Kananaskis Lake. Most trout caught are in the 20-30 cm range.

Invincible Lake

Upper Elbow Sub-Region

This Sub-Region is centered on Elbow Pass and the headwaters of the Elbow River, and sits amid the rugged peaks east of Highway 40 at Highwood Pass. All angling prospects require hiking, with the shortest and most popular being the steep 1 km walk from Highway 40 to Elbow Lake. The Elbow River begins in Elbow Lake and flows east, before eventually emptying into the Bow River at Calgary. The Elbow River offers fair stream fishing in its upper reaches. Other lake fishing opportunities in the Sub-Region require day hikes at a minimum and include Lower Tombstone, Talus, and Burns Lakes, all of which contain cutthroat trout.

Elbow Lake (AB)
Brook trout to 35 cm
Cutthroat trout to 35 cm
Elbow Lake is situated at the summit of Elbow Pass, and is a steep 1 km by trail from Highway 40. The pretty blue waters of Elbow Lake attract numerous visitors every summer, so don't expect solitude. Brook trout predominate, with most fish taken from the lake averaging 20-25 cm in length. There have been a number of projects undertaken in recent years to enhance the lake's habitat, which hopefully will result in larger trout. Forest cover and extended shallows around much of the lake will deter many fly fishers. However, fish can be taken very close to shore in many spots, particularly in the deeper waters off the scree slopes along the north side.

Elbow Lake

Elbow River (AB)
(Headwaters to confluence with Little Elbow River)
Brown trout to 45 cm
Brook trout to 35 cm
Rainbow trout to 35 cm
Cutthroat trout to 35 cm
Bull trout to 50 cm (1.5 kg)
Whitefish to 30 cm
The upper reaches of the Elbow River flow northeast from Elbow Lake, and are overlooked by most anglers. Access is along a hiking trail that parallels the river between the Elbow Pass region and Elbow Falls Trail (Highway 66) at Little Elbow Campground. Cutthroat, brook and bull trout are all present in this upper section, which near Elbow Lake is little more than a small creek. Brown and rainbow trout become more prevalent in the heavily fished lower reaches of the Elbow River that is accessible via Elbow Falls Trail from Bragg Creek.

Rae Lake (AB)
Status: Devoid of fish
The dark waters of Rae Lake lie tucked into the side of Mt. Rae's eastern outlier. The lake is approximately 10 km by trail from Highway 40, and received attention from anglers as long as the lake was stocked regularly. Winter kill has effectively eliminated the remnants of Rae Lake's cutthroat trout population, and its seems unlikely that the lake will be restocked in the future.

KANANASKIS REGION: Upper Elbow Sub-Region

Rae Lake

Tombstone Lakes (AB)
Cutthroat trout to 35 cm (Lower Lake only)
Despite their ominous name, the Tombstone Lakes are set in a delightful basin. They are located 10 km by trail from Highway 40 via Elbow Lake. There is a small backcountry campground at the lower lake. The tiny Lower Tombstone Lake, surrounded on three sides by forest, contains plenty of small cutthroat trout averaging 20-25 cm in length. Dramatically set beneath the towering east face of Tombstone Mountain, the shallow Upper Tombstone Lake has never been stocked and contains no fish.

Lower Tombstone Lake

Burns Lake (AB)
Cutthroat trout to 50 cm (1.5 kg)
Burns Lake is located in a rocky basin at the head of a minor tributary of the upper Sheep River. The lake is a distant 15 km by trail from Elbow Lake, and 16 km by trail from Highway 546 (Sheep River Trail). A steep scramble up a headwall protects Burns from all but the most enterprising hikers. Those who do reach the lake will be rewarded by plentiful cutthroat trout averaging 25-35 cm in length.

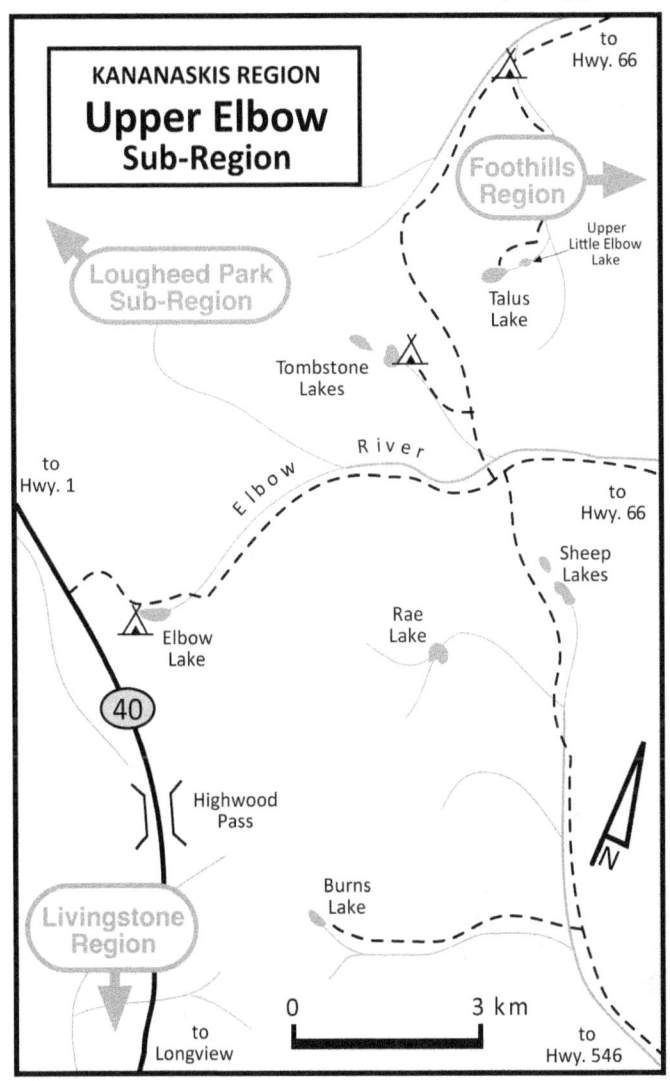

Burns Lake (cutthroat trout)

Jim Rennels photos

KANANASKIS REGION: Upper Elbow Sub-Region

Sheep River (AB)
(Headwaters to Junction Creek)
Rainbow trout to 35 cm
Brook trout to 35 cm
Cutthroat trout to 35 cm
Bull trout to 50 cm (1.5 kg)
Whitefish to 35 cm

The upper Sheep River is accessed by trails from Bluerock Campground at the end of the Sheep River Trail (Highway 546). Although there is a good variety of fish, angling is regarded only as fair in the upper Sheep River. Expect to catch rainbow, cutthroat or brook trout in the 15-25 cm range.

Sheep Lakes (Sheep and Cougar Lake) (AB)
Status: Devoid of fish

These two shallow lakes are located at the headwaters of the Sheep River. Fish would be unable to over winter in either lake.

Sheep Lakes

Talus Lake (AB)
Cutthroat trout to 45 cm

Talus Lake is located at the head of a minor tributary stream that enters the Little Elbow River approximately 10 km upstream from Little Elbow Campground. Ill-defined trails lead south along Talus Lake's outlet creek from the main hiking trail along the Little Elbow River to the shores of this appropriately named body of water. Talus (scree) slopes make up virtually the entire shore of the lake. Cutthroat trout in the 25-35 cm range are the normal catch from Talus Lake, and fly fishing is the most effective technique.

Talus Lake

(cutthroat trout)

Upper Little Elbow Lake (AB)
Status: Doubtful

Little Upper Elbow Lake is the small pond located below the Talus Lake headwall. It has never been stocked, and likely contains no fish.

Barrier Sub-Region

Highway 40 (Kananaskis Trail) runs through the core of this Sub-Region, from the Trans-Canada Highway in the north, to Peter Lougheed Provincial Park in the south. Limited supplies are available at Fortress Junction and Ribbon Creek Alpine Village. The area has several major frontcountry campgrounds as well as a Travel Alberta Information Centre at Barrier Lake. Winding its way north to its confluence with the Bow River, the beautiful Kananaskis River and its multitude of accompanying beaver ponds are within easy walking distance of Highway 40 for most anglers. Barrier Lake, formed by a dam on the Kananaskis River, is one of only a handful of lakes in the Canadian Rockies that contain brown trout, and for this reason attracts many anglers. Travelling south along Highway 40 you pass the Mt. Lorette Ponds and Wedge Pond, both of which offer good roadside fishing and are stocked annually. The Ribbon Creek-Galatea Creek loop presents a challenging hike with some fine backcountry fishing en route in Ribbon, Galatea and Lillian Lakes.

Barrier Lake (AB)
Brown trout to 60 cm (2.5 kg)
Brook trout to 50 cm (1.5 kg)
Rainbow trout to 50 cm (1.5 kg)
Whitefish to 40 cm

The Barrier Dam on the Kananaskis River creates Barrier Lake, a beautiful green coloured body of water. The level of the water in the lake fluctuates with the seasons and with the use of the dam. Late in the fall and early in the spring, the area around the inlet of the Kananaskis River becomes one large mud flat intersected by the river winding back and forth. As the dam fills with melt water, the mudflats disappear and the lake gains almost 2 km in length. Barrier Lake holds brown trout and whitefish in the 25-35 cm range as well as a few brook and rainbow. Fishing is best from a boat, although there are a few locations where shore-bound anglers do well. Any one of a number of points that jut out into the lake hold decent possibilities, as does the area around the inlet and the main bay near Barrier Dam.

Barrier Lake

KANANASKIS REGION: Barrier Sub-Region

Kananaskis River (AB)
Brook trout to 40 cm
Cutthroat trout to 40 cm
Brown trout to 45 cm
Rainbow trout to 40 cm
Whitefish to 40 cm
Bull trout to 60 cm (2.5 kg)

The Kananaskis River flows from the Kananaskis Lakes to the Bow River, and is paralleled by Highway 40 for much of its length. The Kananaskis River has many deep pools and nice riffle sections, but does not have a good reputation for angling. The river holds a variety of fish, with brook trout predominating, although cutthroat and brown are taken regularly. Be aware that the release of water from the dam on Lower Kananaskis Lake can cause changes in water levels over a few hours which in addition to being hazardous, usually disrupts fishing. The changing water levels in the river create a poor habitat, and this affects the overall quality of the fishery.

Kananaskis River

Kananaskis Ponds (AB)
Brook trout to 35 cm
Rainbow trout to 35 cm

There is a seemingly endless maze of beaver ponds that parallel the Kananaskis River between Barrier Lake and Ribbon Creek. Although some are subject to winter kill, most hold small brook trout averaging 20-30 cm in length. The ponds closest to the highway are generally over fished and reaching the more productive ponds usually means working through a tangle of brush and deadfall. Wet feet are a sure bet. Major clusters of ponds are found along the river south of Barrier Lake, including Beaver Ponds Picnic Area, and near the junction of the Kananaskis River with Porcupine, Wasootch, Grizzly and Rocky Creeks.

Kananaskis Ponds
(brook trout)

Mount Lorette Ponds (AB)
Rainbow trout to 35 cm
Brook trout to 35 cm

The Mount Lorette Ponds are series of small man-made lakes that were built to provide children, handicapped and elderly persons the opportunity to fish. A network of paved trails leads from the parking lot past a picnic area to all the ponds, where rainbow and brook trout (depending upon what has been stocked) in the 20-30 cm range are the normal catch. The ponds are stocked annually and are usually fished out by mid-summer unless supplemented by fall plantings.

Mount Lorette Ponds

Wedge Pond (AB)
Arctic grayling to 35 cm

Wedge Pond is a man-made lake situated alongside Highway 40. Winter kill has been a problem in the past, but Wedge Lake has been re-stocked with arctic grayling, which appear to be thriving. The arctic grayling taken from the pond average 20-30 cm in length. Fly fishing is usually effective in taking grayling from Wedge Pond.

Wedge Pond

Evan-Thomas Creek (AB)
Brook trout to 25 cm
Bull trout to 30 cm
Rainbow trout to 25 cm

Evan-Thomas Creek is a major tributary of the Kananaskis River, and has fair angling in its lower sections. Brook trout in small sizes predominate, with the occasional cutthroat or rainbow trout or whitefish also taken.

KANANASKIS REGION: Barrier Sub-Region

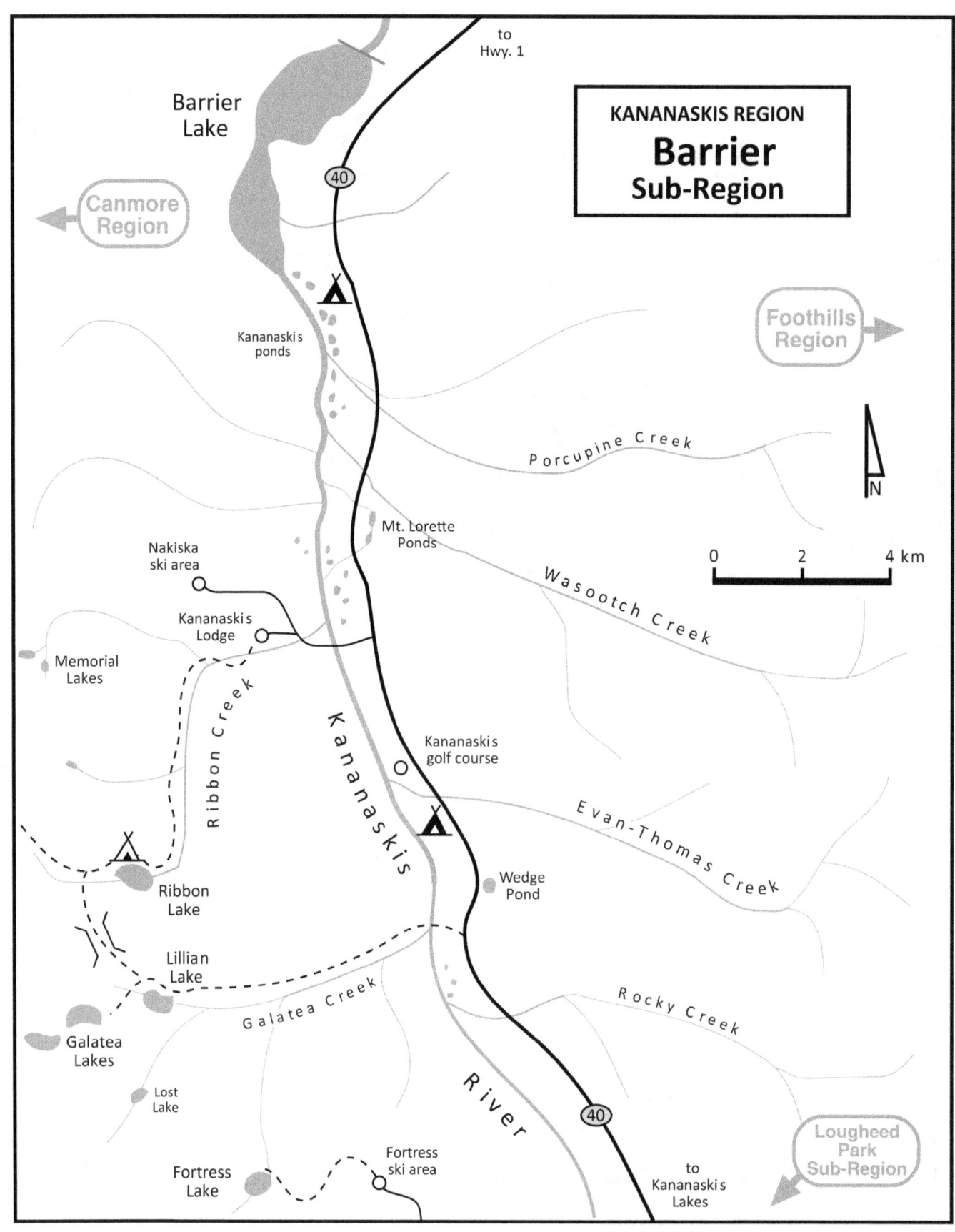

KANANASKIS REGION: Barrier Sub-Region

Ribbon Creek (AB)
Cutthroat trout to 25 cm
The lower reaches of Ribbon Creek hold a few small cutthroat trout and may also hold the odd brook, rainbow or bull trout. Fishing is best restricted to the waters within a kilometre of the Kananaskis River. This section also includes a number of beaver ponds.

Ribbon Lake (AB)
Cutthroat trout to 45 cm
Ribbon Lake is an exquisite body of water set on a lip above Ribbon Falls. The lake is guarded by dangerous cliffs, which make access very difficult. The first 11 km of the 13 km trail are a straightforward hike up Ribbon Creek at a very moderate grade to the delightful Ribbon Falls. Once past the falls, the trail rises steeply, soon coming to a series of exposed ledges and cliff faces to which chains have been attached to aid climbing. Even so, it is still a dangerous section, particularly in wet weather, and those faint-of-heart are strongly advised to pass on this lake or to use the longer Guinn's Pass or Buller Pass access routes. Ribbon Lake holds cutthroat averaging 25-35 cm in length. Casting a fly is difficult around much of the shoreline due to heavy brush, although there are enough suitable locations to keep fly fishers happy. A distinctive drop-off can be seen around the entire lake and fishing this zone where the shallow meets the deep is usually very productive.

Ribbon Lake

Memorial (Bogart) Lakes (AB)
Cutthroat trout to 40 cm
The three Memorial Lakes are located in a secluded basin at the head of the North Fork of Ribbon Creek. Access to the lakes is on a 10 km trail that begins at Ribbon Creek. The two lower Memorial Lakes hold cutthroat trout that average 20-30 cm in length, with the middle lake having by far the best potential for anglers. The upper lake drains dry each fall.

Middle Memorial Lake

Lillian Lake (AB)
Cutthroat trout to 50 cm (1.5 kg)
Lillian Lake is a very popular backcountry destination, and is crowded with hikers throughout the summer. Located 6 km by trail from Highway 40, the shallow, olive coloured waters hold cutthroat averaging 20-30 cm in length. Due to water clarity, fish can be seen far out into the lake and casting ahead of cruising fish will produce positive results even though heavy forest cover around much of the shore will inhibit fly casting. Under low light conditions, keen-eyed anglers can very often take fish within a few metres of shore.

Lillian Lake

Galatea Lakes (AB)
Cutthroat trout to 45 cm
The twin gems of Lower and Upper Galatea Lakes are located little more than a kilometre by ill-defined trail above Lillian Lake. Both of these turquoise bodies of waters hold cutthroat in the 20-30 cm range. Lower Galatea Lake offers better quality angling than its upper sibling does. The lakes are set in rockbound basins at tree line, and there is plenty of fly casting room is available around the lakes. Both lakes are very clear and drop off quickly, and a wet fly fished deep generally gets strikes.

Lower Galatea Lake

KANANASKIS REGION: Barrier Sub-Region

Galatea Creek (AB)
Cutthroat trout to 25 cm
Bull trout to 30 cm
Brook trout to 25 cm
The lower 2 km of Galatea Creek contains a few small cutthroat, bull and brook trout.

Lost (South Galatea) Lake (AB)
Status: Doubtful
This small lake is situated at the headwaters of Galatea Creek. The lake has never been stocked, but trout may have made their way in from the creek.

Fortress Lake (AB)
Cutthroat trout to 50 cm (1.5 kg)
Beautiful Fortress lake is set beneath the imposing north wall of The Fortress, and is reached by a 4 km hike from Fortress Ski Area. Fortress Lake holds cutthroat trout averaging 25-35 cm in length. Scree slopes from The Fortress make up half of the lake's shore, with the rest a mixture of forest and meadow, allowing for reasonable fly casting opportunities. Due to the proximity of its mountain backdrop, Fortress Lake is often in shadow, and usually is not ice-free until July.

Fortress Lake

CANAL FLATS

Columbia Lake, the headwaters of the Columbia River, is physically the centerpiece of this Region. The logging-oriented community of Canal Flats is situated at the south end of Columbia Lake and is the service centre for the immediate area. Bisecting the Region is Highway 93/95, which leads south to Cranbrook and north to Invermere. Whitetail and Whiteswan Lakes are the two most popular angling destinations, although there are many fine trout lakes in the Region.

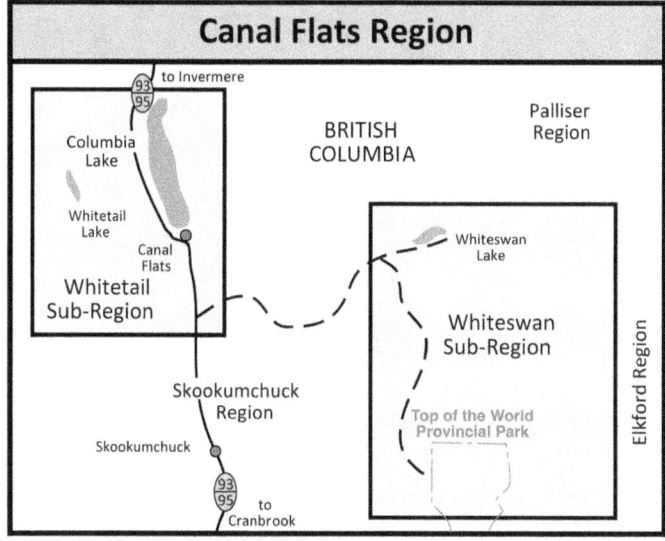

Columbia Lake

Whitetail Sub-Region

Columbia Lake has never been renowned for great fishing, although large bull trout are taken on occasion. The Kootenay River is the main waterway, and the quality of fishing is generally determined by the clarity of the water. Dutch Creek, a tributary of the Columbia, and Findlay Creek, a tributary of the Kootenay, both offer good river fishing. Whitetail Lake, 28 km by gravel road from Highway 93/95, is the Sub-Region's angling masterpiece, with large rainbow trout plentiful in this Rockies' classic.

Columbia Lake (BC)
Bull trout to 90 cm (10.0 kg)
Cutthroat trout to 50 cm (1.5 kg)
Rainbow trout to 50 cm (1.5 kg)
Whitefish to 40 cm

The pretty, aquamarine waters of Columbia Lake serve as the source of the mighty Columbia River, which eventually flows into the Pacific Ocean at Astoria, Oregon. Although Columbia Lake's fishing is generally regarded as substandard due to the coarse fish population, anglers are occasionally rewarded with huge bull trout often weighing 7 kg or more. The waters where Dutch Creek empties into the north end of Columbia Lake tend to be the most productive, although cutthroat and rainbow trout can be taken from many locations on the lake. Trolling will be the most effective angling technique.

Kootenay River (BC) *(Kootenay National Park to Canal Flats)*
Cutthroat trout to 50 cm (1.5 kg)
Bull trout to 75 cm (5.0 kg)
Whitefish to 40 cm

The Kootenay River flows out of the Kootenay Valley into the Rocky Mountain Trench at Canal Flats. The Kootenay River continues to flow south, and by a quirk of geography, misses Columbia Lake by less than two kilometres. The two river systems eventually reconnect at Castlegar after each river has traveled hundreds of kilometres. The Kootenay is a relatively large river as it flows south from Canal Flats, and it receives heavy run-off in the spring. The river is often muddy until mid to late summer, after which cutthroat and bull trout can be taken in increasing numbers as the river clears. Fall is the best time for whitefish.

Kootenay River

Dutch Creek (BC)
Cutthroat to 50 cm (1.5 kg)
Bull trout to 75 cm (5.0 kg)
Whitefish to 40 cm

Dutch Creek is regarded by many as the "true source" of the Columbia River, as it is the main tributary flowing into Columbia Lake. Dutch Creek has gained a reputation over time as an excellent trout stream. Cutthroat in the 30-40 cm range can be taken from the many pools along the entire length of the creek, while bull trout exceeding 60 cm in length are found in some of the larger holes. The lower reaches of Dutch Creek in the vicinity of Highway 93/95 tend to get over fished. The upper river, which is accessed by logging roads branching from the Westside Road, sees lesser numbers of anglers and holds the promise of great fishing. Water clarity is stunning in the late summer and fall and Dutch Creek's cutthroat are always eager to rise to a well-presented dry fly.

Dutch Creek

CANAL FLATS REGION: Whitetail Sub-Region

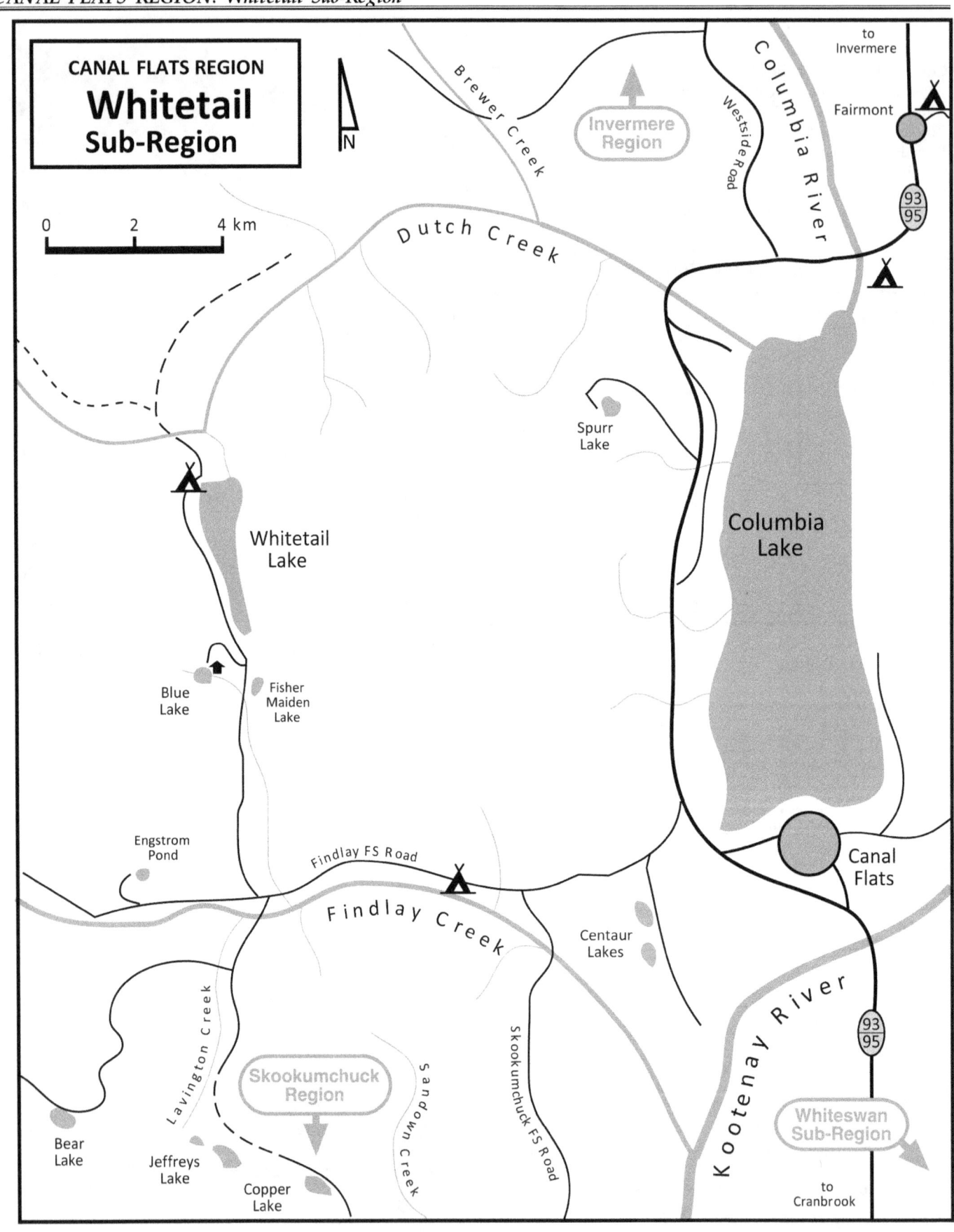

CANAL FLATS REGION: Whitetail Sub-Region

Brewer Creek (BC)
Cutthroat trout to 40 cm
Bull trout to 60 cm (2.5 kg)
Whitefish to 35 cm
Brewer Creek is a major tributary of Dutch Creek and can be reached from logging roads connecting with the Westside Road. Cutthroat averaging 20-30 cm in length are the dominant species, with a few bull trout and whitefish present as well.

Spurr Lake (BC)
Rainbow trout to 55 cm (1.5 kg)
This small forest encircled lake is located approximately 6 km by rough road from Highway 93/95. Spurr Lake holds an abundance of rainbow trout, most in the 25-35 cm range. Although fish can generally be taken fairly close to shore, fishing from a boat or float tube is preferable. Lures and flies will do equally well in Spurr Lake.

Whitetail Lake

Spurr Lake

Whitetail (Deer) Lake (BC)
Rainbow trout to 70 cm (4.0 kg)
Brook trout to 55 cm (2.0 kg)
Whitetail Lake is set in a valley between the Dutch and Findlay Creek watersheds. Access is via a good gravel road from Highway 93/95 at Thunder Hill, above the south end of Columbia Lake. A sizable forestry campground is located at the north end of the lake. Whitetail Lake has been designated as a trophy lake, and consequently special limits on number and size of trout kept are in effect, as well as restrictions on bait and type of hook. The quality of fishing in Whitetail Lake has been increasing every year, and it presently ranks as one of the best lakes in the Rockies. Rainbow trout upwards of 50 cm in length are taken with amazing regularity, and trophy fish of 60 cm or more are not uncommon. Fly fishing enthusiasts love Whitetail Lake's extended shallows and crystal clear water, where large rainbows cruise constantly. A boat or float tube is essential to fish Whitetail effectively.

Tyler Ambrosi with Whitetail Lake rainbow

Blue Lake (BC)
Rainbow trout to 40 cm
Blue Lake, a small but colourful lake located 2 km south of Whitetail Lake, contains rainbow trout averaging 25-35 cm in length. The Blue Lake Forestry Education Centre, which is at the lake, is busy throughout the summer. Blue Lake is usually a hive of canoeing, swimming and fishing activity.

Blue Lake

Fisher Maiden Lake (BC)
Rainbow trout to 35 cm
Tiny Fisher Maiden Lake is located alongside the Whitetail Lake road, and its population of rainbow trout is restricted to youngsters and senior citizens only. Casting room is limited around this small pond. The rainbow trout in Fisher Maiden Lake will average 20-30 cm in length.

Fisher Maiden Lake

Findlay Creek (BC)
Cutthroat trout to 50 cm (1.5 kg)
Bull trout to 70 cm (4.0 kg)
Whitefish to 40 cm
Findlay Creek is a major tributary of the Kootenay River, and joins the Kootenay approximately 5 km south of Canal Flats. Although several kilometres of Findlay Creek are virtually impossible to access due to a deep canyon, there are many stretches of fishable water. Cutthroat trout averaging 20-30 cm in length predominate, with bull trout and whitefish present in fair numbers as well. A gravel road beginning at Thunder Hill off Highway 93/95, above the south end of Columbia Lake, leads up the Findlay Creek drainage.

CANAL FLATS REGION: Whitetail Sub-Region

Engstrom (Burks) Pond (BC)
Rainbow trout to 35 cm
Brook trout to 35 cm

Tiny Engstrom Pond is reached via some rough dirt roads that lead off the Findlay Creek Forest Service Road. The almost perfectly circular pond is crystal clear, and fish can easily be seen cruising along the seam between the shallows and deeper water. Rainbow and brook trout inhabit Engstrom Pond in relatively equal numbers, and the size of the fish will average 20-30 cm in length. For those who are fly fishing, roll casting will be essential, as the forest cover hugs the lake in the areas where the shallows are least extensive. Lures and bait are also effective.

Engstrom Pond

Bear (Shallow) Lake (BC)
Brook trout to 40 cm

Bear Lake is located in Lavington Creek drainage, and can be reached on logging roads from the Findlay Creek Forest Service Road. As its name alternate suggests, the lake is not very deep, and shallow water extends far out from the shoreline. Brook trout are present in the lake in the 20-30 cm range.

Bear Lake

Lavington Creek (BC)
Cutthroat trout to 35 cm

Lavington Creek is a tributary of Findlay Creek, and can be reached by following logging roads that branch south off of the main Findlay Creek Road. Lavington Creek holds small cutthroat trout, and few are larger than 25 cm in length.

Jeffreys Lake (BC)
Cutthroat trout to 55 cm (1.5 kg)

Jeffreys Lake is located at the height of land separating Lavington and Sandown Creek, and can only be reached through private property. The lake's colouration is particularly stunning, with the dark blues of the depths contrasted against the light greens of the shallows. The margin separating the deep and shallow waters is productive for cutthroat trout that average 30-40 cm in length.

Jeffreys Lake

Copper Lake (BC)
Cutthroat trout to 40 cm

Copper Lake is situated at the head of Sandown Creek, and can be reached by a rough road that leads up Sandown Creek. Copper Lake is not heavily fished, and does hold cutthroat trout in the 20-30 cm range.

Centaur Lakes (BC)
Brook trout to 50 cm (1.5 kg)

The Centaur Lakes are a series of shallow, interconnected lakes situated on the benches above the southwest corner of Columbia Lake. Access is on poorly maintained roads off the main Findlay Creek Road. A wide margin of bull rushes around the lakes makes fishing awkward in many places. The brook trout in the lake are favourable to lures and bait. Most fish taken will be less than 35 cm in length, although there are larger fish present.

Centaur Lakes

CANAL FLATS REGION: Whiteswan Sub-Region

Whiteswan Sub-Region

Whiteswan Lake Provincial Park is located southeast of Canal Flats, and is the core of this Sub-Region. The park is reached by following the 24 km long gravel access road that branches east from Highway 93/95, approximately 5 km south of Canal Flats. Whiteswan Lake itself receives heavy fishing pressure all season long. Nearby Alces Lake is popular with fly fishers. Top of the World Provincial Park, located in the rugged backcountry south of Whiteswan Lake, attracts hikers and anglers to appropriately named Fish Lake. The White River, and its numerous tributaries, are found to the north of Whiteswan Lake, and offer some outstanding stream fishing for cutthroat trout.

Whiteswan Lake (BC)
Rainbow trout to 75 cm (4.0 kg)

Whiteswan Lake and its provincial park are enormously popular during the summer, and the campgrounds are invariably filled to overflowing every weekend. Whiteswan is a long, narrow lake sandwiched between the rugged peaks of the Hughes and Van Nostrand Ranges. Whiteswan's deep, dark waters hold rainbow trout averaging 30-45 cm in length, with larger individuals present in good numbers. Gang trolls and flatfish predominate among fishing equipment on Whiteswan Lake, although fly fishing continues to become more popular each year. There are some excellent fly fishing opportunities at Whiteswan: simply trolling a wet fly behind a boat at a slow speed is usually productive. In the late evening, if wind conditions are favourable, there is superb dry fly fishing in the shallow waters at the eastern end of the lake. Wind can be a problem at Whiteswan as it generally picks up in intensity by mid-day and remains strong throughout much of the afternoon. All of Whiteswan's inlet and outlet creeks are closed to angling. Check regulations, as there are special limits on trout taken from the lake. Be aware of logging and ore trucks on the main access road from Highway 93/95.

Whiteswan Lake (rainbow trout)

Alces (Moose) Lake (BC)
Rainbow trout to 60 cm (2.5 kg.)

Alces Lake is situated alongside the Whiteswan Lake Forest Service road, 2 km before reaching Whiteswan Lake. Alces Lake is restricted to fly-fishing only and motors are not permitted, factors that keep it much less busy than nearby Whiteswan Lake. Alces Lake's pleasing blue-green waters hold plenty of rainbow trout averaging 30-40 cm in length. Trolling a fly along the margin that separates the shallows from the deeper water is generally an effective technique. Working the shallows in the evening with a dry fly also produces well.

Alces Lake (rainbow trout)

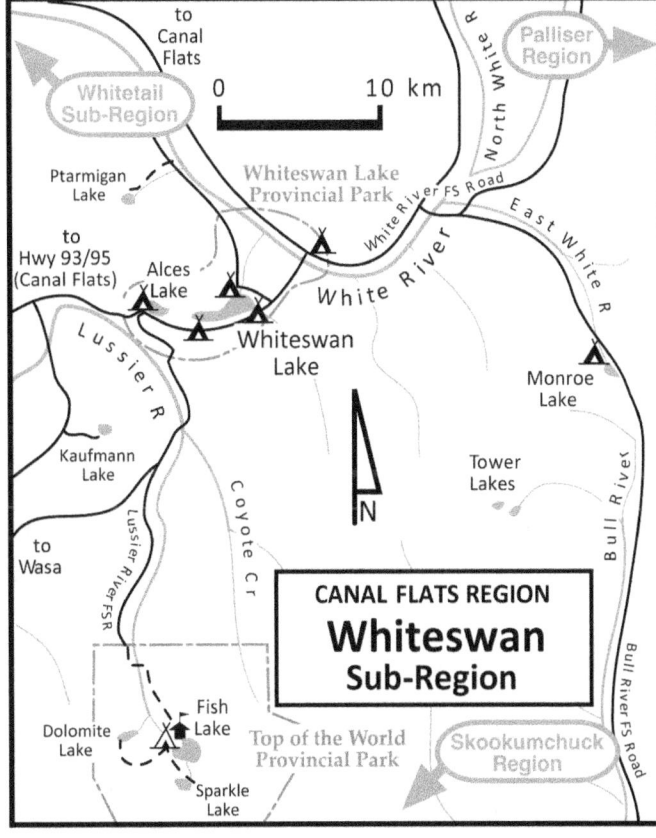

CANAL FLATS REGION: Whiteswan Sub-Region

Kaufmann Lake (BC)
Brook trout to 40 cm
Kaufmann Lake is hidden in a small side valley above the Lussier River, and can be reached by following a confusing series of logging roads that lead south and east off of the Whiteswan Lake Forest Service Road. A very steep hill is encountered just before the lake, and it is best to walk the hill rather than drive it. Kaufmann Lake is a secluded gem of emerald green water, encircled by a pleasant mixed forest. Fly fishing is difficult from shore due to the forest cover, but those spin casting with lures or bait should do well. Brook trout in Kaufmann Lake are plentiful, but tend to be small, with the average in the 20-25 cm range.

Kaufmann Lake

Ptarmigan Lake (BC)
Cutthroat trout to 40 cm
Ptarmigan Lake is set in an alpine basin north of Whiteswan Lake, and is reached by following a 6 km trail, half of which is an abandoned logging road. Ptarmigan was stocked in the past with cutthroat trout, which are doing well. The trout average 25-35 cm in length and can be taken from most locations around the lake. Forest, meadow, brush and avalanche slope make up the shoreline, and there are numerous locations from which to fish.

Ptarmigan Lake

White River (BC)
(Downstream from Height of the Rockies Park boundary)
Cutthroat trout to 50 cm (1.5 kg)
Rainbow trout to 60 cm (2.5 kg)
Bull trout to 70 cm (4.0 kg)
Whitefish to 40 cm
The White River is major flowing water of the Sub-Region, rushing south and west from headwaters along the Continental Divide before swinging north to join the Kootenay River. Logging roads from the Kootenay River and from Whiteswan Lake make their way up all the branches of the White River. The upper portions of the White River offer outstanding fishing for cutthroat trout, and are far removed from heavy fishing pressure. Cutthroat caught in the White River will average 25-35 cm in length. Bull trout and whitefish are also found along the river's entire length, with rainbow trout populating the area below the White River's confluence with Whiteswan Lake's outlet creek.

White River

North White River (BC)
Cutthroat trout to 50 cm (1.5 kg)
Bull trout to 70 cm (4.0 kg)
Whitefish to 40 cm
The North White River possesses the characteristics of the upper White River, and is accessed from logging roads branching off the White River. Cutthroat trout averaging 25-35 cm are plentiful, with bull trout and whitefish also present in fair numbers.

East White River (BC)
Cutthroat trout to 45 cm
Bull trout to 60 cm (2.5 kg)
Whitefish to 35 cm
The East White River is a major tributary of the White River, which flows northwest from its source at Monroe Lake to join the White River. Logging roads parallel the East White River for its entire length, making river access relatively easy. Road access to the East White River drainage is from the White River and also from the Bull River. Cutthroat, whitefish and bull trout can be caught in the many fine pools along the entire length of the East White River. Cutthroat trout predominate, and average 20-30 cm in length.

Monroe Lake (BC)
Cutthroat trout to 45 cm
Monroe Lake is a small, placid body of water at the head of the East White River. Monroe's stunning green waters receive little fishing pressure each season due to the lengthy access. The lake is not very productive, and the trout tend to grow slowly. Partial winter kill has also been a problem in the past. Cutthroat trout in Monroe Lake will average 25-35 cm in length.

Monroe Lake

Tower Lakes (BC)
Cutthroat trout to 45 cm

The diminutive Tower Lakes are located in the shadow of Mt. Harrison, the highest mountain in the Region. The lakes are reached after bushwhacking from logging roads in the extreme upper Bull River drainage. Map, compass and wilderness experience are prerequisite for anyone planning to fish Tower Lakes. The lakes have been stocked with cutthroat trout, which are now reproducing naturally. Fish caught from the two Tower Lakes (individually named as Tower #1 and Tower #2) will average 25-35 cm in length. Fishing is equally good in each lake.

Lussier River (BC) *(Headwaters to Diorite Creek)*
Cutthroat trout to 45 cm
Bull trout to 60 cm (2.5 kg)
Whitefish to 35 cm

The Lussier River flows from its headwaters in Top of the World Provincial Park and eventually joins the Kootenay River. The upper section, above the junction with Diorite Creek, offers fine streamside angling over much of its course. The canyon section, which is paralleled by the Whiteswan Lake road, is very difficult to access. Above the canyon, the Lussier River can be reached by following the Top of the World Provincial Park road. The upper Lussier is crisscrossed with logging roads and is readily accessible. Cutthroat trout predominate in the Lussier, with average specimens running in the 25-35 cm range.

Lussier River

Coyote Creek (BC)
Cutthroat trout to 40 cm
Bull trout to 55 cm (2.0 kg)
Whitefish to 35 cm

Coyote Creek is a major tributary of the upper Lussier River, and can be reached from logging roads that branch off of the Top of the World Provincial Park road. Coyote Creek has many fine pools, and cutthroat trout of 20-30 cm in length will be the average catch.

Fish Lake (BC)
Cutthroat trout to 50 cm (1.5 kg)
Bull trout to 75 cm (6.0 kg)

Fish Lake is a very popular backcountry hiking destination, and is located in the heart of Top of the World Provincial Park. Fish Lake is reached via a 6 km trail, after a 55 km drive on a gravel road from Highway 93/95. There is a backcountry campground at the lake, as well as a B.C. Parks cabin, which is available for a minimal fee on a first-come, first-served basis. Fishing is usually excellent, as cutthroat trout in the 20-35 cm range abound in the lake's sparkling green waters. Large bull trout are also present in small numbers. Fishing from shore is limited in most locations due to the heavy forest cover, which rings the lake. In the past, however, a few rafts have been available, from which the quality of fishing improves greatly. Despite the seemingly remote location, Top of the World Provincial Park, and Fish Lake in particular, are busy throughout the summer months.

Fish Lake

Dolomite Lake (BC)
Cutthroat trout to 50 cm (1.5 kg)

Dolomite Lake is set in a narrow basin north of Fish Lake. The lake is reached by hiking a heart-pounding 2 km trail up to the crest of Wild Horse Ridge, and then descending steeply down the other side of the ridge. Those anglers who reach Dolomite Lake are rewarded with chunky cutthroat trout ranging from 30-40 cm in length. The bottom drops off quickly all around the lake, and there are several good spots from which to cast a fly and reach the fish-holding waters. Be forewarned that the hike to Dolomite Lake, although not particularly long, is very strenuous.

Sparkle Lake (BC)
Status: Devoid of fish

Sparkle Lake is set in a windswept basin above the inlet to Fish Lake, and is very popular as a half-day hike from the Fish Lake campground. Sparkle Lake has never been stocked and contains no fish.

PALLISER REGION

This is one of the most rugged and unspoiled Regions of the Rockies, and includes two of British Columbia's most spectacular Provincial Parks: Mount Assiniboine and Height of the Rockies. Access into the Region is by hiking trails only. There are numerous excellent cutthroat trout lakes, rivers and streams in the Region. Connor Lakes in the south, and the lakes in the core area of Mount Assiniboine Park in the north, are truly outstanding. Anyone planning to fish this corner of the Rockies can expect to do a significant amount of legwork prior to the reward of great fishing.

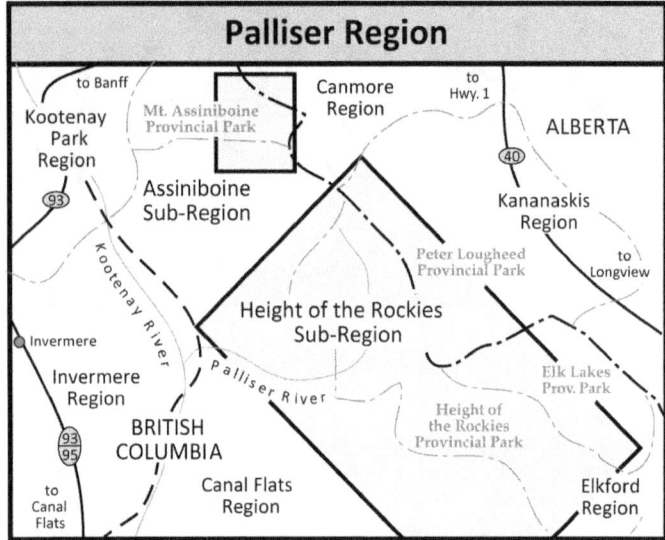

Height of the Rockies Sub-Region

This Sub-Region includes the recently created Height of the Rockies (HOTR) Provincial Park, and sits amid some of the most striking mountain scenery on the continent. The Height of the Rockies runs from Palliser Pass and Banff National Park in the north to Connor Lakes in the south, taking in peaks, valleys, lakes and rivers on the British Columbia side of the Continental Divide. All of the fishing opportunities in this Sub-Region are remote, and virtually all will require a hike of some magnitude. Cutthroat trout are the predominant species in the area's rivers and lakes.

Palliser River (BC)
Cutthroat trout to 50 cm (1.5 kg)
Bull trout to 75 cm (5.0 kg)
Whitefish to 40 cm
The Palliser River is a major tributary of the Kootenay River, and joins the Kootenay approximately 20 km south of Kootenay National Park. The primary road access up Palliser River watershed is from Settlers Road in Kootenay National Park. The Palliser Forest Service Road branches east from Settlers Road, and ascends the Palliser River drainage to the provincial park boundary near Joffre Creek. Although the river is very fast in sections, there are many excellent pools that hold sizeable cutthroat trout. Trout in the Palliser River will average 25-35 cm in length. Large bull trout up to 5 kg can be found in the large pools.

Albert River (BC)
Cutthroat trout to 45 cm
Bull trout to 60 cm (2.5 kg)
Whitefish to 35 cm
The Albert River is a major tributary of the Palliser, and is accessible from a B.C. Forest Service road that branches off the Palliser Forest Service Road. The Albert River is a fast-flowing river much like the Palliser River, and it likewise holds cutthroat and the occasional bull trout in its many pools. From roads on the upper reaches of the Albert, a short but ill-defined trail leads to Leman Lake and the upper Spray River in Banff National Park.

Albert River

Fenwick Lake (BC)
Rainbow trout to 35 cm
Fenwick Lake is located 6 km west of the Kootenay Forest Service Road along a rough but passable track. Set in marshy surroundings, Fenwick Lake contains good numbers of rainbow trout averaging 20-25 cm in length. Fish can be taken from the shoreline of this narrow lake, although using a boat will increase angling prospects. Fenwick is relatively shallow and subject to winter kill on occasion.

Fenwick Lake

Belgium Lake (NP)
Status: Doubtful
Belgium Lake is set in the alpine environs of Palliser Pass at the extreme southern end of Banff National Park. Access is via a trail south from the Spray River or north from the Palliser River. This shallow lake at one time had a small population of cutthroat trout that faced the annual threat of winter kill. Recent reports indicate no signs of fish in Belgium Lake.

Belgium Lake

PALLISER REGION: Height of the Rockies Sub-Region

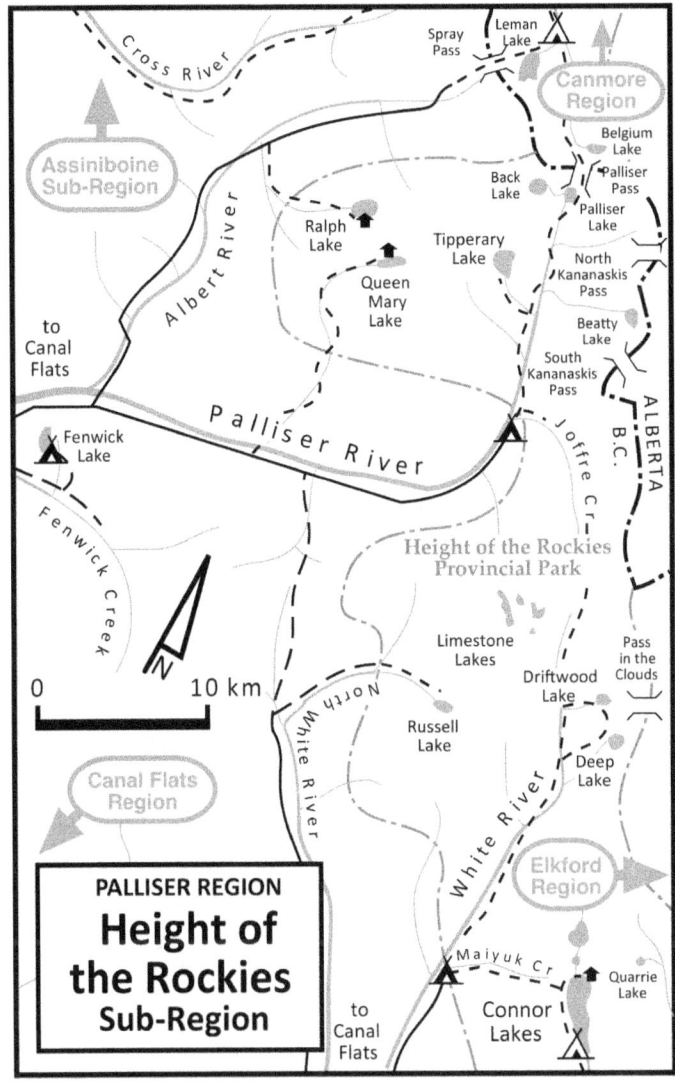

PALLISER REGION
Height of the Rockies Sub-Region

Tipperary Lake (BC)
Cutthroat trout to 45 cm
Tipperary Lake is located in a basin west of the Palliser River and is accessible only by trail. Few parties make it to Tipperary Lake each year. The silted waters of Tipperary Lake hold plenty of cutthroat trout, with most specimens averaging 25-35 cm in length.

Beatty Lake (BC)
Status: Devoid of fish
Beatty Lake is set in a forested basin on the western side of South Kananaskis Pass. The main trail access is from Three Isle Lake in Peter Lougheed Park in Alberta. There is no record of Beatty Lake ever being stocked, and it is not possible for fish to enter the lake from the Palliser drainage.

Ralph Lake (BC)
Cutthroat trout to 50 cm
Ralph Lake is set high in an alpine basin above the Albert River. Access is on a very steep 5 km trail from the Albert River Forest Service Road. Much of the shoreline around Ralph Lake is treeless, and the lake affords itself well to fly casting. The cutthroat trout in the lake are numerous, with most averaging 25-35 cm in length. Be aware that the Ralph Lake basin is prime grizzly bear habitat.

Ralph Lake (cutthroat trout)

Queen Mary Lake (BC)
Cutthroat trout to 50 cm
Queen Mary Lake is set in the midst of the spectacular peaks of the Royal Group. The main access is via a rough horse trail that leads up Queen Mary Creek from the Palliser River. There are numerous creek crossings on this route. For those on foot, an alternate route into the lake is south from Ralph Lake. This requires a serious hike into Ralph Lake and then some good route finding over to Queen Mary Lake. The cutthroat trout fishing at Queen Mary Lake is excellent. Most trout taken from the lake will be in the 25-35 cm range, with larger fish present in good numbers.

Limestone Lakes (BC)
Status: Devoid of fish
The Limestone Lakes are located on a barren plateau at the head of Joffre Creek. They are accessed via long and difficult trails either from Joffre Creek in the north, or from the White River in the south. The lakes have never been stocked, and they do not hold any fish.

Palliser Lake (BC)
Status: Devoid of fish
Palliser Lake is an appealing body of water on the B.C. side of Palliser Pass, but it has never been stocked and contains no fish.

Palliser Lake

Back Lake (BC)
Status: Devoid of fish
Back Lake is an algae-infested pond that sits in a rocky basin less than a kilometre above Palliser Lake. It holds no fish.

PALLISER REGION: Height of the Rockies Sub-Region

Limestone Lakes

White River (BC) *(Headwaters to HOTR park boundary)*
Cutthroat trout to 45 cm

The extreme upper reaches of the White River, which are inside the Height of the Rockies Provincial Park, can only be accessed by trail. Fishing is good for cutthroat trout in any of the pools on the river. Most trout caught will be in the 20-30 cm range.

Maiyuk Creek (BC)
Cutthroat trout to 35 cm

Maiyuk Creek is a tributary of the upper White River. Logging roads off the White River branch up Maiyuk Creek as far as the Height of the Rockies boundary. From the end of the road, a 7 km trail leads up Maiyuk Creek to Connor Lakes. Maiyuk Creek holds cutthroat trout in small sizes.

Connor Lakes (BC)
Cutthroat trout to 60 cm (3.0 kg)

The three Connor Lakes are the angling gems of the area. Access is by trail only, either 7 km up Maiyuk Creek from the White River, or 10 km up Forsyth Creek from the Elk River. There are several primitive campsites on the lower lake, as well as a small B.C. Forest Service cabin that is available on a first-come, first-served basis. For many years, Connor Lakes have been regarded as some of the finest cutthroat trout waters in the Rockies. The lower lake is the largest, extending over 3 km in length. The middle lake is small, little more than 200 m across. The upper lake is almost 1 km in length. Cutthroat trout in all three lakes grow to very large sizes, with fish over 2 kg caught each season. Lures and flies are the standard fishing gear. Although a few intrepid hikers and some horse parties bring belly boats to Connor Lakes, most anglers are relegated to shore. Fishing from shore is not a major disadvantage as the fish can be taken in the crystal clear waters close to shore. For those uncomfortable fishing a very large lake from shore, the small middle lake is a good option.

Upper Connor Lake (cutthroat trout)

Quarrie Lake (BC)
Cutthroat trout to 45 cm

Quarrie Lake is located in the Quarrie Creek valley, immediately west of the valley that holds Connor Lakes. Access is difficult, either along a rough trail up Quarrie Creek itself, or through a rocky gap from Connor Lakes. Quarrie Lake sees few anglers each year. The lake holds cutthroat trout that average 20-30 cm in length.

Deep Lake (BC)
Cutthroat trout to 35 cm

Deep Lake is situated in the upper White River drainage, and can be reached on trails from the White River. The lake can also be accessed by a rough trail from the Abruzzi Creek drainage through the Pass in the Clouds. As its name suggests, the lake is has significant depth, as the bottom drops off quickly on all sides. Cutthroat trout in Deep Lake are numerous but small, averaging 20-30 cm in length.

Deep Lake

Driftwood Lake (BC)
Cutthroat trout to 35 cm

Driftwood Lake is located one small valley north of Deep Lake, and is accessed by the same trail from the White River. Avalanche slopes make their way down to Driftwood Lake, and each winter and spring debris is strewn out onto the ice-covered lake. In early summer the ice melts, and the driftwood is deposited at the high water mark. As with neighbouring Deep Lake, the cutthroat trout in Driftwood Lake are numerous, but few will be larger than 30 cm in length

Driftwood Lake

Russell Lake (BC)
Status: Doubtful

Russell Lake is set in a basin at the head of the North White River, and is accessed via a trail up the North White River. Russell Lake has never been stocked, and it is doubtful if there are any fish in the lake.

Russell Lake

PALLISER REGION: Assiniboine Sub-Region

Cross River (BC)
Cutthroat trout to 45 cm
Bull trout to 60 cm (2.5 kg)
Whitefish to 35 cm

The Cross River joins the Kootenay River just outside the Kootenay National Park boundary. The Cross River offers some excellent fishing particularly in its lower reaches where a series of falls and pools within 2 km of the Cross' confluence with the Kootenay usually produce well. Although both bull trout and whitefish are present, cutthroat trout averaging 20-35 cm in length are taken in greater numbers.

Assiniboine Sub-Region

The Assiniboine area is one of the true gems in the Canadian Rockies, and has been a favourite of backcountry travellers since the turn of the century. Despite lengthy access routes, incredible scenery and good fishing ensure that the Assiniboine area will be crowded each summer. Lake Magog, set beneath the awe-inspiring summit of Mt. Assiniboine, represents the heart of the Sub-Region. The main campground is located on the bench above Magog's northwest shore, while Assiniboine Lodge (reservations only) and the government-run Naiset Cabins (first come-first served) are found on the lake's northeast corner. Sunburst, Cerulean, Elizabeth and Gog Lakes are all within the Assiniboine core area, and Wedgwood and Og Lakes are easy half-day trips from Lake Magog. Access to the Assiniboine core area is by trail. The most popular route in is up Bryant Creek from the Mt. Shark trailhead and Spray Lakes Reservoir. Other routes into Assiniboine include Sunshine Village and Ferro Pass. All routes into the Assiniboine core area require a hike of at least 28 km.

Magog Lake (BC)
Cutthroat trout to 60 cm (2.0 kg)

Magog Lake, at 2 km in length, is the largest lake of the Assiniboine area. Its treeless shoreline offers ample room for fly casting, and its waters hold some fine cutthroat trout. Trout taken from the lake will average 30-45 cm in length. As with most lakes in the area, water clarity dictates that low light periods (early morning and late evening) will be the most productive, as this is the time fish enter the shallower water to feed. High winds are often a problem for fly fishermen on Magog during the daytime. Magog Lake has no outlet stream, but the area around several inlet creeks often hold fish.

Magog Lake and Mount Assiniboine

Gog Lake (BC)
Cutthroat trout to 35 cm

Gog Lake is located just over 1 km south of the Naiset Cabins in a quiet basin on the trail to Wonder Pass. Much of Gog's shoreline allows fly casting, and its sheltered setting usually protects it from the strong winds that prevail on other lakes of the region. The cutthroat trout in the lake average 25-30 cm, which are small by Assiniboine standards, and their numbers have been significantly reduced in recent years by over harvest. Trout seem to be evenly distributed throughout the lake, but most anglers will choose to work from the accessible north and east shores despite the prospect of wet feet.

Gog Lake

(cutthroat trout)

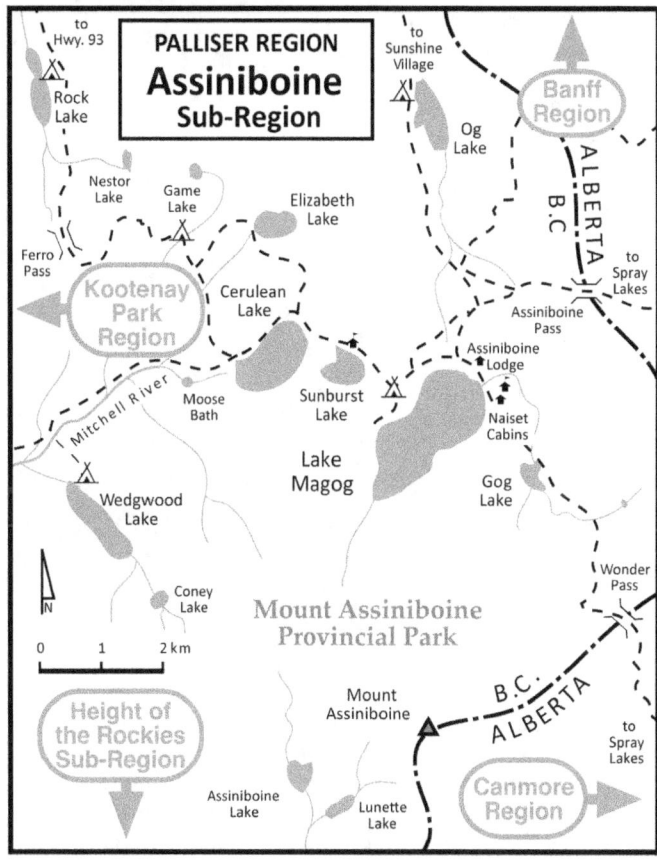

PALLISER REGION: Assiniboine Sub-Region

Og Lake (BC)
Cutthroat trout to 40 cm
Og Lake is located amid the near moonscape at the south end of the appropriately named Valley of the Rocks. The rockbound waters of Og Lake have been stocked with cutthroat trout which now average 25-35 cm in length. Fish can be taken from all locations around the lake, although those fly fishing will have casting problems on the steeper talus slopes.

Og Lake

(cutthroat trout)

Sunburst Lake (BC)
Rainbow trout to 75 cm (4.0 kg)
Located just over 1 km west of Magog Lake by trail, Sunburst Lake was long regarded as one of the premier fly fishing lakes in the Rockies. Sunburst Lake was closed for study for a number of years, but has been reopened to fishing since the 1980's. Large rainbow trout (and a few rainbow-cutthroat hybrids) in the 2-3 kg range are taken regularly from Sunburst Lake. Most trout caught will average 35-45 cm in length. Anglers' preference for casting locations range from the scree slopes on the south side of the lake to the wooded north and west shores.

Sunburst Lake

Cerulean Lake (BC)
Cutthroat trout to 70 cm (3.0 kg)
Cerulean Lake is located a short walk west of Sunburst Lake, and in the past attracted many anglers because of its reputation for trophy-sized trout. Although small in number, some extremely large cutthroat trout and rainbow-cutthroat hybrids still inhabit the lake's deep, blue-green waters. Fish exceeding 2 kg are caught each year. Special regulations are presently in effect in Cerulean. The shoreline offers few opportunities for fly casting, so roll casting ability is a must for those using fly rods. Lures can be very effective in Cerulean at times. As Cerulean Lake has no inlet creek and only a tiny outlet, fish in the lake tend to keep to a boundary that separates the shallow water from the deep. At most locations around the shore this zone is within casting distance, and if wind and light conditions are right, the large fish can often be sighted from shore.

Cerulean Lake

(cutthroat trout)

Elizabeth Lake (BC)
Cutthroat trout to 35 cm
The remarkably clear waters of Elizabeth Lake are found in a small larch-filled basin less than 1 km north of Cerulean Lake. Elizabeth Lake is an outstanding lake for novice anglers, as small cutthroat in the 20-25 cm range can be caught from virtually any spot along the lakeshore. Expect lots of action at Elizabeth Lake.

Elizabeth Lake

Moose Bath (BC)
Status: Devoid of fish
Moose Bath is a small, shallow pond below the western end of Cerulean Lake. Moose Bath has long been rumoured to contain trout. Despite the rumours, Moose Bath dries up in summer to the point of being incapable of holding trout.

Wedgwood Lake (BC)
Cutthroat trout to 60 cm (2.0 kg)
Forest enclosed Wedgwood Lake is located in a side valley south of the Mitchell River, some 4 km by trail below Cerulean Lake. Less heavily fished than other lakes in the Assiniboine area because of its location, Wedgwood holds cutthroat trout

averaging 30-35 cm in length. With the exception of a few isolated openings, casting a fly is difficult due to the proximity of the forest cover to the lakeshore. A very distinctive drop-off dividing the shallow water from the deep is visible from shore. This zone usually holds fish, although both the outlet and inlet areas can also be very productive at times. The fish in Wedgwood tend to travel in schools and because of the clarity of the water, it is often more useful to walk along the shore keeping an eye on the water than to cast into an area where no fish can be seen.

Wedgwood Lake
(cutthroat trout)

Coney Lake (BC)
Status: Doubtful
Coney Lake is situated in a rocky amphitheatre, half a kilometre upstream from the inlet of Wedgwood Lake. The lake is algae-infested and it is doubtful that it holds fish.

Mitchell River (BC)
Cutthroat trout to 35 cm
Bull trout to 70 cm (4.0 kg)
Whitefish to 30 cm
The Mitchell River flows westward from Assiniboine to its confluence with the Cross River, and possesses numerous fine pools that hold fish. Access is easy along a horse trail that parallels the Mitchell River downstream of Wedgwood Lake, and eventually reaches logging and mining exploration roads at the provincial park boundary. Seldom fished, the Mitchell River is generally productive by mid-summer after the spring runoff is complete.

Game Lake (BC)
Status: Unknown
This small tarn at the head of Nestor Creek, a tributary of the Mitchell River, may contain small populations of cutthroat trout that have entered from Nestor Creek. No trails to the lake exist. Those interested in reaching the lake should simply follow Nestor Creek upstream from the Ferro Pass trail. Game Lake is set in an enclosed basin, and remains frozen until mid-July.

Nestor Lake (BC)
Status: Unknown
Nestor Lake, the headwaters of Surprise Creek, receives few or no visitors each year. The lake likely holds a few cutthroat trout that have made their way in from Surprise Creek.

Rock Lake (BC)
Cutthroat trout to 25 cm
Rock Lake is situated halfway along the Ferro Pass trail access to Assiniboine, and is popular as a stopover point. Rock Lake is a good spot for novice anglers, as it holds plenty of small cutthroat in the 15-20 cm range. The shoreline is forgiving in terms of fly casting from most locations, although wet feet are likely on the eastern side of the lake. The rockslide on the western side allows casting without wet feet, but be aware that rocks will claim the hooks of those anglers with sloppy back casts. Even though they are tiny, the eager trout in Rock Lake will give pleasure to beginners, as casting distance and technique are not important. Surprise Creek, which is the outlet for Rock Lake, holds trout for a kilometre or so downstream from the lake before becoming too steep and rapid on its descent to the Simpson River.

Rock Lake

Assiniboine Lake, Lunette Lake (BC)
Status: Devoid of fish
These two small, remote lakes are accessible by a rough trail from logging roads on the Mitchell River. They have never been stocked, and do not contain any trout. An ill-defined trail leads east up Aurora Creek, a tributary of the Mitchell River, before turning north at Assiniboine Creek into the basin containing Assiniboine and Lunette Lakes. Be forewarned that this is very rugged and isolated country, and it is home to many a grizzly bear.

Lunette Lake

INVERMERE REGION

This Region is set in the heart of the Rocky Mountain Trench, and Windermere Lake serves as its focal point. Invermere is the business centre of the valley, and offers numerous services including several sporting goods stores. The main valley also harbours the small towns of Athalmer, Wilmer and Windermere and is linked by Highway 95, north to Golden, Highway 93 east to Banff, and Highway 93/95 south to Cranbrook. Fifteen kilometre long Windermere Lake is more renowned for its warm waters, boardsailing and water skiing than for its fishery. The Columbia River, flowing downstream from Windermere Lake, holds plenty of whitefish and some large bull trout. Nearby Toby and Horsethief Creeks offer fine stream fishing. The Region is divided into two Sub-Regions: Windermere, which encompasses the eastern side of Windermere Lake; and Westside, which is west and north of Windermere Lake, and includes Invermere.

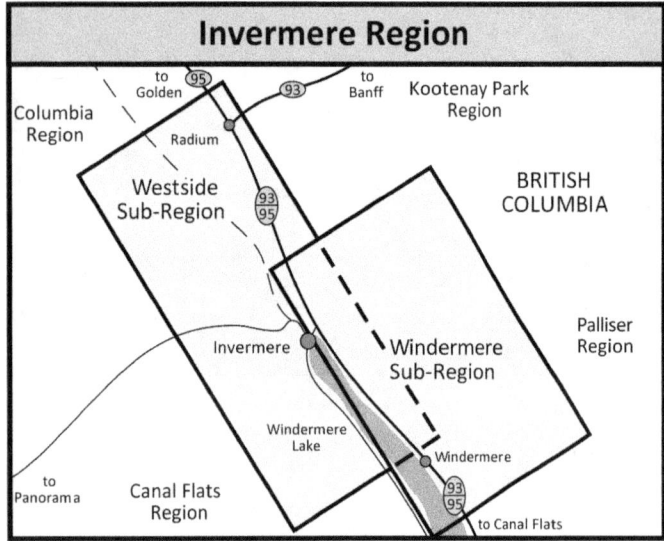

Windermere Sub-Region

This Sub-Region includes Windermere Lake and the area to the east of the lake. The small community of Windermere is located on Highway 93/95, and does offer basic tourist services. Other than Windermere Lake, fishing opportunities are limited to creeks and a few small lakes in the Windermere Creek watershed.

Windermere Lake (BC)
Rainbow trout to 50 cm (1.5 kg)
Cutthroat trout to 45 cm
Brook trout to 45 cm
Bull trout to 70 cm (3.5 kg)
Kokanee to 50 cm (1.5 kg)
Largemouth bass to 50 cm (1.5 kg)
Whitefish to 40 cm
Windermere Lake has never gained a good reputation for fishing, despite the wide variety of game fish available. The lake also has a large population of coarse fish. Kokanee have been stocked in the lake, and their population has grown in recent years and this has increased the lake's angling popularity somewhat. Rainbow trout can usually be taken in the spring, in the weeks immediately after ice-out. During the summer, trolling in the areas around the lake's many inlet creeks such as Goldie Creek and Windermere Creek will often produce trout. Anglers can also catch the occasional largemouth bass, chub, or burbot. Winter sees the most angling activity on Windermere Lake.

Windermere Lake

Columbia River (BC) *(Windermere Lake to Radium)*
Bull trout to 70 cm (3.5 kg)
Whitefish to 40 cm
The Columbia River flows north from Windermere Lake and possesses numerous deep pools. It offers fair fishing for bull trout and whitefish. Cutthroat, rainbow and brook trout are also present. The best spots are where major tributaries, such as Toby and Horsethief Creeks, join the Columbia River. The Wilmer Sloughs, a series of large, shallow lakes approximately 5 km north of Windermere Lake, hold little in the way of fish and are best left to the ducks.

Wilmer Sloughs

Windermere Creek (BC)
Cutthroat trout to 35 cm
This small stream flows from headwaters above Twin and Lost Lakes to Windermere Lake. The upper portion of the creek can be accessed from the Westroc Mine Road. Windermere Creek contains plenty of small cutthroat trout, most in the 15-25 cm range.

INVERMERE REGION: Windermere Sub-Region

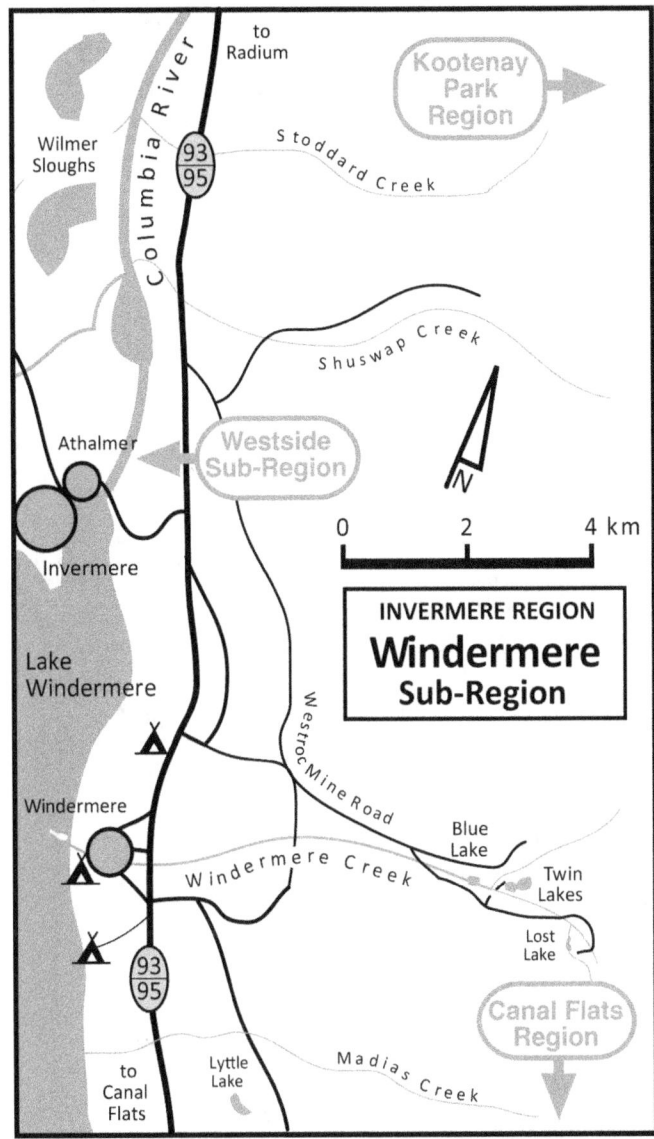

Note: *To reach Blue Lake, Twin Lakes, Lost Lake, and upper Windermere Creek, the Westroc Mine Road must be driven. During working hours, the road is very dangerous due to the many large trucks that haul gypsum ore. Check with the mine office for hours of operation, and for procedure for driving the mine road.*

Blue Lake (BC)
Cutthroat trout to 30 cm

At one time, this small but incredibly deep lake, was a most amazing shade of blue, due to its mineral content. In recent years, road construction and the unsightly realignment of Windermere Creek has ruined Blue Lake's natural beauty, and severe silting is causing the lake to fill up rapidly. A small number of cutthroat trout can still be taken from the lake.

Blue Lake

Twin Lakes (BC)
Cutthroat trout to 35 cm

Twin Lakes is a popular picnic spot and receives some fishing pressure during the summer. Cutthroat trout in the lakes average 20-25 cm in length, although bigger trout are often caught from the larger of the two lakes. The larger lake is an extremely deep body of water that is almost completely encircled by a high cliff. For those fly fishing, there are a few locations to cast from, the most popular being the narrow point between the two lakes.

Twin Lakes

Lost Lake (BC)
Cutthroat trout to 35 cm

In a blatant display of industrial pollution, the gypsum mine above Lost Lake virtually filled in the entire lake with debris, and has totally destroyed what was at one time an excellent cutthroat fishery. Upstream and downstream from the former site of Lost Lake there are small beaver dams that still hold a few small cutthroat trout.

Stoddart Creek (BC)
Cutthroat trout to 20 cm
Bull trout to 25 cm

Stoddart Creek is a small stream that flows west to join the Columbia River. Access is from abandoned logging roads that intersect with Highway 93/95. Stoddart Creek holds a few small cutthroat and bull trout.

Shuswap Creek (BC)
Cutthroat trout to 20 cm
Bull trout to 25 cm

Old logging roads that extend high into the Shuswap Creek drainage offer access to prospective anglers. Small bull trout are present in the upper reaches with small cutthroat predominant downstream.

Lyttle Lake (BC)
Cutthroat trout to 35 cm

Lyttle Lake is a shallow pond located east of Highway 93/95 just south of Fairmont. Private property restricts access to the lake. Lyttle Lake holds cutthroat trout in small sizes.

INVERMERE REGION: Westside Sub-Region

Westside Sub-Region

The community of Invermere is located on the north end of Windermere Lake. It is accessed by paved road off of Highway 93/95. Golfing and water sports dominate the outdoor lifestyle around Invermere. Most fishing opportunities in the Westside Sub-Region are in the lakes on the benches west of the Columbia River. Lillian Lake and Enid Lake hold excellent rainbow trout, and are heavily fished.

Toby Creek (BC)
Cutthroat trout to 40 cm
Bull trout to 70 cm (3.5 kg)
Whitefish to 35 cm
Toby Creek parallels the road to Panorama Resort. However, direct access to Toby Creek is difficult, as it flows through a deep canyon for much of its course. After run-off is complete, fishing is usually good for cutthroat and bull trout. There is excellent angling for whitefish in the fall.

Lillian Lake (BC)
Rainbow trout to 60 cm (2.5 kg)
Brook trout to 40 cm
Lillian Lake is located west of Invermere, just off the Panorama ski hill road. Lillian Lake is popular with locals, especially in the first weeks immediately after ice-out, usually late April. Lillian Lake's pretty blue-green waters hold plenty of rainbow and brook trout in the 25-35 cm range, with rainbows over 2 kg caught regularly. The zone dividing the deep water from the shallows usually holds fish. Trolling through the deeper waters can also be productive at times. During low light periods, many of the larger fish make their way into the shallow waters to feed. A boat is strongly advised, as fishing from shore at Lillian Lake is difficult because of access problems due to private land.

Lillian Lake (rainbow trout)

Barbour's Rock (Bluff Lake) (BC)
Brook trout to 30 cm
Barbour's Rock is located three kilometres beyond Lillian Lake, north of the Panorama Resort road. The lake sits at the base of a towering and impressive cliff face. Access is restricted due to private land around the lake. In the past, Barbour's Rock held brook trout in the 20-25 cm range.

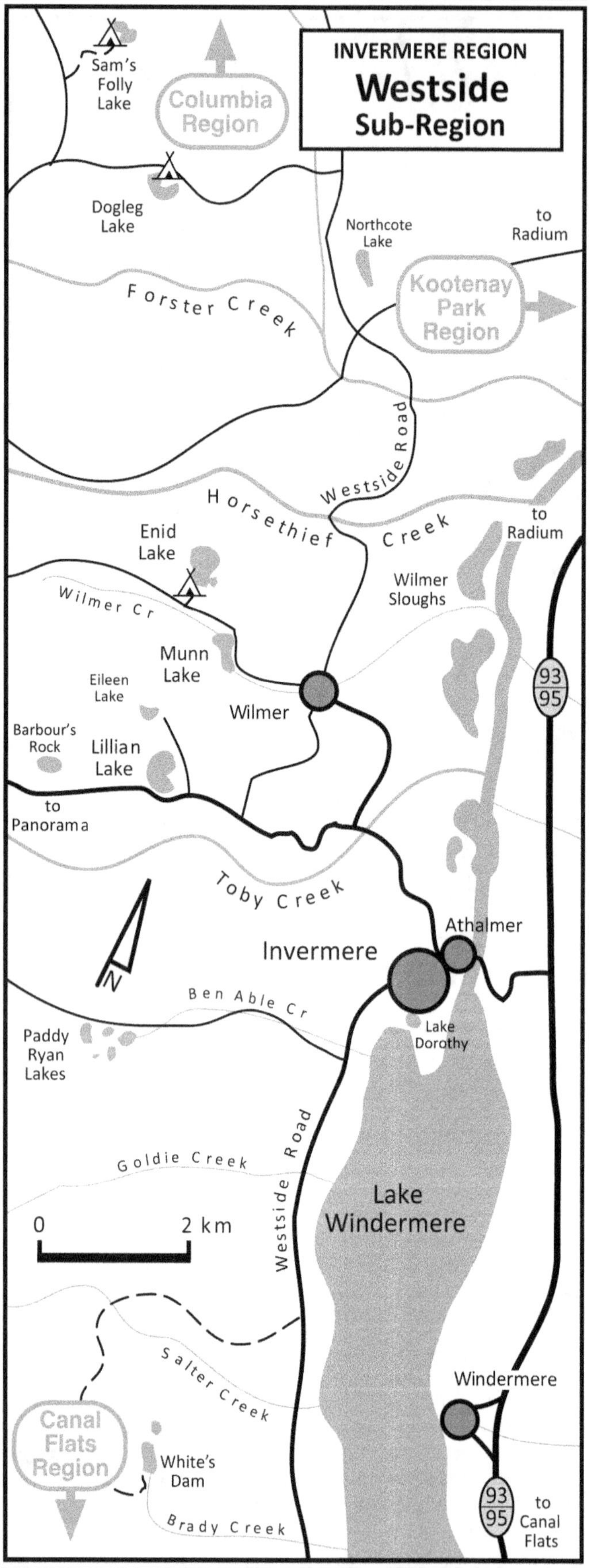

INVERMERE REGION: Westside Sub-Region

Eileen Lake (BC)
Status: Devoid of fish
Little more than an overgrown marsh, shallow Eileen Lake located 1 km north of Lillian Lake contains no fish.

Munn (Wilmer) Lake (BC)
Brook trout to 60 cm (2.5 kg)
Rainbow trout to 60 cm (2.5 kg)
The elongated form of Munn Lake is located 1 km west of the townsite of Wilmer. Munn Lake is popular in the spring as soon as the ice melts. Munn Lake's murky waters hold brook and rainbow trout averaging 30-40 cm in length. Although fishing is possible from many locations along the shore, a boat is recommended. Trolling is the normal method of angling at Munn Lake.

Munn Lake

Enid Lake (BC)
Rainbow trout to 65 cm (3.5 kg)
Brook trout to 55 cm (2.0 kg)
Enid Lake is a popular picnic spot, and is situated 2 km beyond Munn Lake on a good gravel road. Rainbow trout are in the majority in Enid Lake, with most averaging 30-40 cm in length. Very large trout are taken from the lake on occasion. As with nearby Lillian Lake, the margin between the deep and shallow waters is often productive, although many anglers prefer to troll the deep waters. Fly fishers using boats or float tubes tend to work the shallows along the eastern side of the lake.

Enid Lake
(rainbow trout)

Horsethief Creek (BC)
Cutthroat trout to 40 cm
Bull trout to 70 cm (3.5 kg)
Whitefish to 35 cm
Horsethief Creek is similar to all of the major creeks in the area that join the Columbia River from the west. Horsethief Creek offers fair fishing in the late summer and early fall, particularly during whitefish runs. The lower portion of Horsethief Creek is reached by taking the Westside Road north from Wilmer. The upper sections of Horsethief Creek are accessed from the Horsethief Creek F.S. Road. Due to its glacial origins, Horsethief Creek is notorious for being muddy later into the summer than other local creeks.

Horsethief Creek

Forster Creek (BC)
Cutthroat trout to 40 cm
Bull trout to 70 cm (3.5 kg)
Whitefish to 35 cm
Forster Creek is another one of the many large creeks that enter the Columbia River from the west. It is accessed from the Westside Road and from logging roads. Forster Creek holds cutthroat trout that average 20-30 cm in length.

Northcote Lake (BC)
Status: Doubtful
This shallow lake is located east of the Westside Road. Although Northcote Lake has held brook and rainbow trout in the past, it is unlikely that there are any fish in the lake today.

Dogleg Lake (BC)
Status: Devoid of fish
Dogleg Lake is a promising body of water situated several kilometres west of the Westside Road. At one time Dogleg Lake held a healthy population of brook trout, but they were winter killed. Subsequent plantings suffered the same fate. Rumours persist that Dogleg Lake may be used as a test lake for largemouth bass at some point in the future.

Dogleg Lake

INVERMERE REGION: Westside Sub-Region

Sam's Folly Lake (BC)
Rainbow trout to 50 cm (1.5 kg)
Sam's Folly Lake is located approximately 5 km north of Dogleg Lake, and is reached by following a rough dirt road. Sam's Folly is in fact two interconnected lakes. The first lake is very shallow with extensive wed beds, and the second lake is a much deeper with less weed growth. Both lakes hold rainbow trout in the 25-35 cm range. The first lake is more suited to fly fishing, with lures more productive in the second lake. A boat is a must for fishing either lake.

Sam's Folly Lake (first lake)

Jonathan Shandrowsky and dad, Don, with Sam's Folly Lake rainbow trout

Dorothy Lake (BC)
Brook trout to 35 cm
Dorothy Lake is located in Invermere next to the Kinsmen Beach and Windermere Lake. The lake is open for angling for those aged 12 and under, and is stocked regularly with brook trout. Trout caught in the lake will average 20-30 cm in length. Weeds extend out all around this small lake, making fishing from shore somewhat difficult for youngsters.

Dorothy Lake and its fountain

Paddy Ryan Lakes (BC)
Brook trout to 30 cm
The Paddy Ryan Lakes are the source of Invermere's water supply. As such, most of the Paddy Ryan Lakes are closed to angling and are fenced off. The fifth and largest of the lakes is still open to fishing and holds brook trout averaging 20-25 cm in length as well as the occasional rainbow, remnants of past stockings.

Ben Able Creek (BC)
Brook trout to 20 cm
Rainbow trout to 20 cm
Tiny Ben Abel Creek is the outlet creek for Paddy Ryan Lakes. It contains small brook and rainbow trout, and has traditionally been a favourite of local youngsters.

White's Dam (BC)
Cutthroat trout to 40 cm
White's Dam is reached by following a veritable maze of logging roads on the western side of Windermere Lake. Today, White's Dam retains little of is past fishing glory. Cutthroat trout exceeding 80 cm in length were taken from this overgrown beaver pond in the past, but over harvest led to a severe decline in both number and size of trout taken. At present, White's Dam holds a small population of cutthroat averaging 25-35 cm in length.

Graham Tyler at White's Dam

COLUMBIA REGION

The Region in the upper Columbia River Valley to the west of the small towns of Brisco, Spillimacheen and Parson has many excellent trout lakes. The main route through the area is the Westside Road, a gravel and dirt road that can be accessed from Highway 95 at Brisco, Spillimacheen, Parson, Radium and Wilmer. Since virtually all of the lakes can be reached by vehicle, they are favourites of local anglers, and most spots are busy spring through fall. The most popular of the lakes include Cartwright, Jade, Cleland, Mitten, Wilbur and Rocky Point. The region divides into two Sub-Regions: the southern half, which is west of Brisco; and the northern half, which is west of Parson.

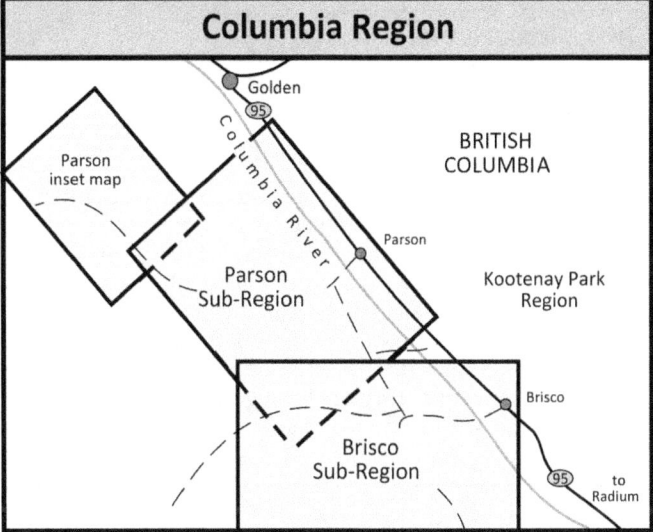

Brisco Sub-Region

The lakes to the west of Brisco are known collectively as the Fish Lakes. Most can be accessed from short roads that branch off the Westside Road. The lakes in this Sub-Region are found in several clusters. Cleland, Jade, Topaz and Cub Lakes form one cluster. Farther south, Dunbar, Twin and Botts Lakes, form another group. Farther south still, Hall, Halgrave and Steamboat Lakes are bunched together on the flank of Steamboat Mountain. Cartwright Lake is known for its great rainbow trout fishery, and receives the heaviest angling pressure of all the lakes in the area.

Hall Lakes (BC)
Cutthroat trout to 35 cm
Brook trout to 35 cm

These two shallow lakes are located 1 km east of the Westside Road. The Hall Lakes contain a few cutthroat and brook trout in small sizes, averaging 20-30 cm in length. Most of the fish are concentrated in the larger lake, and are very spooky due to their shallow habitat. Although fly fishing from shore is possible from a number of locations, a boat is recommended.

Halgrave Lakes (BC)
Cutthroat trout to 45 cm

A good logging road branches east off the Westside Road just before the crossing of Frances Creek, and it leads to a campsite at Upper Halgrave Lake. Shallows around the entire lake make the use of a boat essential. The shoreline mud can even make the launching of a boat very difficult. Wet flies are particularly effective in taking the lake's cutthroat, which average 30-40 cm in length. Lower Halgrave Lake can be reached via a short walk through a logged-out area approximately 1 km past Upper Halgrave on the road to Steamboat Lake. As with the Upper Lake, shallows extend far out from shore around Lower Halgrave. Cutthroat trout in Lower Halgrave are not as plentiful as in the upper lake, and most are in the 25-35 cm range.

Lower Halgrave Lake

Steamboat Lake (BC)
Rainbow trout to 35 cm

Steamboat Lake is nestled high on the side of Steamboat Mountain. The lake is reached by taking the Halgrave Lakes cutoff from the Westside Road. While most of the rainbow trout in Steamboat Lake are less than 25 cm in length, they are plentiful. Flies are very effective, but a boat is necessary for any angling success.

Steamboat Lake

Lead Queen Lake (BC)
Cutthroat trout to 40 cm
Brook trout to 35 cm

Lead Queen Lake is located north of Frances Creek, approximately 2 km off the Westside Road. Lead Queen is a very shallow lake bordered by marsh on its western side, and is little more than a very large beaver pond. Lead Queen contains cutthroat and brook trout ranging from 25 to 35 cm in length. If fishing from shore, the best opportunities are found near the dam at the lake's outlet. From a boat, schools of fish can usually be seen in the main part of the lake. However, due to the shallow nature of the lake, the trout are very wary, and many anglers will no doubt be frustrated.

Lead Queen Lake

COLUMBIA REGION: Brisco Sub-Region

Whary Lake (BC)
Status: Doubtful
Whary Lake is situated in a forested depression alongside the Frances-Cartwright F.S. Road, approximately 2 km past the turnoff to Lead Queen Lake. Looking down from the road, Whary Lake looks promising. However, it has never been stocked and it likely contains no fish.

Whary Lake

Frances Creek (BC)
Cutthroat trout to 30 cm
Frances Creek parallels the Westside Road for several kilometres. It is well-known by locals as an excellent trout stream. Cutthroat trout averaging 20-25 cm in length are abundant, especially in the numerous pools and log jams along the creek. A few brook trout may be present as well.

Halfway Lake (BC)
Rainbow trout to 40 cm
A rough road through a thick lodgepole pine forest leads west from the Westside Road into Halfway Lake. A boat is preferable for fishing at Halfway Lake, as there is substantial reed growth around most of the lake. Rainbow trout in the 25-35 cm size are plentiful. Trolling a fly behind a boat or canoe is usually very effective, especially for novices who haven't mastered all the intricacies of casting.

Halfway Lake

Note: Twin, Dunbar, Botts, Hall and Lead Queen Lakes at one time were excellent cutthroat trout fisheries. Illegal plantings of brook trout in these waters in recent years has negatively affected the existing cutthroat trout populations.

Twin Lakes (BC)
Cutthroat trout to 40 cm
Brook trout to 35 cm
The Twin Lakes are oddly named, as they in fact actually consist of three lakes all joined by narrow channels. All three lakes hold cutthroat and brook trout in the 20-30 cm range. The small, shallow first lake usually has a few trout that congregate around one of several natural springs. The second lake is the deepest and holds the most trout. The third lake is the largest, but is very shallow, and its best potential is in its northeast corner, where Dunbar Creek flows through. The completion of a dam on the third lake stabilized water levels, but caused a major drowning of trees around all three lakes. As the trees died and fell into the lakes, the fish habitat was improved, as the fish tend to seek the security of the deadfall. Although fishing from shore is possible, a boat is recommended for all of the lakes. Both dry and wet flies will work very well at Twin Lakes.

Twin Lakes (second lake) (cutthroat trout)

Dunbar (Big Fish) Lake (BC)
Cutthroat trout to 60 cm (2.0 kg)
Brook trout to 35 cm
Dunbar Lake was renowned in past years for its large cutthroat, many topping the 2 kg mark. Over harvest decimated Dunbar's trout, and the lake has never been able to fully recover. Dunbar is a strikingly beautiful lake, and holds cutthroat and brook trout that average 20-30 cm in length. On occasion, beauties of up to 60 cm in length are still caught. For those anglers without a boat, the best opportunities are found in the series of dams below the lake's outlet. If you're fishing from a boat, the margin separating the shallow water from the deep holds the best potential.

Dunbar Lake

Botts Lake (BC)
Cutthroat trout to 40 cm
Brook trout to 35 cm
Tiny, marsh-rimmed Botts Lake is little more than a widening of Dunbar Creek. Botts Lake holds cutthroat and brook trout in the 20-30 cm range and usually produces well throughout the summer and fall. Fly fishers will need a boat to reach trout holding waters. A small, deep lake is located only a few hundred metres from the southwest corner of Botts Lake, and it also holds cutthroat and brook trout in fair numbers. You will have to drag your boat through marshy ground to reach the back lake.

COLUMBIA REGION: Brisco Sub-Region

Botts Lake (main lake)

Botts Lake (back lake)

Dunbar Creek, Outlet Creek (BC)
Cutthroat trout to 35 cm
Brook trout to 35 cm

Outlet Creek connects Dunbar to Twin Lakes, where it joins Dunbar Creek. Dunbar Creek connects Twin and Botts Lakes. Dunbar Creek is never more than a short hike from the Westside Road. Both creeks have plenty of log jams and deep pools that hold small cutthroat and brook trout in the 20-30 cm range.

Dunbar Creek

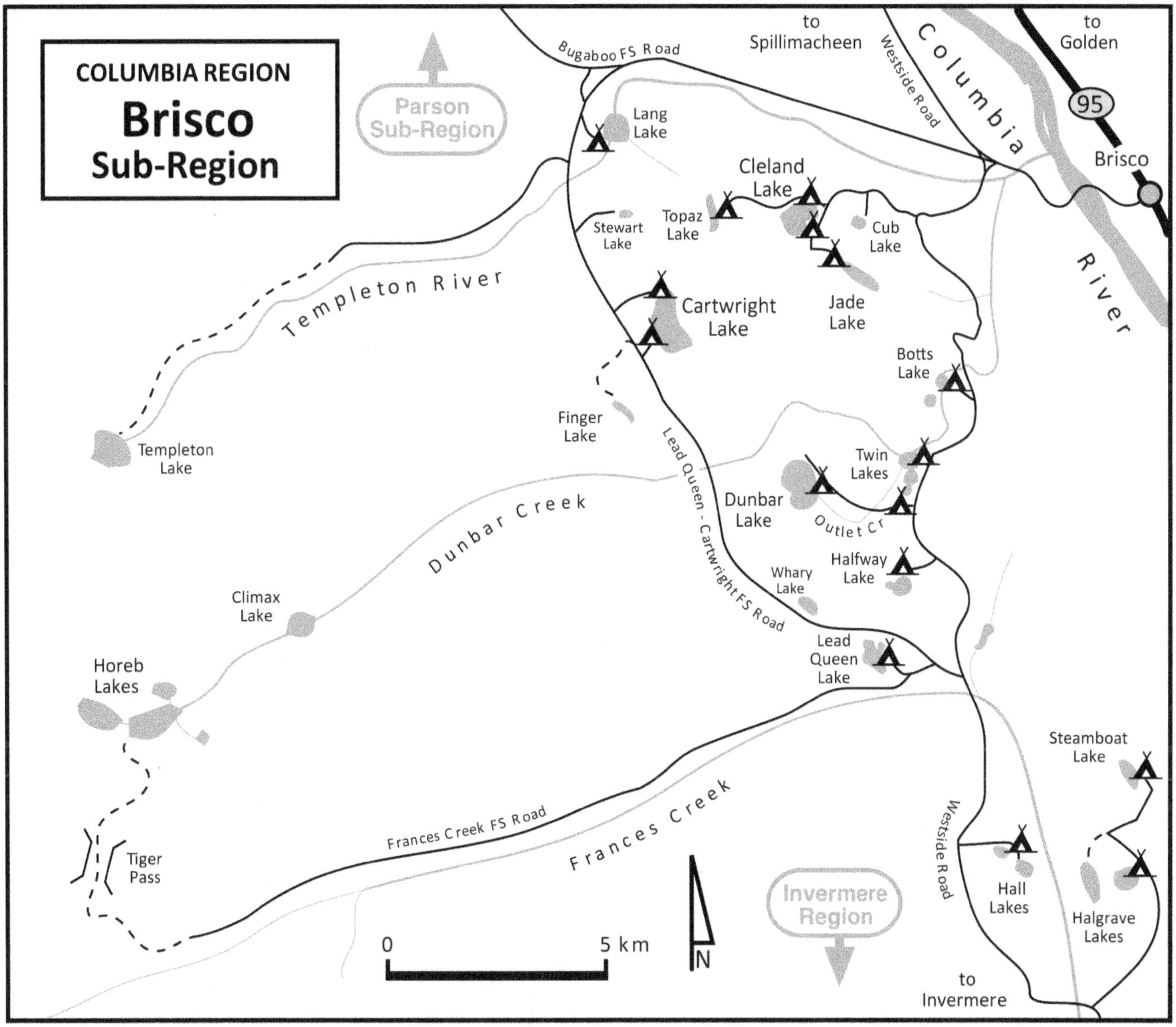

135

COLUMBIA REGION: Brisco Sub-Region

Cleland Lake (BC)
Rainbow trout to 60 cm (2.5 kg)

Cleland Lake is the largest of the Cleland-Jade-Topaz-Cub cluster, and receives significant attention from anglers. All four of the lakes are reached by taking the rough road that branches northwest from the Westside Road just over 1 km above the Templeton River bridge. Cleland Lake's translucent blue-green waters hold rainbow trout averaging 30-40 cm in length. Much larger fish are taken regularly. A boat is a must for fishing at Cleland Lake. During the day, most fish are taken from the shelf separating the shallows from the deep, but as daylight fades, many of the larger fish make their way into the shallow waters to feed, making evenings a prime time for dry fly enthusiasts.

Cleland Lake

(rainbow trout)

Jade Lake (BC)
Rainbow trout to 60 cm (2.5 kg)

Jade Lake is located approximately 2 km by road beyond the campsite on the eastern side of Cleland Lake. Jade Lake is restricted to fly fishing, and attracts many anglers each year. Jade's stunning green waters hold plenty of hard-fighting rainbows averaging 35-45 cm in length. From a boat, fish can generally be seen feeding in the shallows at both ends of the lake all during the day with increased activity in the shallows during low light periods. Patiently working the shallows with a wet line will usually produce positive results. In the deep middle section of the lake, trolling a fly is generally an effective technique.

Jade Lake

(rainbow trout)

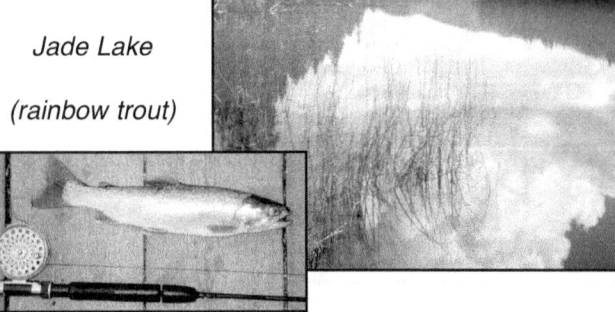

Topaz Lake (BC)
Rainbow trout to 45 cm

Topaz Lake is located at the end of a rough and often muddy 2 km access road from the campsite on the north side of Cleland Lake. Topaz Lake is very shallow, and has been prone in the past to winter kill. Topaz is stocked regularly, and rainbow trout are still present in the lake, with most averaging 30-35 cm in length. Topaz is a long and narrow lake that is best fished from a boat, although fish can occasionally be taken from shore when they are feeding in the shallows.

Topaz Lake

Cub Lake (BC)
Rainbow trout to 40 cm

Cub Lake is a small, round, sinkhole lake ringed by marsh, and does not overwhelm anyone with its beauty. Fishing from shore is a near impossibility due to extensive lily pads. Trolling or casting from a boat is necessary. Cub does hold small rainbows in good numbers, most averaging 20-30 cm in length.

Cub Lake

Cartwright Lake (BC)
Rainbow trout to 70 cm (4.0 kg)

Cartwright Lake is the most popular lake in the Brisco Sub-Region. It is busy with anglers from June through to October. Rainbow trout averaging 35-45 cm in length cruise the shallower water for food throughout the day, and from a boat those fly fishing will get numerous opportunities to hook into a big fish. Trolling in the deeper water can also be extremely effective. Extended shallows around the entire lake make fishing from shore very inefficient.

Cartwright Lake

COLUMBIA REGION: Brisco Sub-Region

Finger (Slide, Wendy) Lake
Rainbow trout to 35 cm

This shallow lake is located approximately 2 km by trail from the Cartwright Lake road. Rainbow trout have been stocked in Finger Lake, but winter kill is a potential problem. Expect to find a few rainbow trout in the 20-30 cm range. Fishing from shore is possible at many locations around the lake.

Finger Lake

Stewart Lake (BC)
Rainbow trout to 30 cm

Stewart Lake is little more than an overgrown beaver pond located between Cartwright and Lang Lakes. Stewart Lake's waters are often murky, but hold small rainbow averaging 20-25 cm in length.

Lang (Lang's) Lake (BC)
Cutthroat trout to 40 cm
Rainbow trout to 40 cm

Lang Lake is located north of Cartwright Lake, and is accessed from the Bugaboo F.S. Road. Lang Lake is very shallow, and a boat is required to reach the fish holding waters. Cutthroat trout have been stocked in Lang Lake, and most caught will be in the 25-35 cm range. Rainbow trout were stocked in the past, and there still may be a few rainbow trout present. Lures and flies both work well at Lang Lake.

Lang Lake

Templeton River (BC)
Cutthroat trout to 40 cm
Rainbow trout to 40 cm

The best fishing on the Templeton River is found in the area above Lang Lake, where a seemingly infinite series of small beaver ponds exist. Cutthroat and rainbow trout in the 25-35 cm range can be taken at most spots along the river. The lower Templeton River, near the bridges on the Westside Road, has some fine pools.

Templeton River

Horeb Lakes (BC)
Cutthroat trout to 40 cm

The Horeb Lakes are series of pristine alpine tarns at the head of Dunbar Creek. The lakes are set in a magnificent basin appropriately named Shangri-La. Cutthroat trout have been stocked in the past, and can now be taken in fair numbers. Not all of the lakes in the basin were stocked, but trout seem to have made their way into most of the lakes. Anglers are advised to watch the waters for trout activity. The lower lakes tend to be less silted, and hold more trout. The main access routes to the Horeb Lakes are difficult: One route is over Tiger Pass and Glacier from the Frances Creek drainage; and the second is a long hike/bushwhack up Dunbar Creek. Both are for route-finders armed with map and compass.

Climax Lake (BC)
Cutthroat trout to 40 cm

Climax Lake is located on Dunbar Creek, approximately 2 km downstream from the Horeb Lakes, has been stocked with cutthroat trout that have seldom been tested by anglers. Access to Climax Lake is the same as for Horeb, either over Tiger Pass or up Dunbar Creek.

Climax Lake

Templeton Lake (BC)
Cutthroat trout to 40 cm

Templeton Lake is a seldom-visited lake that is the source of its namesake river. A rough 6 km trail to the lake begins from logging roads that head west from the Cartwright Lake road. Templeton Lake has been stocked in the past with cutthroat trout. Trout taken from the lake's silted waters average 20-30 cm in length.

Templeton Lake

Columbia River (BC) *(Radium to Spillimacheen)*
Bull trout to 80 cm (7.0 kg)
Whitefish to 40 cm

The slow-moving Columbia River runs muddy for much of the year. The Columbia contains plenty of bull trout and whitefish, as well as the occasional rainbow or cutthroat trout.

COLUMBIA REGION: Parson Sub-Region

Parson Sub-Region

The area to the west of the small community of Parson holds a number of lakes with excellent records as producers of large rainbow trout. Primary access is on Highway 95 from Golden in the north and Radium in the south. Logging roads that are rough in spots lead to a majority of the lakes. Rocky Point and Mitten Lakes are the most popular of the Sub-Region's waters, and hold some big trout. Other lakes include Loon, Nixon and Redcliff to the north; Wilbur, Summit and Three Island in the central portion; and Bittern, Nine Bay, Moose and Jordan to the south. Some excellent stream fishing opportunities exist in the Parson region, the most notable being the Spillimacheen River and Bobbie Burns, Bugaboo and Driftwood Creeks.

Wilbur Lake (BC)
Rainbow trout to 60 cm (2.5 kg)
Wilbur Lake is the closest of the west side lakes to Parson. It is located 10 km from Parson by logging road. Wilbur is stocked regularly and holds hard-fighting rainbow trout which average 25-40 cm in length. Wilbur fishes best from a boat, whether trolling or casting a fly. The small bay off the northeast end of the lake is fairly shallow, and fish can be seen cruising. Using a wet fly line and casting ahead of cruising trout with a nymph can be dynamite.

Wilbur Lake

(rainbow trout)

Hobo Lake (BC)
Rainbow trout to 35 cm
Hobo Lake is a small lake located northeast of Wilbur Lake, and accessed by rough roads. Hobo Lake holds a small population of rainbow trout averaging 20-30 cm in length.

Rocky Point Lake (BC)
Rainbow trout to 75 cm (5.0 kg)
The Rocky Point-Three Island-Summit complex is just under 30 km from Parson by logging road. Rocky Point Lake is named for a number of prominent points jutting out along the lakeshore. It holds good numbers of rainbow trout which average 30-40 cm in length. Much larger specimens are caught very frequently. Although rainbows can be taken all season long, autumn is particularly productive, especially for those fly fishing. A boat is necessary for fishing at Rocky Point.

Rocky Point Lake

Summit (Bridal) Lake (BC)
Brook trout to 50 cm (1.5 kg)
Summit Lake is situated just a few kilometres to the west of Rocky Point Lake at a height of land between Bobbie Burns Creek and the Spillimacheen River watersheds. The shallow waters of Summit Lake hold brook trout, as well as possible remnants of a previously stocked cutthroat trout population. Although the brook trout only average 20-30 cm in length, they are plentiful. From a boat, trout can be taken from most locations around the lake.

Three Island Lake (BC)
Rainbow trout to 60 cm (3.0 kg)
Three Island Lake is located in the forested basin immediately southwest of Rocky Point Lake. Three Island Lake holds good-sized rainbow trout in its numerous bays and around its three prominent islands. Rainbows in the lake average 30-40 cm in length, with larger ones taken regularly. A boat is recommended, although shore bound anglers may have some success from one of the points that jut out into the lake, or in one of the many small inlets.

Three Island Lake

COLUMBIA REGION: Parson Sub-Region

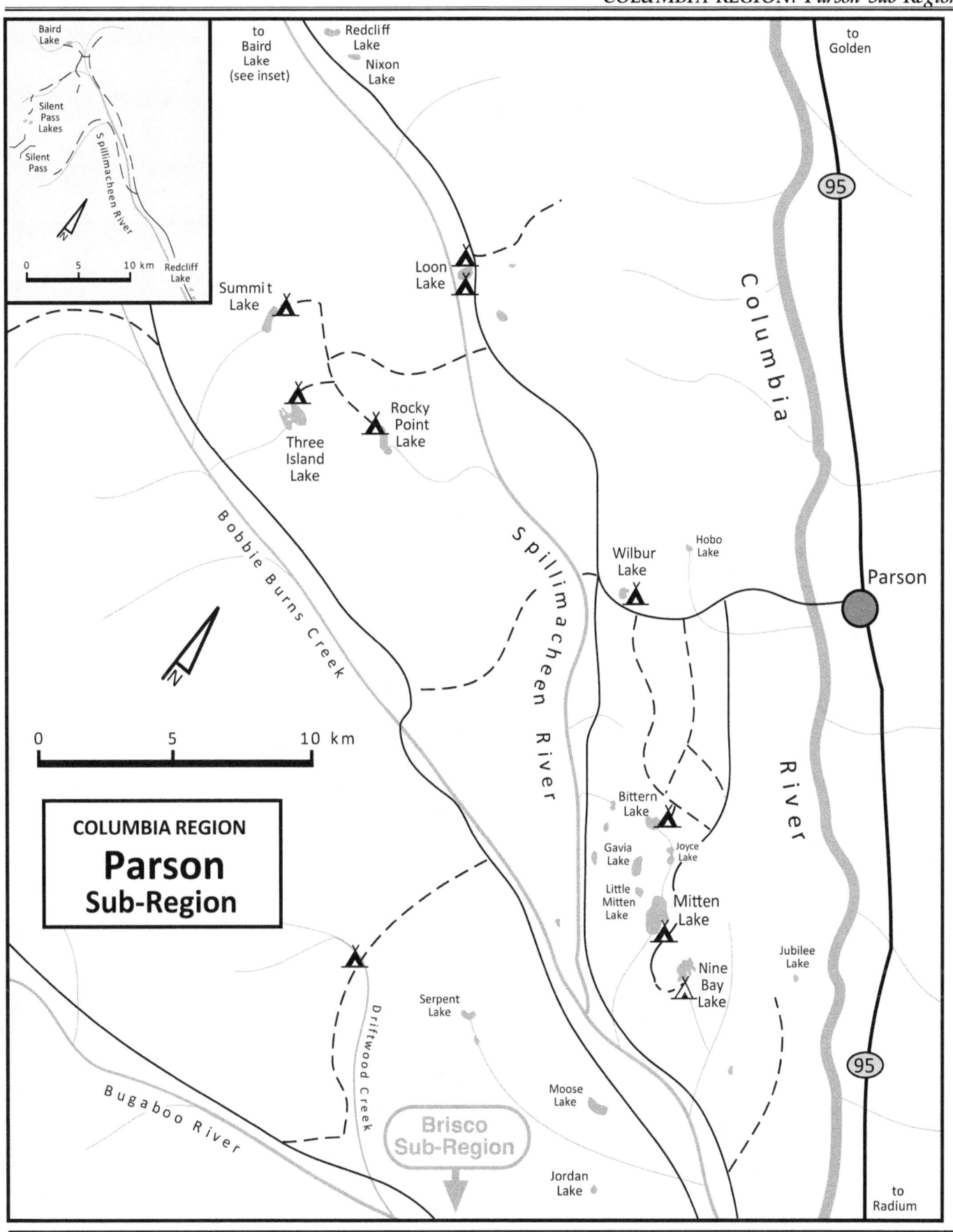

COLUMBIA REGION: Parson Sub-Region

Loon Lake (BC)
Rainbow trout to 55 cm (1.5 kg)
Diminutive Loon Lake is set alongside logging roads approximately 3 km beyond the Rocky Point Lake cut-off on the Spillimacheen River. The lake holds rainbow trout in good numbers. The rainbow trout in Loon's shallow waters average 25-35 cm in length, with larger ones present. Although trolling is the normal technique, fly fishers should keep an eye on the shallows for hungry trout cruising for food.

Loon Lake

Nixon Lake (BC)
Rainbow trout to 40 cm
Nixon Lake is a small pond located approximately 35 km from Parson on the north side of the Spillimacheen River. Nixon holds good numbers of small rainbows, most in the 20-30 cm range. A boat is recommended, and trolling a fly will produce positive results.

Nixon Lake

Redcliff Lake (BC)
Rainbow trout to 40 cm
Intrepid anglers will find the quiet waters of Redcliff Lake 2 km beyond Nixon Lake on the Spillimacheen River road. Redcliff Lake holds rainbow trout averaging 20-30 cm in length, which can generally be taken from shallows around the lake. Working the area between the shallower and deeper waters from a boat is usually productive.

Redcliff Lake

Baird (Moose) Lake (BC)
Rainbow trout to 35 cm
Tiny Baird Lake is located near the very head of the Spillimacheen River, some 60 km by road from Parson. There is little fishing pressure at Baird Lake for its rainbow trout, which average 20-30 cm in length.

Baird Lake

Silent (Silent Pass) Lakes (BC)
Cutthroat trout to 40 cm
These two small lakes are found in the McMurdo Creek drainage, below the alpine environs of Silent Pass. A trail leads from logging roads to the upper lake, which is just below the pass. The Silent Lakes have been stocked with cutthroat trout, and fish caught from the lakes will average 20-30 cm in length.

Spillimacheen River (BC)
Rainbow trout to 40 cm
Cutthroat trout to 40 cm
Bull trout to 60 cm (3.0 kg)
Whitefish to 35 cm
The Spillimacheen River enters the Columbia River at Spillimacheen. It possesses many kilometres of fine fishing, and is easily accessed for its entire length from logging roads from Parson. Rainbow and cutthroat trout are the dominant species, and average 20-30 cm in length. Large bull trout are taken on occasion. In the fall, the Spillimacheen River is noted for its excellent angling for whitefish.

Mitten Lake (BC)
Rainbow trout to 75 cm (5.0 kg)
Mitten Lake is located approximately 15 km by road from Parson. Mitten Lake is one of the most popular angling spots in the Region. Rainbow trout, which average 30-40 cm in length, can be taken throughout the season. Large trout, upwards of 3 kg, are taken regularly. Trolling is the standard fishing method on Mitten, although dry fly fishing aficionados usually do well in the fall in the lake's extended shallows.

Mitten Lake

Little Mitten Lake, Gavia Lake, Joyce Lake (BC)
Rainbow trout to 50 cm (1.5 kg)
These three lakes are located just north of Mitten Lake. Access generally requires some footwork through swampy ground, and the lakes are seldom fished. All three have been stocked with rainbow trout, which are present in good numbers. Expect to catch rainbow trout in the 25-35 cm range.

Little Mitten Lake

Bittern Lake (BC)
Rainbow trout to 45 cm
Bittern Lake lies 2 km northwest of Mitten Lake. It holds rainbow trout that average 20-30 cm in length. Shallows around the lake require the use of a boat. The deeper waters on the western side of the lake hold the most potential, especially along the boundary of the deep and shallow waters.

Bittern Lake

Nine Bay Lake (BC)
Rainbow trout to 70 cm (4.0 kg)
Nine Bay Lake is situated 2 km past Mitten Lake, at the southern end of the Mitten-Bittern-Nine Bay, and is reached via a short trail. The lake contains rainbow trout in good numbers and sizes. Averaging 25-35 cm in length, rainbows of over 2.0 kg are taken frequently. The southern end of the lake is the deepest and generally holds the most trout, which are susceptible to trolling. Large rainbow trout that cruise the bays and shallows at the north end of the lake can be taken by fly fishers who exercise plenty of patience.

Nine Bay Lake

Hobo Creek (BC)
Rainbow trout to 25 cm
Hobo Creek connects Bittern Lake to Mitten Lake before emptying into the Spillimacheen River. Hobo Creek holds small rainbow trout.

Moose Lake (BC)
Rainbow trout to 40 cm
Moose Lake is a seldom fished lake located south of the Spillimacheen River approximately 12 km west of the hamlet of Spillimacheen. Moose Lake contains rainbow trout that average 20-30 cm in length.

Jordan Lake (BC)
Rainbow trout to 40 cm
Jordan Lake is an overgrown beaver pond, located approximately 2 km southeast of Moose Lake. Jordan Lake was stocked in the past with rainbow trout, which can be taken in good numbers and average 20-30 cm in length. The lake's small size allows reasonable angling opportunities from shore.

Serpent Lake (BC)
Rainbow trout to 40 cm
Serpent Lake is located 2 km southwest of the confluence of Bobbie Burns Creek with the Spillimacheen River. Serpent Lake receives few visitors, and fishing reports are non-existent. This lake is for enterprising anglers only.

Bobbie Burns Creek (BC)
Rainbow trout to 35 cm
Cutthroat trout to 35 cm
Bull trout to 55 cm (2.0 kg)
Whitefish to 30 cm
Bobbie Burns Creek is accessible from logging roads for most of its fishable length. Bobbie Burns Creek is a major tributary of the Spillimacheen River, and possesses the same variety of game fish. Rainbow and cutthroat trout can be taken from most locations, with the odd bull trout present as well. Whitefish become more plentiful in the fall.

Jubilee Lake (BC)
Rainbow trout to 35 cm
Tiny Jubilee Lake is located on the forested bench on the western side the Columbia River. Jubilee Lake was stocked in the past, and contains limited numbers of rainbow trout in the 20-30 cm range.

Jubilee Lake

Bugaboo Creek (BC)
Cutthroat trout to 35 cm
Bull trout to 55 cm (2.0 kg)
Whitefish to 30 cm

Bugaboo Creek is born high amid the glaciers of the spectacular Bugaboo Mountains. Bugaboo Creek flows east, eventually emptying into the Columbia River just south of Spillimacheen. Although it is silted much of the year due to its glacial origins, Bugaboo Creek generally clears up enough by late-summer to offer decent stream fishing in its lower reaches. Cutthroat trout in the 20-30 cm range are the normal catch, with bull trout and whitefish present as well.

Bugaboo Glacier

Driftwood Creek (BC)
Cutthroat trout to 30 cm

Driftwood Creek is a tributary of Bugaboo Creek. It is accessible from logging roads in the Bugaboo and Bobbie Burns Creek drainages. Driftwood Creek holds plenty of small cutthroat trout, although few are larger than 25 cm in length. This is an excellent creek to gain some fishing experience on.

Columbia River (BC) *(Spillimacheen to Parson)*
Bull trout to 80 cm (7.0 kg)

The slow-moving Columbia River is of little interest to most anglers as it continues north on its roll to the Pacific. Bull trout and whitefish are caught in the river, along with the occasional rainbow or cutthroat trout.

KOOTENAY PARK REGION

The upper Kootenay River and its main tributary, the Vermilion River, serve as the main arteries for this Region, which includes all of Kootenay National Park. Highway 93 (Banff-Windermere Highway) connects the Region east to the Trans-Canada Highway and Banff, and south to Radium and the Columbia Valley. Fishing opportunities in the Region are limited, with small lakes and large rivers being the main sites. Cutthroat trout are the predominant species. Sub-Regions are based on the watersheds of the two main rivers - the Kootenay and the Vermilion.

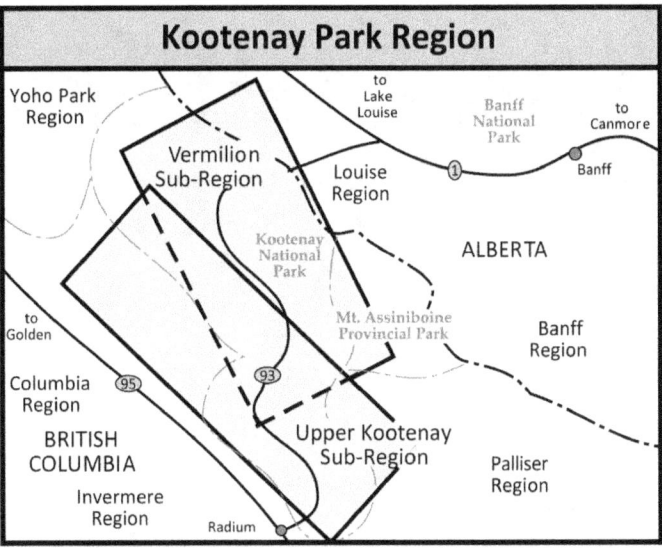

Upper Kootenay Sub-Region

The upper Kootenay River, from its headwaters and through Kootenay National Park (KNP), is the main waterway through the Sub-Region. Within Kootenay National Park, short side trails lead from Highway 93 to Dog and Cobb Lakes, while pretty Olive Lake lies alongside the highway at the crest of Sinclair Pass. The upper Kootenay River valley, which is outside the National Park, connects over a very low height of land with the Beaverfoot River. The upper Beaverfoot River is accessible from roads that branch south off the Trans-Canada Highway east of Golden. There are a number of good fishing lakes in this area, including Dainard, Diana and Marion.

Kootenay River (NP-BC)
(Headwaters to KNP boundary [south])
Cutthroat trout to 50 cm (1.5 kg)
Bull trout to 70 cm (3.5 kg)
Whitefish to 40 cm

The Kootenay River, which flows south from headwaters in the Vermilion Range, offers many kilometres of fine stream fishing. Cutthroat trout in the 25-35 cm range predominate, with both whitefish and bull trout also present in good numbers. North of the Kootenay Park boundary, the Kootenay River has a slow flow and frequent marshy areas. The river is still relatively small as it crosses the park boundary, but begins to drop in elevation and loses most of its marshy features. After joining the Vermilion River (which is larger than the Kootenay at the confluence), the Kootenay possesses enough volume to genuinely be given river status. Flowing back and forth across the wide Kootenay Valley, the river develops into a series of pools and riffles. The junctions of the Kootenay with minor tributaries are generally productive, especially when the main river is silted. Within Kootenay National Park these minor tributaries include Dolly Varden, Daer, Pitts, Swede and Rubie Creeks.

Kootenay River

Olive Lake (NP)
Brook trout to 25 cm

Olive Lake is a delightful little pond of a particularly pleasing shade of green. It sits alongside Highway 93 at the summit of Sinclair Pass. Although stocked in the past with rainbow and cutthroat trout, only brook trout are present today. Most of the fish are small, and few reach 25 cm in length. The waters of Olive Lake are particularly unproductive, with fish growing only a few centimetres each year. Casting a fly is a difficult proposition around most of the shoreline due to the proximity of the forest cover. As Olive is a very shallow and clear lake, and fish can easily be seen swimming in and around the submerged deadfall, casting ahead of cruising fish is generally effective.

Olive Lake

Cobb Lake (NP)
Brook trout to 45 cm

Cobb Lake is located 3 km by trail from Highway 93, and lies in a quiet opening in the forest. The boggy shoreline will ensure that most anglers end up with wet feet. Cobb's dark waters hold brook trout averaging 20-30 cm in length. Flies are very effective at Cobb Lake, but fly casting is difficult, with the exception of the few locations where forest cover opens up slightly. As the lake's bottom drops off quickly, one of the better tactics for this lake is to use a wet fly and let it sink deep before retrieval. Lures also work well at Cobb Lake.

Cobb Lake

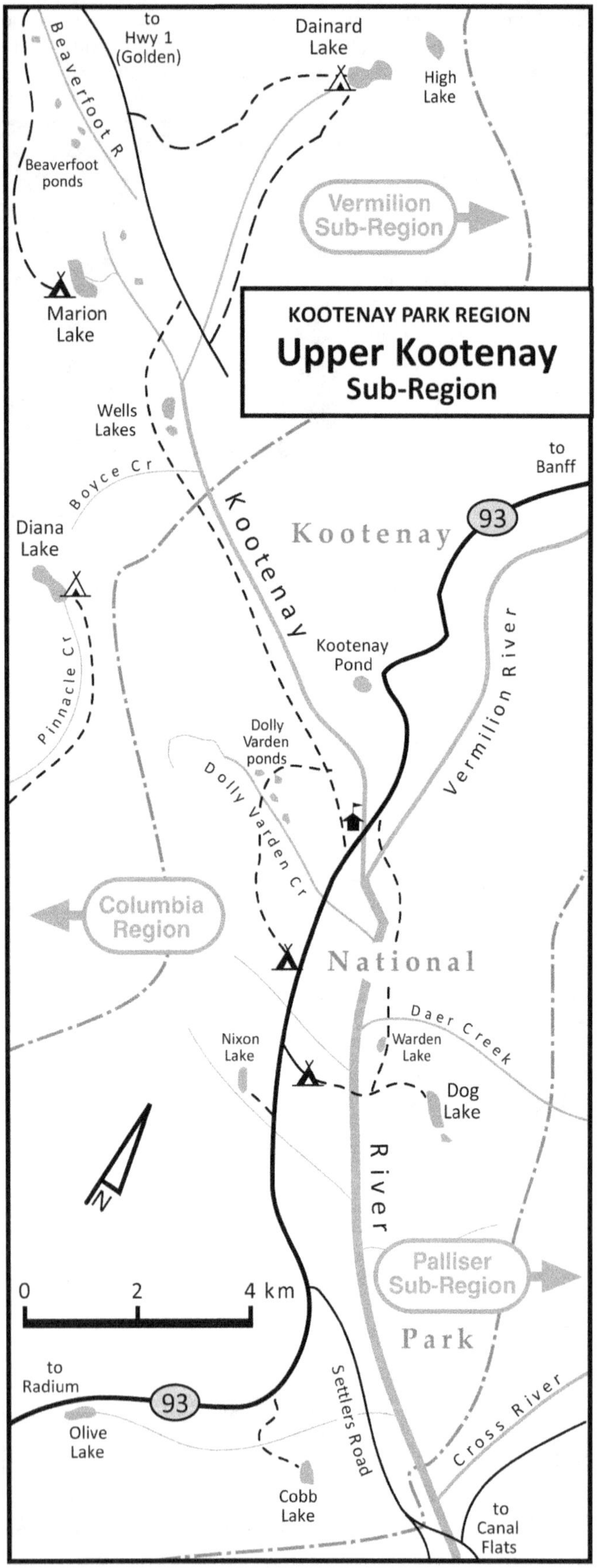

KOOTENAY PARK REGION: *Upper Kootenay Sub-Region*

Dog Lake (NP)
Brook trout to 40 cm

Lovely Dog Lake, located 3 km by trail from the McLeod Meadows campground, is one of the Sub-Region's more popular hiking destinations. It is also popular with anglers, as it holds a healthy population of brook trout in the 25-35 cm range. Lures and flies are effective, and fish can be taken close to shore in many locations. On a calm day, fish can easily be seen swimming about in Dog Lake's pretty green waters.

Dog Lake

Warden Lake (NP)
Status: Doubtful

Tiny Warden Lake is located amid heavy forest cover on the western side of the Kootenay River north of Dog Lake. Access is on the West Kootenay Fire Road, which connects to the Macleod Meadows Campground. Although Warden Lake looks promising, it has never been stocked, and likely contains no fish.

Warden Lake

Nixon Lake (NP)
Status: Devoid of fish

This small, shallow pond located less than a kilometre west of Highway 93 by trail has never been stocked and contains no fish.

Dolly Varden Creek and Ponds (NP)
Cutthroat trout to 25 cm
Bull trout to 30 cm

Despite its name, Dolly Varden Creek holds far more cutthroat trout than bull trout (formerly known as Dolly Varden). Several kilometres upstream from the Kootenay lies a series of small beaver dams where cutthroat in the 15-25 cm range are plentiful. Fishable waters can be reached by either following the creek upstream through very thick brush, or by following the fire road that connects Kootenay Crossing with Crook's Meadow.

KOOTENAY PARK REGION: Upper Kootenay Sub-Region

Kootenay Pond (NP)
Status: Devoid of fish
Kootenay Pond was a popular angling location in the past, but required regular plantings, as the trout did not reproduce. No trout exist in the lake today.

Beaverfoot River (BC)
Cutthroat trout to 40 cm
Rainbow trout to 40 cm
Bull trout to 60 cm (3.0 kg)
Whitefish to 35 cm
The Beaverfoot River is a major tributary of the Kicking Horse River, and forms the southwestern boundary of Yoho National Park. Access to fishable waters in the upper reaches is via the Beaverfoot Forest Service Road, which heads south from the Trans-Canada Highway just west of the park gates at the western entrance to Yoho National Park. The river holds cutthroat and rainbow, with a few good-sized bull trout lurking about. Fine meadows and great pools characterize the upper Beaverfoot River.

Beaverfoot River

Beaverfoot Ponds (BC)
Rainbow trout to 35 cm
Cutthroat trout to 35 cm
There are an extended series of beaver ponds attached to the upper Beaverfoot River that can be accessed from the Beaverfoot F.S. Road. The ponds hold both rainbow and cutthroat trout in the 20-30 cm range.

Marion Lake (BC)
Rainbow trout to 45 cm
Cutthroat trout to 45 cm
Marion Lake is reached after a long drive on the Beaverfoot F.S. Road from the Trans-Canada highway just outside the west entrance to Yoho National Park. The lake is surrounded by a combination of marsh, logged-out and burned-out forest. Marion holds plenty of rainbow trout in the 25-30 cm range, with a few cutthroat trout present as well. A boat is recommended, as shallows extend well out from the shoreline. Sticking to the edge between the deep and shallow waters will be productive.

Marion Lake

Diana Lake (BC)
Cutthroat trout to 45 cm
Set high in the Brisco Range, spectacular Diana Lake and its accompanying basin are generally overlooked by anglers because of awkward access. The most common access is via logging roads up Pinnacle Creek east of the town of Edgewater in the Columbia Valley. At the end of the road, a 4 km hike up Diana's outlet creek is required to reach the lake. An alternate route, which requires good route-finding skills, leads up from Boyce Creek, just outside the Kootenay Park boundary north of Kootenay Crossing. Diana Lake is seldom ice-free until early July due to its sheltered location. The lake holds plenty of finicky cutthroat trout averaging 25-35 cm in length. Fly fishing is effective, and fly casting is possible from numerous locations around the lake, with a few large boulders being the preferred locations. Hordes of horseflies are unwanted summer companions at Diana Lake.

Diana Lake

Dainard Lake (BC)
Cutthroat trout to 40 cm
Dainard Lake is hidden high in the Vermilion Range near the headwaters of the Kootenay River, and receives little attention from anglers despite the prospect of good fishing. Access is via logging roads up the Beaverfoot River from the Kicking Horse River, followed by a short 1 km trail. Located just outside the western boundary of Kootenay National Park in the Rockwall region, Dainard Lake contains cutthroat trout averaging 25-35 cm in length. Fish are numerous, and can be taken from almost any spot around the lake.

Dainard Lake

KOOTENAY PARK REGION: Upper Kootenay Sub-Region

High Lake (BC)
Status: Doubtful
Appropriately named, High Lake is set in a rocky pocket very high on the mountain above Dainard Lake. It is very unlikely that there are any fish in High Lake.

Wells (Carol) Lakes (BC)
Cutthroat trout to 35 cm
The Wells Lakes are a series of small, interconnected shallow lakes just off the upper Kootenay River. Access is via a long 20 km trail from Kootenay Crossing in Kootenay National Park, or by a long 50 km drive up the Beaverfoot River and down the upper Kootenay River. Small cutthroat trout in the 20-25 cm range are present in the lakes.

Wells Lake

Vermilion Sub-Region

The Vermilion Sub-Region encompasses the northern half of Kootenay National Park, and holds limited possibilities for anglers. The Vermilion River, which parallels Highway 93 (Banff-Windermere Highway), is silted for much of the year and has never been noted for good fishing. Trying some of the Vermilion's small tributaries, or taking a short hike to the Simpson River, represent much more worthwhile ventures in terms of stream fishing potential. The most popular backcountry destinations in the area are Kaufmann Lake and Floe Lake, both of which are noted more for their splendid scenery than their fishing.

Kaufmann Lake (NP)
Brook trout to 40 cm
Kaufmann Lake is located 14 km by trail from the popular tourist attraction of Marble Canyon on Highway 93. Kaufmann Lake lies tucked away in a hanging valley beneath the towering peaks of the Continental Divide. The lake is very popular with backpackers throughout the summer months. Kaufmann is long, narrow lake that contains brook trout ranging from 20-30 cm in length, which can be taken from most locations around the lakeshore. The area around the inlet creek at the far end of the lake usually holds fish and offers plenty of casting room for those who are fly fishing. Flies and lures will work well at Kaufmann Lake.

Kaufmann Lake

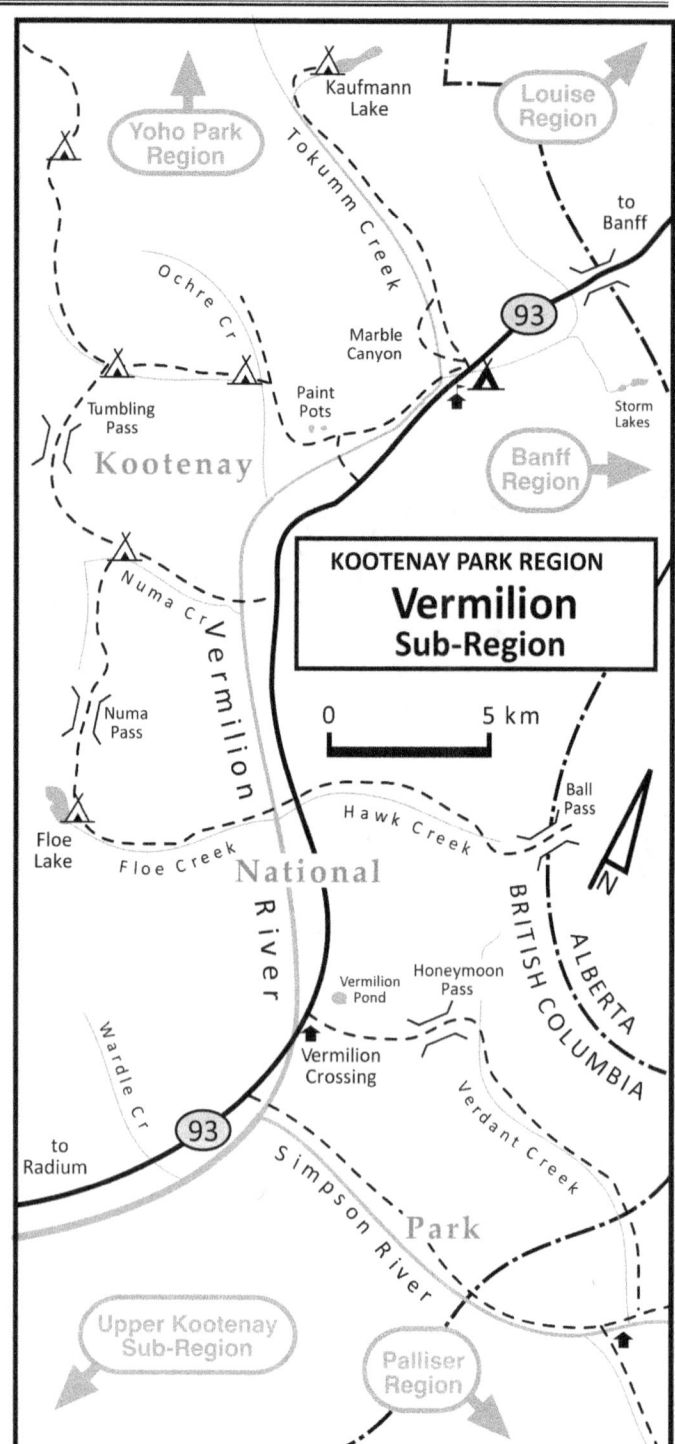

Tokumm Creek (NP)
Bull trout to 40 cm
Cutthroat trout to 30 cm
Tokumm Creek parallels the Kaufmann Lake trail for almost its entire distance, and at a glance appears to have plenty of potential as a trout stream. Unfortunately, fish cannot make it upstream past the falls in Marble Canyon, so the only fishing in Tokumm Creek is in the last half kilometre before it joins the Vermilion River.

KOOTENAY PARK REGION: Vermilion Sub-Region

Vermilion River (NP)
Bull trout to 60 cm (2.5 kg)
Cutthroat trout to 35 cm
Whitefish to 35 cm

The Vermilion River is very accessible as it flows alongside Highway 93 (Banff-Windermere Highway). The river remains very silted for much of the year, due to its glacial origins. However, the Vermilion does possess some fine holes and for a few brief weeks each autumn, it clears enough to allow the prospect of reasonable fishing. Bull and cutthroat trout and whitefish in the 20-30 cm range are normally taken, although large bull trout to 60 cm can also be caught on occasion. The best fishing spots tend to be where one of the tributary streams join the Vermilion River, particularly if the side creeks are clearer than the main river. The junction of the Vermilion and Simpson Rivers, in particular, is a prime fishing location.

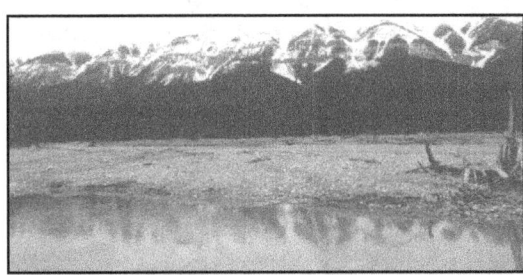
Vermilion River

Ochre Creek, Numa Creek, Floe Creek, Hawk Creek, Wardle Creek (NP)
Bull trout to 25 cm
Cutthroat trout to 20 cm

Once their waters have cleared after run-off, all of the major tributaries of the Vermilion River contain small cutthroat and bull trout in their lower reaches within a kilometre of their confluence with the river.

Paint Pots (NP)
Status: Devoid of fish

The Paint Pots have historical interest, but have no angling value. The ochre beds at the Paint Pots were worked by natives, and the ochre was used to make paint. The tiny springs that flow from the Paint Pots hold no fish.

Vermilion Pond (NP)
Cutthroat trout to 20 cm

Tiny Vermilion Pond is located just off Highway 93 approximately 1 km north of Vermilion Crossing. The pond, amazingly, always seems to hold a few small cutthroat trout in its shallow waters. Most of the fish tend to keep to the middle of the pond beyond the reach of all but the most expert angler.

Floe Lake (NP)
Status: Doubtful

Floe Lake is one of the most beautiful spots in all the mountain parks. The magnificent Rockwall towers above stunning blue waters dotted with ice floes. Floe Lake and its surrounding alpine meadows are reached by a 10 km trail from Highway 93, and the area is popular with hikers throughout the summer. Floe Lake's waters at one time held a small population of cutthroat trout, averaging 35-40 cm in length. Reports indicate that there is little natural reproduction in Floe Lake, and it is unlikely that any trout remain. Go for the scenery.

Floe Lake

Storm Lakes (NP)
Status: Devoid of fish

The two tiny Storm Lakes are located at the head of the Vermilion River beneath the western face of Storm Mountain. Bushwhacking through the deadfall of the massive fire of 1968 is required to reach the lakes. The Storm Lakes have never been stocked, and it is unlikely that they hold any fish.

Storm Lake

Simpson River (NP-BC)
Cutthroat trout to 40 cm
Bull trout to 75 cm (4.0 kg)
Whitefish to 30 cm

The Simpson River, which flows from the Golden Valley in Mount Assiniboine Provincial Park to the Vermilion River in Kootenay Park, has long stretches of fishable waters. The 8 km stretch above its confluence with the Vermilion River is within the boundaries of Kootenay National Park, and contains many large pools home to cutthroat and whitefish, and usually a large bull trout or two. Expect to catch cutthroat trout averaging 25-35 cm in length. Above the 8 km-mark (signs mark the boundary), the Simpson flows inside Mount Assiniboine Provincial Park and a B.C. license is required. This stretch of river is characterized by faster waters and less pools. Because no glaciers feed the Simpson River, it is generally very clear and the spring run-off usually short-lived.

Simpson River (bull trout)

Verdant Creek (NP-BC)
Cutthroat trout to 25 cm
Bull trout to 40 cm

Verdant Creek is a major tributary of the Simpson River, and can be reached by trails on the upper Simpson River or by the Honeymoon Pass trail, north of Vermilion Crossing. The many pools on Verdant Creek are home to cutthroat and bull trout that average 20-25 cm in length.

CANMORE REGION: Three Sisters Sub-Region

CANMORE REGION

The bustling community of Canmore serves as the centre of the Region, and offers complete tourist facilities. The Trans-Canada Highway, leading east to Calgary and west to Banff is the main transportation artery. The 1-A Highway and the Smith-Dorrien/Spray Trail provide access to areas off of the Trans-Canada Highway. The Bow River and the Spray Lakes Reservoir are the most significant water features in the Region. Angling opportunities in the Region are good, and range from river to stream to lake, and access varies from highway to gravel road to trail. The Region is divided into three Sub-Regions: the Three Sisters Sub-Region in and around Canmore; the Smith-Dorrien Creek drainage; and the backcountry surrounding Marvel Lake.

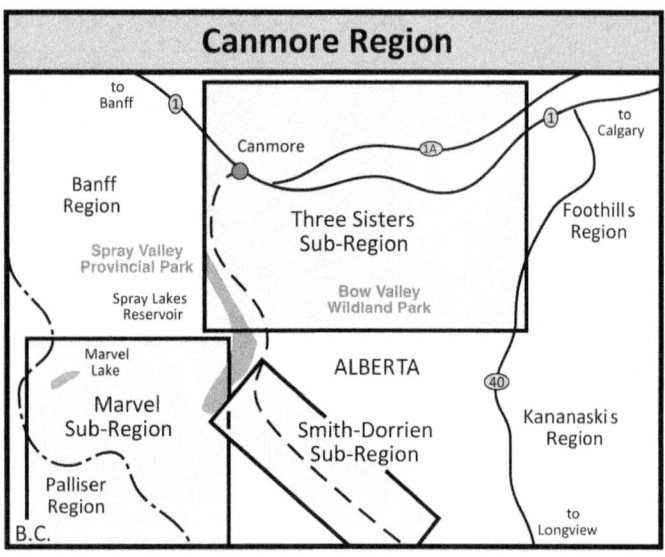

Three Sisters Sub-Region

This Sub-Region extends from the Spray Lakes Reservoir to Canmore and then east along the Bow River valley as far as Chief Hector Lake. Vehicular access is on the Trans-Canada Highway, the 1-A Highway and the Smith-Dorrien/Spray Trail. The Bow River, which flows through Canmore, receives heavy fishing pressure. From Canmore, the graveled Smith-Dorrien/Spray Trail heads directly west through Whiteman Gap into the newly created Spray Valley Provincial Park. The road leads past Whiteman Pond in short order to Goat Pond and the Spray Lakes Reservoir. Spray Lakes Reservoir is a very popular spot with anglers and is busy all year long. Gap Lake, Grotto Mountain Pond, Canmore beaver ponds and the Steele Brothers Ponds are all located east of Canmore and are accessed from the 1-A Highway. Continuing east on the 1-A, one reaches Chief Hector Lake and its monstrous rainbow trout.

Spray Lakes Reservoir (AB)
Lake trout to 85 cm (8.0 kg)
Cutthroat trout to 60 cm (2.5 kg)
Whitefish to 50 cm (1.5 kg)

The Spray Lakes Reservoir, which measures over 20 km in length, is located southwest of Canmore in a deep valley between the Goat and Kananaskis Ranges, in the heart of the new Spray Valley Provincial Park. The reservoir is accessed by the Smith-Dorrien/Spray Trail that connects Canmore with the Kananaskis Lakes. Due to the lake's size, a boat is useful for fishing, but boaters should be aware that very strong winds are common and often keep all crafts off the water for days at a time. Huge lake trout inhabit the lake, with whitefish also present in good numbers, as well as a few cutthroat trout. Most lake trout caught will be in the 40-50 cm range. Early spring and late fall is generally the best time for lake trout. Winter also sees significant activity at Spray Lakes Reservoir. Bait and lures are generally effective for lake trout. For shore bound anglers, areas around the many inlet creeks hold trout.

Spray Lakes Reservoir

Lorenda Jahoda with Spray Lakes lake trout

Goat Pond (AB)
Lake trout to 60 cm (2.0 kg)
Whitefish to 45 cm

Goat Pond is a man-made lake 2 km northwest and downstream of Spray Lakes Reservoir. It is part of the reservoir/power complex, and sits alongside the Smith-Dorrien/Spray Trail. Most of the shoreline and lake is cluttered with deadfall and although lake trout and whitefish are there for the catching, most anglers will likely catch more snags than fish. Cutthroat and brook trout may be present in small numbers as well.

Goat Pond

CANMORE REGION: Three Sisters Sub-Region

Whiteman Pond (AB)
Brook trout to 35 cm
Lake trout to 50 cm (1.5 kg)
Whitefish to 40 cm

Whiteman Pond is a very narrow stretch of water alongside the Smith-Dorrien/Spray Trail at Whiteman Gap. It holds brook and lake trout as well as the odd whitefish. Angling is possible only from the road side of the pond.

Grassi Lakes (AB)
Brook trout to 30 cm

These two tiny charming lakes of exquisite color are set in the basin immediately beneath Whiteman Gap. The lakes are a very popular hiking destination for locals. Both Grassi Lakes contain a very limited number of brook trout in the 20-30 cm range.

Grassi Lakes

Quarry (Canmore Mines No. 3) Lake (AB)
Arctic grayling to 35 cm

Quarry Lake, as one might expect, is a water-filled abandoned rock quarry. It is located in a meadow approximately 1 km south of the Smith-Dorrien/Spray Trail just west of Canmore. The lake was stocked at one time with rainbow trout, which failed to reproduce. It is now stocked with arctic grayling, which average 20-30 cm in length. Although these fish can be taken by a number of methods, they seem particularly susceptible to the fly, and fly casting room is available around the entire lake.

Canmore Creek (AB)
Brook trout to 30 cm
Brown trout to 30 cm
Cutthroat trout to 30 cm
Whitefish to 30 cm

The waters of Canmore Creek begin at the bottom of the power complex below Whiteman Gap and flow for a few short kilometres before joining the Bow River. Alberta Fish and Wildlife is attempting to reintroduce cutthroat trout to the creek. In addition to the stocked cutthroat, brook and brown trout are also present. Most trout caught will be in the 15-25 cm range. Check your regulations, as special restrictions apply on Canmore Creek.

Policeman Creek (AB)
Brown trout to 30 cm
Brook trout to 30 cm

Policeman Creek flows under the Trans-Canada Highway and into Canmore. Within Canmore, it is very popular with local youngsters, in particular the area around the bridge that leads to downtown Canmore. Brown and brook trout averaging 15-30 cm in length are caught in the creek.

Bow River (AB)
(Downstream from Banff Park east boundary)
Brown trout to 75 cm (4.0 kg)
Rainbow trout to 65 cm (3.0 kg)
Brook trout to 50 cm (1.5 kg)
Bull trout to 75 cm (4.0 kg)
Whitefish to 55 cm (1.5 kg)

The stretch of the Bow River downstream from the Banff National Park boundary is a high quality fishery, and is steadily gaining more attention from anglers. Although this section of the Bow River is accessible on foot from the Trans-Canada and 1-A Highways, drift boats have become very popular. The Bow River provides some excellent river fishing for brown trout, with large individuals in the 2-3 kg range taken regularly. Whitefish can be taken in good numbers in the fall. The area around the Trans-Canada Highway bridge and the old C.P.R. bridges seem inordinately popular and are heavily over fished. Excellent pools are waiting just around the bend, both upstream and downstream. Fishing slows dramatically during run-off, which lasts from June through late-July. Early season fishing from mid-April to late-May is usually very productive, the action picking up again in August through October.

Bow River and Three Sisters

Alan Brice with Bow River brown trout

Canmore Beaver Ponds (AB)
Rainbow trout to 35 cm
Brown trout to 35 cm

The Canmore beaver ponds are interconnected with various channels of the Bow River, and are located alongside the 1-A Highway 4 km east of Canmore. The ponds contain rainbow trout along with a few brown trout. Trout caught in the ponds will average 20-30 cm in length.

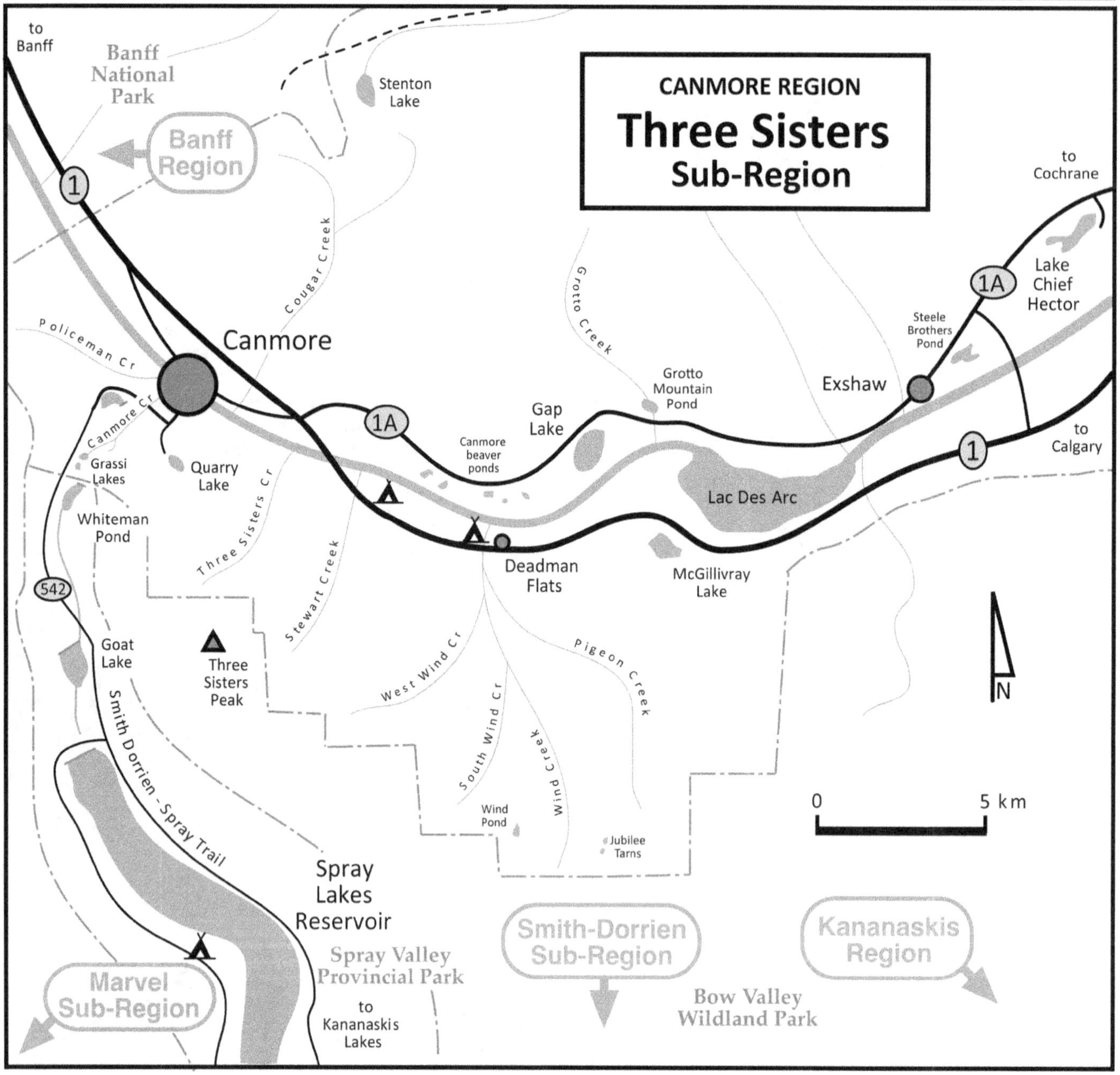

CANMORE REGION: Three Sisters Sub-Region

CANMORE REGION
Three Sisters
Sub-Region

Pigeon Creek, Wind Creek, West Wind Creek, Stewart Creek, Three Sisters Creek (AB)
Brook trout to 30 cm
Brown trout to 30 cm
Whitefish to 30 cm
These small tributaries of the Bow River are located south of Canmore. They hold small numbers of brook and brown trout, and the occasional whitefish. These creeks may dry up completely in some years.

Wind Pond, Jubilee Tarns (AB)
Status: Devoid of fish
Wind Pond and the Jubilee Tarns are very small lakes located high in the Wind and West Wind Creek watersheds. They have never been stocked and contain no fish.

Grotto Mountain Pond (AB)
Rainbow trout to 35 cm
Brook trout to 35 cm
Grotto Mountain Pond and its nearby picnic area are situated on the north side of 1-A Highway just west of Lac Des Arc. The pond is stocked regularly, usually with rainbow or brook trout. Trout caught in the pond are not large, averaging 20-30 cm in length. A few whitefish may also be present in the pond. Grotto Mountain Pond is a pleasant location, and always seems busy with families.

Grotto Mountain Pond

CANMORE REGION: Smith-Dorrien Sub-Region

Gap Lake (AB)
Brown trout to 60 cm (2.5 kg)
Brook trout to 40 cm
Whitefish to 55 cm (2.0 kg)

Gap Lake is sandwiched between the 1-A Highway and the C.P.R. mainline, 8 km east of Canmore. Brown and brook trout in the 25-35 cm range predominate, with large whitefish present in fair numbers as well. A boat is recommended for those fishing Gap Lake.

Gap Lake
(brown trout)

Lac Des Arc (AB)
Brown trout to 55 cm (2.0 kg)
Whitefish to 50 cm (1.5 kg)

Lac Des Arc is merely an overflow basin for the Bow River during high water, and is no more than 1-2 m deep. The lake itself almost dries up completely on occasion. Accordingly, any fish population will tend to keep near the river on the north side, although whitefish and brown trout might be taken from a boat in the shallow waters that make up the main part of the lake.

McGillivray Pond
Status: Doubtful

McGillivray Pond is the small lake that sits on the south side of the Trans-Canada Highway at the western end of Lac Des Arc. McGillivray Pond has never been stocked, and likely holds no fish.

Steele Brothers Ponds (AB)
Brook trout to 50 cm (1.5 kg)
Rainbow trout to 40 cm
Brown trout to 55 cm (2.0 kg)

This series of large, interconnected beaver ponds is located immediately east of the Steele Brothers lime plant on the 1-A Highway. The ponds contain good numbers of brook trout, with browns, rainbows and the occasional whitefish present as well. As with most beaver dams, the surrounding vegetation growth is heavy and finding a spot to cast from effectively may prove difficult, and wet feet are likely.

Chief Hector (Hector) Lake (Fee required to fish)
Rainbow trout to 75 cm (5.0 kg)

Chief Hector Lake is located on the Morley Reserve, and is accessed from the 1-A Highway at Nakoda Lodge. The lake is on a First Nations' reserve, and as such is beyond federal or provincial jurisdiction for angling licenses. As such, a license is not required, but a fee must be paid for angling at Chief Hector Lake. The lake is catch-and-release only. Chief Hector Lake is shallow and an aeration system prevents winter kill. It is possible to fish from shore, but a watercraft is a superior option. The rainbow trout in the lake are huge, with average trout being 50-60 cm in length and 2-3 kg in weight. Most fish are very wary, as they have been caught several times. However, an angler who shows a bit of patience will be rewarded. Fly fishing is the most effective method of angling at Chief Hector Lake. Be prepared for some screaming reels!

Chief Hector Lake

(rainbow trout)

Stenton (South Ghost, Astral) Lake
Cutthroat trout to 45 cm

Stenton Lake is located at the headwaters of South Ghost River, and is accessed by a 10 km trail up the South Ghost River. Although the lake is situated almost due north of Canmore, road access to the trail is via the Forestry Trunk Road west of Cochrane. Stenton Lake contains a good population of cutthroat trout that average 25-35 cm in length.

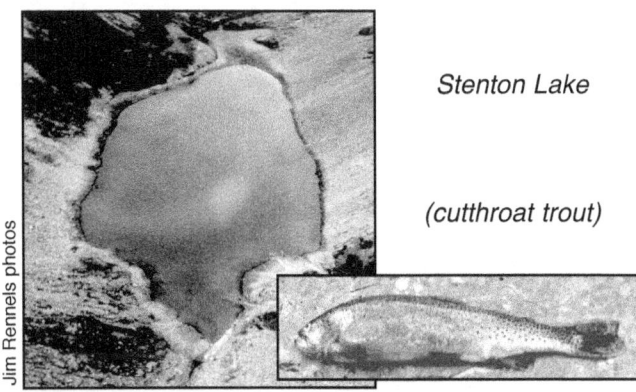

Stenton Lake

(cutthroat trout)

Jim Rennels photos

Smith-Dorrien Sub-Region

The Smith-Dorrien/Spray Trail is a gravel road connecting Canmore with Peter Lougheed Provincial Park, and it provides access to this rugged area noted for its outstanding day and half-day hikes. Mud Lake and the Hogarth Lakes are located in the wide valley at the head of the Smuts and Smith-Dorrien watersheds. Spur valleys to the west of the Smith-Dorrien valley hold Commonwealth Lake and the Burstall Lakes, while to the east, consecutive side valleys hold Rummel, Chester and Headwall Lakes.

CANMORE REGION: Smith-Dorien Sub-Region

Warspite Lake (AB)
Status: Doubtful
Warspite Lake is located on the western side of the Smith-Dorrien valley approximately 5 km west of Lower Kananaskis Lake. A 2 km trail leads from the Mt. Black Prince Day Use area to Warspite Lake. Warspite Lake held small cutthroat trout in the past.

Black Prince Lakes, Construction Lake (AB)
Status: Devoid of fish
The Black Prince Lakes are set in a high basin above Warspite Lake. The Upper Black Prince Lake is also known as Construction Lake. None of the lakes have ever been stocked and they contain no fish.

Headwall (Ranger) Lakes (AB)
Cutthroat trout to 45 cm
The Headwall Lakes are located 7 km by trail from the Chester Lake parking area. The lakes are set in rocky, windswept basins with a general lack of vegetation around the shoreline. Both the lower and upper lakes hold plenty of cutthroat trout averaging 25-35 cm in length. The trout tend to keep to the area around the distinctive drop-off zone. Flies and lures work well in Headwall Lakes.

Lower Headwall Lake

Chester Lake (AB)
Northern Dolly Varden to 70 cm (4.0 kg)
Cutthroat trout to 55 cm (1.5 kg)
Chester Lake and its appealing larch-filled valley are reached by a 6 km walk-in from the Smith-Dorrien/Spray Trail. The lake attracts numerous day hikers and anglers throughout the summer. Chester Lake was stocked in 1974 with Northern Dolly Varden, a close relative of the bull trout, which are now reproducing naturally. Cutthroat trout have also been stocked in Chester Lake, and are doing well. North Dolly Varden from Chester will average 35-45 cm in length, with the cutthroat trout averaging 25-35 cm in length. Fly fishing is effective for both the dollies and the cutthroat. Check your regulations, as special restrictions are in effect at Chester Lake.

Chester Lake

Rummel (West Galatea Lake) Lake (AB)
Cutthroat trout to 55 cm (1.5 kg)
Rummel Lake is reached by following a 5 km trail from the Smith-Dorrien/Spray Trail opposite Mt. Engadine Lodge. Alternate access involves bushwhacking south from the Chester Lake trail. Rummel Lake is set in a charming basin, and its clear waters hold cutthroat trout in good numbers in the 25-35 cm range. Open shoreline of meadow and scree offer ample room for fly casting.

Rummel Lake

Smith-Dorrien Creek (AB)
Status: Closed to angling
Smith-Dorrien Creek has been recognized as the primary spawning location for bull trout from Lower Kananaskis Lake. As such, it has been permanently closed to angling.

Mud Lake (AB)
Cutthroat trout to 35 cm
Bull trout to 50 cm (1.5 kg)
Northern Dolly Varden to 45 cm.
Whitefish to 30 cm
Mud Lake is fed by the melt waters of Robertson Glacier, and true to its name, remains chocolate coloured for most of the year. Accordingly, fishing is usually slow for cutthroat, bull trout and whitefish that inhabit Mud's roadside waters. It has been reported that Northern Dolly Varden have made their way down Chester Creek and now inhabit Mud Lake.

Burstall Lakes (AB)
Cutthroat trout to 35 cm
Northern Dolly Varden to 40 cm
This series of fine lakes sits in a meadowed valley 2 km west of Mud Lake on the Burstall Pass trail. The lakes contain cutthroat trout in the 20-30 cm range, and may also contain a few Northern Dolly Varden that have migrated from Chester Creek and Mud Lake. Burstall Creek, which flows from Burstall Lake to Mud Lake, contains a few small trout.

Upper Burstall Lake

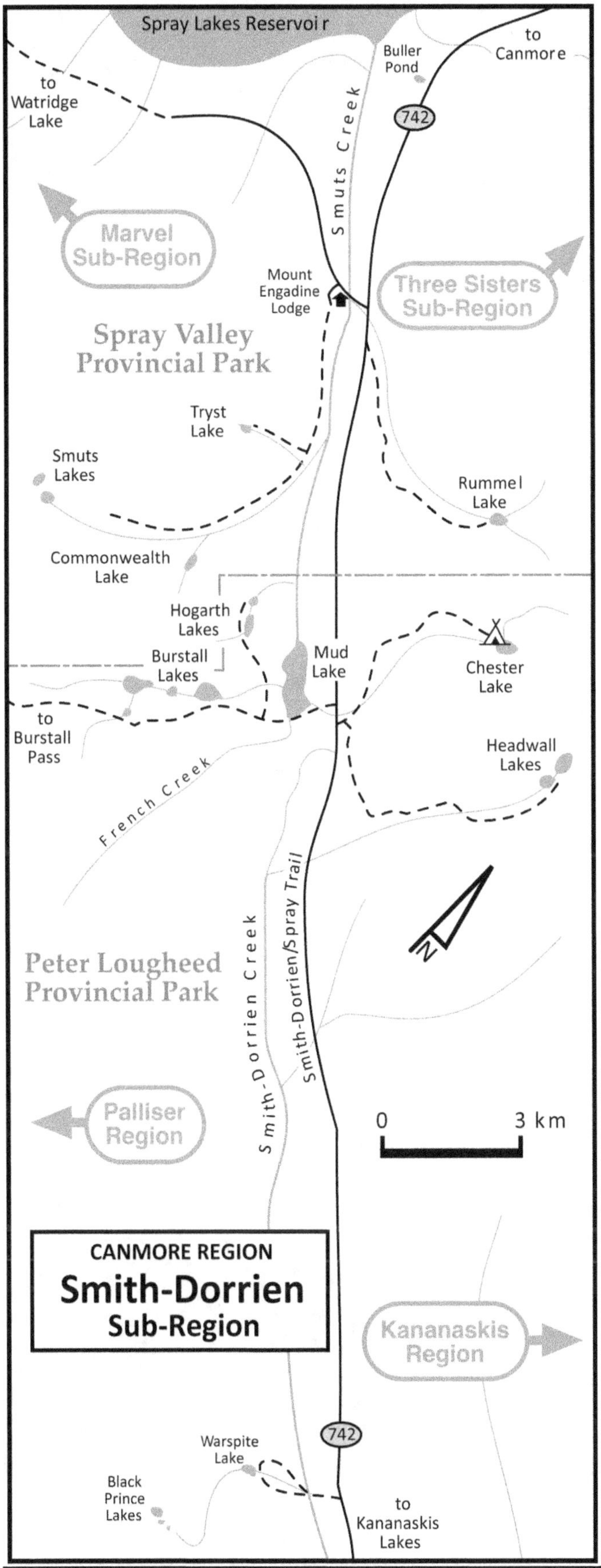

CANMORE REGION: Smith-Dorrien Sub-Region

Hogarth Lakes (AB)
Cutthroat trout to 40 cm

These three emerald-green bodies of water are located 2 km by trail from the Mud Lake Parking area. The lakes receive surprisingly little attention from anglers despite their proximity to the Smith-Dorrien/Spray Trail. The lakes contain a population of native cutthroat trout averaging 20-30 cm in length, and extreme water clarity allows the angler to see fish cruising about. Flies are effective, and casting room is adequate around the larger lake.

Commonwealth (Lost) Lake (AB)
Cutthroat trout to 40 cm

Commonwealth Lake is situated in a secluded side valley off Commonwealth Creek. It receives few visits from anglers each season because of a lack of defined trails. Commonwealth Lake holds cutthroat in the 20-30 cm range and is encircled by forest, making fly casting difficult from most locations. Nearby Commonwealth Creek contains small cutthroat trout, and can be reached along abandoned logging roads from the Smith-Dorrien/Spray Trail.

Commonwealth Lake

Tryst Lake (AB)
Status: Devoid of fish

Tryst Lake is a small tarn set in a hanging valley to the north of Commonwealth Creek and Lake. A 2 km trail leads to the lake from the Smith-Dorrien/Spray Trail. The lake has never been stocked and contains no fish.

Smuts Creek (AB)
Cutthroat trout to 25 cm
Bull trout to 40 cm
Whitefish to 25 cm

Smuts Creek flows alongside the Smith-Dorrien/Spray Trail downstream to the Spray Lakes Reservoir, and offers a few stretches of good stream fishing. Cutthroat trout in small sizes predominate, with the odd bull trout or whitefish also present.

Smuts Creek

CANMORE REGION: Smith-Dorrien Sub-Region

Smuts (Birdwood) Lakes (AB)
Cutthroat trout to 45 cm

These two small lakes are located at the head of Commonwealth Creek and are reached by a poorly-defined 7 km trail. Both lakes are set in distinctive alpine cirques with little vegetation. The upper lake has better quality angling, although cutthroat trout average 25-35 cm in length can be taken from both lakes. Flies and lures are both very effective in the Smuts Lakes.

Upper Smuts Lake

Buller Pond
Rainbow trout to 35 cm

This small pond and its picnic site are located alongside the Smith-Dorrien/Spray Trail on the south end of the Spray Lakes. Rainbow trout are stocked in Buller Pond, and they average 20-30 cm in length.

Marvel Sub-Region

The Marvel Sub-Region is always close to the peaks of the Continental Divide, and possesses some incredible mountain scenery. The main access into Marvel Lake is via a hiking trail that begins at the Mt. Shark trailhead. Stunning Marvel Lake, with its beautiful translucent blue-green waters, is the dominant feature to the north. To the south are the upper Spray River and Leman Lake. Large cutthroat trout are present in several lakes in the Sub-Region, including Marvel, Leman and Watridge Lakes.

Marvel Lake (NP)
Cutthroat trout to 75 cm (4.0 kg)

Marvel Lake is set in a long, narrow valley, 15 km by trail from the Mt. Shark trailhead. The lake is over 4 km in length and 75 m in depth. Marvel Lake holds some immense cutthroat trout, upwards of 4 kg. Most trout taken from the lake, however, will average 30-40 cm in length. Due to the lake's size, however, fishing from shore is often a frustrating proposition. Anglers generally have the most success at the eastern end of the lake, although those willing to expend the energy will find fish all around the lake. Fly fishing is very productive at Marvel Lake, and packing in a float tube is a very worthwhile venture.

Marvel Lake

Alan Brice with Marvel Lake cutthroat trout

Terrapin Lake (NP)
Cutthroat trout to 40 cm

Terrapin Lake is sandwiched between Marvel Lake to the east and Gloria Lake to the west. It is reached via a short spur trail off the Marvel Pass trail. The silted blue waters of Terrapin Lake hold a small number of cutthroat trout, for which the angling is generally poor. Tall grass along the shoreline makes angling very difficult.

Terrapin Lake

Gloria Lake (NP)
Cutthroat trout to 50 cm (1.5 kg)

Gloria Lake is one of the most exquisitely coloured lakes in the Canadian Rockies. Gloria's rich blue waters hold some fine cutthroat trout, but few anglers make it to the lake each year. Cutthroat trout in the lake average 30-40 cm in length. Fish will tend to keep near shore because of the silted nature of the water, and fishing near one of the many inlet streams can be particularly effective. The quality of trails diminishes rapidly beyond the area of the outlet stream and those anglers travelling along the shoreline will encounter heavy brush.

Gloria Lake

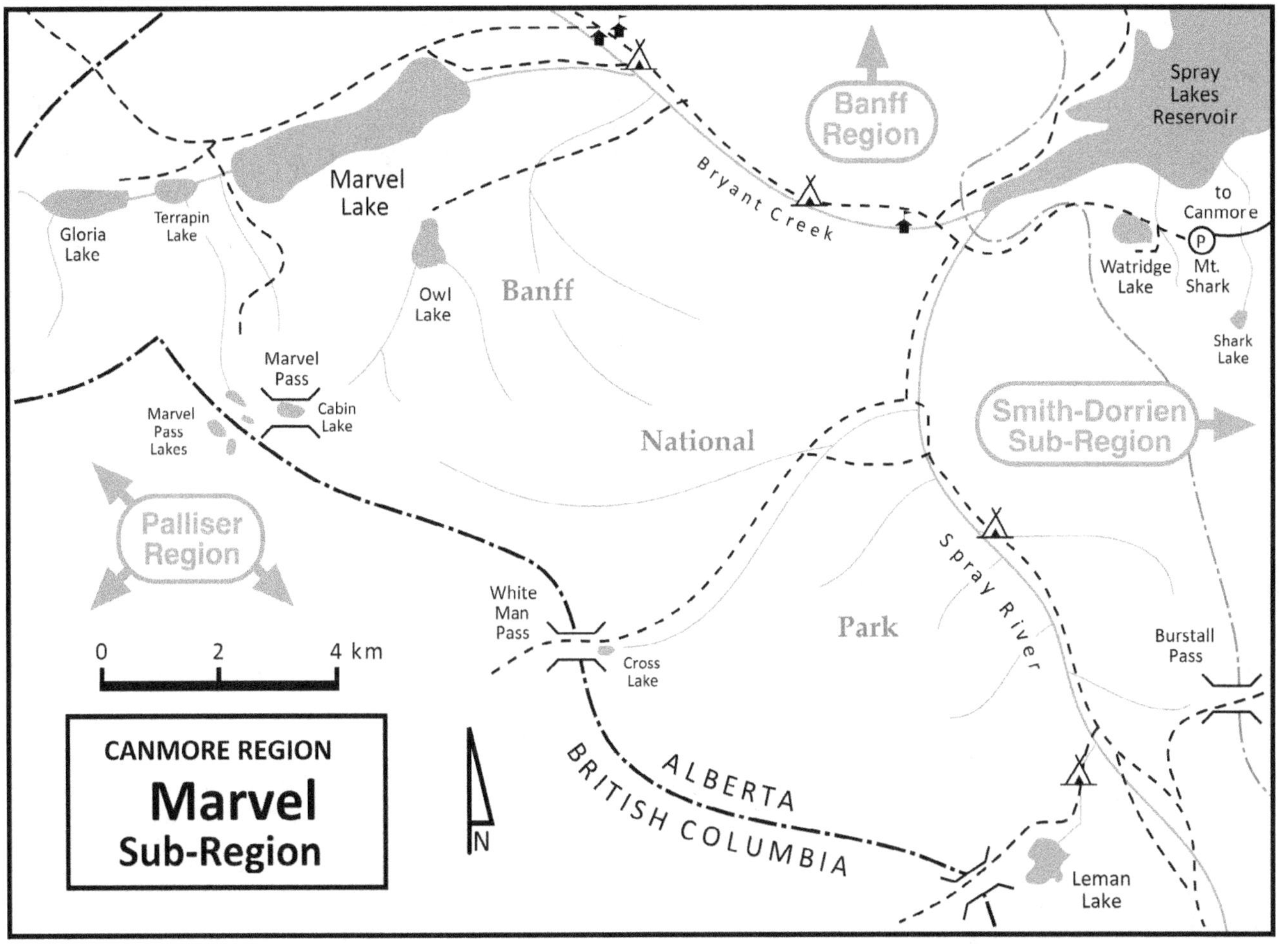

CANMORE REGION: Marvel Sub-Region

CANMORE REGION
Marvel Sub-Region

Marvel Pass Lakes (NP-BC)
Status: Devoid of fish
Situated in the alpine meadows of Marvel Pass, these promising looking waters have never been stocked and contain no trout.

Marvel Pass Lakes

Cabin Lake (NP)
Status: Devoid of fish
Cabin Lake is the largest of the Marvel Pass lakes and lies just inside the boundary of Banff National Park. Cabin Lake has never been stocked and contains no trout.

Cabin Lake

Owl Lake (NP)
Brook trout to 50 cm (1.5 kg)
Owl Lake is located in a side valley west of Bryant Creek. Access is via a 15 km hike from the Mt. Shark trailhead. Water levels in Owl fluctuate dramatically both seasonally and annually. Brook trout inhabit the lake, and they average 25-35 cm in length.

Owl Lake

Bryant Creek (NP)
Cutthroat trout to 35 cm
Bull trout to 60 cm (2.5 kg)
Whitefish to 35 cm
Bryant Creek is a noisy companion to hikers travelling to either Marvel Lake or Mt. Assiniboine Provincial Park. Bryant Creek's sparkling waters hold small cutthroat trout, most in the 20-30 cm range. The creek is very popular in its lower reaches, within a kilometre or two of the Spray Lakes Reservoir, where bull trout and whitefish can also be taken. In the meadow section upstream from the Bryant Creek Warden Cabin, there are several kilometres of slow, fishable water as well as numerous beaver ponds.

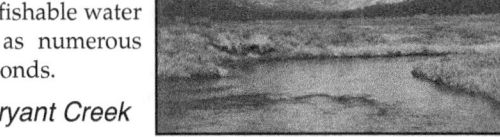

Bryant Creek

CANMORE REGION: Three Sisters Sub-Region

Watridge Lake (AB)
Cutthroat trout to 70 cm (4.0 kg)
Watridge Lake is situated in Kananaskis Country, just outside the boundary of Banff National Park. Access to the lake is on a 2 km long trail from the Mt. Shark trailhead. Watridge Lake is very popular with anglers who fish its clear, green waters for fine cutthroat trout averaging 30-40 cm in length. Larger trout, in the 2-3 kg range, are caught regularly from Watridge Lake. Fishing pressure is usually heavy throughout the season. For those who will be fly fishing, a belly boat is a good option for Watridge, as fly casting room is limited around much of the lake.

Watridge Lake

(cutthroat trout)

Upper Spray River

Cross Lake (NP)
Status: Devoid of fish
Petite Cross Lake is located in a meadow just below the summit of White Man Pass. Cross Lake has never been stocked and contains no fish.

Cross Lake

Leman Lake (NP)
Cutthroat trout to 75 cm (4.0 kg)
Leman Lake is located on the western side of the upper Spray River valley, near the summit of Spray Pass. The standard access to Leman Lake is either via the 14 km trail from the Spray Lakes Reservoir or the 13 km Burstall Pass trail. A shorter 2 km access route begins on the B.C. side from logging roads on the upper Albert River, and alternates between game trails and bushwhacking. A topographic map is strongly recommended for this route. Leman Lake was very popular in the past due to its large trout, and it subsequently suffered badly through a period of over harvest. With the dramatic decline in the quality of fishing, the number of anglers also declined. Legislation protecting cutthroat trout in Banff National Park will hopefully restore Leman Lake to its past glory. Leman Lake holds some very large cutthroat trout in its striking waters, and most fish taken average 35-45 cm in length. Fishing the obvious divide between the shallow and deep waters is the best strategy. Lures and flies will both be effective.

Shark (Marushka) Lake (AB)
Cutthroat trout to 35 cm
Shark Lake is a diminutive, forest enclosed lake set beneath the northeast face of Mt. Shark. The lake is accessible from the Watridge Lake trail by following game trails along Shark Lake's outlet stream. Shark Lake holds cutthroat trout in the 20-30 cm range.

Shark Lake

Spray River (NP) *(Headwaters to Spray Lakes Reservoir)*
Cutthroat trout to 30 cm
The upper Spray River, which flows from the Palliser Pass region down to the Spray Lakes Reservoir, has many stretches of excellent fishing. The upper Spray valley is accessed by a hiking trail from the Mt. Shark trailhead. The upper Spray River offers kilometres of excellent stream fishing for cutthroat trout. The trout are not large, averaging 20-30 cm in length, but they are plentiful. Although heavy brush may be a hindrance in spots, most fly fishers will have little difficulty casting into trout-holding waters.

Leman Lake

(cutthroat trout)

BANFF REGION

This Region is centered on the world-renowned tourist resort of Banff. Services of all types can be obtained in the Banff Townsite, including the sale of fishing tackle. Access is on the Trans-Canada Highway, which continues east to Calgary and west to Lake Louise. Lake Minnewanka is a favourite of anglers who come in search of its huge lake trout. The Bow River also attracts plenty of attention. Backcountry lakes make up the much of the rest of the Region's angling opportunities. The Region is divided into four Sub-Regions. The first is in the immediate vicinity of Banff and includes Lake Minnewanka. The other three Sub-Regions are largely backcountry, and have many popular day hiking and overnight destinations. These Sub-Regions include the Cascade River drainage and the area north of Banff; the Sunshine Village area; and the Egypt Lake environs.

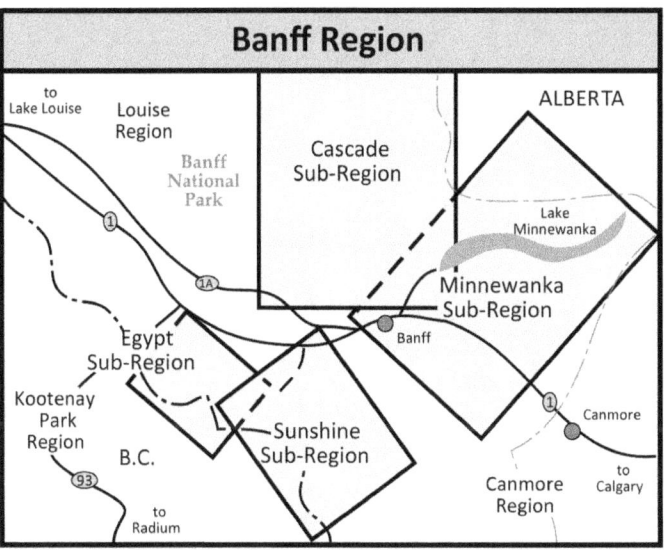

Minnewanka Sub-Region

The Banff Townsite is the hub of the Sub-Region. Dining, bars and shopping generally take precedence over angling among visitors. The Trans-Canada Highway provides Banff's link to the outside world. Lake Minnewanka is the primary fishing destination for most anglers. Two Jack and Johnson Lakes, just off the Lake Minnewanka Road, are also active during the summer. The Bow River is readily accessible near the Townsite, and is usually alive with canoeists and sightseers.

Lake Minnewanka (NP)
Lake trout to 1.2 m (20.0 kg)
Bull trout to 80 cm (6.0 kg)
Rainbow trout to 65 cm (3.0 kg)
Whitefish to 45 cm

Lake Minnewanka, at 20 km in length, is one of the largest lakes in the Canadian Rockies. The lake is reached by taking the paved road that branches north from the Trans-Canada Highway at the western entrance to Banff. Lake Minnewanka's depths hold lake trout of immense proportions that each year tempt innumerable anglers to test their skills against these monsters. The first weeks after ice-out are generally the most productive, as the lake trout move into shallower water (still up to 20 m deep) and begin feeding actively. Trolling or jigging in the areas around inlet creeks at this time of year can be very productive. As summer progresses, the lake trout tend to move out to deeper waters and fishing slows noticeably. Although lake trout in the 15-20 kg range have been taken on occasion, most will average 50-60 cm in length and 2-3 kg in weight. Aside from lake trout, Minnewanka holds rainbow trout, bull trout and whitefish in good numbers. Boats are available for rent at Lake Minnewanka. Due to the size and location of the lake, boaters should be very aware of changing weather conditions, and of the strong winds that can appear suddenly.

Lake Minnewanka

Blair Walberg with Lake Minnewanka lake trout

Ghost Lakes (NP)
Lake trout to 75 cm (5.0 kg)
Bull trout to 70 cm (4.0 kg)
Rainbow trout to 60 cm (2.5 kg)
Whitefish to 45 cm

The Ghost Lakes are simply an extension of the extreme eastern end of Lake Minnewanka. The actual Ghost Lakes vary in size and number with fluctuating water levels. The variety of fish in Ghost Lakes is identical to those in Minnewanka, although generally in slightly smaller sizes. Reaching the Ghost Lakes requires either a long boat trip down the entire length of Minnewanka, or an 8 km hike-in from the Ghost River Road. If fishing from shore, the best areas tend to be those where the lakes are at their narrowest point.

Two Jack Lake (NP)
Rainbow trout to 55 cm (1.5 kg)
Lake trout to 70 cm (4.0 kg)

Two Jack Lake is located less than 1 km south of Lake Minnewanka, and offers a pleasant respite for those fishermen overwhelmed by the size of Minnewanka. Rainbow trout

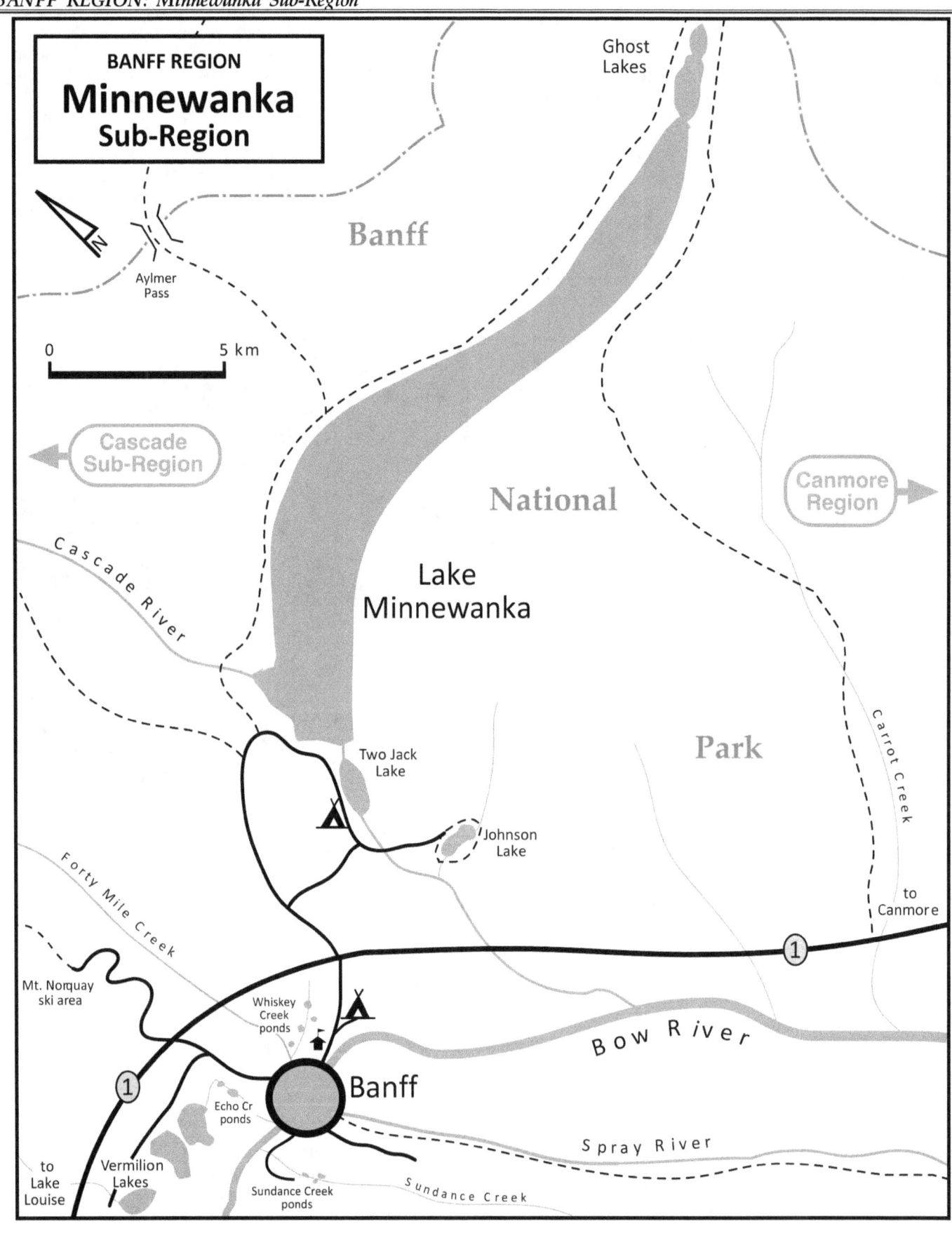

predominate, and average 30-40 cm in length. Lake trout are also present in fair numbers. The nearby campground ensures that Two Jack's shores will be busy all summer long.

Two Jack Lake

Johnson Lake (NP)
Rainbow trout to 40 cm
Brook trout to 40 cm
Johnson Lake is located two kilometres south of Two Jack Lake, and has received far fewer visitors in recent years since the closing of the alternate access to Lake Minnewanka from the Trans-Canada Highway. Angling has never been highly regarded at Johnson Lake, although there are still likely rainbow and brook trout in the lake.

Vermilion Lakes (NP)
Rainbow trout to 60 cm (2.5 kg)
Brook trout to 60 cm (2.5 kg)
Bull trout to 75 cm (5.0 kg)
Whitefish to 40 cm
These three shallow lakes located west of Banff alongside the Bow River have gained a reputation over the years for inconsistent fishing. The two most easterly lakes have extended shallows and are of little value to fishermen relegated to shore. From a boat, fishing is most productive in the deeper water that is accentuated by its darker colouration. The most westerly lake is the deepest of the three, but still not deep by normal standards being seldom more than 4-5 m in depth. Fishing is possible from a number of shoreline locations although getting there will require getting a little soggy. While large brook and rainbow trout are taken on occasion, most fish taken average 25-35 cm in length.

Vermilion Lakes and Mount Rundle

BANFF REGION: Minnewanka Sub-Region

Bow River (NP) *(Redearth Creek to Banff Park east boundary)*
Bull trout to 70 cm (5.0 kg)
Brown trout to 50 cm (1.5 kg)
Rainbow trout to 60 cm (2.5 kg)
Brook trout to 60 cm (2.5 kg)
Cutthroat trout to 50 cm (1.5 kg)
Whitefish to 40 cm
This section of the Bow River flows from Redearth Creek to the east park boundary. It includes the Banff Townsite, and is characterized by slower water and deep pools. Canoeists frequent the river throughout the summer and anglers can usually be seen working the shoreline for a wide variety of trout, including rainbow, brook, cutthroat and bull, most in the 25-35 cm range. Downstream from Bow Falls, brown trout can be caught in good numbers. Brown trout from this section of the Bow River will average 30-40 cm in length. The pool at the confluence of the Spray River with the Bow has lots of potential.

Bow River

Echo Creek ponds (NP)
Brook trout to 25 cm
Rainbow trout to 25 cm
The network of beaver ponds on Echo Creek that connect the Vermilion Lakes with the Bow River holds the promise of solitude due to difficult access and the guarantee of wet feet. Small brook and rainbow trout predominate, although bull trout are also present.

Whiskey Creek ponds (NP)
Brook trout to 25 cm
Rainbow trout to 25 cm
The maze of beaver ponds on Whiskey Creek is located between Banff townsite and the Trans-Canada Highway. Despite their proximity to the townsite, they see few anglers each season. The ponds hold small brook and rainbow trout.

Forty Mile Creek (NP) *(Mt. Norquay to Bow River)*
Brook trout to 25 cm
Cutthroat trout to 25 cm
Bull trout to 25 cm
Forty Mile Creek joins the Whiskey Creek pond complex north of Banff, after crossing under the Trans-Canada Highway just west of the Buffalo Paddock. Forty Mile Creek holds brook, cutthroat and bull trout, as well as the odd rainbow trout. Be aware that the creek is closed to angling in the vicinity of the Banff townsite water intake.

Sundance Creek ponds (NP)
Brook trout to 25 cm

This series of beaver dams extend for 3 km along Sundance Creek above its confluence with the Bow. The ponds are readily accessible from the Cave and Basin road. Small brook trout predominate, with cutthroat and rainbow present as well.

Spray River (NP) *(Spray Lakes Reservoir to Bow River)*
Brook trout to 50 cm (1.5 kg)
Brown trout to 45 cm
Rainbow trout to 50 cm (1.5 kg)
Cutthroat trout to 45 cm
Bull trout to 70 cm (5.0 kg)

The lower Spray River is a major tributary of the Bow River. It flows from the Spray Lakes Reservoir and joins the Bow just west of Banff. The river can be accessed for virtually its entire length from the Spray River Fire Road, which is closed to vehicular traffic. The Spray River offers good fishing for cutthroat trout in its upper reaches. In the lower section, closer to the Bow River, brook, rainbow and brown trout in the 25-35 cm range are the normal catch. Large bull trout are taken on occasion along all stretches of the river.

Carrot Creek (NP)
Brown trout to 25 cm
Bull trout to 30 cm
Rainbow trout to 25 cm

Carrot Creek joins the Bow River 3 km west of the Banff Park boundary. In its lower reaches, it holds bull, brown and rainbow trout in small sizes.

Cascade Sub-Region

The Cascade River, and its accompanying fire road, run directly through the heart of the Front Ranges of the Rockies. The southern end of the fire road meets the Lake Minnewanka Road approximately 1 km west of the lake itself, and 5 km east of the Trans-Canada Highway overpass. Although the upper Cascade Valley is very popular with outfitters, the area receives relatively few hikers each year because of the huge distances involved. Everyone entering the area should be aware that the Cascade Valley contains one of the highest concentrations of grizzly bears anywhere in the Rocky Mountains. All of the lakes in this Sub-Region require a significant hiking effort to be reached. The most popular of the lakes include Elk, Mystic and Sawback Lakes.

Cascade River (NP)
Cutthroat trout to 35 cm
Brook trout to 35 cm
Rainbow trout to 30 cm
Bull trout to 60 cm (2.5 kg)
Whitefish to 30 cm

The Cascade River flows for over 35 km from headwaters before emptying into Lake Minnewanka. The Cascade River has innumerable excellent pools, and offers good fishing along its entire length. Cutthroat and brook trout in the 20-30 cm range will be the normal catch. The Cascade Fire Road, which is closed to vehicular travel, parallels the river for much of the distance and offers direct access. The lower sections of the river receive some fishing pressure, while only outfitters and seasoned backpackers visit the headwaters area.

Cascade River

Stenton Pond (NP)
Brook trout to 20 cm

Stenton Pond is actually several small, shallow interconnected beaver ponds located alongside the Cascade Fire Road just over 2 km from the road's southern terminus on the Lake Minnewanka Road. The ponds hold small brook trout, few larger than 15 cm in length. Due to the shallow water, the fish are very wary, and an abundance of shoreline vegetation and deadfall make fly fishing a difficult, but interesting, proposition.

Stony Creek (NP)
Cutthroat trout to 20 cm
Bull trout to 25 cm

Stony Creek is a major tributary of the Cascade River, and enters the Cascade approximately 15 km upstream from Lake Minnewanka. Fast-flowing Stony Creek holds both cutthroat and bull trout in small sizes and numbers.

Stony Creek ponds (NP)
Brook trout to 25 cm

The Stony Creek ponds are located just over 2 km north of the bridge over Stony Creek on the Cascade Fire Road. Set in somewhat marshy surroundings between the fire road and the Cascade River, these beaver ponds hold a fair number of small brook trout. Reaching the ponds without getting wet will take some skill, as will casting to the easily spooked trout. Fly casting room is generally available except around the odd deadfall.

Cuthead Creek (NP)
Cutthroat trout to 20 cm
Bull trout to 25 cm

Cuthead Creek enters the Cascade River approximately 20 km upstream from Lake Minnewanka. The Cascade Fire Road follows the course of Cuthead Creek. The most fishable waters are in the lower reaches of Cuthead Creek, where it holds some small bull and cutthroat trout.

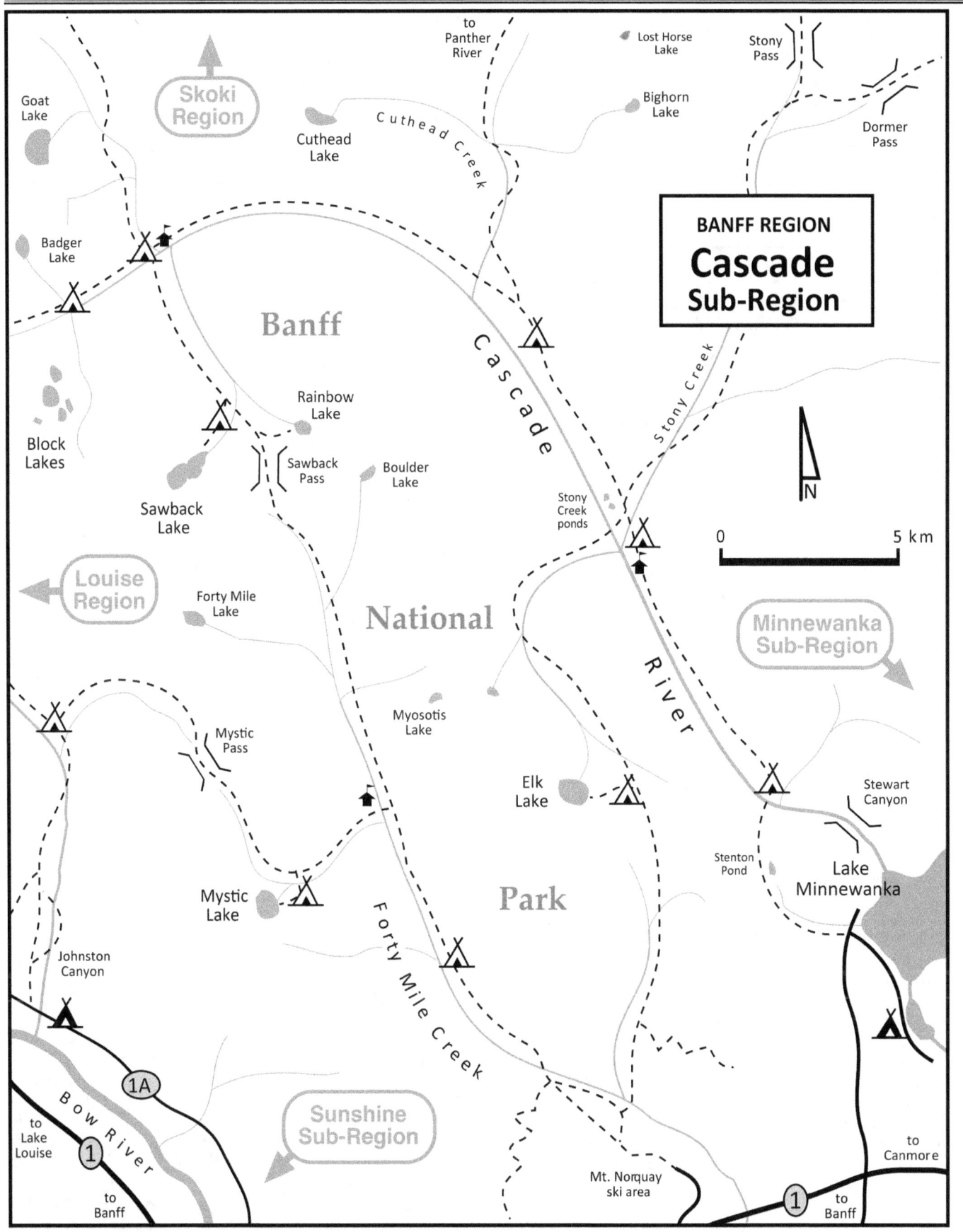

BANFF REGION: Cascade Sub-Region

Cuthead Lake (NP)
Cutthroat trout to 40 cm
Bull trout to 60 cm (2.5 kg)
Cuthead Lake lies in a secluded basin, far from civilization. The route to Cuthead Lake leaves the Cascade Fire Road 45 km north of Lake Minnewanka, and ascends the Cuthead Creek drainage. From the fire road, the 4 km route to Cuthead Lake alternates between bushwhacking and game trail. Cuthead Lake's silted waters hold cutthroat trout averaging 25-30 cm in length as well as a few bull trout. Sparsely treed meadows around the lake offer ample room for fly casting.

Cuthead Lake

Bighorn Lake (NP)
Brook trout to 30 cm
Bighorn Lake is located in a barren cirque, 4 km east of Cuthead Creek along an ill-defined trail. The route begins from the Cascade Fire Road, opposite Cuthead Lake valley. The trail winds its way through heavy timber, eventually emerging above tree line. The route then works its way steeply alongside Bighorn's tiny outlet creek, finally reaching the small basin holding the lake. The brook trout in Bighorn Lake are small, most in the 20-25 cm range.

Lost Horse Lake (NP)
Status: Devoid of fish
Lost Horse Lake is a small tarn located in the valley to the north of Bighorn Lake. Lost Horse Lake has never been stocked and contains no fish.

Goat Lake (NP)
Status: Devoid of fish
Goat Lake is located in a valley west of Cuthead Lake. Goat Lake has never been stocked and contains no fish.

Block Lakes (NP)
Cutthroat trout to 40 cm
The Block Lakes are located near the headwaters of the Cascade River, and are set in a basin gouged high into the side of Block Mountain. Guarded by a 150 m-high cliff face, the lakes are only accessible to skilled climbers who register with the warden service before attempting the climb. At one time, the Block Lakes were stocked with Quebec Red Trout, which flourished for a short period of time but failed to reproduce. At present, cutthroat trout averaging 25-35 cm in length populate the lakes.

Badger Lake (NP)
Brook trout to 30 cm
Three kilometres of bushwhacking in a northerly direction from the upper Cascade River/Block Lakes campsite leads to isolated Badger Lake. The final half kilometre into Badger's rockbound surroundings requires negotiating a 150 m cliff. Registration with the warden service is mandatory. Difficult and dangerous access, along with recent reports indicating that few trout remain in Badger Lake, will keep it off most anglers' "must-visit" list.

Sawback Lake (NP)
Cutthroat trout to 55 cm (2.0 kg)
Sawback Lake has been known for many years for its fine cutthroat trout fishery. Lengthy access trails protect Sawback Lake from over fishing. The lake is located almost 30 km from Mt. Norquay via Forty Mile Creek or 40 km from Lake Minnewanka via the Cascade Fire Road. Sawback Lake is most popular with outfitters, although determined hikers will be equally rewarded for their efforts. The lake is set in a beautiful basin just below Forty Mile Summit (Sawback Pass). The translucent green waters of Sawback Lake hold cutthroat trout averaging 25-35 cm in length, with larger ones taken quite regularly. The deeper waters off of the scree slopes on Sawback's south shore are usually productive.

Sawback Lake

Rainbow Lake (NP)
Rainbow trout to 50 cm (1.5 kg)
Rainbow Lake sits in a prominent bowl a little over a kilometre north and east of Forty Mile Summit. As its name suggests, the lake contains rainbow trout, which are plentiful and average 30-35 cm in length. Fly fishing is productive, and fly casting room is available around much of the shoreline, as the lake is situated in a pleasant basin amid open stands of larches.

Rainbow Lake (rainbow trout)

BANFF REGION: Cascade Sub-Region

Forty Mile Creek (NP) *(Headwaters to Mt. Norquay)*
Cutthroat trout to 25 cm
Brook trout to 25 cm
Bull trout to 30 cm

The upper sections of Forty Mile Creek flowing between Forty Mile Summit (Sawback Pass) and Mt. Norquay hold plenty of cutthroat trout in small sizes. Hiking trails parallel Forty Mile Creek for its entire length, and offer easy access to the numerous pools.

Forty Mile Creek

Boulder Lake (NP)
Status: Doubtful
Diminutive Boulder Lake sits in a desolate cirque at an elevation of nearly 2400 metres, and can be reached by following game trails along its outlet creek from the south side of Forty Mile Summit. The cutthroat trout once stocked in the lake either no longer exist, or are present in very small numbers.

Forty Mile Lake (NP)
Brook trout to 30 cm
Forty Mile Lake is nestled in a high sub-alpine valley west of the main Forty Mile Creek valley. The lake sees very few human visitors each year. The most direct access is via ill-defined and often non-existent game trails that work up the small outlet creek, which enters Forty Mile Creek approximately 3 km above the Mystic Pass trail junction. The lake itself contains a small population of brook trout, few larger than 25 cm in length.

Myosotis Lake (NP)
Status: Doubtful
Tiny Myosotis Lake is set in a barren cirque 2 km east of the upper Forty Mile Creek valley. The lake was stocked a number of years ago with rainbow trout and some may still exist, maintaining themselves through natural propagation. Access is for route finders armed with map and compass.

Mystic Lake (NP)
Cutthroat trout to 40 cm
Bull trout to 60 cm (2.5 kg)
Mystic Lake is located 17 km from Johnston Canyon and 19 km from Mt. Norquay, near the midway point on the Mystic Pass trail. The lake is set in a sheltered basin 3 km below Mystic Pass. Despite the lake's relatively remote location, numerous hikers and horse parties make their way to Mystic Lake each year. Anglers who reach these waters will find cutthroat averaging 25-35 cm in length as well as a few large bull trout. The area around the outlet creek is always productive.

Mystic Lake

Elk Lake (NP)
Cutthroat trout 45 cm
The impressive east face of Mt. Brewster towers over the pretty larch-filled basin containing Elk Lake. Elk Lake is located 14 km by trail from the Mt. Norquay parking area, and has been a favourite with Banff anglers for many years. Cutthroat trout are plentiful in the lake, and average 20-30 cm in length. Flies work very well in Elk Lake, and there is adequate fly casting room around the entire lake.

Elk Lake

Sunshine Sub-Region

The Sunshine Village ski area and its flower-filled meadows are the hub of the Sub-Region. Sunshine Village is accessed from the Bourgeau Parking lot by one of three methods. A gondola connects the parking area and the Village, but it has not been operational during the summer in recent years. If the gondola is not running, a bus service may be operating to take visitors up to Sunshine Village. If the gondola or busses are not operating, it is a steep 6 km road walk to reach Sunshine Village. Most day hikers make their way through the Sunshine Meadows to nearby Rock Isle, Larix and Grizzly Lakes, although return trips to Howard Douglas and Citadel Lakes are well within a day's limit for most hikers. Sunshine Village is also the trailhead for the Citadel Pass route to Mount Assiniboine, with the Lake Magog campground 27 km distant.

BANFF REGION: Sunshine Sub-Region

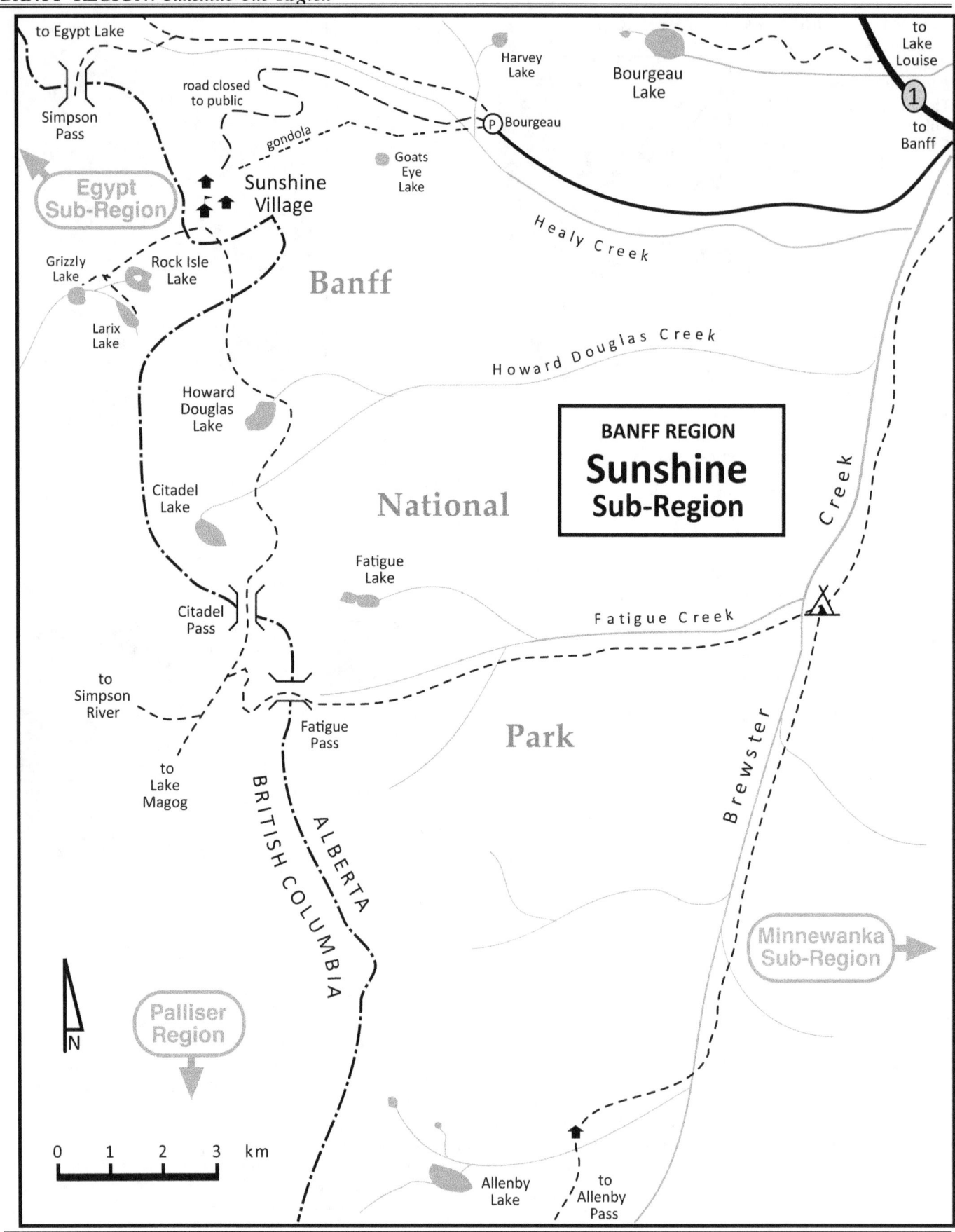

BANFF REGION: Sunshine Sub-Region

Bourgeau Lake (NP)
Brook trout to 45 cm

Bourgeau Lake is set in a deep, rocky amphitheatre just over 7 km by trail from the Trans-Canada Highway. In the past, numerous large trout were taken from Bourgeau Lake, and the lake became very popular with anglers, which inevitably led to a decline in the quality of fishing. Today, most brook trout will only average 20-30 cm in length and are in very limited supply. Flies and lures are both productive at Bourgeau Lake. Fly casting room is adequate along much of the shoreline, although rocks will take the point off the hook of many a disgruntled fly fisher.

Bourgeau Lake

Harvey Pond (NP)
Status: Devoid of fish

Harvey Pond is the tiny body of water set in a high pass above Bourgeau Lake. It can be reached by rough trails that lead up the steep valley from Bourgeau Lake. Harvey Lake contains no fish.

Goat's Eye Lake (NP)
Status: Devoid of fish

Goat's Eye Lake is a small tarn hidden high on the flank of Goat's Eye Peak. The lake was stocked in the past with rainbow trout, which failed to reproduce. A difficult scramble up the side of Goat's Eye Peak generally deters most hikers.

Rock Isle Lake (BC)
Status: Closed to angling

Picturesque Rock Isle Lake is located in the beautiful Sunshine Meadows, just over a kilometre from Sunshine Village. The lake is closed to angling due to its use as water supply for the Village.

Rock Isle Lake

Larix Lake (BC)
Status: Closed to angling

Larix Lake lies in a quiet, meadowed basin less than a kilometre below Rock Isle Lake. Larix Lake is closed to angling.

Grizzly Lake (BC)
Status: Closed to angling

Grizzly Lake is a small, round body of water that is reached by following the outlet stream of Larix Lake. Grizzly Lake is closed to angling.

Howard Douglas Lake (NP)
Brook trout to 45 cm

Howard Douglas Lake is located on the Citadel Pass trail, 6 km from Sunshine Village. The lake is often overlooked by anglers passing through on their way to the more renowned waters of Assiniboine. Howard Douglas Lake holds a fair number of brook trout, most ranging from 15-25 cm, although trout upwards of 40 cm are caught on occasion. The fish are equally distributed throughout the lake, and can be taken from virtually any location

Howard Douglas Lake

Citadel (Sunset) Lake (NP)
Rainbow trout to 45 cm

Citadel Lake lies less than half a kilometre south of the Citadel Pass trail and is hidden by a small knoll. Citadel Lake is seldom seen, much less visited by most hikers. The lake is set in a small basin with half its shoreline comprised of scree and half of meadow, the latter offering an abundance of fly casting spots. Uniquely marked rainbow trout in the lake average 30-35 cm in length, and are plentiful

Citadel Lake (rainbow trout)

BANFF REGION: Egypt Sub-Region

Brewster Creek (NP)
Bull trout to 30 cm
Cutthroat trout to 25 cm
Brewster Creek is paralleled by horse trails for its entire length, and possesses many kilometres of fishable waters. Small bull and cutthroat trout can be taken from most stretches, with brook and rainbow trout also taken occasionally in the lower reaches.

Fatigue Lake (NP)
Status: Devoid of fish
Fatigue Lake is set in an alpine basin beneath Fatigue Peak. The lake is reached by following ill-defined game trails up a tributary branching west off the Fatigue Pass trail. It is rarely visited due to its isolated location. Fatigue Lake was stocked with rainbow trout, but it is reported that they are no longer are found in the lake.

Allenby Lake (NP)
Rainbow trout to 35 cm
Allenby Lake is set in a hanging valley, 2 km west of the Brewster Creek-Allenby Pass trail to Mt. Assiniboine Provincial Park, and is overlooked by most hikers. Rumours persist that Allenby Lake holds good numbers of rainbow trout in the 20-30 cm range.

Egypt Sub-Region

Egypt Lake is located at the core of one of Banff National Park's most popular backpacking destinations. The Egypt Lake vicinity is crowded with hikers and anglers from mid-June through the end of September. The main access into this superb area begins at Sunshine Village's Bourgeau Parking Lot, and follows the 13 km trail over Healy Pass to Egypt Lake. Lakes within the immediate Egypt Lake complex include Egypt, Scarab, Mummy, Pharaoh, Black Rock and Sphinx. Shadow Lake, at the northern end of the Egypt Lake area, is accessed by a 14 km trail that begins at Redearth Parking Lot on the Trans-Canada Highway. This route also serves as an alternate but longer access into the Egypt Lake complex.

Egypt Lake (NP)
Brook trout to 40 cm
Cutthroat trout to 40 cm
Egypt Lake is located less than 1 km from the shelter and campground, and is the most heavily fished lake of the area. Its deep, clear waters hold a good number of brook and cutthroat, most in the 25-35 cm range. The deep waters off the rockslide along the north shore generally hold the larger trout. Brook trout are in the majority, but both cutthroat and brookies can be taken from most spots, particularly around the area of the inlet creek that falls from Scarab Lake. The outlet pond and the outlet stream usually hold a few trout that can be spotted from shore, but due to their shallow habitat, the fish are very wary. Flies work well, but fly casting room is at a premium, so roll casting will be the order of the day from many locations.

Egypt Lake

Scarab Lake (NP)
Cutthroat trout to 50 cm (1.5 kg)
Scarab Lake is situated in a large basin above Egypt Lake, and is reached by following the steep trail that winds its way up the cliff band above Egypt's northwest corner. Silt from snowmelt accounts for Scarab's striking blue-green colour. The lake does not hold a large number of cutthroat trout, but they will average 30-40 cm in length. Scarab Lake's location near the tree line ensures ample fly casting room. Due to the lake's high elevation and shaded position beneath Haiduk Peak, Scarab is often ice-covered well into July, and spawning often occurs in late July.

Mummy Lake (NP)
Cutthroat trout to 50 cm (1.5 kg)
Mummy Lake is accessible from nearby Scarab Lake on an ill-defined and rocky trail, or along a route that crosses the low gap northwest of Natalko Lake. Mummy Lake is long and narrow, and is set in a rocky, windswept valley located a few hundred metres above Scarab Lake. Its high elevation and absence of vegetation allow for fly casting around most of the shoreline. The lake is usually ice-covered until mid-July and spawning can occur as late as early August. The cutthroat trout in Mummy Lake are very limited in number, and average 30-35 cm in length.

Steve Fediow with Mummy Lake cutthroat trout

Mummy Lake

BANFF REGION: Egypt Sub-Region

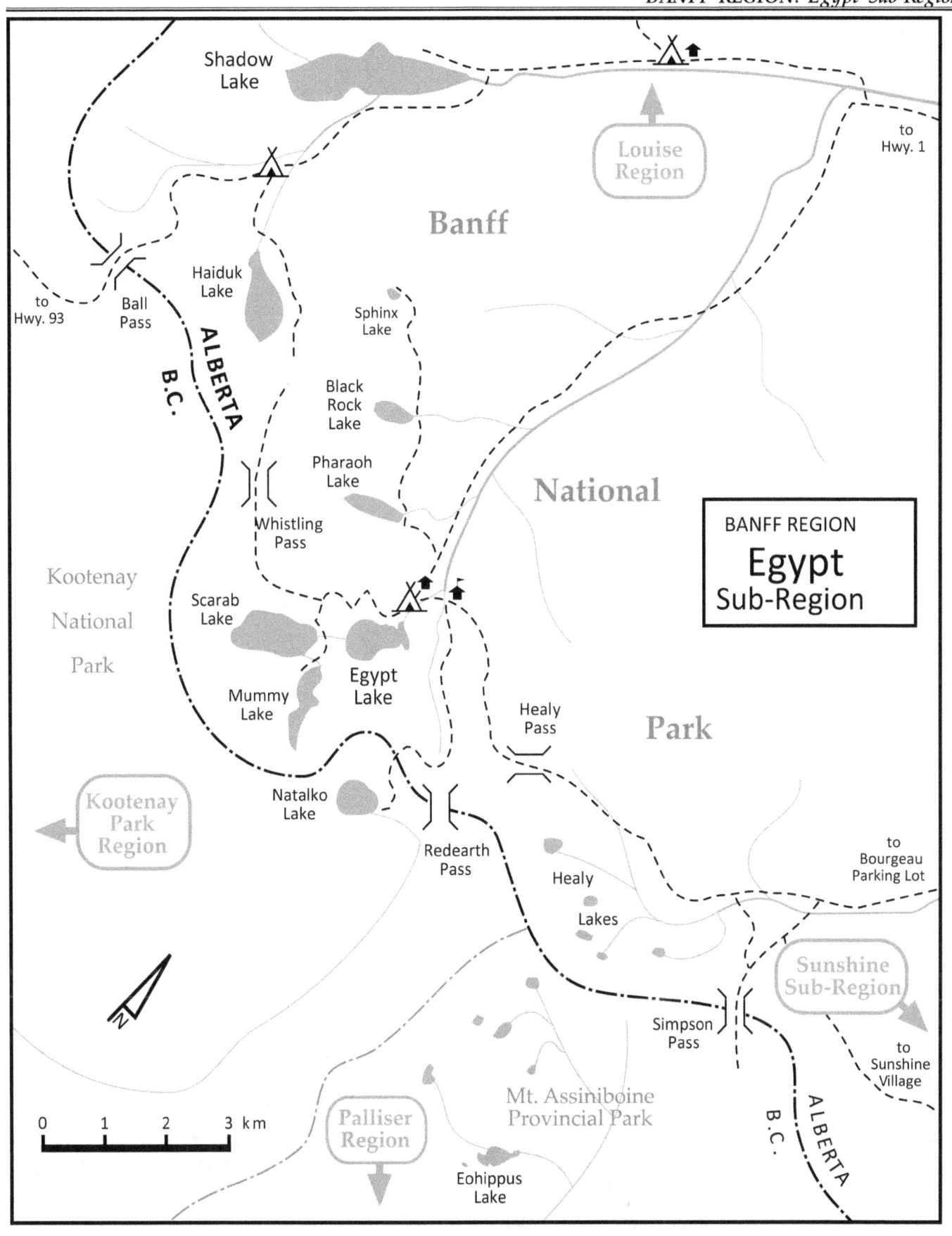

BANFF REGION: Egypt Sub-Region

Pharaoh Creek (NP)
Cutthroat trout to 30 cm
Brook trout to 25 cm
The upper waters of Pharaoh Creek hold a fair number of trout downstream of the Egypt Lake outlet. For several kilometres Pharaoh Creek winds its way back and forth across open meadows. Cutthroat trout in the 15-20 cm range are caught, as well as a few brook trout.

Pharaoh Lake (NP)
Cutthroat trout to 45 cm
Pharaoh, Black Rock and Sphinx Lakes are located in successive side valleys north of Egypt Lake. The trail winds its way up the flank of Pharaoh Peak for just over a kilometre to the notch containing the deep, dark waters of Pharaoh Lake. The lake is set beneath the sheer cliffs of the Pharaoh Peaks. Scree slopes make up much of the shoreline, but there are a few spots that will permit a reasonable back cast for fly fishing. Cutthroat trout in the 30-35 cm range are present in limited numbers.

Pharaoh Lake

Black Rock Lake (NP)
Cutthroat trout to 35 cm
Black Rock Lake lies one kilometre beyond Pharaoh Lake, and is set in a very similar basin as its neighbour. Black Rock Lake is named for the dark cliffs above the western end of the lake. It holds good numbers of cutthroat trout averaging 20-25 cm in length. Trout can be seen well out into the lake due to the clarity of the water. Fly casting room is adequate along much of the shoreline. A few large boulders in the shallows along the north shore may tempt a few anglers to wade out in search of a better casting position.

Black Rock Lake (cutthroat trout)

Sphinx Lake (NP)
Status: Devoid of fish
Tiny Sphinx Lake is situated in a small basin 2 km beyond Black Rock Lake. Sphinx Lake at one time had a breeding population of cutthroat trout, but recent examination tends to indicate that no trout presently exist. A very poor and ill-defined trail leads past Black Rock Lake for those hardy souls wishing to check the lake out for themselves.

Natalko (Talc) Lake (NP)
Brook trout to 35 cm
Natalko Lake is reached by following a 4 km trail south from the Egypt Lake campground. The lake itself is situated just within the boundary of Kootenay National Park. Natalko's waters are incredibly clear, even for a mountain lake, and as a result fish are easily spooked. Meadows form much of the shoreline, which allows plenty of room for fly casting. The scree slopes on the far side of the lake will test roll casting abilities of fly fishers. Although the lake holds plenty of brook trout averaging 25-30 cm, the wariness of the fish will surely test most anglers' patience.

Natalko Lake

Healy Lakes (includes Square Lake) (NP)
Cutthroat trout to 20 cm
This series of interconnected ponds and small lakes are set in the beautiful meadows beneath the Monarch Ramparts southwest of Healy Pass. Access is by trail from the Bourgeau Parking lot. The Healy Lakes contain small cutthroat trout. The size and number of trout varies with each lake, but few fish are larger than 15 cm in length. The marshy nature of the shoreline around most of the lakes will result in wet feet for most anglers.

Upper Healy Lake

Eohippus Lake (BC)
Rainbow trout to 50 cm

Eohippus Lake is a seldom-visited body of water, nestled beneath the prominent east face of The Monarch. The most straightforward access involves hiking the crest of the Ramparts south from Healy Pass and dropping down to the lake from above. However, be aware that lingering snow packs and dangerous cornices on the Ramparts prevent the use of this route until mid-summer. The lake is named for its outline's striking resemblance to a prehistoric species of horse. Rainbow trout are present in good numbers, and average 30-35 cm in length. Flies work well, and open meadows surround the lake, providing ample room for back casting.

Eohippus Lake

Haiduk Lake
Cutthroat trout to 55 cm (1.5 kg)

Secluded Haiduk Lake is situated 4 km northwest of Scarab Lake through Whistling Pass. It is also accessible by trail from Shadow Lake and Ball Pass. Haiduk Lake contains some fine cutthroat trout, with average fish being in the 30-40 cm range. Fishing is best along the scree slopes on the western side of the lake. The areas around the inlet creeks are also productive. Haiduk Lake is shaded much of the day by the high wall to the west, and remains frozen into early July and access trails are snowbound.

Haiduk Lake

(cutthroat trout)

Shadow Lake (NP)
Cutthroat trout to 45 cm
Brook trout to 40 cm
Rainbow trout to 40 cm

Shadow Lake is strikingly beautiful body of water, set in a forested valley beneath the east face of Mt. Ball. Shadow Lake is reached via the 14 km trail from Redearth Creek trailhead on the Trans-Canada Highway. Although it is the largest of the lakes in the Egypt/Sunshine complex, and in turn holds some good-sized trout, Shadow Lake has never gained a reputation for outstanding fishing. Trout in the lake will average 25-35 cm in length. Cutthroat and brook trout are caught with more regularity than rainbow, the areas around inlet creeks being some of the better waters. The outlet bay also holds fish, particularly during the low light periods of early morning and late evening when fish enter the shallower waters to feed.

Shadow Lake and Mount Ball

Redearth Creek (NP)
Cutthroat trout to 20 cm
Brook trout to 20 cm

Redearth Creek flows from Shadow Lake to the Bow River. It holds both cutthroat and brook trout, although small in size and limited in number. Best fishing opportunities exist in the few kilometres of slow water below Shadow Lake, and in the last half kilometre before Redearth Creek flows into the Bow River.

Redearth Creek

LOUISE REGION: Castle Junction Sub-Region

LOUISE REGION

This Region encompasses the heart of Banff National Park. Primary access is on the Trans-Canada Highway. The small village at Lake Louise provides limited tourist services. The majority of this Region is backcountry, and hiking is required to reach most of the fishable waters. Three Sub-Regions make up the Louise region. To the south is Castle Junction, which is highlighted by Taylor, Arnica and Twin Lakes. North of Castle Junction is the Temple Sub-Region, which is centred on Lake Louise and Moraine Lake. To the north of Lake Louise is the Hector Sub-Region, which includes Hector and Bow Lakes.

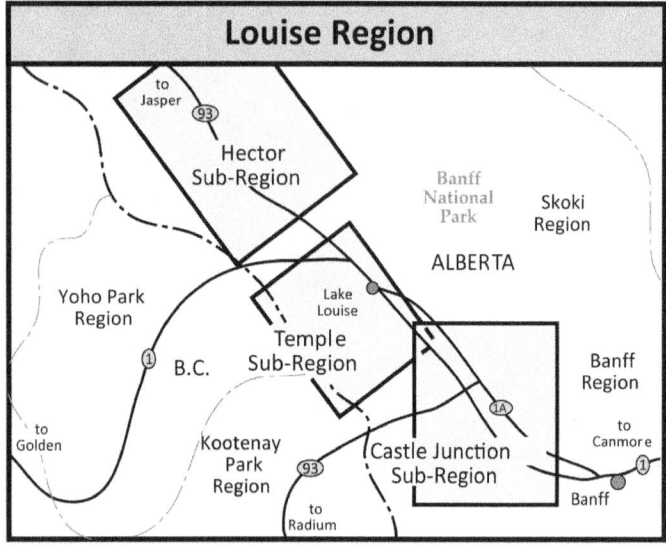

Taylor Lake

Castle Junction Sub-Region

The Castle Junction Sub-Region is centered on the impressive form of Castle Mountain and the junction of Highway 93 with the Trans-Canada Highway. This area has many popular fishing spots within easy hiking distance of major highways. Altrude, Vista, Boom, Arnica and Twin Lakes can all be reached by trails originating from Highway 93 (Banff-Windermere Highway). The Taylor Lake trail is accessed from the Trans-Canada Highway, and Rockbound and Tower Lakes have their trailheads on the Bow Valley Parkway. Luellen Lake is the only major backpacking destination in the Castle Junction Sub-Region, and its trail begins at Johnston Canyon.

Taylor Lake (NP)
Cutthroat trout to 50 cm (1.5 kg)
Beautifully coloured Taylor Lake is nestled in a high side valley 6 km by trail from the Trans-Canada Highway. Taylor Lake is a popular destination for day hikers throughout the summer months. Its icy waters hold cutthroat trout that generally range from 25-35 cm in length. The area around the outlet is the most popular with anglers. For those willing to make the effort, the waters off the scree slopes on the south side of the lake are usually productive.

O'Brien (Larch) Lake (NP)
Cutthroat trout to 50 cm (1.5 kg)
O'Brien Lake is located only 2 km by trail from the outlet of Taylor Lake, but is overlooked by most hikers visiting the area. O'Brien Lake holds feisty cutthroat trout in good numbers that average 30-40 cm in length. Great fishing and pleasant surroundings make O'Brien one of the gems of the entire Sub-Region. Flies work well at O'Brien, and sparse forest cover around much of the lake allows plenty of room for fly casting. Fish can be taken from most spots around the lake, although larger ones seem to prefer the deeper water off the scree slopes along the west shore. Much of the shoreline in the vicinity of the outlet creek is marshy, causing most people to avoid the area.

O'Brien Lake

(cutthroat trout)

Boom Lake (NP)
Cutthroat trout to 50 cm (1.5 kg)
Boom Lake is a large body of water set beneath the impressive cliffs of Boom Mountain. The lake is reached on a 5 km hiking trail from Highway 93. Boom Lake holds cutthroat trout averaging 25-35 cm in length. Patient anglers willing to work the shoreline are usually rewarded with fish. During low light

LOUISE REGION: Castle Junction Sub-Region

periods trout can often be seen feeding among the logs in the shallow waters around the outlet. Boom Creek, which flows from Boom Lake to Highway 93 contains a limited number of small cutthroat trout.

Boom Lake

Altrude Lakes (NP)
Cutthroat trout to 35 cm

The Altrude Lakes are passed daily by hundreds of vehicles on nearby Highway 93. However, very few visitors stop and make the short hike down to the lakes. The upper lake, which is visible from the highway, holds a dwindling population of cutthroat trout, with recent reports indicating that few or none remain. The lower lake, located a few hundred metres off the highway, offers relatively poor fishing for cutthroat trout averaging 20-30 cm in length. The best potential is in the area along the distinctive drop-off zone.

Vista Lake (NP)
Brook trout to 40 cm
Cutthroat trout to 40 cm

Vista Lake sits at the bottom of a deep valley south of Highway 93. It is reached by a short, steep 1.5 km trail. Brook trout are the dominant species in the lake, although cutthroat are present as well. Looking down at the lake from the trailhead at the highway, you will notice Vista's two-toned colouration. Those anglers who make the trek down to the lake's shore are advised to fish the zone along the obvious drop-off. Flies work well in Vista Lake. Fly casting room is limited, although lengthy casts are not required in the vicinity of the outlet creek, where extensive submerged deadfall offers cover for trout.

Vista Lake

Altrude Creek (NP)
Brook trout to 25 cm
Cutthroat trout to 25 cm
Bull trout to 35 cm

Altrude Creek, which flows from the Altrude Lakes through Vista Lake before entering the Bow River, contains brook, cutthroat and bull trout in small sizes. Fish can be taken along the entire course of the creek. The best potential is in the lower reaches, near the confluence with the Bow River.

Arnica Lake (NP)
Cutthroat trout to 50 cm (1.5 kg)

Arnica Lake is set beneath the ominous cliffs of Storm Mountain's north shoulder. It is reached by a 5 km trail from Highway 93. Anglers heading for nearby Twin Lakes often overlook tiny Arnica Lake. Despite its size, some fine cutthroat trout inhabit Arnica's blue waters. Most trout taken will average 30-35 cm in length. Fly casting is a problem around much of the shoreline because of trees. Arnica Lake is usually frozen into early July because of its sheltered location.

Arnica Lake

(cutthroat trout)

Twin Lakes (NP)
Cutthroat trout to 40 cm

The striking east face of Storm Mountain rises above Twin Lakes, and keeps the area in shadow much of the time. As a result, the lakes thaw late and area trails are usually snowbound well into July. Access is via two 8 km-long hiking trails: one beginning at the Vista Lake trailhead on Highway 93; and the other from the Altrude Creek picnic site near Castle Junction. Both lakes contain cutthroat trout in good numbers averaging 20-30 cm in length. The Lower (south) Lake holds better potential for fly fishers as it offers more backcasting room along its shoreline than its elevated counterpart.

Lower Twin Lake

Upper Twin Lake

LOUISE REGION: Castle Junction Sub-Region

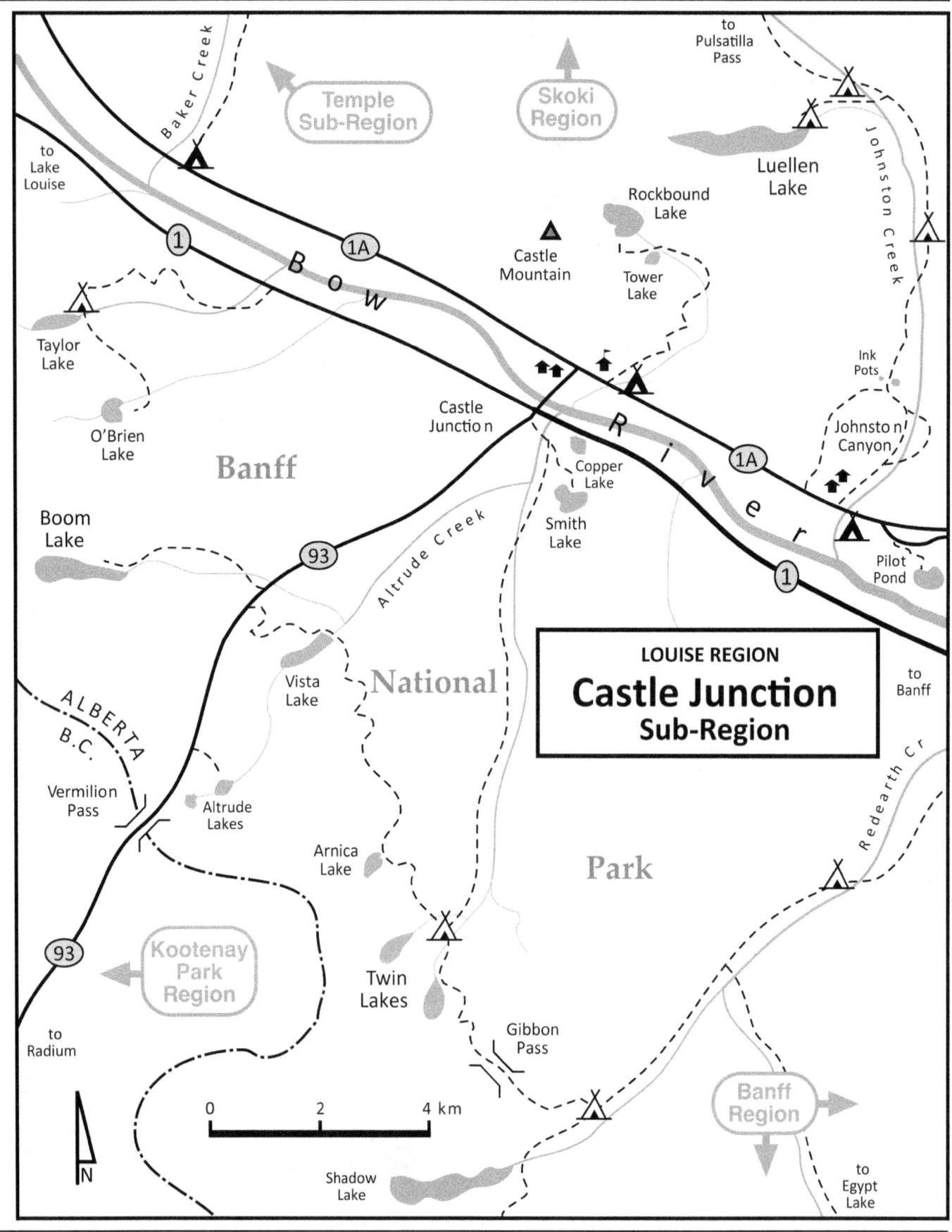

LOUISE REGION: Castle Junction Sub-Region

Copper Lake (NP)
Rainbow trout to 40 cm
Copper Lake is a small lake set in a sink hole less than a hundred metres from the busy Trans-Canada Highway. Despite its proximity to the highway, Copper Lake does not see much angling activity each year. A short trail leads from the Altrude picnic area to Copper Lake. Rainbow trout averaging 20-25 cm in length likely are still present in the lake in very limited numbers. Although casting conditions are not ideal because of the vegetation and the sloped terrain near the shoreline, Copper's trout usually feed fairly close to shore, and tend to be very willing to strike at a fly.

Copper Lake

Smith Lake (NP)
Cutthroat trout to 45 cm
Brook trout to 55 cm (2.0 kg)
Tranquil Smith Lake is located less than 2 km by trail from the Altrude Creek picnic site. Smith Lake sits amid forested surroundings which will be a source of consternation for most fly fishers, as heavy tree cover makes its way down to the water's edge around much of the lake. The marshy nature of the lakeshore presents an additional barrier when trying to cast to the fish-holding waters. . Brook trout in large sizes were once prominent in Smith Lake, but now cutthroat trout seem to be in the majority, and most fish average 20-30 cm in length.

Smith Lake

Tower Lake (NP)
Cutthroat trout to 30 cm
Tower Lake is located 8 km by steep trail from the Eisenhower Warden Station on the Bow Valley Parkway. It lies hidden behind the massive turrets of Castle Mountain. Tower Lake holds a very small population of cutthroat trout. Trout caught will average 20-25 cm in length. Although the trout can generally be seen from shore, they will be wary because of shallow waters, and will be spooked by most casts. The terrain is favourable for fly casting, and the best tactic here is to cast a fly well ahead of the fish as they cruise the shoreline for food.

Tower Lake

Rockbound Lake (NP)
Brook trout to 55 cm (1.5 kg)
Cutthroat trout to 40 cm
Rockbound Lake sits in a rugged amphitheatre, less than 1 km above Tower Lake. Brook trout far outnumber cutthroat trout, with most fish taken averaging 25-35 cm in length. Fish can be seen from many locations along the shore in Rockbound's crystal clear waters. Flies work well, and there is plenty of back casting room available.

Rockbound Lake

Luellen Lake (NP)
Cutthroat trout to 55 cm (2.0 kg)
Luellen Lake is set in a long narrow valley, 18 km by trail from the Bow Valley Parkway at Johnston Canyon. It has been popular with backcountry fishermen for many years, on account of its plentiful supply of good-sized cutthroat. Most fish taken from the lake will average 30-40 cm in length. The lake is ringed by forest, so roll casting will be the order of the day for those that fly fish. Anglers working up either the north or south side of the lake can generally sight schools of fish from shore. Due to less fishing pressure, the far end of the lake offers better prospects.

LOUISE REGION: Castle Junction Sub-Region

Luellen Lake

Johnston Creek (NP)
Cutthroat trout to 20 cm
Bull trout to 30 cm

Small cutthroat trout are plentiful in the upper Johnston Creek, above Johnston Canyon. The many fine pools are easily reached from the Luellen Lake/Pulsatilla Pass trail, which parallels Johnston Creek for its entire length. In the lower reaches of the creek, between Johnston Canyon and the Bow River, bull trout predominate.

Johnston Creek

Ink Pots (NP)
Status: Devoid of fish

The miniscule Ink Pots are a series of tiny, spring fed pools that are found above Johnston Canyon, and are accessed by a popular hiking trail. The Ink Pots contain no fish.

Pilot Pond (Lizard Lake) (NP)
Rainbow trout to 50 cm (1.5 kg)
Brook trout to 45 cm

Pilot Pond sits in a quiet forest-encircled basin half a kilometre below the Bow Valley Parkway. The trailhead for Pilot Pond is at the viewpoint on the eastbound one-way section of the Bow Valley Parkway. Pilot Pond's clear waters at one time held plenty of rainbow and brook trout averaging 30-40 cm in length. Recent reports indicate a significant decline in fish numbers. A distinctive drop-off is visible and any fish in the lake will keep to the deeper waters most of the day, venturing into the shallows to feed during low light periods.

Bow River (NP) *(Baker Creek to Redearth Creek)*
Cutthroat trout to 40 cm
Brook trout to 40 cm
Rainbow trout to 40 cm
Bull trout to 70 cm (5.0 kg)
Whitefish to 35 cm

The section of the Bow River flowing between Baker Creek and Redearth Creek holds many kilometres of fishable waters with its numerous deep pools. Cutthroat trout are usually taken in greater numbers by fly fishers than other species, although brook, rainbow and bull trout and whitefish are also present. At first glance, this section of the river looks like it has enormous angling potential, but it does not match the quality of the Bow River downstream from Canmore.

Temple Sub-Region

Fishing amid some of the most exquisite settings anywhere in the mountain world will tend to distract many anglers. Although more renowned for its scenery than for its fishing, this Sub-Region does possess a few good fishing spots. The Trans-Canada Highway, heading west to Field and southeast to Banff, is the area's main thoroughfare. As for fishing, the ever popular Bow River can be reached from many locations along both highways. Despite the relatively poor angling offered by the twin jewels of Lake Louise and Moraine Lake, anglers are attracted to their shores each summer.

Lake Louise (NP)
Whitefish to 35 cm
Bull trout to 60 cm (2.5 kg)

With Mts. Victoria and Lefroy providing a dazzling backdrop, Lake Louise's brilliant emerald coloured waters have gained a world-wide reputation for scenic excellence. Unfortunately, Lake Louise's fishing is worthy of little acclaim. Whitefish in the 20-30 cm range, and the occasional bull trout, are all that are taken from Louise. Stocked in the past with splake, rainbow, cutthroat, and brook trout, it is possible, although unlikely, that very limited numbers of some of these species still exist. Canoes are available for rent at the lake during the summer.

Lake Louise

Mirror Lake (NP)
Status: Devoid of fish

This small lake along the trail from Lake Louise to Lake Agnes contains no fish and has never been stocked.

LOUISE REGION: Temple Sub-Region

Lake Agnes (NP)
Status: Closed to angling
Lake Agnes is nestled in a hanging valley behind the Beehives. It serves as the water supply for the Chateau Lake Louise, and is therefore closed to angling. The fish you see swimming in the lake are either brook trout or hybridized splake.

Minewakun Lake (NP)
Status: Devoid of fish
Tiny Minewakun Lake sits in a secluded basin beneath the north face of Mt. St. Piran, 2 km northwest of Lake Louise. The reproductive success of brook trout stocked in the lake was poor. There are no access trails, and few visitors make their way into Minewakun.

Moraine Lake (NP)
Bull trout to 70 cm (4.0 kg)
Cutthroat trout to 55 cm (2.0 kg)
Moraine was widely recognized for many years as "the lake on the back of the Canadian twenty dollar bill". Today, it is one of the main tourist attractions in the Region, rivaled only by Lake Louise itself. Fishing is very slow in Moraine Lake. There are small numbers of cutthroat in the 30-40 cm range, and the occasional bull trout of 50 cm or more in Moraine Lake's appealing turquoise waters. Canoes are available for rent at the lake during summer months.

Moraine Lake

Consolation Lakes (NP)
Brook trout to 40 cm
Cutthroat trout to 40 cm [Lower Lake only]
The beautiful Consolation Lakes are located 3 km by trail from the Moraine Lake parking lot. The lakes are set in a secluded subalpine valley beneath Mt. Babel. Both lakes contain brook trout averaging 20-30 cm in length, the lower lake also holding a few cutthroat trout in the same size range. Flies work well, and there is ample fly casting room available from scree slopes which make up much of the shoreline. The large boulders at the lower lake's outlet provide good casting platforms. Fish are also found in the outlet creek in good numbers.

Lower Consolation Lake

Eiffel Lake (NP)
Status: Devoid of fish
Eiffel Lake sits in the middle of barren Desolation Valley, and is 6 km by trail from the Moraine parking area. Eiffel Lake has never been stocked and contains no fish.

Eiffel Lake

Minnestimma Lakes (NP)
Status: Devoid of fish
This series of shallow tarns in Larch Valley have never been stocked and are devoid of fish.

Moraine Creek (NP)
Brook trout to 25 cm
Cutthroat trout to 25 cm
Bull trout to 30 cm
The outlet for Moraine Lake contains brook and cutthroat trout that are most plentiful in the vicinity of the confluence with Babel Creek. On the lower part of Moraine Creek, within a kilometre of the Bow River, limited numbers of small brook and cutthroat as well as bull trout can be taken.

Temple Lake (NP)
Brook trout to 25 cm
Diminutive Temple Lake is located on the eastern flank of magnificent Mt. Temple. It is reached by following a rough trail on the banks of its outlet stream, but is seldom visited by hikers or anglers. The lake was stocked in the past with both rainbow and brook trout, and small brook trout in the 15-20 cm range are still present in Temple Lake. Partial winter kill is annually a problem at Temple Lake.

LOUISE REGION: Temple Sub-Region

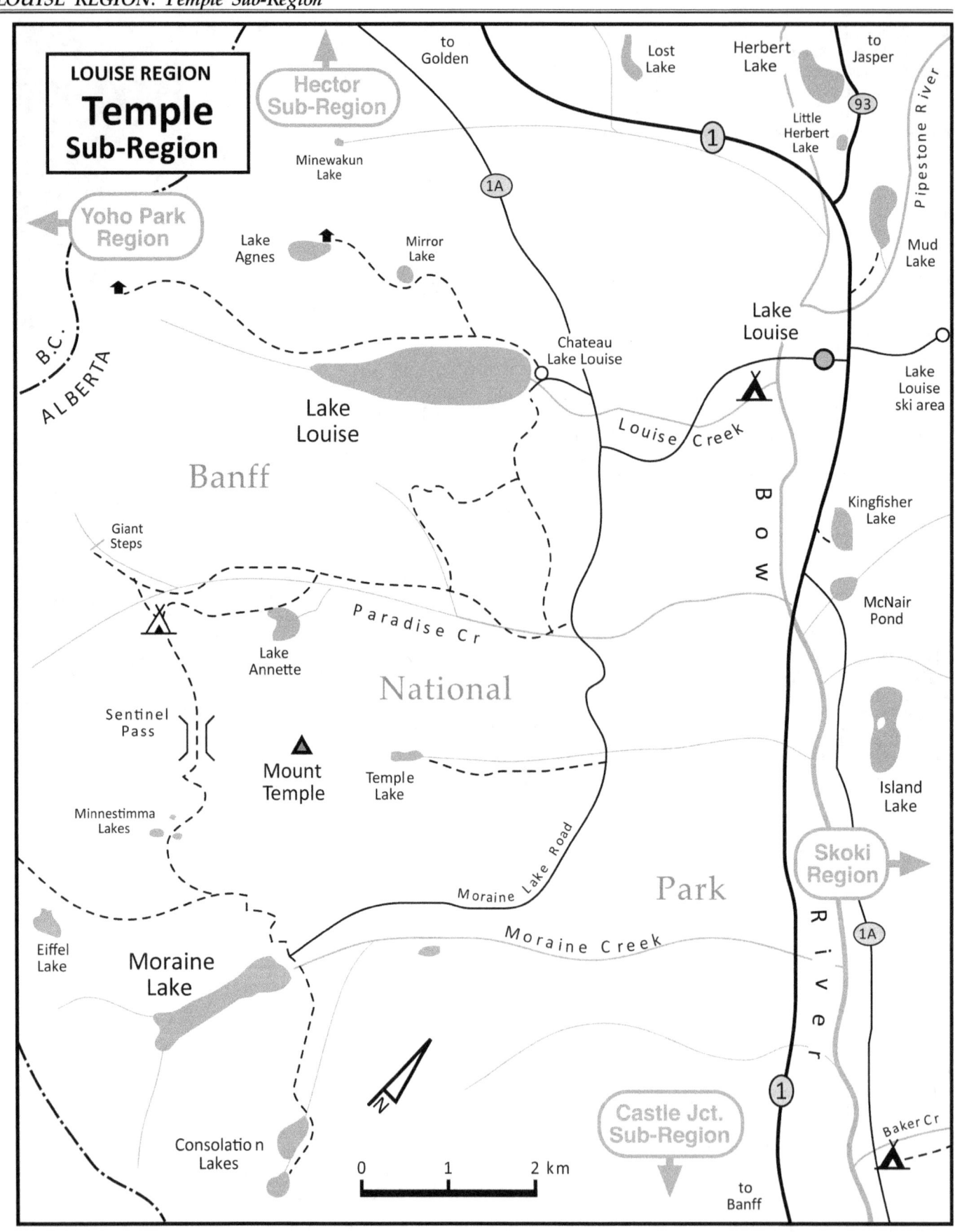

176

LOUISE REGION: Temple Sub-Region

Temple Lake

Lake Annette (NP)
Cutthroat trout to 35 cm
Rainbow trout to 35 cm

Lake Annette sits directly below the foreboding north face of Mt. Temple, in the heart of Paradise Valley. Its deep, dark waters hold a very limited number of cutthroat and rainbow trout in the 20-30 cm range. Heavy brush around much of the shoreline inhibits fly casting, although there are a few tolerable locations.

Annette Lake

Paradise Creek (NP)
Cutthroat trout to 25 cm
Bull trout to 25 cm

Paradise Creek flows through the entire length of Paradise Valley. It contains small cutthroat in the middle section, between the Giant Steps and the Moraine Lake Road. It holds small cutthroat and bull trout in the lower reaches, near its confluence with the Bow River.

Bow River (NP) *(Pipestone River to Baker Creek)*
Cutthroat trout to 40 cm
Brook trout to 40 cm
Rainbow trout to 40 cm
Bull trout to 70 cm (4.0 kg)
Whitefish to 35 cm

This section of the Bow River is accessible from both the Trans-Canada and the Bow Valley Parkway. The river contains some really fine looking stretches of fishable water, although numbers of trout are not high. Cutthroat and brook trout predominate in this section of the Bow River, although a variety of fish are present

Island Lake (NP)
Status: Doubtful

Shallow Island Lake is located just east of the Bow Valley Parkway. Island Lake has been stocked in the past with a variety of trout, none of which have been able to take hold. Most reports indicate that Island Lake is devoid of fish.

McNair Pond (NP)
Cutthroat trout to 30 cm
Rainbow trout to 30 cm
Brook trout to 30 cm

McNair Pond is situated alongside the Bow Valley Parkway just east of the Trans-Canada/Parkway junction. The pond was formed during highway construction that resulted in the damming of a small creek. Much of McNair Pond's shoreline consists of dead trees that allow for very little fly casting room. Cutthroat and rainbow from 15-25 cm in length are present, with the occasional brook trout taken as well.

McNair Pond

Kingfisher Lake (NP)
Rainbow trout to 40 cm
Brook trout to 35 cm

Kingfisher Lake is reached by a short 300 m trail from the Trans-Canada Highway. Rainbow trout averaging 20-30 cm in length are caught in greater number than brook trout in Kingfisher Lake. A wide margin of shallow water along with heavy forest cover around the shore makes Kingfisher unpopular with most fly fishing enthusiasts. However, casting distance is significantly reduced during low light conditions when trout enter the shallower waters to feed.

Kingfisher Lake

Mud Lake (NP)
Status: Devoid of fish

Mud Lake is located west of the Trans-Canada Highway in the Pipestone River drainage, and sits amid forested surroundings. Mud Lake was stocked in the past with brook, cutthroat and rainbow trout, but their existence was dependent upon regular plantings. No fish are present in Mud Lake today.

LOUISE REGION: Temple Sub-Region

Pipestone River (NP)
Cutthroat trout to 35 cm
Bull trout to 50 cm (1.5 kg)

The Pipestone River flows southwest from its headwaters, in alpine meadows below Pipestone Pass, to Lake Louise where it joins the Bow River. It holds small cutthroat and the occasional bull trout over its entire length.

Jackie Brice on the Pipestone River

Herbert Lake (NP)
Brook trout to 50 cm (1.5 kg)

Herbert Lake is a popular roadside picnic spot along the Icefields Parkway. Herbert Lake's crystal clear waters hold brook trout averaging 30-40 cm in length. Remnants of cutthroat and rainbow populations from previous plantings may also be present, although unlikely. Fishing from shore requires long casts to reach deeper water where the fish hold for most of the day due to water clarity. Working around to the side of the lake opposite the highway offers slightly better access to deeper waters. Fishing from a canoe is the best plan.

Little Herbert Lake (NP)
Rainbow trout to 30 cm

Little Herbert Lake is little more than a roadside pond, located less than a kilometre south of Herbert Lake on the western side of the Icefields Parkway. Little Herbert Lake contains a limited population of small rainbow trout. Because long casts are not required, Little Herbert is a favourite of novice anglers. A boggy shoreline will likely cause wet feet.

Little Herbert Lake

Lost Lake (NP)
Status: Devoid of fish

Lost Lake is a seldom-visited body of water located on the north side of the Trans-Canada Highway, 2 km east of Kicking Horse Pass. It is a very shallow lake completely encircled by forest. Lost Lake has been stocked in the past with cutthroat and brook trout, both of which have failed to reproduce. As it has not been stocked in recent years, there are no fish in the lake.

Hector Sub-Region

There are some excellent backcountry fishing opportunities in this area, which is characterized by glaciers and rugged mountains. The Icefields Parkway runs through the middle of the Sub-Region, paralleling the Bow River, and passing close to popular Bow Lake. Farther south, a short spur trail leads from the Icefields Parkway down to Hector Lake. The Fish Lakes area, which includes nearby Moose and Pipestone Lakes, is a favourite of backpackers. Another area popular with hikers is Dolomite Pass, which contains Helen, Katherine and Dolomite Lakes.

Bow Lake (NP)
Lake trout to 75 cm (5.0 kg)
Bull trout to 75 cm (5.0 kg)
Cutthroat trout to 50 cm (1.5 kg)
Whitefish to 40 cm

Bow Lake has been a long-time favourite of anglers due to its roadside location, and has consequently suffered a decline in the quality of fishing over the years. However, large lake and bull trout are still present in good numbers and patient anglers are usually rewarded with fish averaging 35-45 cm in length. Trolling is the standard angling method at Bow Lake. Areas around inlet creeks usually produce well as do the "narrows" where Bow Lake tapers down to Bow River width. Num-ti-jah Lodge, its bright red roof visible from the highway, provides lakeside accommodations and canoe rentals.

Bow Lake

Mary Lake (NP)
Brook trout to 30 cm

Mary Lake is a small tarn hidden behind Crowfoot Mountain. It is 5 km distant from Bow Lake, and remains a mystery to most anglers due to its isolated location. Mary Lake has been stocked in the past with both cutthroat and brook trout, and only small brook trout are present today. Expect a tough hike and small brook trout in the 20-25 cm range.

Mary Lake

LOUISE REGION: Hector Sub-Region

Bow River (NP) *(Headwaters to Pipestone River)*
Cutthroat trout to 40 cm
Brook trout to 40 cm
Bull trout to 70 cm (4.0 kg)
Whitefish to 35 cm

The section of the Bow River flowing between Bow Lake and Pipestone River offers mediocre fishing at best. As the water clears and levels begin to drop in late summer, cutthroat and brook trout in the 20-30 cm range can be taken. Although this stretch of the Bow possesses an abundance of fine pools, the fish population is less numerous than farther downstream and many anglers will be disappointed after working likely looking waters without positive results.

Bow River

Hector Lake (NP)
Lake trout to 75 cm (5.0 kg)
Bull trout to 75 cm (5.0 kg)
Cutthroat trout to 50 cm (1.5 kg)
Brook trout to 50 cm (1.5 kg)
Whitefish to 40 cm

Although it is only 2 km by trail from the Icefields Parkway, and noted for its splendid setting, Hector Lake receives little or no pressure from anglers each summer. The trail to Hector Lake includes a ford of the Bow River. Hector Lake is a large lake by mountain standards, and is an imposing sight to shore bound anglers. Its silted waters hold a variety of fish, including large lake and bull trout. Areas around major inlet creeks and the lake's outlet hold the most potential for anglers.

Hector Lake

Margaret Lake (NP)
Brook trout to 50 cm (1.5 kg)
Cutthroat trout to 40 cm

Margaret Lake lies hidden in a quiet side valley south of Hector Lake. Access is difficult including two fords of the Bow River and a tedious hike along the south shore of Hector Lake, and it tends to keep the number of anglers to a minimum each season. The lake's clear waters hold plenty of brook trout in the 25-35 cm range, and a few cutthroat trout may be present as well.

Margaret Lake

Turquoise Lake (NP)
Splake to 40 cm

The beautifully coloured waters of Turquoise Lake are set in a rocky basin guarded by high cliffs, and are seldom seen by anglers. Intrepid individuals attempting to reach Turquoise from Margaret Lake are required to register out with the warden service, due to the exposed and dangerous nature of the climb. The lake was stocked in the past with splake, and they are apparently still present in good numbers, averaging 20-30 cm in length.

Mosquito Pond (NP)
Status: Devoid of fish

This small pond is located below North Molar Pass on the Fish Lakes trail. It generally serves as a watering hole for thirsty hikers. Mosquito Pond was stocked in the past with rainbow trout, which failed to reproduce.

Mosquito Pond

Fish Lakes (NP)
Status: Closed to angling

The two Fish Lakes (Upper and Lower) are located 15 km by trail from the Icefields Parkway, and are set in a pleasant subalpine valley below North Molar Pass. The area is very popular with backpackers, who crowd the Fish Lakes campsite during summer months. Cutthroat trout inhabit both lakes.

Upper Fish Lake

LOUISE REGION: Hector Sub-Region

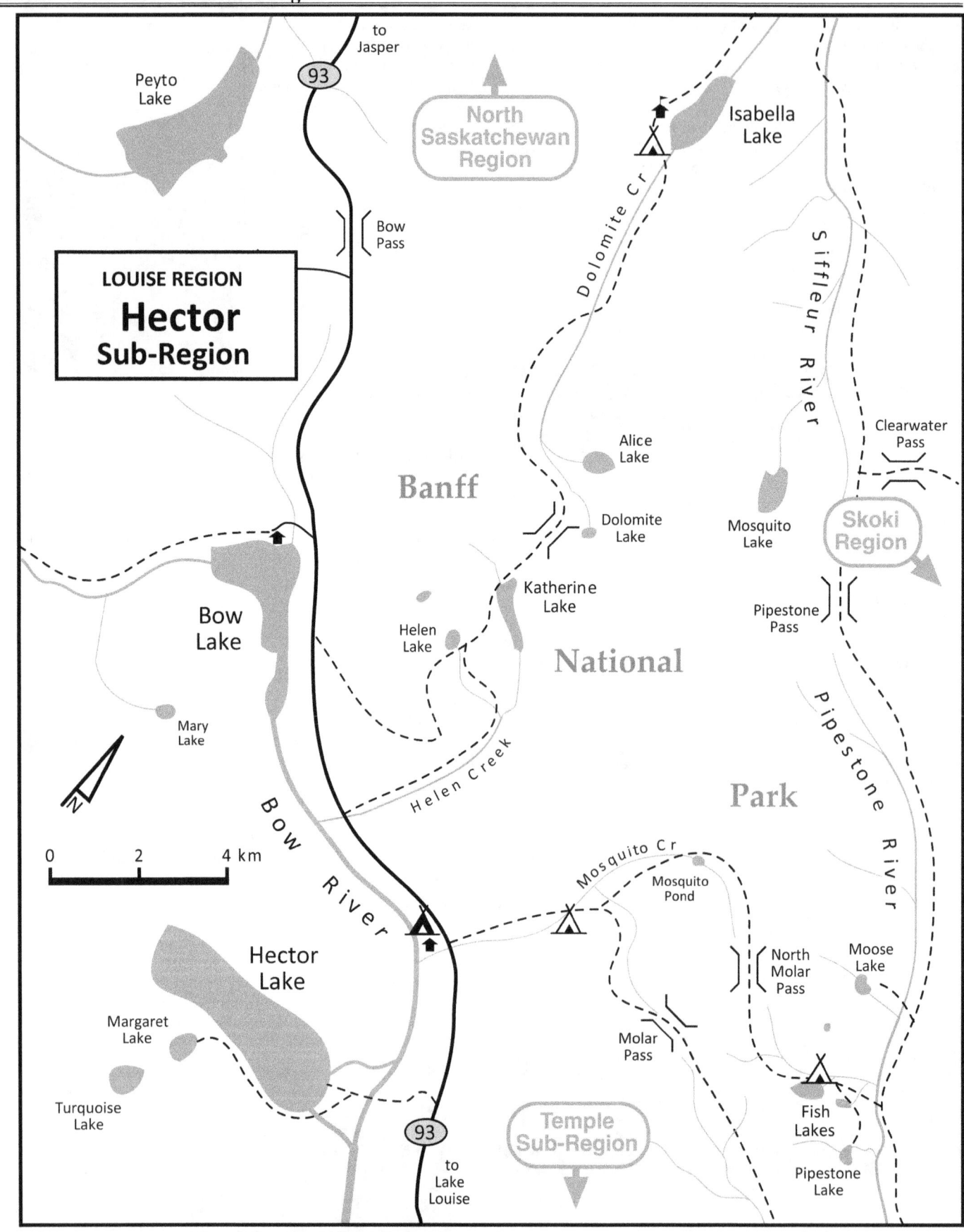

LOUISE REGION: Hector Sub-Region

Pipestone (Deer) Lake (NP)
Cutthroat trout to 45 cm
Pipestone Lake is located 2 km southeast of Lower Fish Lake along an ill-defined trail. It is an easy half-day excursion for hikers based at the Fish Lakes. Pipestone Lake holds plenty of cutthroat trout averaging 25-35 cm in length. Flies are very effective, and fly casting room is available at numerous locations around the lake.

Pipestone Lake

(cutthroat trout)

Moose Lake (NP)
Cutthroat trout to 40 cm
Moose Lake is located on a bench amid mixed forest and meadow west of the Pipestone River. It can be reached by a 5 km trail from the Fish Lakes campground. Moose Lake's silted, green waters hold an abundance of cutthroat trout, mostly in the 20-30 cm range. Moose's cutthroat trout are easy to catch and offer good sport, especially for anglers who haven't yet fully mastered casting skills. For fly fishers, there is ample back casting room around most of the lake.

Moose Lake

Mosquito Lake (NP)
Status: Unknown
Mosquito Lake is set in alpine surroundings on the northwest side of Pipestone Pass, near the headwaters of the Siffleur River. A 2 km trek over open ground from the main Pipestone Pass trail leads to the lake, which usually remains frozen until mid-July. Rainbow trout were stocked in the past, but their reproductive success has never been determined. Few anglers, if any, make it into this isolated lake each year.

Siffleur River (NP) *(Headwaters to National Park boundary)*
Bull trout to 60 cm (2.5 kg)
Whitefish to 35 cm
The Siffleur River flows northwest through a long, wide valley from the lofty heights of Pipestone Pass. The river has long stretches of babbling riffles, interspersed with quiet pools. Although the upper Siffleur is attractive to the eye of the angler, its fish population is small, being made up of bull trout in the 25-35 cm range along with whitefish.

Isabella Lake (NP)
Rainbow trout to 60 cm (2.5 kg)
Bull trout to 60 cm (2.5 kg)
Picturesque Isabella Lake, which has Dolomite Creek as both its inlet and outlet, stands out as the Sub-Region's hidden treasure in terms of angling. Infrequently visited due to long approach routes, the quality of angling in Isabella Lake should remain high. The lake's silted waters hold plenty of rainbow trout in the 30-40 cm range. Larger trout are present in substantial numbers. Although rainbow trout can be taken from most spots around the lake, the area around the inlet usually proves to be the most productive. Flies and lures are both effective. Fly casting room is generally available around the lake.

Isabella Lake
(rainbow trout)

J. Rennels photo

Dolomite Creek (NP)
Bull trout to 50 cm (1.5 kg)
Rainbow trout to 40 cm
This fast-flowing glacial stream offers little in the way of fishing. Immediately above and below Isabella Lake the occasional rainbow can be taken, while bull trout are present in the creek between Isabella Lake and the Siffleur River.

LOUISE REGION: Hector Sub-Region

Alice Lake (NP)
Status: devoid of fish
Alice Lake is located in a stark, rocky basin above Dolomite Creek, and has never been stocked. The lake contains no fish.

Dolomite Lake (NP)
Status: Devoid of fish
The striking blue waters of tiny Dolomite Lake are set in the flowered alpine meadows of Dolomite Pass. Few anglers ever make their way to Dolomite Lake. Although rainbow trout were stocked in the past, fishing was generally regarded as very poor for many years, and it is highly doubtful that any trout remain in this tiny pond.

Dolomite Lake

Katherine Lake (NP)
Cutthroat trout to 50 cm (1.5 kg)
The long, narrow form of Katherine Lake sits amid treeless surroundings just south of Dolomite Pass, 8 km by trail from the Icefields Parkway. Due to its alpine environment, Katherine Lake is usually frozen into July. The lake's sparkling blue waters hold plenty of uniquely-marked cutthroat trout in the 25-35 cm range. The waters in the vicinity of the several inlet creeks hold trout. Around most of the lake, the bottom drops off quickly, and a wet fly fished deep usually attracts some attention. With no tree cover, fly casting room is available from every location.

Katherine Lake (cutthroat trout)

Helen Lake (NP)
Brook trout to 35 cm
Delicate Helen Lake is set in an appealing alpine meadow, 6 km by trail from the Icefields Parkway. Brook trout in the 20-30 cm range inhabit Helen's translucent green waters in fair numbers. Fish can generally be taken within a few metres of shore. If wind and light conditions are ideal, fish can be seen cruising about for food. Flies work well, and fly casting room is available around the entire lake.

Helen Lake

SKOKI REGION

The Region immediately east of Lake Louise is highlighted by some outstanding backcountry. The Skoki and Baker Valleys, with their network of sparkling lakes and alpine meadows, have been popular with hikers for over 60 years. Beyond Skoki Valley is the remote Front Ranges area. This includes the drainages of the upper Red Deer, Clearwater and Panther Rivers. Access to the Region is by trail only. Angling opportunities are limited, with Baker, Redoubt, Douglas and Red Deer Lakes being the most promising locations.

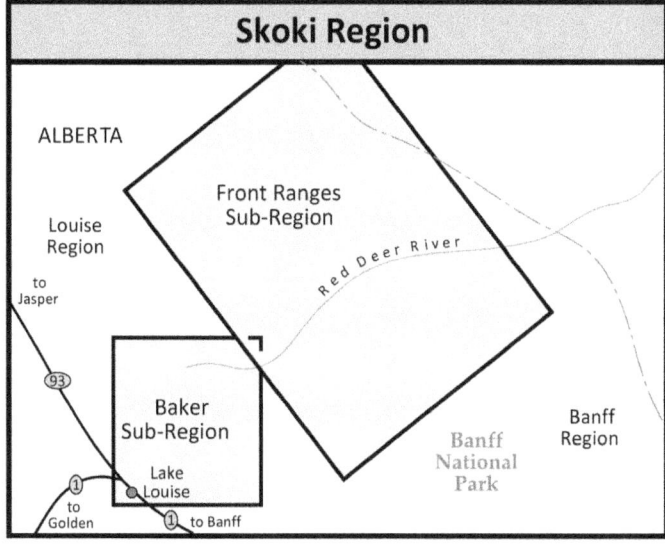

Baker Sub-Region

The main access into Skoki Valley and the Baker Sub-Region begins at the Lake Louise ski area. It is a 15 km hike to Skoki Lodge, a historic backcountry chalet that is available by reservation only. Hidden, Redoubt, Baker, Skoki, Merlin, Castilleja and Red Deer Lakes are all reached by short side trails en route to the lodge. Although cutthroat and rainbow are present in good numbers in many lakes, most anglers come in pursuit of the large brook trout inhabiting Redoubt, Baker and Ptarmigan Lakes. Longer trails radiate out from Skoki Valley, extending deep into the backcountry of Banff National Park along the Red Deer and Pipestone Rivers and Baker Creek.

Baker Lake (NP)
Brook trout to 55 cm (2.0 kg)
Cutthroat trout to 45 cm

Baker Lake is the largest lake in the Skoki area, and there is a backcountry campground at the eastern end of Baker Lake. It is set in a wide basin near tree line, and holds both cutthroat and brook trout ranging from 30-40 cm in length. Brook trout are caught more often than cutthroat trout, although both species inhabit all areas of the lake. The western end of the lake is usually productive, particularly near the inlet creek. Lures and wet flies fished deep tend to attract more brook trout, whereas cutthroat are more favourable to dry flies. Due to its high elevation and lack of tree cover around the shore, Baker is susceptible to strong winds.

Baker Lake

Little Baker Lake (NP)
Brook trout to 45 cm
Cutthroat trout to 45 cm

Little Baker Lake is located less than a kilometre from Baker Lake. Little Baker Lake holds small numbers of brook and cutthroat trout. Fly casting room is adequate along much of the shoreline, although fish holding waters tend to be beyond the range of an average cast.

Little Baker Lake

Tilted Lake (NP)
Brook trout to 40 cm
Cutthroat trout to 40 cm

Tilted Lake is set in the same basin as Little Baker Lake. Tilted Lake reportedly has a small population of brook and cutthroat trout, although few fish have been taken in recent years. General lack of tree cover allows for backcasting a fly.

Tilted Lake

Brachiopod Lake (NP)
Status: Devoid of fish

Despite rumours to the contrary, Brachiopod Lake contains no fish, and dries up completely on occasion.

Brachiopod Lake

SKOKI REGION: Baker Sub-Region

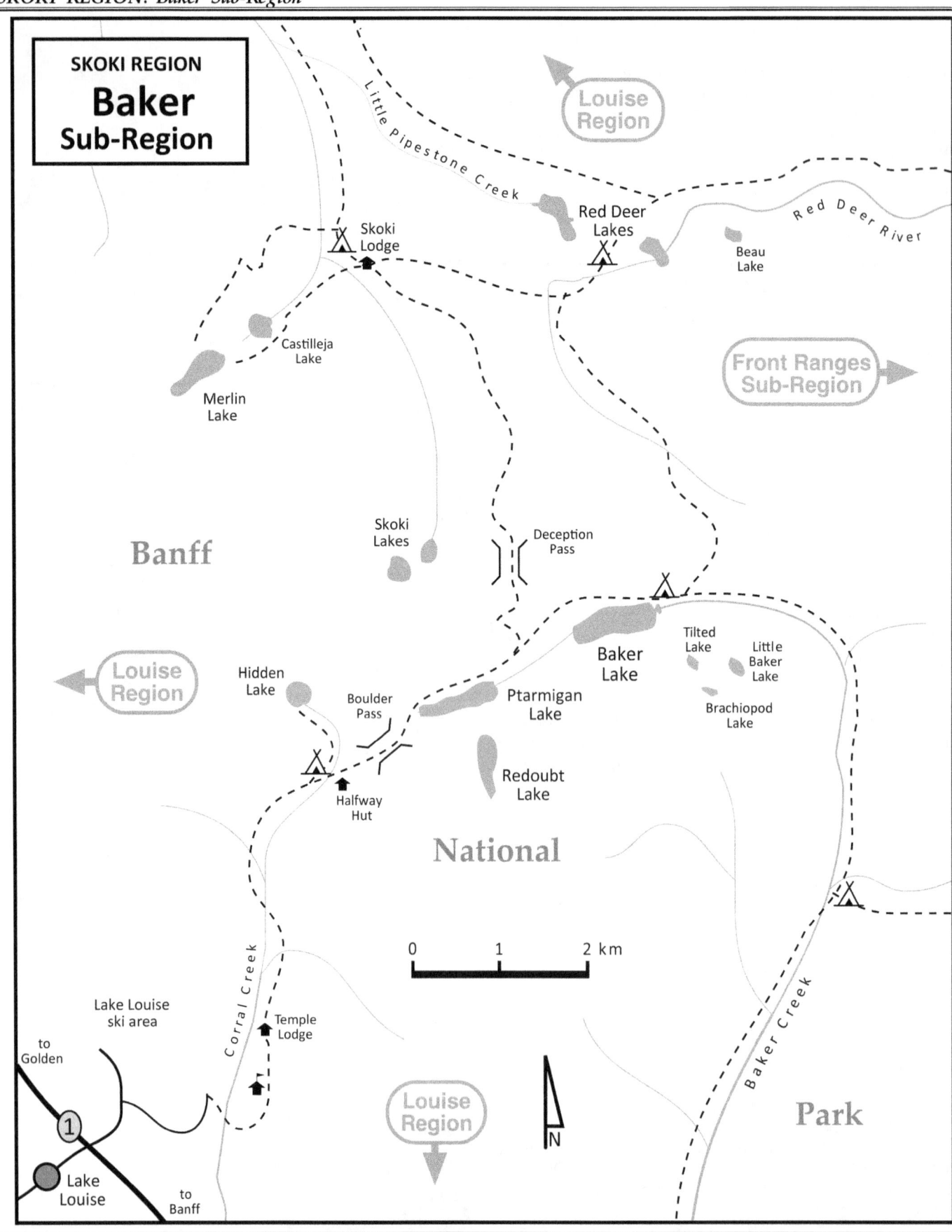

SKOKI REGION: Baker Sub-Region

Baker Creek (NP)
Cutthroat trout to 25 cm
Brook trout to 25 cm
Bull trout to 30 cm
Whitefish to 25 cm

Baker Creek is best in its upper reaches, particularly in the meadows below Baker Lake. Baker Creek holds a variety of fish, with cutthroat and brook trout predominant in the upper sections, and bull trout more numerous downstream. Baker Creek is accessible from a trail that parallels the creek over its entire course.

Ptarmigan Lake (NP)
Brook trout to 40 cm
Cutthroat trout to 40 cm

Ptarmigan Lake is set in windswept Boulder Pass, 9 km from the trailhead at the Lake Louise ski hill. The sparkling waters of Ptarmigan Lake hold both brook and cutthroat trout averaging 25-30 cm in length, with brook trout in the majority. Although fly casting room is available around the entire lake, this advantage is offset by frequent strong winds that make life miserable for most fly fishers. A drop-off zone within casting distance tends to hold most of the fish.

Ptarmigan Lake

Redoubt Lake (NP)
Brook trout to 60 cm (2.5 kg)
Cutthroat trout to 40 cm

Redoubt Lake is perched in a high, alpine basin less than a kilometre south of Ptarmigan Lake by trail. Redoubt Lake has earned a reputation for holding large brook trout. The lake is popular with backcountry anglers following ice-out, which generally occurs in early July. Brook trout taken from the lake will average 30-45 cm in length. Lures and flies work well in Redoubt Lake. Redoubt Lake's tundra-like setting allows for fly casting from all locations around the lake.

Redoubt Lake

Hidden Lake (NP)
Cutthroat trout to 30 cm

Hidden Lake is set in a rocky amphitheatre, less than a kilometre along a side trail from Halfway Hut. Hidden Lake likely holds a very limited number of small cutthroat trout. A general lack of success by fishermen over the past few years has tended to produce rumours proclaiming the final demise of fish in Hidden Lake. For those anglers willing to put this rumour to the test, the best potential lies in the deep waters along the rocky north shore.

Hidden Lake

Corral Creek (NP)
Cutthroat trout to 25 cm
Brook trout to 25 cm

Corral Creek has a small population of brook and cutthroat trout in its upper reaches and also at its lower end near its confluence with the Bow River. The fast waters in the middle section hold very few fish.

Skoki Lakes:
Zigadenus Lake (NP)
Status: Devoid of fish
Myosotis Lake (NP)
Rainbow trout to 30 cm

The beautifully coloured Skoki Lakes (Zigadenus and Myosotis), are located high on the western side of Skoki Valley beneath the east face of Ptarmigan Peak. The lakes are visible to the west as you descend the north side of Deception Pass. They can be reached either by leaving the trail and working across the valley, or by following a rough trail that begins half a kilometre south of Skoki Lodge. Both lakes are heavily silted which accounts for their striking green colour. Zigadenus Lake, the upper lake, was once stocked with rainbow trout that failed to reproduce. Myosotis Lake has a dwindling population of rainbow trout. Reports indicate poor fishing.

Skoki Lakes

SKOKI REGION: Baker Sub-Region

Castilleja Lake (NP)
Brook trout to 40 cm
Castilleja Lake is a small lake encountered on the trail to Merlin Lake from Skoki Lodge. Castilleja Lake was at one time stocked with rainbow trout, but evidence indicates that brook trout now inhabit the lake, probably migrating downstream from Merlin Lake over time.

Castilleja Lake

Merlin Lake (NP)
Brook trout to 40 cm
Picturesque Merlin Lake is set in a hanging valley above Castilleja Lake, and is protected by a small cliff band requiring scrambling ability. Merlin Lake has a population of brook trout that average 20-30 cm in length. Rainbow trout may also be present in small numbers. Due to its elevation and sheltered location, Merlin is usually icebound until mid-July and freeze-up occurs early in the fall.

Merlin Lake

Red Deer Lakes (NP)
Brook trout to 60 cm (3.0 kg)
Cutthroat trout to 55 cm (2.0 kg)
Rainbow trout to 50 cm (1.5 kg)
The two Red Deer Lakes are set in a wide, open valley 4 km by trail from Skoki Lodge. The upper lake, the larger of the two, lies west of the trail and contains good-sized brook and cutthroat trout. Fish from the lakes will average 25-35 cm in length. Flies and lures work well in both lakes. Although room for fly casting is available, the upper lake is very shallow for a fair distance out from shore, which makes it difficult for those fly fishing to reach deeper waters holding the fish. The best opportunities for fly fishing from shore are in the areas around the inlet and outlet streams. The lower lake, situated just east of the main trail, has a very limited population of brook trout. The marshy nature of the area almost ensures wet feet, and the abundance of reeds makes fly casting difficult at the lower lake. Several streams wind back and forth across the marshy flats around the lower lake, and most hold a few trout.

Red Deer Lake

Beau (Hatchet) Lake (NP)
Status: Doubtful
This small lake is located just east of lower Red Deer Lake. Beau Lake at one time held brook and rainbow trout, but there appears to be few, if any, fish remaining in the lake.

Front Ranges Sub-Region

The Front Ranges Sub-Region covers the watersheds of the upper Red Deer, Panther and Clearwater Rivers. This Sub-Region lies deep within the Front Ranges of the Rocky Mountains in Banff National Park, and is home to many grizzly bears. Visitors entering the Sub-Region are generally limited to horse parties and a few enterprising hikers, who should be aware that major river fords are to be expected on most trails, and that there are no easy escape routes back to civilization. From the upper Red Deer River, which can be accessed from Skoki Valley, side trails branch to Douglas and Horseshoe Lakes. The Cascade Fire Road, although lengthy, provides an alternate approach to the Sub-Region. Fishing opportunities are limited to remote backcountry lakes with limited trout populations.

Clearwater River (NP)
Bull trout to 75 cm (5.0 kg)
Whitefish to 40 cm
Brook trout to 35 cm
The Clearwater River flows eastwards from humble beginnings at the Devon Lakes at Clearwater Pass, and eventually joins the North Saskatchewan River at Rocky Mountain House as a major tributary. The section of the Clearwater River within the boundaries of Banff National Park is seldom fished due to long approach routes, all of which require a minimum of two days

SKOKI REGION: Front Ranges Sub-Region

of hiking. In its upper reaches, the river holds bull trout and whitefish, with brook trout becoming more plentiful downstream from Trident Lake. Horse trails parallel the Clearwater for its entire length. A dangerous ford of Martin Creek above Trident Lake will cause problems for most hikers.

Devon Lakes (NP)
Lake trout to 75 cm (5.0 kg)
Bull trout to 75 cm (5.0 kg)
Cutthroat trout to 35 cm
Whitefish to 40 cm

The Devon Lakes are set in alpine surroundings, immediately east of Clearwater Pass. The Devon Lakes were for many years regarded as one of the Sub-Region's best fishing destinations. The largest lake at one time contained plenty of big lake and bull trout. However, over harvest severely depleted fish stocks. The two smaller Devon Lakes, located in a basin just to the south of the main lake, were both stocked in the past with cutthroat and brook trout. Cutthroat trout are reported to be present in the upper lake.

Clearwater Lake (NP)
Status: Closed to angling

Clearwater Lake is set in wide valley, 10 km below Clearwater Pass on the Clearwater River. Clearwater Lake is merely a widening of the river. Clearwater Lake and its neighbours, Trident and Martin Lakes, are visited by few hikers each season. Lake trout, bull trout and whitefish are present in the lake.

Trident Lake (NP)
Status: Closed to angling

Two kilometres downstream from Clearwater Lake the Clearwater River again widens, this time into the form of Trident Lake. Lake trout, bull trout and whitefish are present in the lake.

Martin Lake (NP)
Status: Closed to angling

Martin Lake is located less than a kilometre above Trident Lake on Martin Creek. Brook trout likely still inhabit the lake.

Red Deer River (NP) *(Headwaters to National Park boundary)*
Brook trout to 35 cm
Cutthroat trout to 35 cm
Bull trout to 70 cm (4.0 kg)
Whitefish to 40 cm

The Red Deer River offers fair fishing as it flows east from its source at the Red Deer Lakes to the Banff National Park boundary. While the main river is often very clouded until mid to late summer due to glacial run-off, many of the side channels and ponds provide better opportunities to catch trout at this time. The river is noticeably silted downstream from the Drummond Glacier tributary. Brook trout predominate in the upper sections, with bull trout and whitefish becoming more plentiful downstream. In the vicinity of Red Deer Lakes, the occasional rainbow or cutthroat may also be caught. Horse trails along the upper Red Deer connect with the Cascade Fire Road.

Red Deer River

Douglas Lake (NP)
Cutthroat trout to 55 cm (1.5 kg)

This relatively large lake is set in a wide valley to the south of the main Red Deer River valley. Douglas Lake usually attracts a few eager anglers each season, despite a tricky ford of the Red Deer prior to reaching the Douglas Lake spur trail. Cutthroat trout averaging 25-35 cm in length inhabit the lake's silted waters in good numbers. Although brook trout were also stocked at one time in Douglas, reports indicate that few or none remain. The areas around the lake's inlet and outlet are generally the most productive, although cutthroat can be taken from most spots along the shore. The trout tend to keep fairly close to the shore in search of food due to silted waters and lures will work well.

Douglas Lake

Donald Lake, Alfred Lake, Gwendolyn Lake (NP)
Status: Devoid of fish

These three remote lakes are located in the Valley of the Hidden Lakes, which is south of Douglas Lake. The lakes have never been stocked and contain no fish.

Horseshoe (Skeleton) Lake (NP)
Rainbow to 40 cm
Brook trout 40 cm

Horseshoe Lake is located 6 km downstream from Douglas Lake, and is overlooked by most hikers because of the dangerous ford of the Red Deer River. However, a cable car crossing of the Red Deer River is found in the canyon just downstream from Horseshoe's outlet. This distinctly U-shaped lake holds plenty of rainbow and brook trout averaging 25-35 cm in length. For fly fishers, there is casting room available from many locations around the lake.

SKOKI REGION: Front Ranges Sub-Region

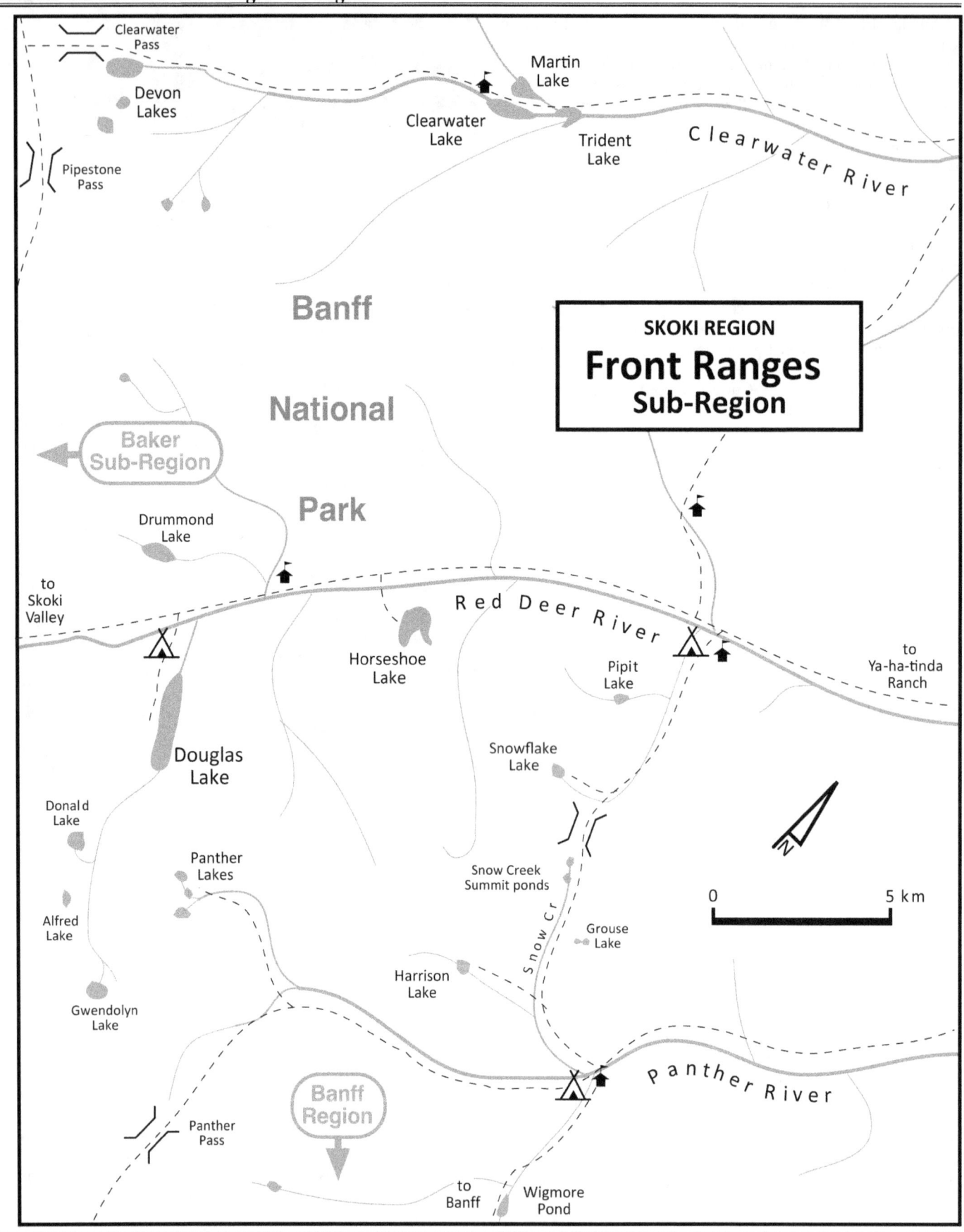

SKOKI REGION: Front Ranges Sub-Region

Horseshoe Lake

Drummond Lake (NP)
Status: Devoid of fish
Drummond Lake is hidden in a side valley northwest of the Red Deer River. The lake has never been stocked and contains no fish.

Drummond Glacier

Pipit Lake (NP)
Rainbow trout to 40 cm
This small, isolated lake sits west of the Cascade Fire Road on the northern side of Snow Creek Summit. It receives very few two-legged visitors each summer. Although the route is fairly obvious, a map and compass are recommended, as no trails lead to the lake. Reports indicate that Pipit holds a small population of rainbow trout averaging 20-30 cm in length.

Snowflake Lake (NP)
Status: Doubtful
Snowflake Lake is set in a beautiful alpine basin west of Snow Creek Summit. Snowflake Lake has been stocked several times, but has been unable to maintain a stable population of trout. Both rainbow and brook trout have been planted in the past without success, and reports indicate that the lake is likely barren.

Snow Creek Summit ponds (NP)
Bull trout to 40 cm
This series of beaver ponds is located on the western side of Snow Creek Summit, and are overlooked by most parties passing through. The ponds hold plenty of small bull trout averaging 20-30 cm in length.

Snow Creek Summit

Grouse Lake (NP)
Status: Devoid of fish
Grouse Lake lies hidden in a narrow side valley just east of the Cascade Fire Road. The brook trout stocked in the past failed to reproduce, and the lake is now devoid of fish.

Harrison Lake (NP)
Bull trout to 50 cm (1.5 kg)
Harrison Lake is nestled high on the flank of an unnamed peak at the south end of the Vermilion Range. Harrison Lake is one of the Sub-Region's hidden treasures, and it is accessed by a 3-km side trail from the Cascade Fire Road. Despite the long distances involved, Harrison Lake is still visited by a few anglers each season. The lake has an abundance of bull trout averaging 30-40 cm in length, making it worth the long distances traveled.

Panther River (NP)
Bull trout to 70 cm (4.0 kg)
Whitefish to 40 cm
The Panther River flows east to its junction with the Red Deer River, and offers average stream fishing at best. Bull trout and whitefish are found in pockets along the entire length of the river, but never in great numbers. Progressing downstream, the fishing generally picks up, and nearing the park boundary, the odd brook trout and rainbow can also be caught. Horse trails parallel the Panther River, intersecting with the Cascade Fire Road at Wigmore Creek.

Panther Pass

Panther Lakes (NP)
Status: Doubtful
This series of lakes set amid spectacular scenery at the head of the Panther River have never been stocked. It is possible, although unlikely, that a few bull trout have worked their way into the lakes.

Wigmore Pond (NP)
Status: Doubtful
The man-made dam holding the waters in tiny Wigmore Pond has been breached, and there is little left other than marshy flats. It is highly unlikely that any trout remain.

YOHO PARK REGION

This Region encompasses the entirety of spectacular Yoho National Park. The Trans-Canada Highway bisects the Region and provides access. The tiny community of Field offers very limited services for visitors. There are few quality fisheries in the Region. Most of the rivers are glacial, and run silted much of the year. Lakes tend to be small, backcountry lakes with very limited populations of trout. The Region is divided into three Sub-Regions: The area around exquisite Lake O'Hara; the territory around Emerald Lake; and the main Kicking Horse River valley.

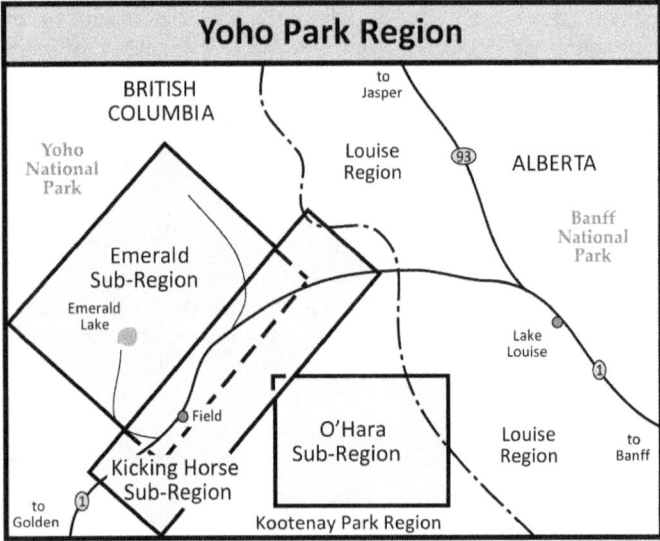

O'Hara Sub-Region

O'Hara's jeweled setting of pristine mountain lakes set beneath the spectacular peaks of the Continental Divide is equal to that of any area in the Rockies. The Lake O'Hara vicinity is renowned for its quality hiking and climbing opportunities, and not for fishing. However, prospective anglers coming to this corner of Yoho National Park need not be disappointed. Lake O'Hara is the focal point of the region, and is reached via a 13 km limited access fire road from the Trans-Canada Highway. Arrangements can be made with Lake O'Hara Lodge to reserve a space on the shuttle bus during summer months. Both Lake O'Hara Lodge and the Alpine Club of Canada's Elizabeth Parker Hut require reservations, as does the park campground, located a half kilometre below Lake O'Hara, alongside Cataract Brook. From the shores of beautiful Lake O'Hara, trails radiate out to nearby lakes, including Mary, Schaeffer, McArthur, Morning Glory, Linda, Vera and Oesa.

Lake O'Hara (NP)
Cutthroat trout to 45 cm
The turquoise waters of Lake O'Hara are situated beneath the same impressive peaks that form the backdrop for Lake Louise. The O'Hara locale is a favourite destination of backcountry visitors. Unfortunately, Lake O'Hara's fishing has never been able to match its beauty. The lake contains small cutthroat trout in the 20-25 cm range. The tangle of sunken logs in the area of the lake's outlet is a popular spot that usually holds trout. Canoes can be rented from the Lake O'Hara Lodge, but fishing from a boat is not usually a great aid here, as the fish tend to stay close to shore due to the silted nature of the water.

Lake O'Hara

Lake Oesa (NP)
Status: Devoid of fish
Lake Oesa remains ice-covered for ten months each year. The lake was stocked in the past with rainbow trout, but they probably just froze to death! There are no fish in Lake Oesa.

Lake Oesa

Yukness Lake, Lake Victoria, Lefroy Lake (NP)
Status: Devoid of fish
These three small, silted bodies of water alongside the trail to Lake Oesa have never been stocked and contain no fish.

Hungabee Lake, Opabin Lake (NP)
Status: Devoid of fish
Set in the alpine environs of the Opabin Plateau, neither Hungabee nor Opabin Lake has ever been stocked.

Lake McArthur (NP)
Brook trout to 35 cm
Lake McArthur is the largest lake of the Sub-Region, and it lies hidden in a hanging valley 3 km south of Lake O'Hara. It is noted for its exceptional blue colouration, a result of heavy silting from nearby glaciers. Although the lake holds brook trout averaging 25-30 cm in length, anglers at McArthur do not usually enjoy much success. Reports indicate that a very small number of trout still exist in McArthur.

YOHO PARK REGION: O'Hara Sub-Region

Lake McArthur

Schaeffer Lake (NP)
Status: Devoid of fish
Schaeffer Lake was stocked in the past with both rainbow and cutthroat trout, but no reproductive success has ever been recorded. It is very likely that Schaeffer Lake is devoid of fish.

Mary Lake (NP)
Status: Devoid of fish
Mary Lake is located on a bench just south of Lake O'Hara. It has never been stocked and contains no fish.

Morning Glory Lakes (NP)
Cutthroat trout to 30 cm
The Morning Glory Lakes are a series of three shallow lakes situated beneath the impressive north face of Mt. Odaray. All three contain limited populations of small cutthroat trout. Most fish are in the 20-25 cm range. The fish spook easily due to the shallow nature of the water, making patience an important asset for anglers. For persons fly fishing, there is plenty of casting room around all three lakes.

Linda Lake (NP)
Cutthroat trout to 50 cm (1.5 kg)
Linda Lake is set in a quiet subalpine basin northwest of Lake O'Hara, and offers the best angling potential of any lake in the area. Its clear blue waters hold plenty of cutthroat trout in the 20-30 cm range, with larger fish taken regularly. Flies work very well here. Numerous openings in the forest cover along the shoreline allow for fly casting. No one area seems to be best, and anglers are advised to keep a close eye on the water while working around the lake.

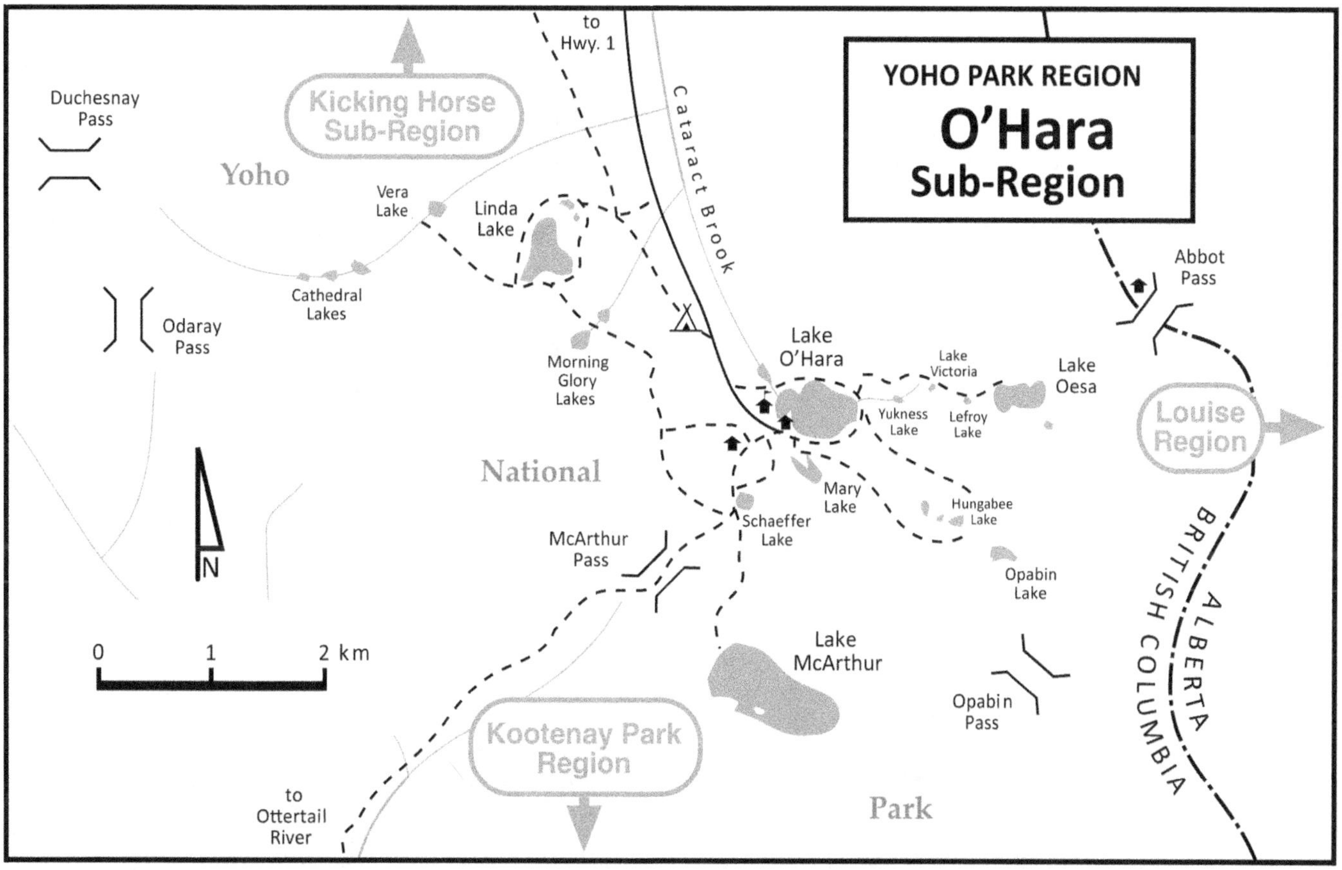

YOHO PARK REGION: O'Hara Sub-Region

Linda Lake

(cutthroat trout)

Vera Lake (NP)
Cutthroat to 35 cm
Vera Lake is located a little over 4 km by trail from Lake O'Hara. It is seldom visited by anglers, as most do not venture beyond nearby Linda Lake. Vera Lake's placid waters hold a small population of cutthroat trout averaging 20-25 cm in length. The areas around the inlet and outlet creeks are usually productive.

Cathedral Lakes (NP)
Status: Unknown
The diminutive Cathedral Lakes are located half a kilometre above Vera Lake. They have never been stocked with trout. However, it is possible that fish could have migrated upstream over time from Vera Lake.

Cataract Brook (NP)
Cutthroat trout to 25 cm
Cataract Brook parallels the Lake O'Hara Fire Road. As its name indicates, Cataract Creek contains numerous falls and rapids. The creek holds small cutthroat trout in its upper section, particularly in the 2 km stretch below Lake O'Hara, where there are several large pools just below the lake's outlet.

Cataract Creek

Emerald Sub-Region

This Sub-Region encompasses the northern half of Yoho National Park. It possesses an abundance of superb scenery, and a scarcity of good fishing opportunities. The main access is via the Yoho Valley Road or the Emerald Lake Road, both of which branch north off the Trans-Canada Highway. Charming Emerald Lake is a favourite with sightseers, and is the hub of hiking trails leading to Hamilton Lake and Yoho Lake. From the terminus of the Yoho Valley Road, at 380 m high Takakkaw Falls, the main Yoho Valley trail leads past Celeste, Duchesnay and Marpole Lakes, none of which hold much promise for anglers.

Emerald Lake (NP)
Brook trout to 50 cm (1.5 kg)
Rainbow trout to 50 cm (1.5 kg)
Emerald Lake's dazzling setting attracts hordes of visitors each summer, and its shoreline always seems to be busy with hikers and photographers. Although Emerald is not an outstanding fishing lake, its rich green waters contain fair numbers of both brook and rainbow trout averaging 25-35 cm in length, with brook trout in the majority. The occasional bull trout may also be present. As the water is silted, fish can generally be taken close to shore, particularly in the area around the outlet and bridge to Emerald Lake Lodge. From a canoe, which can be rented at the lake, the best tactic is to keep fairly close to shore while trolling a fly or lure.

Emerald Lake

Lone Duck Lake (NP)
Brook trout to 35 cm
Rainbow trout to 35 cm
Lone Duck Lake is simply a widening of the Emerald River half a kilometre downstream from Emerald Lake. It holds brook and rainbow trout in small sizes.

Emerald River (NP)
Brook trout to 35 cm
Rainbow trout to 35 cm
Bull trout to 40 cm
The Emerald River flows from Emerald Lake to the Kicking Horse River, and possesses long stretches of fishable water. The river is never more than a short walk away from the Emerald Lake Road. Small brook and rainbow trout, in the 20-30 cm range can be caught in the river. A few larger bull trout may be present in the deeper pools.

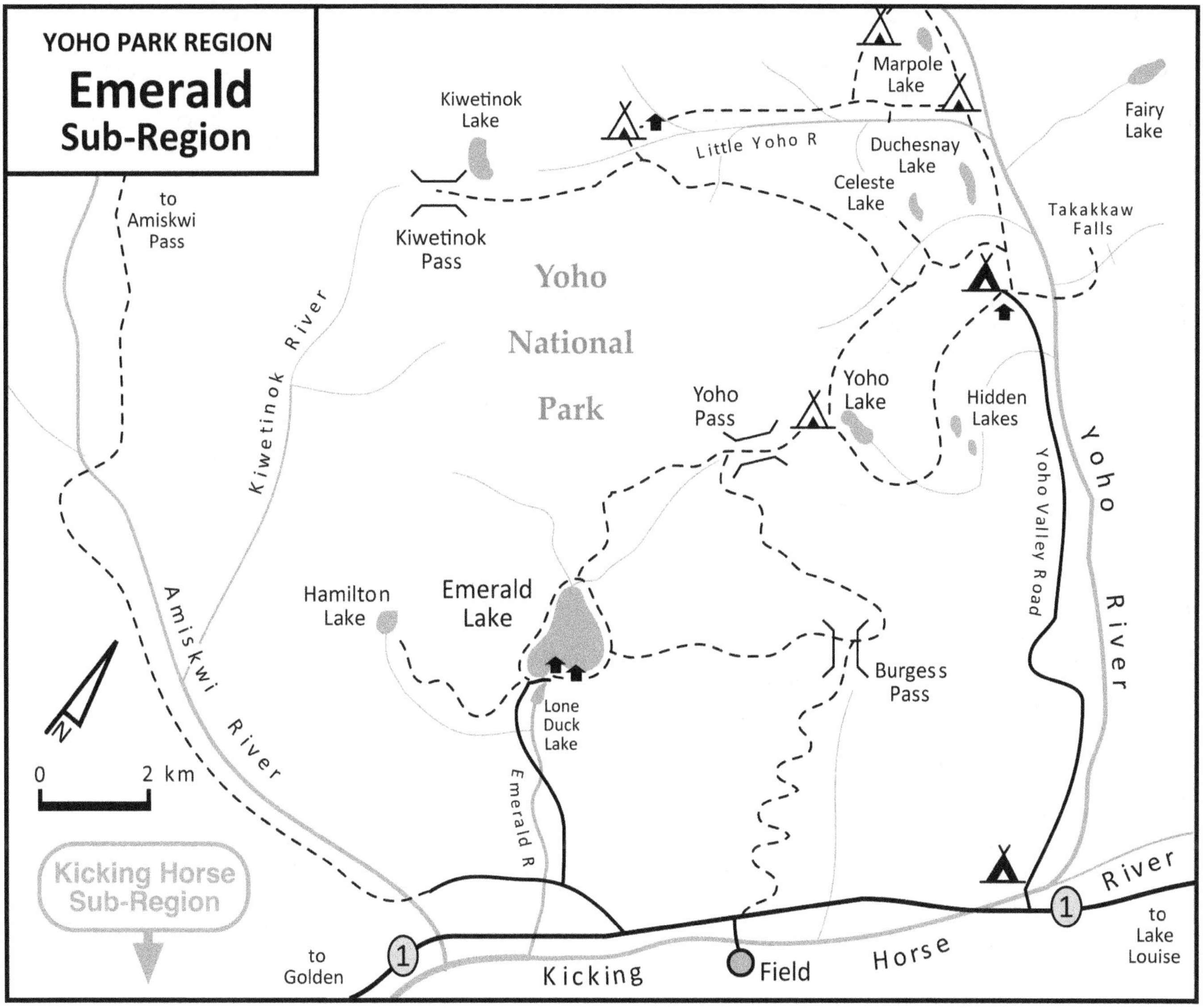

YOHO PARK REGION: Emerald Sub-Region

Hamilton Lake (NP)
Status: Devoid of fish

Delightful Hamilton Lake is located 5 km by trail above Emerald Lake, and is set in a rocky cirque beneath Mount Carnarvon. Hamilton Lake has never been stocked and contains no trout.

Hamilton Lake

Amiskwi River (NP)
Brook trout to 35 cm
Bull trout to 55 cm (2.0 kg)

The Amiskwi River receives little attention from anglers, particularly in the upper sections. Access is along a seldom-hiked fire road that parallels the Amiskwi over its entire length. Small brook and bull trout in the 15-25 cm range are the normal catch, although larger bulls are taken on occasion. Due to high, muddy water, the river is generally not fishable until late July.

Amiskwi River

YOHO PARK REGION: Emerald Sub-Region

Kiwetinok River (NP)
Bull trout to 40 cm
The Kiwetinok River is a tributary of the Amiskwi River. It contains bull trout in small numbers and sizes, but is generally not worth the effort of the long approach up the Amiskwi Fire Road.

Yoho River (NP)
Status: Doubtful
With its headwaters being the Wapta and Yoho Glaciers, the Yoho River is extremely silted throughout the year. In addition to heavy silting, the river is excessively torrential over most of its course and it is very unlikely that trout would proliferate under these conditions. It is possible, however, that small bull trout may live in some pockets near the confluence of clearer running tributary streams.

Little Yoho River (NP)
Status: Devoid of fish
Flowing through much-hiked Little Yoho Valley, the Little Yoho River is too torrential and too silted to hold trout.

Yoho Lake (NP)
Brook trout to 35 cm
Yoho Lake is situated less than a kilometre east of Yoho Pass, and 4 km by trail from the Emerald Lake trailhead. Lovely Yoho Lake is very popular with day hikers throughout summer months. The lake contains plenty of brook trout in smaller sizes, most averaging 20-25 cm in length. The small trout can usually be seen cruising a few metres off shore, and crafty anglers should have no problem catching fish. Flies work very well at Yoho Lake. If wind conditions prevent fish sightings, a wet fly fished deep generally produces well. Fly casting room is limited to the areas where meadows extend down to the shore.

Yoho Lake

Hidden Lakes (NP)
Status: Doubtful
The tiny Hidden Lakes are located on the eastern side of the Yoho Lake-Takakkaw Falls trail. Hidden Lakes have been stocked in the past with both brook and rainbow trout. However, the fish failed to reproduce, and it is very doubtful if any remain.

Fairy Lake (NP)
Status: Devoid of fish
Fairy Lake is tucked high on the flank of Trolltinder Mountain, and is protected by a 300 m high cliff. Fortunately for anglers, Fairy Lake has never been stocked and contains no fish.

Duchesnay Lake (NP)
Status: Doubtful
Forest rimmed Duchesnay Lake is situated on the western side of the Yoho Valley trail, 4 km from the Takakkaw Falls trailhead. This shallow lake was stocked in the past with brook trout, but it is likely the fish succumbed to winter kill.

Lake Celeste (NP)
Status: Devoid of fish
This small, shallow body of water, less than a kilometre due west of Duchesnay Lake, has never been stocked and contains no fish.

Marpole Lake (NP)
Status: Doubtful
Diminutive Marpole Lake is located just south of Twin Falls Chalet. Marpole Lake has been stocked several times in the past with brook, cutthroat and rainbow trout. In recent years, fishing has been very poor in Marpole, leading to speculation that there are no longer any trout in the lake. Aside from reproductive failure, winter kill is also likely a major factor limiting numbers.

Kiwetinok Lake (NP)
Status: Devoid of fish
Kiwetinok Lake is set in the harsh alpine environs of Kiwetinok Pass, and remains ice-covered much of the year. No fish are present.

Kicking Horse Sub-Region

The Kicking Horse River forms a deep valley bounded on the north and south by the imposing peaks of Yoho National Park. The Trans-Canada Highway parallels the river, cutting through the middle of the Sub-Region, connecting Golden and Lake Louise. The village of Field, housing the headquarters for Yoho National Park, offers little in the way of services beyond the essentials of gas and food. Sink, Summit and Ross Lakes are located within a kilometre of Kicking Horse Pass and the Continental Divide. Farther west, Wapta Lake lies alongside the Trans-Canada Highway, and Sherbrooke Lake and the Narao Lakes are only a short hike away.

YOHO PARK REGION: Kicking Horse Sub-Region

Kicking Horse River (NP)
Bull trout to 60 cm (2.5 kg)
Brook trout to 40 cm
Whitefish to 35 cm

The Kicking Horse River forms the main artery through Yoho National Park, and its tributaries extend to the far corners of the park. The Trans-Canada Highway parallels the river. It is readily accessible to anglers, but unfortunately offers only mediocre fishing even on its best days. It is heavily silted most of the year, clearing up only in the late summer-early fall when bull trout and whitefish along with a few brook trout can be taken. Most fish are in the 20-30 cm range, although large bull trout to 60 cm can be caught on occasion. Fishing is best around the Kicking Horse's confluence with its tributary streams, particularly the larger ones such as the Emerald, Amiskwi, Ottertail and Otterhead Rivers.

Kicking Horse River

Ross Lake (NP)
Brook trout to 35 cm

This small, tree fringed lake is located 1 km by trail south of the 1-A Highway. It receives little fishing pressure due to its secluded location. Ross Lake's green waters hold brook trout averaging 20-30 cm in length. The best angling opportunities are found along the scree slopes on the south side of the lake.

Ross Lake

Summit Lake (NP)
Status: Doubtful

Summit Lake is a shallow lake located alongside the 1-A Highway just west of Kicking Horse Pass. It is no longer of much interest to fishermen since its ability to hold fish was entirely dependent on regular plantings, a practice that no longer occurs in Summit. Rainbow, cutthroat and brook trout have all been stocked in the past in Summit Lake, and all have failed to reproduce. Due to the high propensity for winter kill, it is doubtful if any trout are still present in Summit Lake.

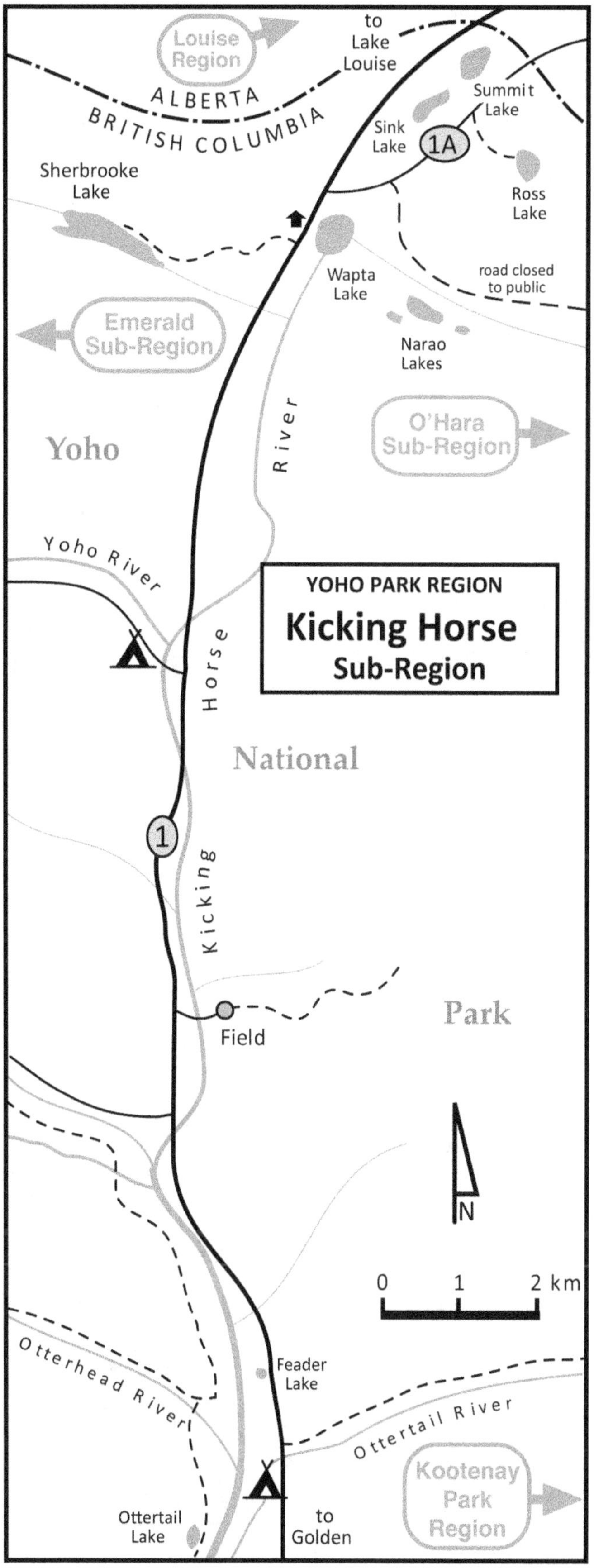

YOHO PARK REGION: Kicking Horse Sub-Region

Sink Lake (NP)
Status: Doubtful

Sink Lake possesses many of the same characteristics as nearby Summit Lake. Winter kill has been a major factor in the demise of fish in the lake over the years. Rainbow, brook and cutthroat trout, as well as splake, have all been planted in Sink Lake, but failed to take hold. Although unlikely, some remnants of rainbow and brook trout plantings may still exist.

Wapta Lake (NP)
Lake trout to 60 cm (2.5 kg)
Rainbow trout to 40 cm
Brook trout to 40 cm

Wapta Lake receives relatively little fishing pressure despite its proximity to the Trans-Canada Highway. Rainbow, brook and lake trout are all present with most fish averaging 25-35 cm. As the lake is silted in nature, the area around the inlet and outlet generally produce the best.

Wapta Lake

Narao Lakes (NP)
Brook trout to 35 cm

The Narao Lakes are set amid marshy surroundings 2 km by trail south of Wapta Lake, and are seldom visited by anglers. Although the lakes were stocked in the past with brook trout, their reproductive success is suspect at best.

Sherbrooke Lake (NP)
Rainbow trout to 50 cm (1.5 kg)
Lake trout to 55 cm (2.0 kg)

The narrow valley between Paget Peak and Mount Ogden holds the elongated form of Sherbrooke Lake. Inlet streams flow from the Daly and Niles Glaciers, and Sherbrooke Lake is very silted. Fishing is slow for rainbow and lake trout that average 30-40 cm in length. Anglers working around the shore can usually take rainbows in the shallow water, particularly in the area of the outlet that is strewn with deadfall. Anglers using lures will have an advantage over fly fishers in catching Sherbrooke's lake trout.

Sherbrooke Lake

Otterhead River (NP)
Bull trout to 40 cm
Brook trout to 30 cm
Whitefish to 30 cm

The Otterhead River joins the Kicking Horse River as a major tributary approximately 5 km west of Field. It can be accessed from a fire road along the north side of the Kicking Horse River. The Otterhead River contains bull and brook trout along with whitefish in its lower reaches and bull trout in its upper waters. Most fish taken are small, averaging only 15-25 cm in length.

Feader Lake (NP)
Brook trout to 30 cm

Feader Lake is a small pond alongside the Trans-Canada Highway. It at one time held a small population of brook trout, which may still exist in limited numbers.

Ottertail Lake (NP)
Brook trout to 35 cm

Ottertail Lake is located on the north side of the Kicking Horse River, just over a kilometre west of the river's confluence with the Otterhead River. The lake is seldom fished, but it does hold a few brook trout in the 15-25 cm range.

Ottertail River (NP)
Bull trout to 40 cm
Brook trout to 30 cm
Whitefish to 30 cm

A fire road branching off the Trans-Canada Highway leads up the Ottertail drainage, where trails link to Lake O'Hara and Kootenay National Park. Whitefish, brook and bull trout all inhabit the lower stretches of the Ottertail River. Small bull trout can be caught in the headwaters.

Ottertail River

NORTH SASKATCHEWAN REGION

This Region takes in much of the upper North Saskatchewan River watershed. The Icefields Parkway (Highway 93), runs north south, and is the main access through the Region. The David Thompson Highway (Highway 11) connects to the Icefields Parkway at Saskatchewan Crossing, and provides a direct connection to Rocky Mountain House and central Alberta. Fishing opportunities in the Region are limited, as fast-flowing rivers and glacial lakes are the norm. The North Saskatchewan Region is divided into three Sub-Regions. The most southerly Sub-Region covers the Mistaya River drainage. The northern Saskatchewan Crossing Sub-Region includes the North Saskatchewan River valley within Banff National Park. The eastern most Sub-Region is centred on the Abraham Lake-Kootenay Plains area, and is located outside the Banff Park boundary.

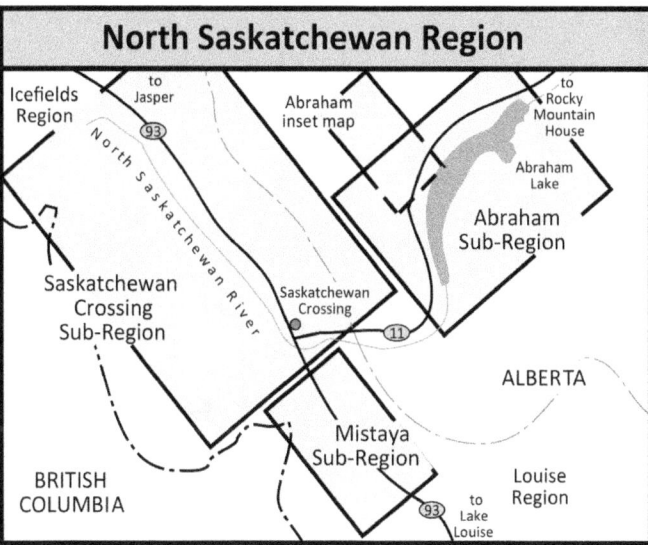

Mistaya Sub-Region

The Mistaya River flows north through the core of the Sub-Region, from Peyto Lake to the North Saskatchewan River, and is paralleled by the Icefields Parkway. The area is well known for the magnificent views of the spectacular mountain and glaciers from the Parkway. The Sub-Region only offers mediocre angling in its best lakes, notably the Waterfowl Lakes and nearby Cirque, Chephren and Mistaya Lakes. The spectacular colouration of the Sub-Region's lakes is attributable to the presence of glacial silt, with the much-photographed blue waters of Peyto Lake being the most prominent example.

Peyto Lake (NP)
Cutthroat trout to 50 cm (1.5 kg)
Although it is admired by thousands of tourists from the viewpoint at Bow Summit each summer, Peyto Lake receives relatively few visitors to its shores. This is no doubt due to the steep 2 km trail, which descends from the Icefields Parkway to lake level. Fishing in Peyto's delightful blue water for cutthroat trout averaging 25-35 cm in length is usually slow. During the heat of the summer, the nearby glaciers deposit large amounts of silt into Peyto Lake. As the temperature begins to cool by autumn, fishing improves somewhat. The area around the lake's outlet is the most productive.

Peyto Lake

Caldron Lake (NP)
Status: Devoid of fish
Caldron Lake lies hidden in an isolated hanging valley west of the Peyto Glacier and 5 km upstream from Peyto Lake. Caldron Lake has never been stocked and contains no fish.

Mistaya River (NP)
Cutthroat trout to 50 cm (1.5 kg)
Rainbow trout to 45 cm
Brook trout to 45 cm
Bull trout to 70 cm (4.0 kg)
Whitefish to 40 cm
The Mistaya River, flowing north from Peyto Lake to the North Saskatchewan River, possesses many long stretches of fishable water, especially in the area between Mistaya and Waterfowl Lakes. The angling season is shortened by the long run-off that brings large amounts of silt down from the icefields to the west. Fishing tends to improve in the late season on the Mistaya River, but still is only fair at best. Depending on which section of river is being fished, a variety of species can be caught. Cutthroat are dominant in the upper reaches and bull trout in the lower, while in the stretch from Mistaya Lake through to the Waterfowl Lakes, cutthroat and brook trout make up the greatest percentage, with rainbow trout present as well. Whitefish can also be taken from many spots along the river throughout its length. Although a short jaunt through the bush is usually required, the Mistaya is always within a kilometre or two of the Icefields Parkway.

Mistaya Lake (NP)
Cutthroat to 55 cm (2.0 kg)
Brook trout to 40 cm
Rainbow trout to 40 cm
Mistaya Lake is hidden by heavy forest, and goes unnoticed by most visitors, despite the crowded campground at Waterfowl Lakes, only 2 km distant. Cutthroat trout averaging 25-35 cm in length predominate in Mistaya, although the odd brook or rainbow trout occasionally makes its way in from Waterfowl Lakes. It's possible whitefish and bull trout may also be present

NORTH SASKATCHEWAN REGION: Mistaya Sub-Region

in limited numbers. As the lake is silted much of the summer, fish tend to keep to the shallower waters in search of food. The waters around the inlet are the most productive if silting isn't too heavy.

Capricorn Lake (NP)
Status: Devoid of fish
Capricorn Lake is set beneath the Capricorn Glacier in a cirque high above Mistaya Lake. Capricorn Lake has never been stocked and is devoid of fish.

Waterfowl Lakes (NP)
Cutthroat trout to 50 cm (1.5 kg)
Brook trout to 50 cm (1.5 kg)
Rainbow trout to 50 cm (1.5 kg)
Upper and Lower Waterfowl are by far the most popular fishing spots in the Sub-Region. A major campground is situated between the two lakes. The Waterfowl Lakes are similar in character to most other major lakes along the Mistaya River. Heavy silting occurs, which accounts for the lake's appealing blue-green colouration. Cutthroat and brook trout averaging 25-35 cm in length are the normal catch. Areas around the inlets and outlets can be productive at times.

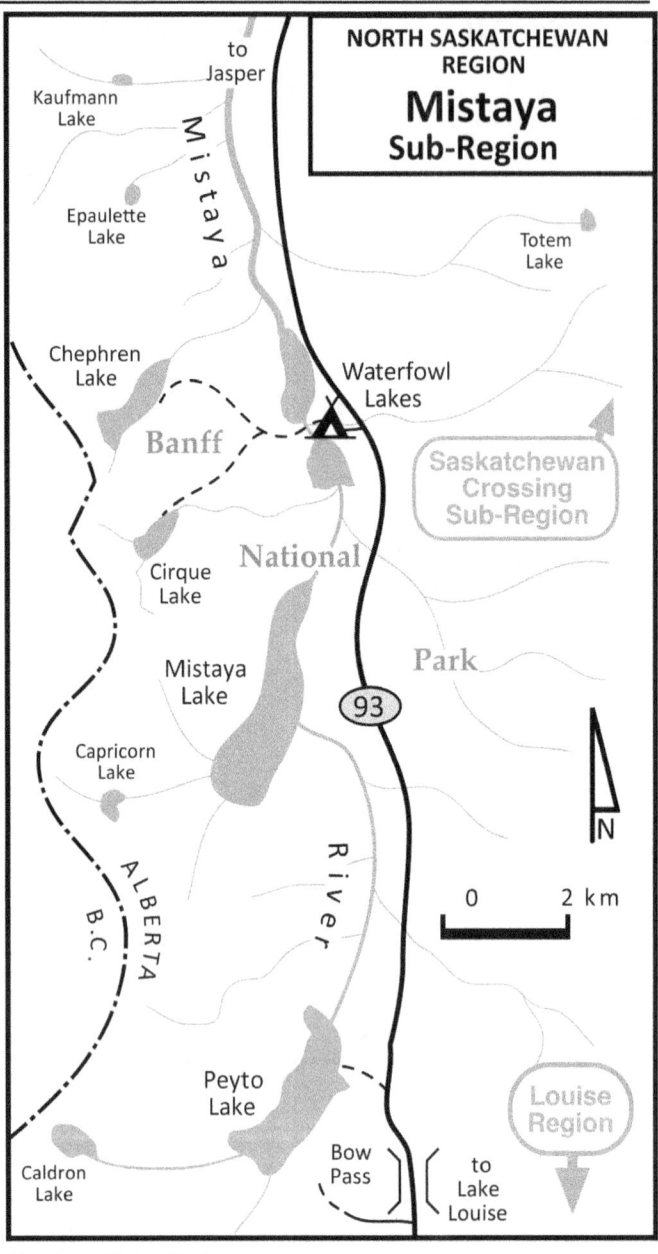

Lower Waterfowl Lake

Cirque Lake (NP)
Brook trout to 50 cm (1.5 kg)
Rainbow trout to 45 cm
Cirque Lake lies tucked away in a side valley 5 km by trail from the Waterfowl Lakes campground. Cirque Lake is generally silted due to run-off from glaciers at the head of the lake. The lake fishes better in the late season for brook and rainbow trout averaging 20-30 cm in length. An extensive outlet strewn with deadfall usually holds trout, although many a fly or lure will be lost to snags.

Cirque Lake

Chephren Lake (NP)
Brook trout to 50 cm (1.5 kg)
Cutthroat trout to 50 cm (1.5 kg)
Rainbow trout to 50 cm (1.5 kg)
Chephren Lake is lightly larger than Cirque Lake, and occupies the next side valley to the north, 4 km by trail from the Waterfowl Lakes. Chephren Lake offers fair fishing for brook, cutthroat and rainbow trout in the 25-35 cm range. Fish can usually be taken close to shore, with the large amount of sunken deadfall providing excellent cover for the trout. Flies work well, and casting is possible from many locations.

Chephren Lake

Epaulette Lake (NP)
Status: Devoid of fish
Epaulette Lake is located 2 km west of the Mistaya River through heavy forest, and is inaccessible to all but the most determined route-finders. Fortunately for anglers, Epaulette Lake has never been stocked and contains no fish.

Kaufmann Lake (NP)
Status: Devoid of fish
No fish are present in this tiny glacial tarn set beneath the east face of Mt. Sarbach.

Totem Lake (NP)
Status: Unknown
Totem Lake is set high in a stark, rocky basin on the flank of Mt. Murchison, and is accessed by an ill-defined, difficult 6 km trail from the Icefields Parkway. Totem Lake is far removed from fishing pressure. Although the lake was stocked in the past with rainbow trout, few confirmed reports about Totem Lake ever make their way out, and it is unknown whether any fish remain.

Saskatchewan Crossing Sub-Region

This Sub-Region encompasses the northern end of Banff National Park, and is dominated geographically by the mighty North Saskatchewan River and its tributaries. The Icefields Parkway (Highway 93) provides the main access into the Sub-Region, and is intersected by Highway 11 (David Thompson Highway), coming in from the east at Saskatchewan River Crossing. Limited tourist supplies of gas, food and lodging can be found at The Crossing. Hiking is required to reach the shores of most lakes in the area. The Howse River, a major tributary to the North Saskatchewan, contains David, Outram, Lagoon and Glacier Lakes within its watershed, while farther north the Alexandra River and Arctomys Creek flow west to join the North Saskatchewan River.

North Saskatchewan River (NP)
(Headwaters to Banff Park boundary)
Bull trout to 70 cm (4.0 kg)
Lake trout to 65 cm (3.0 kg)
Whitefish to 50 cm (1.5 kg)
Brook trout to 40 cm
Rainbow trout to 40 cm
The North Saskatchewan River flows from its source at Saskatchewan Glacier and is joined by a number of other glacial rivers. The North Saskatchewan River is heavily silted much of the year, only clearing in late summer. During run-off, fishing is very slow, and usually confined to waters around clearer flowing tributary streams. When run-off is finally complete, fishing improves along the entire length of the river with large bull and lake trout, along with whitefish, making up the vast majority of fish in the river. Brook and rainbow trout are also caught on occasion. Fishing is usually productive near the mouths of the Mistaya, Howse and Alexandra Rivers.

North Saskatchewan River

Howse River (NP)
Bull trout to 65 cm (3.0 kg)
Lake trout to 60 cm (2.5 kg)
Whitefish to 40 cm
The Howse River flows from headwaters below historic Howse Pass to its junction with the North Saskatchewan River, just west of Saskatchewan River Crossing. Flowing through a broad valley over its final 10 km, the Howse River is characterized by wide gravel flats with extensive braiding where you can fish for bull trout in the 30-40 cm range, plus whitefish and the occasional lake trout. Generally, fishing is very slow in the Howse River, picking up somewhat in late summer and early fall, when water levels recede and the river clears. A major horse trail leading to Howse Pass parallels the river for its entire length.

Howse River

Lagoon Lake (NP)
Bull trout to 65 cm (3.0 kg)
Lagoon Lake lies in marshy meadows east of the Howse River near a backcountry campground and warden's cabin, approximately 20 km by trail from the Icefields Parkway. Lagoon Lake was stocked in the past with rainbow trout that apparently failed to reproduce. At present, the lake contains bull trout and possibly a few whitefish, which have made their way in from the Howse River.

NORTH SASKATCHEWAN REGION: Saskatchewan Crossing Sub-Region

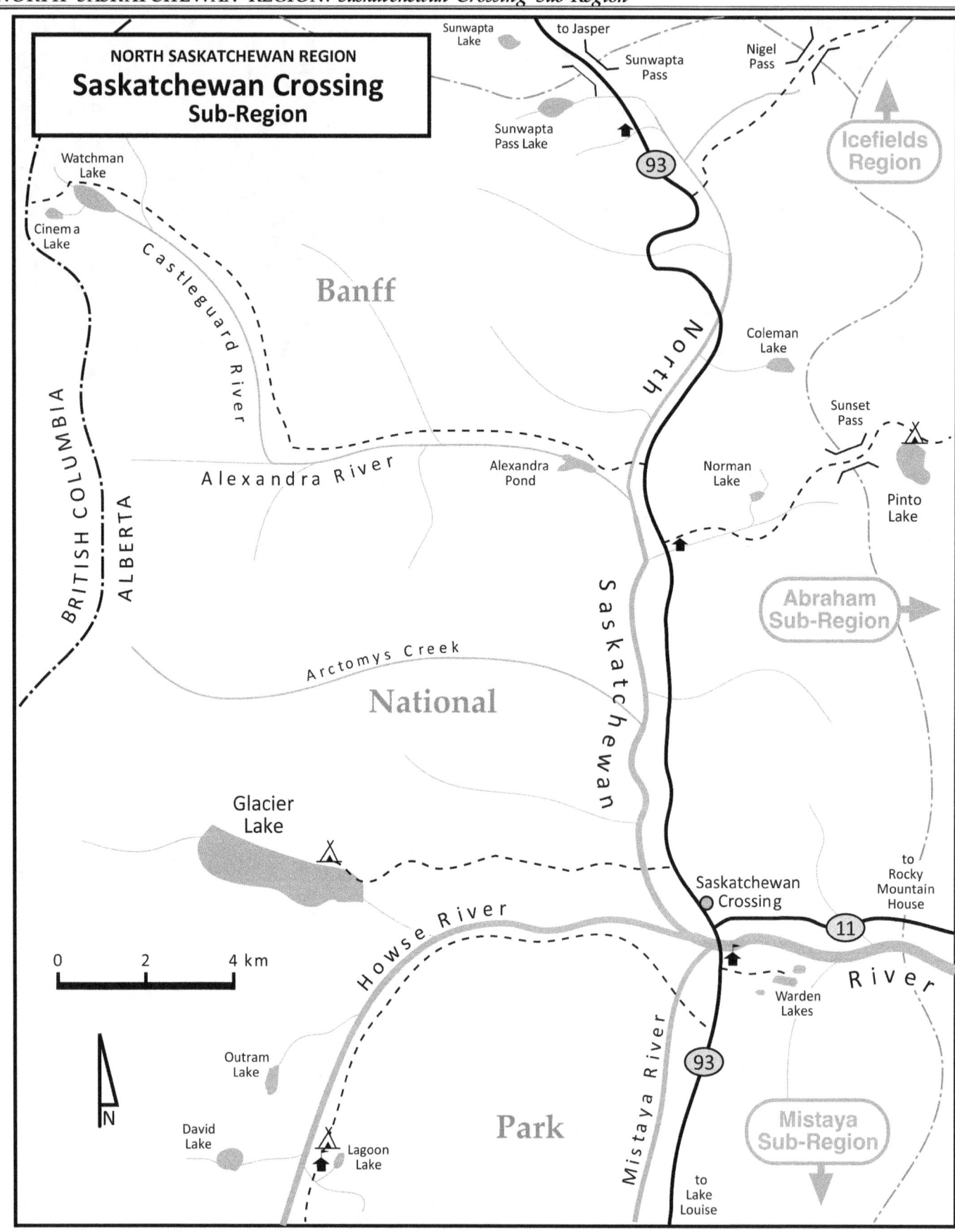

NORTH SASKATCHEWAN REGION: Saskatchewan Crossing Sub-Region

David Lake (NP)
Rainbow trout to 35 cm
David Lake is set in a cirque directly beneath the north face of Mt. David. It is well protected by a major ford of the Howse River, and by steep and difficult terrain over its final 2 km of approach. Very few visitors reach the lake each year. Due to lack of information, it is has never been determined whether the rainbow trout stocked a number of years ago still exist in good numbers.

Outram Lake (NP)
Bull trout to 60 cm (3.5 kg)
Whitefish to 35 cm
Rainbow trout to 35 cm
A ford of the Howse River, which is passable for hikers by late summer, is required in order to reach Outram Lake. Outram Lake is located on a bench above the west bank of the Howse River, opposite the Lagoon Lake warden cabin. The lake holds rainbow and bull trout in good numbers, as well as whitefish. Due to its lengthy and difficult access, Outram Lake offers the promise of solitude.

Glacier Lake (NP)
Lake trout to 80 cm (7.0 kg)
Bull trout to 70 cm (4.5 kg)
Whitefish to 50 cm (1.5 kg)
Glacier Lake is the largest lake in the Sub-Region, but has never gained a favourable reputation for fishing. This is due to run-off from the nearby Lyell Glacier, which ensures the water is heavily silted all year long. When the waters clear in the late season, the area around the outlet is worth a look. Those using lures will have the best success in Glacier, which holds some lake and bull trout of gigantic proportions, as well as whitefish in fair numbers. Although fish can be taken from most locations along the shore, the sheer size of the lake will intimidate most anglers.

Glacier Lake

Warden Lakes (NP)
Rainbow trout to 50 cm (1.5 kg)
Brook trout to 45 cm
The two Warden Lakes are located on a bench south of the North Saskatchewan River, 2 km east of the Icefields Parkway by trail. The Lower Lake was stocked in the past with both rainbow and brook trout, which failed to reproduce, and the lake is now devoid of fish. The larger Upper Warden Lake has been stocked in the past with rainbow trout, cutthroat trout, brook trout and splake. Winter kill is an annual danger, and it is likely that only rainbow or brook trout are now present in very limited numbers.

Upper Warden Lake

Arctomys Creek (NP)
Bull trout to 50 cm (1.5 kg)
Whitefish to 35 cm
Arctomys Creek is born in the Lyell Glacier, high among the peaks of the Continental Divide. Arctomys Creek possesses the same characteristics as other major rivers of the region, as it runs very silted most of the year. It clears up marginally in late summer, when a limited population of bull trout and whitefish can be caught in its lower reaches. Access is difficult, requiring either a near impossible ford of the North Saskatchewan River or a long, ill-defined approach from the Glacier Lake trail.

Norman Lake (NP)
Brook trout to 35 cm
Norman Lake is located 5 km along the Sunset Pass trail from the Icefields Parkway, and is bypassed by most hikers on their way to Pinto Lake. Norman Lake is set in marshy and mosquito infested meadows below Sunset Pass, and holds a small population of brook trout averaging 20-30 cm in length. Flies are effective, and fly casting room is plentiful around the shoreline, although wet feet are a definite possibility.

Norman Lake

Pinto Lake (NP)
Status: Closed to angling
Pinto Lake is located on the north side of Sunset Pass, just outside the Banff National Park boundary. It is very popular with outfitters and backpackers during the summer. A 14 km trail from the Icefields Parkway is the usual route of approach, although outfitters tend to favour the longer access up the Cline River from the David Thompson Highway. Renowned in the past for the angling for its large bull trout, Pinto Lake is at present closed to fishing to protect the remaining bull trout population.

NORTH SASKATCHEWAN REGION: Saskatchewan Crossing Sub-Region

Pinto Lake

Alexandra Pond (NP)
Lake trout to 60 cm (3.0 kg.)
Bull trout to 60 cm (3.0 kg.)
Whitefish to 40 cm
Alexandra Pond is merely a widening of the Alexandra River, and is located less than a kilometre upstream from the Alexandra's confluence with the North Saskatchewan River. It is reached by a trail that bridges the North Saskatchewan, but receives little fishing pressure. The early season is too silted for angling, and even after run-off is over, fishing is slow for lake trout, bull trout and whitefish.

Alexandra River (NP)
Bull trout to 55 cm (2.0 kg)
Lake trout to 55 cm (2.0 kg)
Whitefish to 35 cm
The Alexandra River is a major tributary of the North Saskatchewan River, and offers poor fishing over its entire length. The lower reaches, just above and below Alexandra Pond, provide fair fishing for whitefish, lake trout and bull trout, which are present in limited numbers.

Alexandra River

Castleguard River (NP)
Bull trout to 50 cm (1.5 kg)
Whitefish to 30 cm
The Castleguard River is a tributary of the upper Alexandra River, and presents very few opportunities for anglers. A few bull trout and whitefish may be present in the river.

Watchman Lake (NP)
Status: Closed to angling
Two days of hiking from the Icefields Parkway are required to reach Watchman Lake. It is an attractive body of water, set in subalpine forest 2 km northwest of seldom-visited Thompson Pass. The cutthroat trout in the lake are protected by an angling ban at present.

Cinema Lake (NP)
Status: Devoid of fish
Cinema Lake guards the northwest entrance to Thompson Pass. It has never been stocked and contains no fish.

Coleman Lake (NP)
Status: Devoid of fish
Coleman Lake is defended by a line of cliffs, and is reached by only the most enterprising of individuals. Coleman Lake has never been stocked, and no fish are present in its waters.

Sunwapta Pass Lake (NP)
Status: Doubtful
Although it sits in a sparse forest less than a kilometre from the busy Icefields Parkway, the silted waters of Sunwapta Pass Lake receive very little attention from hikers or anglers. A series of intermittent game trails lead in short order from the Sunwapta Pass parking area to the lake's shoreline. Sunwapta Pass Lake was stocked in the past with cutthroat and brook trout, both of which may still exist in small numbers.

Sunwapta Pass Lake

Sunwapta Lake (NP)
Status: Devoid of fish
This small tarn at the toe of the awe-inspiring Athabasca Glacier is barren.

Abraham Sub-Region

This Sub-Regions lies to the east of Banff National Park along the North Saskatchewan River valley. The Kootenay Plains and Lake Abraham are the most significant natural features. Highway 11 (David Thompson Highway) connects east to Rocky Mountain House and west to Banff National Park and the Icefields Parkway. Fishing opportunities in the Abraham Sub-Region are mixed. There is some excellent backcountry lakes, typified by Landslide Lake and Lake of the Falls. The more prominent waters, such as Abraham Lake and the North Saskatchewan River, offer only fair angling.

NORTH SASKATCHEWAN REGION: Abraham Sub-Region

Abraham Lake (AB)
Bull trout to 75 cm (6.0 kg)
Cutthroat trout to 55 cm (2.0 kg)
Brook trout to 55 cm (2.0 kg)
Lake trout to 70 cm (5.0 kg)
Rainbow trout to 60 cm (2.5 kg)
Whitefish to 50 cm (1.5 kg)

Abraham Lake was created by the construction of the Bighorn Dam on the North Saskatchewan River. Although Abraham Lake contains a wide variety of game fish, it has never been noted for its quality of angling. Hurricane force winds regularly whip down the length of the lake, making it very dangerous for boating. Fishing from shore is most productive where major streams or rivers enter the lake. This includes the Cline River and Tershishner Creek. Bull, cutthroat and brook trout are the most likely catch, although there are other species present.

Abraham Lake

North Saskatchewan River (AB)
(Banff Park boundary to Abraham Lake)
Cutthroat trout to 55 cm (2.0 kg)
Bull trout to 75 cm (6.0 kg)
Brook trout to 55 cm (2.0 kg)
Lake trout to 60 cm (3.0 kg)
Whitefish to 50 cm (1.5 kg)

The North Saskatchewan River is paralleled by Highway 11 as it flows from Banff National Park to Abraham Lake. The lake is very silted for most of the year, clearing up only in the fall. Fishing on this section of the North Saskatchewan River is generally confined to September and October. Angling is poor to fair for cutthroat, bull, brook and lake trout. Some of the deep pools can produce well on occasion.

North Saskatchewan River

Landslide Lake (AB)
Cutthroat trout to 60 cm (2.0 kg)

Landslide Lake is situated 17 km by trail from Highway 11. Its pristine waters hold good numbers of large cutthroat trout. Most trout caught from Landslide Lake will average 30-40 cm in length. Angling is good around virtually the entire lake. The area near the outlet is popular due to its proximity to the main camping areas. The waters around the various inlet creeks at the south end of the lake are very productive.

Landslide Lake

(cutthroat trout)

Lake of the Falls (AB)
Cutthroat trout to 45 cm
Bull trout to 55 cm (2.0 kg)

Lake of the Falls is 17 km by trail from Highway 11, and the first two-thirds of the access trail are the same as for Landslide Lake. Lake of the Falls is set in a beautiful subalpine basin. It holds cutthroat and bull trout that average 25-35 cm in length. Flies work effectively, and there is plenty of casting room available along the shoreline.

Lake of the Falls

Entry (Hidden) Lake (AB)
Cutthroat trout to 45 cm

Entry Lake is a small lake located east of the hiking trail into Landslide Lake. It holds small cutthroat trout, most in the 25-35 cm range.

Entry Creek (AB)
Cutthroat trout to 35 cm
Bull trout to 35 cm

Entry Creek is a tributary of the Cline River, and collects its water from the Lake of the Falls and Landslide Creek. Entry Creek contains small cutthroat trout in its lower reaches, and bull trout as far upstream as its confluence with Landslide Creek.

NORTH SASKATCHEWAN REGION: Abraham Sub-Region

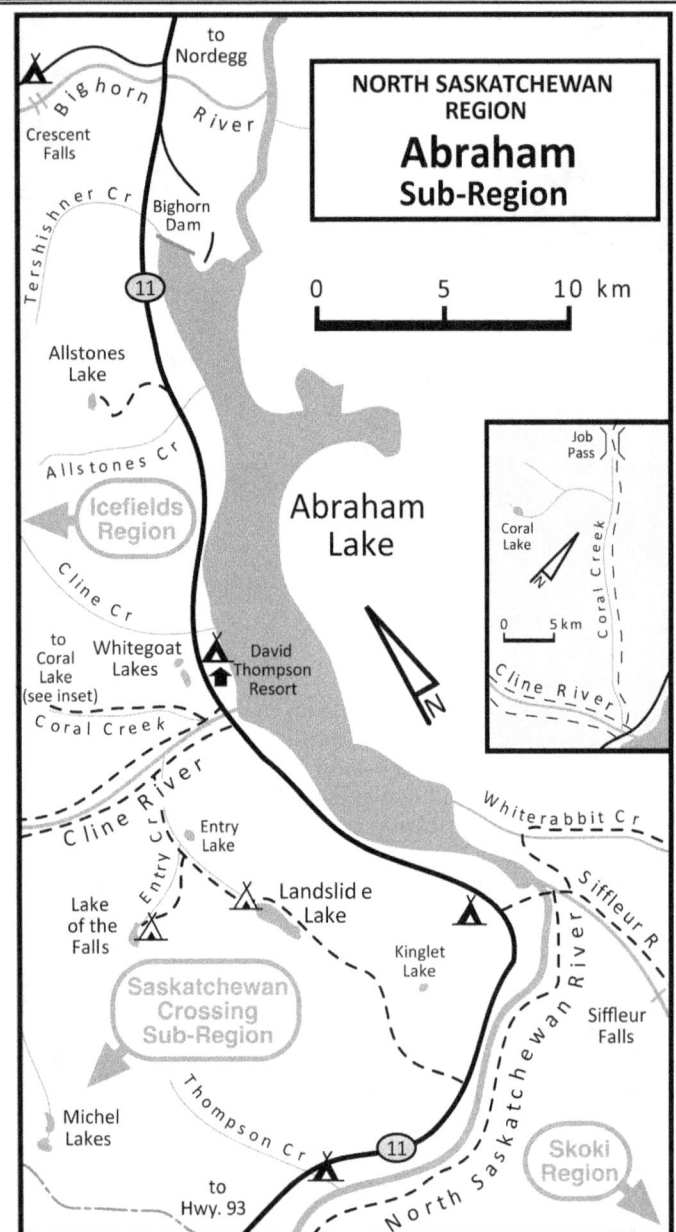

Cline River

Whitegoat Lakes (AB)
Status: Doubtful
The Whitegoat Lakes are located a short distance off Highway 11, opposite the David Thompson Resort. Several short trails lead to the lakes. The Whitegoat Lakes are very shallow, and fish are unable to over winter in the lakes. The occasional trout may make its way into the lakes each summer via the outlet creek.

Whitegoat Lakes

Siffleur River (AB)
(Banff Park boundary to North Saskatchewan River)
Status: Closed to angling
The section of the Siffleur River that flows from Banff National Park to the North Saskatchewan River is closed to angling. Siffleur Falls are located 4 km by trail from Highway 11, and are worth viewing.

Siffleur River

Cline River (AB)
Bull trout to 60 cm (3.0 kg)
Cutthroat trout to 55 cm (2.0 kg)
Brook trout to 50 cm (1.5 kg)
Whitefish to 50 cm (1.5 kg)
The Cline River is a major tributary of the North Saskatchewan River that enters Abraham Lake. There are three distinct sections on the Cline River. The first few kilometres above Abraham Lake are usually good for brook and bull trout. Continuing upstream, the river enters a major canyon, where fishing is difficult due to rough access. Above the canyon, the river is paralleled by a good horse trail. Cutthroat trout are present in good numbers above the canyon, with most in the 20-30 cm range. Fly fishing is the best method of angling on the upper Cline River.

Kinglet Lake (AB)
Cutthroat trout to 35 cm
Kinglet Lake is a small tarn set high in an alpine cirque north of Whirlpool Point on the North Saskatchewan River. Access is difficult, and requires a stiff trek up a rocky ridge from Highway 11. The lake has been stocked on several occasions, and holds small cutthroat trout in the 20-30 cm range.

NORTH SASKATCHEWAN REGION: Abraham Sub-Region

Allstones Lake (AB)
Brook trout to 45 cm

Allstones Lake is set in a forested basin, and is reached by following a very steep 5 km trail up from Highway 11. The lake holds brook trout which average 25-35 cm in length. Lures and flies both work well in Allstones Lake. Fly fishing is difficult in most locations because of the forest cover.

Allstones Lake

Michele Lakes (AB)
Golden trout to 40 cm

The Michele Lakes are reached after a long hike up the Cline River and then a torturous route up Waterfalls Creek. These lakes are for very determined anglers only. The Michele Lakes are unique in that they hold golden trout, one of Alberta's rarest game fish. The golden trout in the lakes have not done particularly well in the Michele Lakes, and they are neither large or numerous. Any trout caught will be in the 20-30 cm size range.

Coral Lake (AB)
Golden trout to 40 cm

Each season Coral Lake attracts anglers in search of the elusive golden trout. Coral Lake is reached by a long and difficult trail up the Cline River and Coral Creek valleys. For those hardy souls who reach Coral Lake, expect golden trout in the 20-30 cm range.

Golden trout

Bighorn River (AB)
Cutthroat trout to 40 cm
Brook trout to 45 cm
Brown trout to 45 cm
Bull trout to 70 cm (4.0 kg)
Whitefish to 50 cm (1.5 kg)

The Bighorn River is a major tributary of the North Saskatchewan River and enters downstream from Abraham Lake and the Bighorn Dam. The spectacular Crescent Falls are an impassable obstacle for fish. Below the falls, bull and brook trout are most likely to be caught. Brown trout and whitefish may be present as well. Above Crescent Falls, cutthroat trout are present in good numbers. Fly fishing is very effective on the upper Bighorn River.

Bighorn River (Crescent Falls)

Tershishner Creek (AB)
Brook trout to 45 cm
Bull trout to 60 cm (3.0 kg)
Whitefish to 45 cm

Tershishner Creek joins the North Saskatchewan River at the north end Abraham Lake, near the Bighorn Dam. Fishing is generally good where Tershishner Creek enters Abraham Lake. Upstream from Abraham Lake, Tershishner Creek holds brook and bull trout in the 20-30 cm range, as well as whitefish.

ICEFIELDS REGION

This Region encompasses the southern half of Jasper National Park. It includes the watersheds of the upper Athabasca, Sunwapta and Brazeau Rivers. The Icefields Parkway (Highway 93) follows the course of the Athabasca and Sunwapta Rivers, and offers prospective anglers direct access to several roadside locations. Beyond the Icefields Parkway, access to most of the rest of the Region is very difficult and requires extended travel by trail. There are some outstanding lakes in the Region, highlighted by Amethyst Lakes in Tonquin Valley and Fortress Lake in B.C.'s Hamber Provincial Forest. The Region is divided into three Sub-Regions. The Upper Athabasca Sub-Region includes the main Athabasca valley upstream (south) of Athabasca Falls. The Brazeau Sub-Region is very remote, and includes the Brazeau River drainage within Jasper National Park. The Tonquin Sub-Region includes the renowned Tonquin Valley and its outstanding backpacking opportunities.

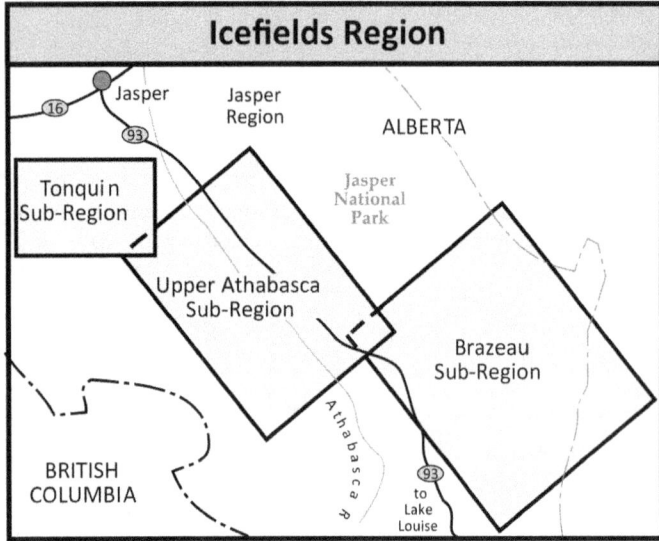

Upper Athabasca Sub-Region

This Sub-Region extends from Banff National Park in the south to Athabasca Falls in the north, and includes the Sunwapta and upper Athabasca River valleys. The Icefields Parkway (Highway 93) is the sole highway access. Angling opportunities are limited to lakes that have been stocked in the past and now have stable trout populations. The best of the Sub-Region include Moab and Fortress Lakes.

Sunwapta River (NP)
Bull trout to 70 cm (4.0 kg)
Rainbow trout to 50 cm (1.5 kg)
Brook trout to 45 cm
Whitefish to 45 cm
The Sunwapta River flows northwest from the Banff-Jasper Boundary at Sunwapta Pass, and joins the Athabasca River 3 km downstream from Sunwapta Falls. The river is readily accessible from the Icefields Parkway, and offers mediocre fishing below the falls for bull, rainbow and brook trout. With its source high among the glaciers of the Continental Divide, the Sunwapta River runs silted for much of the year, clearing only in the fall.

Athabasca River (NP)
Bull trout to 80 cm (7.0 kg)
Rainbow trout to 50 cm (1.5 kg)
Brook trout to 50 cm (1.5 kg)
Whitefish to 50 cm (1.5 kg)
The headwaters of the Athabasca River, upstream from Athabasca Falls, is typically silted much of the year. The river clears long enough in the fall to offer some fishing opportunities. Bull trout and whitefish are the main fare in the upper Athabasca River, with the occasional rainbow and brook trout taken. Anglers are advised to work areas around the confluence with clearer tributaries.

Fortress Lake (BC)
Brook trout to 70 cm (4.0 kg)
A 25 km hike that includes a major ford of the Chaba River leads to Fortress Lake, a beautiful 10-km long body of water situated just west of the Alberta-B.C. boundary at Fortress Pass. Fortress Lake is renowned for its monster brook trout, many of which will top the 2 kg mark. The lake, which is located in Hamber Provincial Forest in B.C., has been popular among fly-in anglers and outfitters' parties for many years. Fortress Lake Lodge, complete with boats, is available for the fly-in crowd. Fortress Lake's remote location ensures that the quality of fishing should remain high for many years to come.

Fortress Lake

(brook trout)

ICEFIELDS REGION: Upper Athabasca Sub-Region

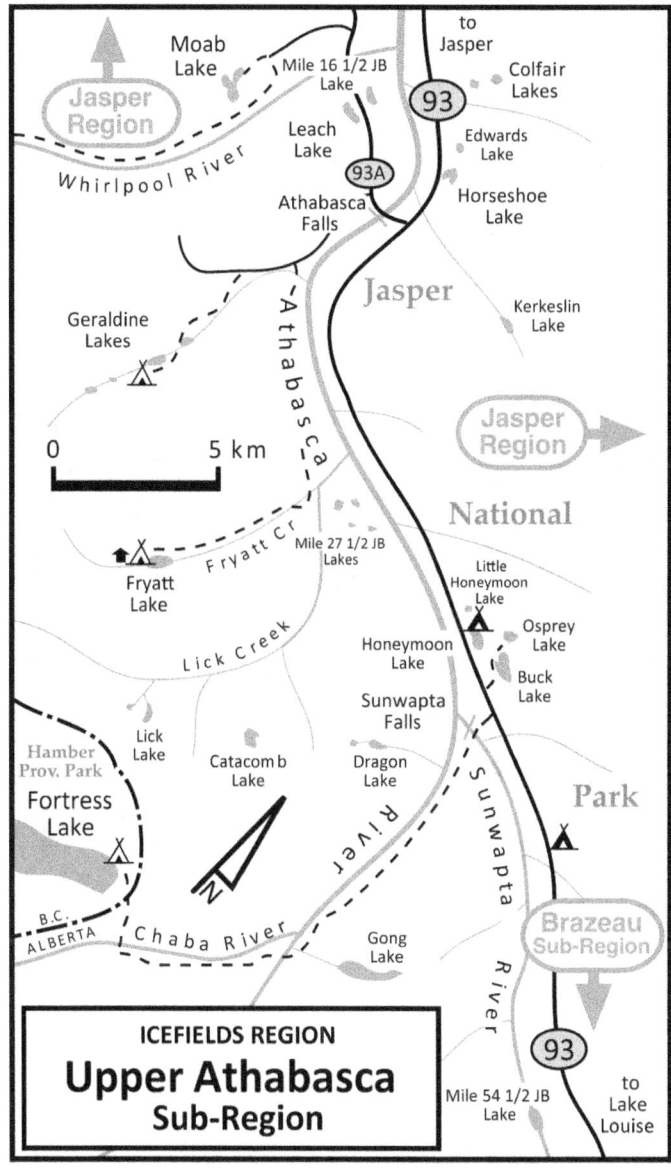

ICEFIELDS REGION
Upper Athabasca Sub-Region

Mile 54 Jasper-Banff Lake (NP)
Brook trout to 40 cm
Mile 54 Lake is located alongside the Sunwapta River and Icefields Parkway, approximately 20 km south of Sunwapta Falls. Although it was stocked in the past with both brook and rainbow trout, it is likely that only a limited number of brook trout remain.

Gong Lake (NP)
Status: Devoid of trout
This large glacial lake near the headwaters of the Athabasca River has never been stocked and contains no fish.

Dragon Lake (NP)
Brook trout to 40 cm
Dragon Lake is protected by a major ford of the Athabasca River and by poorly defined access routes. The lake was stocked in the past with brook trout, and recent reports indicate that some trout still exist, although their numbers are limited.

Buck Lake (NP)
Brook trout to 50 cm (1.5 kg)
Rainbow trout to 50 cm (1.5 kg)
Surrounded by heavy forest, Buck Lake sits less than a kilometre by trail from the Icefields Parkway and is surrounded by heavy forest. Buck Lake holds both rainbow and brook trout, averaging 25-35 cm in length, but since the lake's ability to hold trout has generally been dependent on regular stockings, the quality of fishing has declined significantly in recent years.

Osprey Lake (NP)
Status: Closed to angling
This small reed-fringed lake is a short 15 minute trail walk from the Icefields Parkway. Osprey is closed to angling at the present time.

Honeymoon Lake (NP)
Rainbow trout to 60 cm (2.5 kg)
Honeymoon Lake is situated immediately east of the Icefields Parkway, and has a nice campground on its shore. Honeymoon Lake is a popular fishing spot for anglers. Rainbow trout averaging 25-35 cm in length inhabit Honeymoon's waters. Reports indicate that the quality of fishing has declined somewhat in the past few years, and the lake's ability to hold fish is also in question.

Honeymoon Lake

Little Honeymoon Lake (NP)
Brook trout to 35 cm
Little Honeymoon Lake is located just north of Honeymoon Lake. It was stocked in the past with brook trout, which still may be present in limited numbers.

Lick Lake, Catacomb Lake (NP)
Status: Devoid of fish
These two glacial lakes are set high among the peaks of the Continental Divide at the head of Lick Creek, a minor tributary of the Athabasca River. The lakes have never been stocked and contain no fish.

Moab Lake (NP)
Lake trout to 75 cm (5.0 kg)
Rainbow trout to 50 cm (1.5 kg)

Pretty Moab Lake is reached via a short 1 km hike at the end of a 7 km-long fire road off Highway 93A. Moab Lake is very popular with anglers, and its clear waters hold rainbow trout along with large lake trout. A limited number of arctic grayling may also be present in the lake. Although the lake's distinctive shape allows for fishing from along much of the shoreline, a boat is strongly recommended. Boats are available for rent on Moab Lake through prior arrangements made with one of Jasper's sporting goods stores. Lure fishers generally have good success with Moab's lake trout. Fly fishing is effective on the rainbow trout population. Be sure to check fishing regulations, as the outlet stream and the lake's outlet are permanently closed to angling.

Moab Lake

Whirlpool River (NP)
Bull trout to 60 cm (2.5 kg)
Rainbow trout to 40 cm
Whitefish to 40 cm

The Whirlpool River is paralleled for its entire distance by the historic Athabasca Pass trail. The river receives little pressure from anglers above its confluence with the Athabasca River. Small bull trout are present in the upper reaches, with bull and rainbow trout along with whitefish in the lower river. The waters near the Whirlpool's confluence with the Athabasca usually hold fish.

Whirlpool River

Geraldine Lakes (NP)
Rainbow trout to 55 cm (2.0 kg)
Brook trout to 50 cm (1.5 kg)

These five exquisite lakes strung like pearls in a series of basins separated by short headwalls are one of the Sub-Region's more popular day hikes. The first lake lies less than 2 km from the trailhead on the Geraldine Lakes Fire Road, while the upper (fifth) lake lies another 6 km distant. All five lakes contain both rainbow and brook trout ranging from 25-35 cm in length that can often be sighted well out into the clear waters. Sunken deadfall provides cover in the waters near shore, particularly in the first lake, and anglers are advised to work these areas.

Lower Geraldine Lake

Fryatt Lake (NP)
Rainbow trout to 50 cm (1.5 kg)

Fryatt Lake is pinched in a narrow valley between Brussels Peak and Mt. Fryatt, and is accessed by a tiring 17 km hike from the Geraldine Lakes Fire Road. While the upper Fryatt Creek valley is a favourite haunt of climbers, anglers are more likely to be enticed by Fryatt Lake and its population of rainbow trout. The lake is almost completely encircled by heavy timber that will cause problems for most of those fly fishing.

Colfair Lakes (NP)
Rainbow trout to 50 cm (1.5 kg)

These two small lakes set in the heavily wooded hills north of Hardisty Creek offer good fishing to those who reach their shores. Although an ill-defined trail connects the Colfair Lakes to the Icefields Parkway 2 km distant, finding the trailhead may be a problem. Your best bet is to carry a map and compass. Rainbow trout in the 25-35 cm range are plentiful, and tend to be particularly susceptible to the fly. Although it's doubtful, a few brook trout, remnants of previous plantings, may still exist in the lower lake.

Horseshoe Lake (NP)
Rainbow trout to 50 cm (1.5 kg)

Appropriately-shaped Horseshoe Lake sits alongside the Icefields Parkway 20 km south of Jasper. Although Horseshoe Lake's ability to sustain trout over time has long been questioned, its sparkling blue waters presently hold a few

ICEFIELDS REGION: Brazeau Sub-Region

rainbow trout averaging 25-35 cm in length. The lakeshore is made up of rock rubble that will present problems for those who will be fly casting.

Horseshoe Lake

Edwards Lake (NP)
Rainbow trout to 45 cm
Edwards Lake is located less than a kilometre north of Horseshoe Lake, and is generally overlooked by the area's anglers. Edwards Lake holds rainbow trout in the 25-35 cm range, which can be taken from most locations around the shoreline.

Mile 27 1/2 Jasper-Banff Lake (NP)
Brook trout to 40 cm
This series of ponds are located on the western side of the Icefields Parkway approximately 2 km north of Horseshoe Lake. Brook trout are present in the ponds, and average 20-30 cm in length.

Kerkeslin (Hardisty) Lake (NP)
Bull trout to 60 cm (2.5 kg)
The pristine waters of Kerkeslin Lake are located high in an isolated valley north of Mt. Kerkeslin, and remain virtually untouched. It is reported that Kerkeslin Lake holds a limited population of bull trout that average 35-45 cm in length.

Brazeau Sub-Region

The Brazeau River watershed constitutes the major portion of this Sub-Region, located in the remote southeast corner of Jasper National Park. Extended backpacking trips are required to reach most potential fishing spots in the Sub-Region, which include Brazeau Lake, the Brazeau River and its major tributaries, the Southesk and Cairn Rivers. To the southeast and outside the Jasper National Park boundary are Job and Obstruction Lakes, which can be reached via extended trails from the David Thompson Highway (Highway 11).

Brazeau River (NP/AB)
Bull trout to 65 cm (4.0 kg)
Whitefish to 45 cm
The Brazeau River is a major tributary of the North Saskatchewan River. It has never been noted for its quality of angling in its upper reaches. Access is by trails that parallel the upper river. The Brazeau River is very silted much of the summer, and fishing improves in late August and early September when bull trout and whitefish and the occasional rainbow trout can be taken. Where the Brazeau River forms the boundary of Jasper National Park, national park fishing regulations are in effect.

Brazeau River

Brazeau River bull trout

Brazeau Lake (NP)
Rainbow trout to 70 cm (4.0 kg)
Bull trout to 75 cm (5.0 kg)
Majestic Brazeau Lake is set in a deep valley west of the Brazeau River, and is a remote 30 km by trail away from the Icefields Parkway. As a consequence, Brazeau Lake receives very little attention from anglers. The lake's silted waters contain large rainbow and bull trout in limited numbers. Lures fished deep are often effective in Brazeau Lake, and the area around the outlet can be productive.

Brazeau Lake

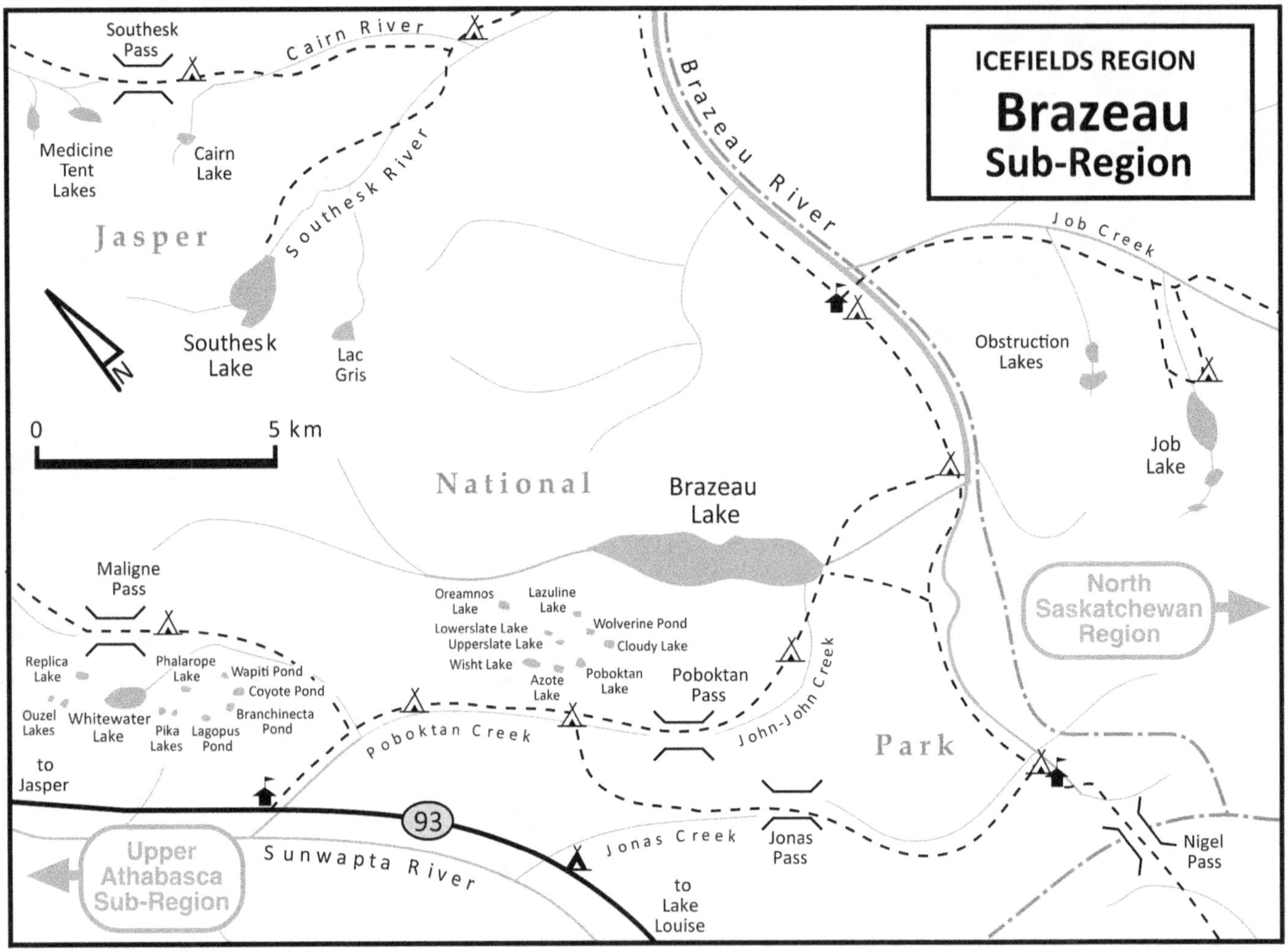

ICEFIELDS REGION: Brazeau Sub-Region

ICEFIELDS REGION
Brazeau Sub-Region

Azote Lake, Wisht Lake, Poboktan Lake, Upperslate Lake, Lowerslate Lake, Wolverine Pond, Cloudy Lake, Oreamnos Lake (NP)
Status: Devoid of fish
This cluster of lakes is located in the valley above Brazeau Lake. None of the lakes have ever been stocked.

Job (Wilson, Blue) Lake (AB)
Status: Closed to angling
Job Lake is exceptional in terms of both beauty and fish habitat. The lake has been popular with outfitters for many years, despite the long 40 km trail from the David Thompson Highway and the even longer 50+ km approach from the Icefields Parkway. For anglers, cutthroat trout in large sizes and good numbers were Job Lake's main attraction. At present, Job is closed to fishing, and anglers should consult the regulations annually to ascertain the lake's status.

Obstruction Lakes (AB)
Cutthroat trout to 40 cm
Tiny Obstruction Lakes, located 4 km southwest of Job Creek by ill-defined trail, receive little attention from anglers each season. The lakes hold cutthroat trout in the 20-30 cm range. Fly fishing is effective, and the lakes have an abundance of fly casting room.

Southesk Lake (NP)
Bull trout to 60 cm (2.5 kg)
Poor trails and restricted access limit travel into Southesk Lake, which is situated in one of the most remote corners of Jasper National Park. Bull trout are present in Southesk, although not in substantial numbers.

Southesk Lake

Lac Gris (NP)
Status: Devoid of fish
Lac Gris is a silted body of water located in the valley south of Southesk Lake. Lac Gris has never been stocked, and contains no fish.

ICEFIELDS REGION: Tonquin Sub-Region

Southesk River (NP)
Bull trout to 55 cm (2.0 kg)
Whitefish to 35 cm
The Southesk River flows east from its headwaters in Southesk Lake, and joins the Brazeau River at the Jasper National Park boundary. The Southesk River is seldom fished due to lengthy access routes. The river holds limited numbers of bull trout and whitefish.

Cairn River (NP)
Bull trout to 40 cm
The Cairn River is a tributary of the Southesk River, and receives virtually no angling pressure. Bull trout are present in small numbers in the river, which begins on the eastern side of Southesk Pass.

Cairn Lake (NP)
Status: Devoid of fish
Cairn Lake is the headwater of the Cairn River. It has never been stocked, and is reported to be devoid of fish.

Medicine Tent Lakes (NP)
Status: Devoid of fish
The Medicine Tent Lakes are set in alpine terrain on the western side of Southesk Pass. The lakes are the source of the Medicine Tent River, which flows northwest to join the Rocky River. The Medicine Tent Lakes have never been stocked, and contain no fish.

Whitewater Lake (NP)
Status: Devoid of fish
Whitewater Lake is the largest of the lakes in the immediate Maligne Pass vicinity. It has never been stocked, and is devoid of fish.

Pika Lakes (North and South), Phalarope Lake, Lagopus Pond, Brachinecta Pond, Coyote Pond, Wapiti Pond, Replica Lake, Ouzel Lakes (Upper and Lower) (NP)
Status: Devoid of fish
This series of small lakes and ponds are located in the alpine environs of Maligne Pass. All of the lakes are devoid of fish.

Tonquin Sub-Region

The magnificent Tonquin Valley is one of Jasper National Park's most popular backcountry destinations. This beautiful area is comparable with any area in the Rockies in terms of scenery. Two 20 km-long trails lead into Tonquin Valley, one via the Astoria River and the other via Portal and Maccarib Creeks. Visitors to the area are able to choose from several fine backcountry campsites as well as permanent outfitters' camps, and an Alpine Club of Canada hut at Outpost Lake. The centrepiece of the Sub-Region is the Amethyst Lakes, which are set beneath the spectacular castellate summits of the Ramparts. The Amethyst Lakes are truly one of the jewels of the Canadian Rockies. Their sparkling waters are home to huge rainbow and brook trout, yet the location is remote enough to ensure the quality of fishing remains high. Many of the other waters in the Tonquin area are devoid of fish, although Moat Lake and the Astoria River hold the promise of good angling.

Amethyst Lakes (NP)
Rainbow trout to 80 cm (5.0 kg)
Brook trout to 70 cm (4.0 kg)
Fortunately for anglers, fishing in Amethyst Lakes rivals the area's scenic splendour. Large rainbow and brook trout, averaging 40-50 cm in length, can be taken in good numbers all summer long. As the lakes are sizable, fishing from shore can be an intimidating proposition. For those anglers having little success from shore, arrangements can generally be made with one of the outfitter camps to rent a boat. Fishing from a boat increases fishing potential many fold, and just trolling a wet fly or lure while admiring the scenery will usually produce results. Early morning and late evening tend to be the most productive times of day. The stretch of the Astoria River between its outlet and a point 400 m downstream is permanently closed to angling. Check regulations before fishing. Be forewarned that the marshy environs of Amethyst Lake support a ravenous mosquito population.

Amethyst Lakes (rainbow trout)

Robin Campbell photo

Moat Lake (NP)
Rainbow trout to 50 cm (1.5 kg)
Moat Lake is reached by a short 2 km side trail from Amethyst Lakes. Moat Lake is set amid very marshy meadows, which contribute to the area's large insect population. The lake holds plenty of rainbow trout averaging 25-35 cm in length. Trout in the lake feed actively on the surface on most days, and a dry fly is usually very effective. Fly casting room is adequate around most of the shoreline. Moat Lake's long, narrow shape is favourable to fly fishing, since a large portion of the fishable water can be reached by shore bound anglers. Boats are available for rent through arrangements with outfitters on Amethyst Lakes.

Moat Lake

211

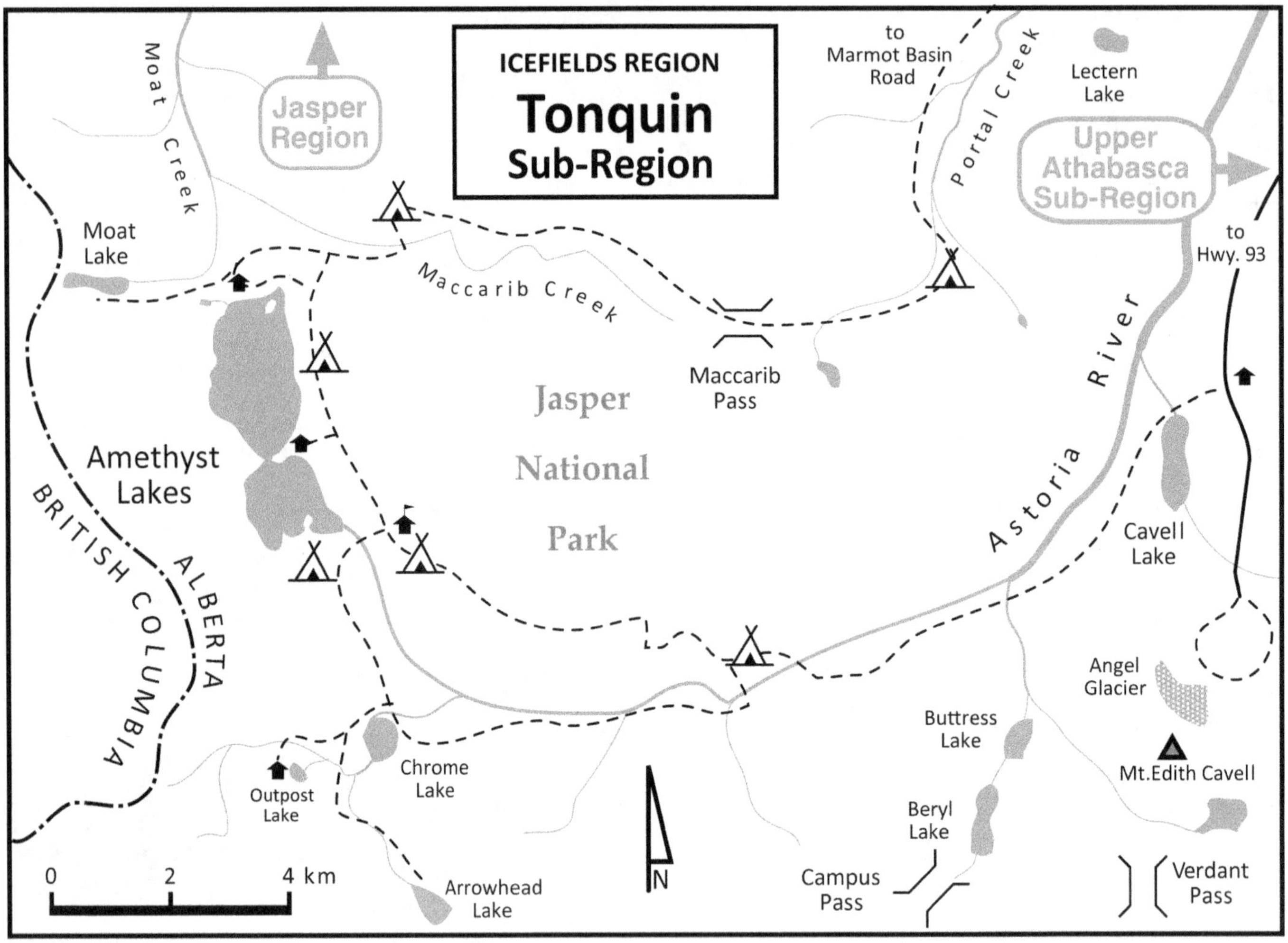

ICEFIELDS REGION: Tonquin Sub-Region

Moat Creek (NP)
Rainbow trout to 35 cm
Moat Creek is the outlet stream for Moat Lake, and it flows north into Meadow Creek, before eventually emptying into the Miette River. In the waters immediately downstream from Moat Lake, the creek holds good numbers of rainbow trout, most averaging 15-25 cm in length.

Maccarib Creek (NP)
Rainbow trout to 30 cm
Maccarib Creek meanders through open meadows below Maccarib Pass before flowing into Moat Creek. It holds small rainbow trout over its entire length. The best fishing is in the waters above the Maccarib campground on the Maccarib Pass trail.

Maccarib Creek

Portal Creek (NP)
Rainbow trout to 35 cm
Brook trout to 35 cm
Portal Creek flows east from the heights of Maccarib Pass to the Athabasca River. Portal Creek has plenty of fine pools that contain small rainbow and brook trout. The upper Portal Creek valley is also prime grizzly habitat, and anglers should be aware at all times.

Portal Creek

ICEFIELDS REGION: Tonquin Sub-Region

Lectern Lake (NP)
Rainbow trout to 30 cm
Lectern Lake is hidden in a forested basin above the Marmot Basin road, midway between Portal Creek and the Astoria River. The lake was stocked in the past with rainbow trout. Few reliable reports are available on Lectern Lake, but it likely still holds a few rainbow trout.

Astoria River (NP)
Rainbow trout to 40 cm
Bull trout to 60 cm (2.5 kg)
Brook trout to 40 cm
The turbulent Astoria River flows from the Amethyst Lakes to the Athabasca River. The Astoria River possesses several fine stretches of fishable water. Most fishing activity takes place in the area of the confluence with the Athabasca and in the upper reaches, within 10 km of Amethyst Lakes. Rainbow trout in the 20-30 cm range are caught in greater numbers than bull and brook trout in the upper section. Near the Athabasca River bull trout tend to predominate, and the odd whitefish may also be taken.

Astoria River

Chrome Lake (NP)
Rainbow trout to 40 cm
Chrome Lake is located 2 km south of Amethyst Lakes by trail, and is surrounded by a pleasant combination of forest and meadow. It holds a small population of rainbow trout averaging 25-30 cm in length. Chrome Lake is generally overlooked by anglers, due to its proximity to the more renowned waters of Amethyst Lakes. It is often very silted due to glacial runoff, and fish are generally taken in the shallower waters close to shore.

Chrome Lake

Outpost Lake (NP)
Status: Devoid of fish
The Alpine Club of Canada's Waites-Gibson Hut is located on the shores of tiny Outpost Lake. Outpost Lake has never been stocked and contains no fish.

Outpost Lake

Arrowhead Lake (NP)
Status: Devoid of fish
Appropriately-shaped Arrowhead Lake lies at the base of Eremite Glacier in Eremite Valley, 3 km south of Chrome Lake. Arrowhead has never been stocked, and is too silted for fish to survive.

Arrowhead Lake

Buttress Lake, Beryl Lake (NP)
Status: Doubtful
Buttress and Beryl Lakes are located in a remote valley off Verdant Creek. Neither lake has been stocked, making it highly improbable that they contain any fish.

Cavell Lake (NP)
Brook trout to 40 cm
Cutthroat trout to 40 cm
The emerald green waters of charming Cavell Lake are most famous as a foreground in photographs of Mt. Edith Cavell. The lake is seldom fished, and reports indicate poor fishing for brook and cutthroat trout in the 25-35 cm range.

Cavell Lake

JASPER REGION

This popular Region offers many excellent fishing opportunities in and around the Jasper townsite. The Icefields Parkway (Highway 93) and Yellowhead Highway (Highway16) provide the primary access to the region. Tourist facilities and fishing equipment are available in Jasper. Large rainbow trout are the main angling attraction, and they can be taken from a number of lakes, including Maligne, Medicine, Annette, and Edith. The Athabasca, Miette and Maligne Rivers provide some good river fishing. The Region is divided into three Sub-Regions. The first is the area west of the Jasper townsite, and includes the Miette River. The Skyline Sub-Region includes the Athabasca River and the areas south of Jasper along the Icefields Parkway, and east along the Yellowhead Highway. The Maligne Sub-Region includes the Maligne River watershed, southeast of Jasper.

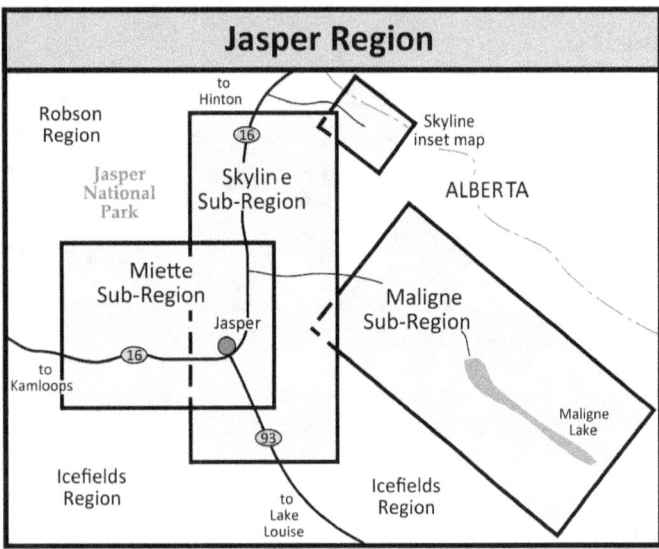

Miette Sub Region

This Sub-Region also includes the Jasper townsite, and extends west to Pyramid Lake, which is very popular with anglers throughout the summer. To the west of Jasper a series of hiking trails radiate out from townsite and from the Pyramid Lake Road, and lead to Riley, Mina, Marjorie, Hibernia, Caledonia, Minnow, High and Saturday Night Lakes. The Miette River and valley stretch to the west and the B.C. border. From Highway 16 west of Jasper, short trails lead to Dorothy, Christine, Iris and Virl Lakes.

Pyramid Lake (NP)
Lake trout to 80 cm (6.0 kg)
Rainbow trout to 55 cm (2.0 kg)
Brook trout to 50 cm (1.5 kg)
Whitefish to 50 cm (1.5 kg)
Pyramid Lake is located six kilometres from Jasper by road, and is the Sub-Region's most popular fishing spot. It is busy with anglers from opening to closing day. Although both rainbow and brook trout are plentiful, it's the large lake trout that attract the attention. In the early season, lake trout can be taken in the shallower waters. The lake trout soon migrate to the colder, deeper waters as soon as the lake begins to warm. By mid-summer, rainbow and brook trout and whitefish become the standard fare. Lake trout are still caught by those anglers fishing the lake's very depths. Rental boats are available at the lake.

Pyramid Lake

Patricia Lake (NP)
Lake trout to 60 cm (2.5 kg)
The striking blue waters of Patricia Lake are situated alongside the Pyramid Lake Road, 5 km from Jasper. Patricia Lake at one time held good numbers of rainbow trout, with some very large individuals taken. Patricia Lake is no longer stocked, and it is unlikely that any rainbow trout are present in the lake. There is still the odd lake trout present, but their numbers are limited.

Patricia Lake

Note: Since Parks Canada no longer stocks trout, many of the great fishing lakes around Jasper retain little of their former glory. The rainbow trout lakes seem to be the hardest hit, particularly those with no inlet or outlet creek available for spawning. Check with On-Line Sports in Jasper for current fishing conditions and advice on tackle.

Cottonwood beaver ponds (NP)
Rainbow trout to 35 cm
Brook trout to 35 cm
This series of beaver ponds extends west from Pyramid Lake Road, 3 km from Jasper. The ponds hold both rainbow and brook trout in the 20-30 cm range. The marshy setting of the ponds, complete with heavy vegetation growth, makes access difficult.

JASPER REGION: Miette Sub-Region

Cottonwood ponds

Riley Lake (NP)
Rainbow trout to 40 cm
Riley Lake is a small reed-encircled lake, 3 km by trail from the Pyramid Lake Road. Riley Lake offers good fishing for rainbow trout averaging 25-35 cm in length. Boats are available for rent through prior arrangement with sporting good stores in Jasper.

Mina Lake (NP)
Rainbow trout to 55 cm (2.0 kg)
Brook trout to 50 cm (1.5 kg)
Mina Lake is located on the Mina-Riley loop trail, 3 km from the Pyramid Lake Road. Mina Lake is typical of many of the smaller lakes on the bench west of Jasper. Both rainbow and brook trout are present in the lake, averaging 20-30 cm in length. Fly fishing is effective, but casting is difficult from much of the shoreline because of heavy tree cover. Long casts are usually required to reach fish-holding waters. Low light periods, when fish tend to feed in the shallows, are generally the best time to fish.

Cabin Lake (NP)
Status: Closed to fishing
Cabin Lake is the source of Jasper's water supply, and is permanently closed to angling.

Hibernia Lake (NP)
Rainbow trout to 55 cm (2.0 kg)
Hibernia Lake is located on a spur trail, less than a kilometre off the main Saturday Night loop. Hibernia Lake attracts anglers in search of rainbow trout in the 25-35 cm range, which inhabit the lake in good numbers. Rental boats are available through arrangements made with sporting goods stores in Jasper.

Hibernia Lake

Marjorie Lake (NP)
Rainbow trout to 65 cm (3.0 kg)
Brook trout to 50 cm (1.5 kg)
Marjorie Lake is a popular fishing destination, as it is an easy 15-20 minute walk from Jasper townsite along the Saturday Night loop. Marjorie Lake holds both rainbow and brook trout in good numbers, with most fish taken averaging 25-35 cm in length. Boats are available through rental arrangements made with one of Jasper's sporting goods stores.

Caledonia Lake (NP)
Rainbow trout to 55 cm (2.0 kg)
Brook trout to 50 cm (1.5 kg)
Caledonia Lake is set on a forested bench, 2 km by trail beyond Marjorie Lake, and 5 km from Jasper. Both rainbow and brook trout are present. Reeds and extended shallows around much of Caledonia's shoreline make fly casting from shore a difficult proposition. Fortunately, boats are available at the lake and can be rented through Jasper's sporting goods stores. Tactics on Caledonia range from trolling a wet fly or lure, to working a dry fly when insects are hatching.

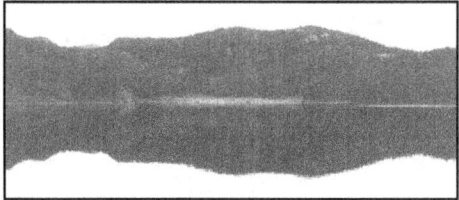
Caledonia Lake

Rathlin Lake, Bench Lake (NP)
Brook trout to 35 cm
These two small lakes are located alongside the Saturday Night loop between Caledonia and Minnow Lakes. Both lakes contain brook trout. There may be some rainbow trout present in Rathlin Lake as well.

Minnow Lake (NP)
Rainbow trout to 50 cm (1.5 kg)
Brook trout to 50 cm (1.5 kg)
Minnow Lake is situated near the upper end of the Saturday Night loop, and receives much less attention from anglers than the more accessible waters of Marjorie, Hibernia and Caledonia. Rainbow and brook trout can both be taken from Minnow Lake, with most averaging 25-35 cm in length.

High Lakes (NP)
Brook trout to 40 cm
Rainbow trout to 35 cm
This series of shallow lakes are located at the upper end of the Saturday Night loop. The seven High Lakes are spread out over 3 km, amid mixed forest and swamp. Although all of the lakes were stocked at one time with both rainbow and brook trout, it is likely that trout are present now only in lakes #4, #5, #6 and #7 (lakes at the western end of the chain), and that brook trout predominate. Soggy feet are a certainty if a good fly casting spot is to be located.

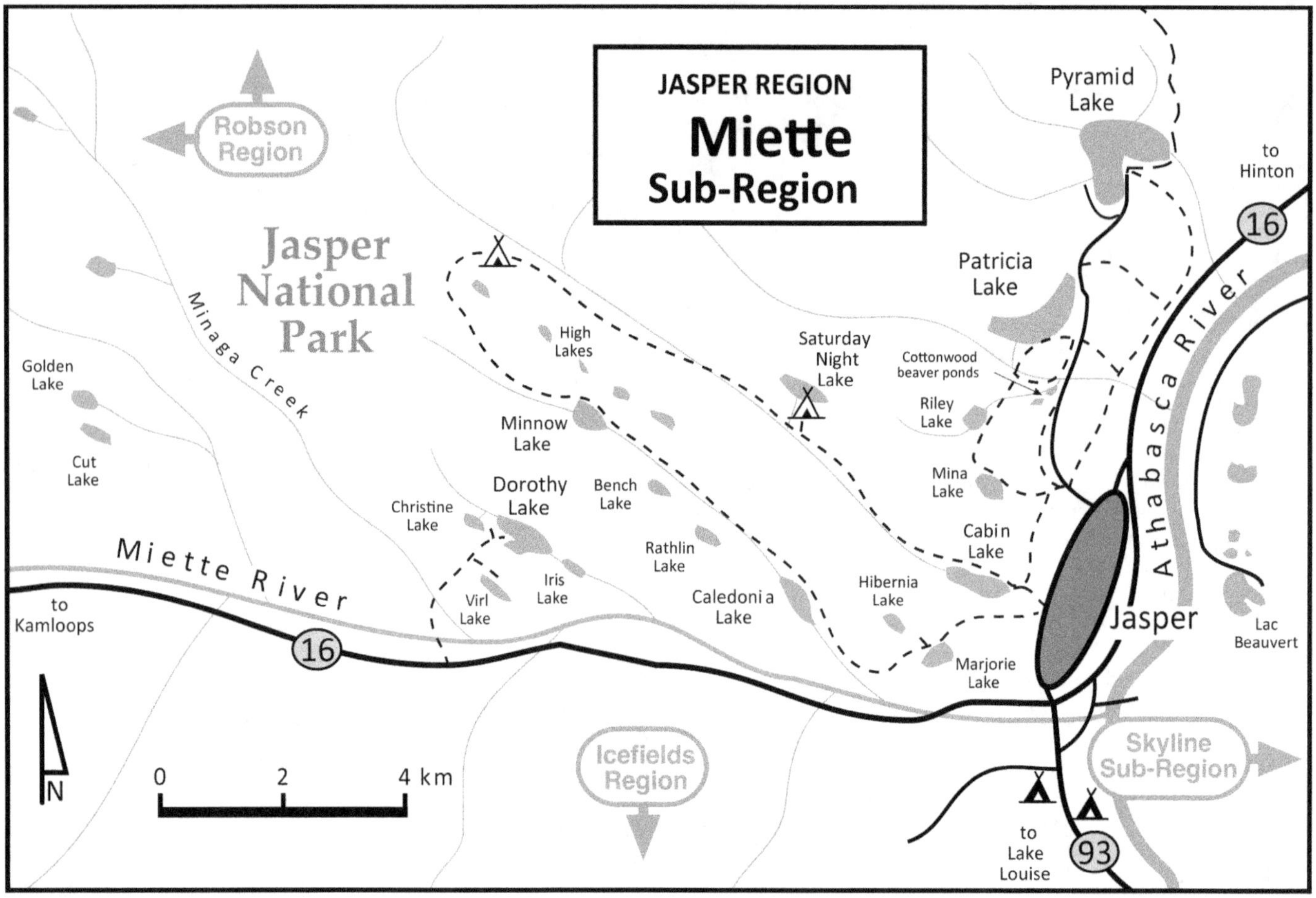

Saturday Night Lake (NP)
Rainbow trout to 60 cm (2.5 kg)
Brook trout to 50 cm (1.5 kg)

Saturday Night Lake is the usual destination for anglers undertaking the Saturday Night loop trail. The lake's shimmering green waters hold plenty of rainbow and brook trout. Trout taken from Saturday Night Lake will average 25-35 cm in length. Fishing from shore is possible from a number of locations, although forest cover will hamper those who are fly casting. Boats can be rented through arrangements made with sporting goods stores in Jasper.

Dorothy Lake (NP)
Rainbow trout to 70 cm (4.0 kg)

Dorothy Lake is accessed by a 4 km trail from the Yellowhead Highway west of Jasper. Dorothy Lake receives much less fishing pressure than other lakes in the immediate vicinity of the townsite. Consequently, rainbow trout are plentiful in Dorothy, most averaging 30-40 cm in length with much larger specimens taken on occasion. Although it's doubtful, the lake may also hold a few brook trout, remnants of past plantings. Boats are available for rent through sporting goods stores in Jasper. Anchoring in one of the numerous sheltered bays and working either a wet fly or lure is generally productive.

Christine Lake (NP)
Rainbow trout to 60 cm (2.5 kg)
Brook trout to 55 cm (2.0 kg)

Christine Lake is located less than half a kilometre by trail from Dorothy Lake. Christine Lake is one of the Sub-Region's few lakes that offers reasonable fishing to the shore bound angler. Fish-holding waters are within easy casting distance from a number of rocky points jutting out into the lake. Brook trout predominated in Christine for many years, but it now appears that rainbow trout are in the majority. Boats are available through rental arrangements made in Jasper.

Saturday Night Lake

JASPER REGION: Skyline Sub-Region

Christine Lake

Iris Lake (NP)
Rainbow lake to 40 cm
Iris Lake is located less than a kilometre below the eastern end of Dorothy Lake, and is reached by ill-defined trails winding around Dorothy Lake. Rainbow trout in the 25-35 cm range are the normal catch.

Virl Lake (NP)
Brook trout to 55 cm (2.0 kg)
Rainbow trout to 50 cm (1.5 kg)
Virl Lake is set in an opening in heavy forest just east of the main Dorothy Lake trail. Virl Lake offers relative solitude for most visitors. Brook and rainbow trout averaging 25-40 cm in length are plentiful. The long, narrow character of the lake allows anglers to cast to fish holding waters with a minimum of effort.

Virl Lake

Miette River (NP)
Rainbow trout to 45 cm
Brook trout to 40 cm
Bull trout to 65 cm (3.0 kg)
Whitefish to 55 cm (2.0 kg)
The Miette River is a major tributary of the Athabasca River, and it flows east from the Alberta-B.C. boundary to its junction with the Athabasca at Jasper. The Yellowhead Highway closely parallels the Miette River for virtually its entire length. The Miette River is very muddy each year during run-off, but it generally clears somewhat by mid-summer. Rainbow, brook and bull trout can be caught from the river's many fine pools. Large whitefish in good numbers can be taken in the fall, when the fishing on the Miette is at its best.

Minaga Creek (NP)
Rainbow trout to 35 cm
Brook trout to 35 cm
This minor tributary of the Miette River is crossed by the Dorothy Lake trail approximately 1 km from Highway 16. Minaga Creek holds both rainbow and brook trout in the 20-30 cm range.

Cut Lake (NP)
Rainbow trout to 40 cm
Cut Lake is reached from trails on upper Minaga Creek. This small lake was stocked long ago with cutthroat trout, hence its name, and more recently with rainbow trout. Reports indicate that rainbow trout measuring 25-35 cm in length are present in good numbers.

Golden Lake (NP)
Rainbow trout to 40 cm
Golden Lake is located less than a kilometre from Cut Lake. It was originally stocked with golden trout, which failed to reproduce. It was later stocked in the past with rainbow trout, which can still be found in fair numbers.

Skyline Sub-Region

The Jasper Townsite is the focal point of the Sub-Region. The Sub-Region includes the Athabasca River and the Jasper Park Lodge environs on the eastern side of the Athabasca River, as well as the territory along the renowned Skyline Trail. Roads or short trails reach most fish-holding waters. The Athabasca River is popular with anglers throughout the year, especially for its plentiful whitefish and large bull trout. Lac Beauvert, Edith, Annette and Trefoil Lakes are located on the bench east of the Athabasca River. To the south, along the Icefields Parkway, a short trail leads to the Valley of the Five Lakes. East of Jasper, the Athabasca and Rocky Rivers, along with Jasper, Talbot, Edna and Mile 14 Lakes, present plenty of opportunities for anglers.

Athabasca River (NP) *(Downstream from Athabasca Falls)*
Bull trout to 80 cm (7.0 kg)
Rainbow trout to 50 cm (1.5 kg)
Brook trout to 50 cm (1.5 kg)
Whitefish to 50 cm (1.5 kg)
Jasper National Park's major river flows from the Columbia Icefields north to Jasper. It swings east and exits the park, eventually turning north en route to the Arctic Ocean. South of Jasper, the Icefields Parkway (Highway 93) follows the course of the upper Athabasca River closely and provides easy access. Although it is very turbulent and muddy for much of the summer, the river does present some good fishing opportunities in the early and late seasons in the waters below Athabasca Falls where whitefish, bull, rainbow and brook trout can all be caught in fair numbers. The whitefish from the river are particularly large. Areas around the Athabasca River's confluence with both major and minor tributaries generally hold fish, especially when the main river is muddy. The Athabasca River's confluence with the Maligne, Snaring and Rocky Rivers are choice spots.

JASPER REGION: Skyline Sub-Region

Edith Lake (NP)
Rainbow trout to 80 cm (6.0 kg)
Brook trout to 60 cm (2.5 kg)

Edith Lake is located just east of the Maligne Lake Road, some 6 km from the Jasper townsite. The translucent blue waters of Edith Lake hold some very large rainbow trout indeed, although most taken are in the 25-40 cm range. Brook trout are also present in limited numbers. Edith Lake is a large lake that drops off sharply in most locations, and fishing is better from a boat. Boats are available for rent through arrangements made with sporting goods stores in Jasper. Trolling is generally productive, especially along the zone around the many deep holes in Edith. On occasion, when there is insect activity on the surface, a dry fly can be particularly effective.

Annette Lake (NP)
Brook trout to 55 cm (2.0 kg)
Rainbow trout to 60 cm (2.5 kg)

This very pretty lake is set amid quiet woods east of the Jasper Park Lodge Road, and attracts plenty of picnickers as well as anglers. The extremely clear waters hold brook and rainbow trout in good numbers, averaging 25-40 cm in length. Boats can be rented through arrangements made in one of Jasper's sporting goods stores, a move that greatly enhances the quality of fishing. Trolling a fly while admiring the scenery is a superb way to get the most out of Annette Lake. For those anglers determined to fish from shore, the eastern side of the lake where the lake bottom drops off very quickly holds the best opportunities.

Annette Lake

Trefoil Lakes (NP)
Rainbow trout to 40 cm
Brook trout to 40 cm

In the past, the fishing potential of three small lakes on the grounds of Jasper Park Lodge has been directly related to artificial stocking. The two larger lakes (Trefoil #1 and #2), still contain limited populations of rainbow trout, and at last report still hold remnants of a brook trout population. The most westerly lake (Trefoil #3) is apparently devoid of fish at present. Although forest cover is sparse around the lakes, a steep shoreline will cause problems for those fly casting.

Mildred Lake (NP)
Status: Devoid of fish

This over-sized duck pond on the western side of the Jasper Park Lodge Road was stocked in the past, but the fish failed to reproduce.

Lac Beauvert (NP)
Rainbow trout to 60 cm (2.5 kg)
Brook trout to 55 cm (2.0 kg)

The sparkling green waters of Lac Beauvert, the scenic centerpiece of the Jasper Park Lodge grounds, have never been renowned for a high quality of fishing. Although a variety of fish have been stocked in the past, only a limited number of rainbow and brook trout are still present.

Valley of the Five Lakes (NP)
Rainbow trout to 80 cm (6.0 kg)
Brook trout to 60 cm (2.5 kg)

The Valley of the Five Lakes is 2 km by trail east of the Icefields Parkway. The lakes are favourite spots for local anglers. All five lakes hold brook trout, which predominate, as well as a fair number of rainbow trout. Some enormous rainbow trout, in the 5-6 kg range, have been taken from the First Lake the past. The First and Fifth Lakes hold the most promise for anglers, with the Fifth Lake being excellent brook trout waters. As all of the lakes are fairly narrow, casting the fish holding waters with a lure or fly is usually not a major problem. Boats are available on the First and Fifth Lakes, and arrangements for their rental can be made in sporting goods stores in Jasper. Check regulations for opening and closing dates of specific lakes.

Valley of the Five Lakes #1

Valley of the Five Lakes #4

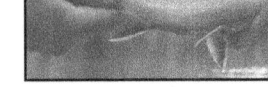

(brook trout)

Wabasso Lake (NP)
Rainbow trout to 55 cm (2.0 kg)
Brook trout to 45 cm

The quiet waters of Wabasso Lake lie less than 3 km by trail from the busy Icefields Parkway. Wabasso Lake is a popular destination for family hikes. It also holds promise for anglers since it contains both rainbow and brook trout in decent numbers. For fly fishers, casting room is somewhat restricted around much of the shoreline, due to heavy reed growth and the proximity of the forest cover.

JASPER REGION: Skyline Sub-Region

Wabasso Lake

Gooseberry Lake (NP)
Brook trout to 35 cm
Gooseberry Lake is located 2 km north of the Valley of the Five Lakes by trail. Gooseberry Lake was stocked in the past with brook trout, which still may be present in small numbers.

Cavern Lake (NP)
Brook trout to 35 cm
Cavern Lake is located south of the Valley of the Five Lakes, near the head of Tekarra Creek. Cavern Lake may hold a few brook trout.

Curator Lake, Tekarra Lake, Centre Lake, Amber Lakes, Excelsior Lake (NP)
Status: Devoid of fish
All of these lakes are companions to hikers on the spectacular Skyline Trail, from Maligne Lake to Jasper. They have never been stocked and contain no fish.

Curator Lake

Leach Lake (NP)
Rainbow trout to 65 cm (3.0 kg)
Leach Lake is located alongside Highway 93A, and has gained a reputation over the years of harbouring some large fish. Rainbow trout in the 30-40 cm range are present in good numbers. Shallows extending far out into the lake make fishing from shore a difficult proposition. During low light conditions when many of the larger fish make their way into the shallows to feed, patient fly fishers can be rewarded with rainbows of 60 cm or more. Boats are available through rental arrangements made at sporting goods stores in Jasper. Working the distinct margin that separates the shallow water from the deep from a boat is usually very effective.

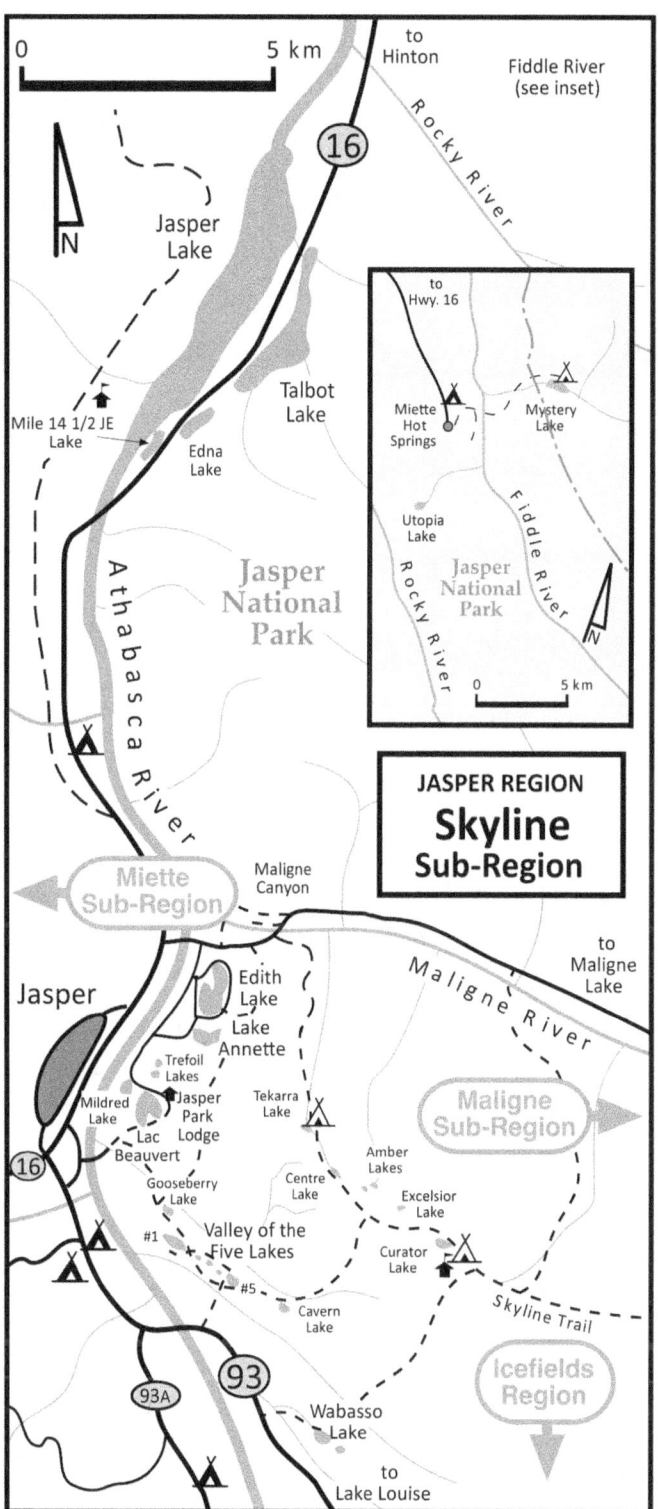

Leach Lake

Jasper Lake

Mile 16 1/2 Jasper-Banff Lake (NP)
Rainbow trout to 60 cm (2.5 kg)
Brook trout to 55 cm (2.0 kg)

Mile 16 1/2 Lake is situated less than a kilometre north of Leach Lake on the opposite side of Highway 93A, and draws high praise from many anglers. Mile 16 1/2 Lake is shallow and similar in character to Leach. Mile 16 1/2 Lake contains large rainbow and brook trout averaging 30-40 cm in length. It is best fished from a boat, which can be rented from sporting goods stores in Jasper. Consistent with other lakes of this nature, the zone between the shallow and deep waters usually holds fish. The north bay is the lake's most promising location, but can only be effectively fished from a boat.

Tyler Ambrosi at Mile 16 1/2 Lake

Jasper Lake (NP)
Bull trout to 70 cm (4.0 kg)
Rainbow trout to 50 cm (1.5 kg)
Brook trout to 50 cm (1.5 kg)
Whitefish to 50 cm (1.5 kg)

The shallow waters of Jasper Lake are merely a widening of the mighty Athabasca River. Jasper Lake attracts little attention from anglers despite its impressive variety of fish which includes whitefish, bull, rainbow and brook trout, as well as pike, ling, chub and suckers. Fishing is generally restricted to the channels through which the main river flows, but unfortunately these areas are usually near impossible to reach due to extensive shallows making up the vast majority of the lake. Anglers are advised to work the waters in and around the lake's inlet and outlet where the Athabasca River is reduced to a more reasonable width.

Mile 14 Lake Jasper-Edmonton Lake (NP)
Rainbow trout to 40 cm
Brook trout to 40 cm

This lake is located, appropriately enough, 14 miles (or 23 km) from Jasper, towards Edmonton, on the north side of the Yellowhead Highway. Mile 14 Lake receives moderate angling pressure each summer for fair numbers of brook and rainbow trout in the 20-30 cm range. Heavy reed growth around much of the shore restricts fishing from shore.

Talbot Lake (NP)
Northern pike to 90 cm (10.0 kg)
Rainbow trout to 50 cm (1.5 kg)
Whitefish to 40 cm

The clear waters of Talbot Lake stand in stark contrast to the silted waters of Jasper Lake, separated only by the Yellowhead Highway. Northern pike are the fish of choice at Talbot Lake, and there are generally a few anglers working the lake at any given time. Boats are available for rent through prior arrangements with sporting good stores in Jasper. Anglers using lures are normally more successful than those fly fishing at Talbot, although fly fishing for pike has become very popular in recent years. Prime time on Talbot Lake is in the first few weeks after the season opens. This is when the large pike enter the shallower waters for spawning.

Talbot Lake

(northern pike)

Edna Lake (NP)
Rainbow trout to 40 cm
Brook trout to 40 cm

Edna Lake is situated less than a kilometre west of Talbot Lake, and is similar in character to other lakes along the Athabasca River. It holds both brook and rainbow trout ranging from 20-30 cm in length. Fish can be taken fairly close to shore during low light conditions.

Rocky River (NP)
Bull trout to 60 cm (2.5 kg)
Rainbow trout to 40 cm
Brook trout to 40 cm
Whitefish to 45 cm

The Rocky River joins the Athabasca River as a major tributary just east of Talbot Lake. The Rocky River generally clears sooner than the Athabasca, offering fine fishing from mid-summer on for bull, rainbow and brook trout, along with whitefish. Fish can be taken in good numbers from the lower reaches of the river, which is within easy walking distance of the Yellowhead Highway. Of particular interest to anglers are the waters around the Rocky River's confluence with the Athabasca - a short hike downstream from Highway 16. Bull trout predominate in the remote upper sections of the Rocky River, accessed by trail from Jacques Lake.

Rocky River

Fiddle River (NP)
Bull trout to 55 cm (2.0 kg)
Rainbow trout to 40 cm
Whitefish to 40 cm

The Fiddle River begins high in the Miette Range and joins the Athabasca River as a minor tributary just inside the eastern boundary of Jasper National Park. The lower reaches are accessible from both the Yellowhead Highway and from the Miette Hot Springs Road. The upper Fiddle is accessed from trails beginning at Miette Hot Springs. Whitefish, bull trout and rainbow trout are all present, with bull trout becoming the dominant species the further upstream you fish.

Fiddle River

Utopia Lake (NP)
Status: Unknown

Utopia Lake is hidden high on the flank of Utopia Mountain, and receives few, if any, visitors each year. The lake was stocked in the past with cutthroat trout but it has never been determined whether any fish still exist. Utopia Lake is recommended for only the most hardy of souls outfitted with a map and compass.

Mystery Lake (AB)
Status: Doubtful

Mystery Lake is located just outside the Jasper National Park boundary, and is protected by a troublesome ford of the Fiddle River. The ford of the Fiddle River can be very dangerous in the early season and during periods of rainy weather. Although it is becoming more popular as a backpacking destination, Mystery Lake is still far removed from the crowds. At one time the lake held plenty of brook and rainbow trout, but a recent winter kill virtually eliminated the trout population.

Mystery Lake

Maligne Sub-Region

Stunning Maligne Lake is set amid some of the most impressive mountain scenery the Rockies has to offer, and stands out as the centerpiece of the Sub-Region. Maligne Lake's world-class rainbow trout attracts anglers from far and wide. The lake is easily accessible via a 45 km-long paved road that leads southeast from Highway 16, five kilometres east of Jasper. Lorraine, Moose, Mona and Evelyn Lakes are all located within easy hiking distance from the Maligne Lake Road terminus. Medicine Lake is situated downstream from Maligne Lake on the Maligne River, and offers superb late summer fishing for large rainbow trout.

Maligne Lake (NP)
Rainbow trout to 90 cm (10 kg)
Brook trout to 65 cm (3.0 kg)

Maligne Lake is situated at the head of the beautiful Maligne Valley, and attracts crowds of visitors to its shores each summer. Tour boats make daily sightseeing excursions down the lake. Maligne Lake is regarded as a very good fishing lake, and contains large rainbow and brook trout. Monster rainbow trout over 7.0 kg have been caught in this lake. Boats and canoes can be rented at the lake, which increases fishing potential enormously. Trolling is very effective, particularly in the famed "Rainbow Alley" which extends from near the outlet of the Maligne River for the first few kilometres down the lake. Almost 10 km down the lake, the Sampson Narrows have also gained renown for fishing, although it is a long trip if you're rowing or paddling. For those who are shore bound, the area around the outlet holds some promise. Maligne Lake is not usually free of ice until mid-June.

JASPER REGION: Maligne Sub-Region

Maligne Lake

(rainbow trout)

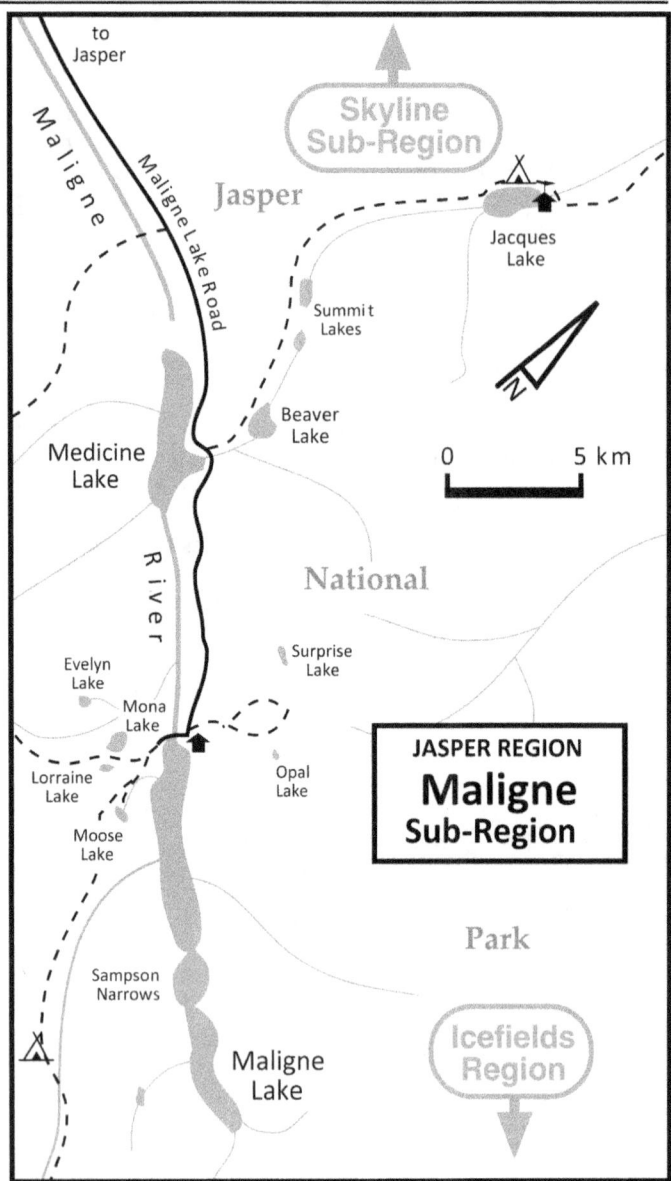

**JASPER REGION
Maligne
Sub-Region**

Moose Lake (NP)
Brook trout to 30 cm
Tiny Moose Lake is less than a kilometre from the Maligne Pass trailhead, and draws little attention from anglers. Brook trout were stocked in the past, but recent reports indicate they are present in very limited numbers at best.

Mona Lake (NP)
Brook trout to 45 cm
Mona Lake is situated 2 km along the Skyline Trail, and is the largest of the lakes located to the west of Maligne Lake. Mona Lake's clear waters hold plenty of brook trout averaging 20-30 cm in length. Mona Lake is ringed by forest, and presents problems for those who will be fly casting.

Mona Lake

Lorraine Lake (NP)
Brook trout to 40 cm
Lorraine Lake is situated opposite Mona Lake, approximately 2 km along the Skyline Trail. This tiny lake attracts many fishermen from nearby Maligne Lake, on account of good numbers of brook trout in the 20-30 cm range. Heavy reed growth and shallows extend around much of the lake. During low light periods, however, the trout tend to work the shallows in search for food, and patient anglers are often rewarded at these times.

Lorraine Lake

Evelyn Lake (NP)
Brook trout to 35 cm
Rainbow trout to 35 cm
This small lake is located less than a kilometre northwest of Mona Lake, and is usually overlooked by the crowds at nearby Maligne Lake. Evelyn Lake holds both brook and rainbow trout in small sizes.

JASPER REGION: Maligne Sub-Region

Surprise Lake (NP)
Status: Doubtful
Only experienced route finders armed with a map and compass find their way into secluded Surprise Lake, located some 4 km east of the Maligne Lake Road. Surprise Lake was stocked in the past with brook trout, which apparently failed to take hold. If any fish were found today in Surprise Lake, it would definitely be a surprise.

Opal (Summit) Lake (NP)
Status: Devoid of fish
This small lake is set in the Opal Hills to the northeast of Maligne Lake. Opal Lake has never been stocked and contains no fish.

Medicine Lake (NP)
Rainbow trout to 70 cm (4.0 kg)
Brook trout to 60 cm (2.5 kg)
Medicine Lake is located alongside the Maligne Lake Road, approximately 10 km downstream from Maligne Lake. When fishing is hot, Medicine Lake ranks favourably with the better fishing lakes in the Rockies. It holds good numbers of large rainbow and brook trout. Rainbow trout taken from the lake will average 35-45 cm in length. Water levels on Medicine Lake fluctuate dramatically during the year, with the lake nearly doubling in size at the height of the run-off in early July. As the lake level recedes in the beginning in August, fishing picks up considerably, and continues to improve into September. In the fall, the upper portion of the lake is little more than a mud flat, crisscrossed by various channels of the Maligne River. During this time of the year, there is excellent fly fishing for large rainbows in Medicine Lake, whether from a boat in the main part of the lake, or from the riverbank in the mud flats. Boats are available for rent through prior arrangement with sporting goods stores in Jasper.

Medicine Lake mud flats (rainbow trout)

Maligne River (NP)
Rainbow trout to 60 cm (2.5 kg)
Brook trout to 55 cm (2.0 kg)
The Maligne River between Maligne Lake and Medicine Lake offers several stretches of outstanding angling for plentiful numbers of rainbow and brook trout in the 25-35 cm range. The best areas are found just below the outlet on Maligne Lake, and just above the inlet on Medicine Lake. Below Medicine Lake, the Maligne River flows underground for a short distance. Soon after reappearing on the surface, the river enters the labyrinth of Maligne Canyon.

Beaver Lake (NP)
Brook trout to 55 cm (2.0 kg)
Rainbow trout to 40 cm
Shallow Beaver Lake is set in a pleasant valley less than 2 km from the Maligne Lake Road. It is a popular spot for family picnics, as well as for fishing. At one time, extremely large brook trout, in the 3-4 kg range, inhabited the lake. Over harvest of the big brookies took its toll, and today it is doubtful if trout of that size exist in the lake. Brook trout are still present, but most are 20-35 cm in length, and tend to be a little finicky. The entire shoreline is made up of heavy reed growth, a strong deterrent to fly casting. Boats are available for rent, and can be reserved through sporting goods stores in Jasper. The outlet stream from Beaver Lake to its junction with the Maligne Lake Road is permanently closed to fishing.

Beaver Lake

(brook trout)

Summit Lakes (NP)
Status: Devoid of fish
These two small lakes are situated at the height of land on the Jacques Lake trail. They have been stocked in the past with brook trout, which failed to reproduce. At present, no fish exist in the lakes.

Jacques Lake (NP)
Bull trout to 70 cm (4.0 kg)
Pretty Jacques Lake is a popular backpacking destination, and is 12 km by trail from the Maligne Lake Road. Jacques Lake contains bull trout averaging 30-40 cm in length in good numbers. Lures work well on the bull trout in the lake. For those fly fishing, try the area around the outlet stream.

Jacques Lake

ROBSON REGION

This Region is dominated by the presence of awe-inspiring Mt. Robson, the highest point in the Canadian Rockies, and represents the pinnacle in mountain scenery. Glacier-mantled peaks towering over pristine lakes attract visitors from all corners of the world. The Yellowhead Highway (Highway 16) is the primary transportation route through the Region. The Region's fishing potential has never gained the stature of the surrounding physical beauty. Berg Lake, set at the base of Mt. Robson is a classic backpacking destination, but attracts no anglers. Beyond Berg Lake, Jasper National Park's noted North Boundary Trail leads adventuresome hikers past Adolphus, Beatrix and Twintree Lakes and the Smoky River, before crossing Snake Indian Pass into the Snake Indian River drainage. The Region is divided into two Sub-Regions; the Yellowhead Sub-Region, encompassing the immediate Mt. Robson area; and a second Sub-Region shadowing the North Boundary Trail.

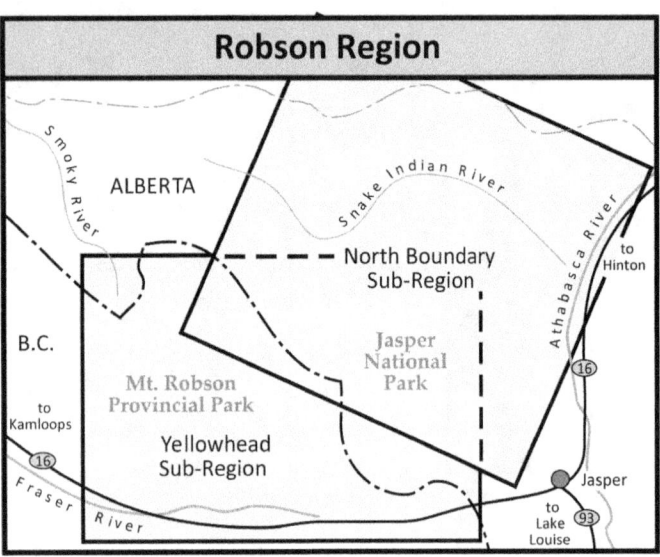

Portal Lake

Yellowhead Sub-Region

Mighty Mt. Robson stands guard over the Sub-Region, which stretches out along the Yellowhead Highway west from Yellowhead Pass and the B.C.-Alberta boundary. The best fishing opportunities are in the string of lakes that parallel the highway, and include Moose, Yellowhead and Lucerne Lakes. Berg Lake and Kinney Lake are popular with hikers, but are of limited value to anglers.

Portal (Flora) Lake (BC)
Rainbow trout to 40 cm

Portal Lake is located alongside the Yellowhead Highway, just west of the B.C.-Alberta border. There is a large parking area and a picnic site beside the lake. Rainbow trout are present in the lake in good numbers, with most averaging 20-30 cm in length. Flies and lures will work well, although those who are fly fishing may have some difficulty finding back casting room anywhere but the picnic area.

Yellowhead Lake (BC)
Lake trout to 75 cm (5.0 kg)
Rainbow trout to 50 cm (1.5 kg)
Whitefish to 40 cm

Yellowhead Lake is situated alongside Yellowhead Highway, a few kilometres west of the Continental Divide at Yellowhead Pass. Yellowhead Lake holds large lake trout, averaging 40-50 cm in length, as well of plenty of smaller rainbow trout and whitefish. In the early season lake trout can be taken in good numbers, but as the season progresses, rainbows and whitefish become the normal catch. Due to the size of the lake the best tactic is trolling from a boat, which are available through rental arrangements made with sporting goods stores in Jasper.

Yellowhead Lake

Lucerne Lake (BC)
Lake trout to 70 cm (4.5 kg)
Rainbow trout to 50 cm (1.5 kg)
Whitefish to 40 cm

Lucerne Lake is little more than a downstream extension of Yellowhead Lake. It offers the same variety of fish, and the same general fishing strategies that work on its larger neighbour to the west. If shore-bound, the areas around the inlet and outlet usually hold some fish.

Witney Lake (BC)
Rainbow trout to 50 cm (1.5 kg)

Witney Lake is located between Yellowhead and Lucerne Lakes, and is beside the highway. Despite its easy access, Witney Lake receives little angling pressure. It holds rainbow trout in the 25-35 cm range.

ROBSON REGION: Yellowhead Sub-Region

Witney Lake

Moose Lake (BC)
Lake trout to 90 cm (10.0 kg)
Bull trout to 75 cm (6.0 kg)
Rainbow trout to 65 cm (3.0 kg)
Kokanee to 60 cm (2.5 kg)
Whitefish to 50 cm (1.5 kg)

Moose Lake is almost 10 km in length, and is a companion to people driving the Yellowhead Highway. Moose Lake's waters, which remains silted much of the summer, hold a variety of fish with lake and bull trout predominating. Large lake and bull trout in excess of 5 kg are taken regularly. Trolling is the most effective method of angling on Moose Lake. Be aware of strong winds that occasionally sweep through Yellowhead Pass.

Moose River
Bull trout to 60 cm (2.5 kg)
Rainbow trout to 45 cm
Whitefish to 50 cm

Moose River has its source high among the peaks that straddle the Continental Divide. It flows south from humble beginnings to join the upper Fraser River as a major tributary just east of Moose Lake. Much of the upper Moose River lies far beyond the reach of most hikers, and remains the domain of grizzly bears, interrupted only by the occasional horse party. Bull and rainbow trout in the 25-35 cm range as well as a few whitefish can be taken along the entire length of the river. Fishing pressure is light in the lower reaches and virtually non-existent along the remote upper Moose River.

Moose River

Grant Brook (BC)
Bull trout to 55 cm (2.0 kg)
Whitefish to 45 cm

Grant Brook is a tributary of the Fraser River, joining midway between Yellowhead Lake and the Moose River. Grant Brook holds a few bull trout and whitefish.

Fraser River (BC) (Headwaters to Robson River)
Bull trout to 70 cm (4.0 kg)
Rainbow trout to 50 cm (1.5 kg)
Whitefish to 40 cm

The upper Fraser River between Yellowhead Lake and Tete Jaune Cache possesses long stretches of fishable water. Bull and rainbow trout predominate, with whitefish present in fair numbers as well. This entire section of the Fraser is paralleled by the Yellowhead Highway, which affords easy access to all of the river's fishing spots. Run-off is usually complete by mid-summer when fishing begins to pick up appreciably. Salmon runs in the fall are spectacular to watch.

Fraser River

Robson River (BC)
Bull trout to 60 cm (2.5 kg)
Rainbow trout to 40 cm
Whitefish to 35 cm

From its source at Berg Lake, the Robson River roars through the Valley of a Thousand Falls into Kinney Lake, before finally emptying into the Fraser River. The upper section is far too torrential to hold fish, and all angling on the Robson should be confined to the final 6 km before its confluence with the Fraser. Whitefish, bull and rainbow trout can all be taken in limited numbers. Due to its glacial source, the Robson River runs silted much longer than most rivers, generally clearing only for a few short weeks in the fall.

Robson River

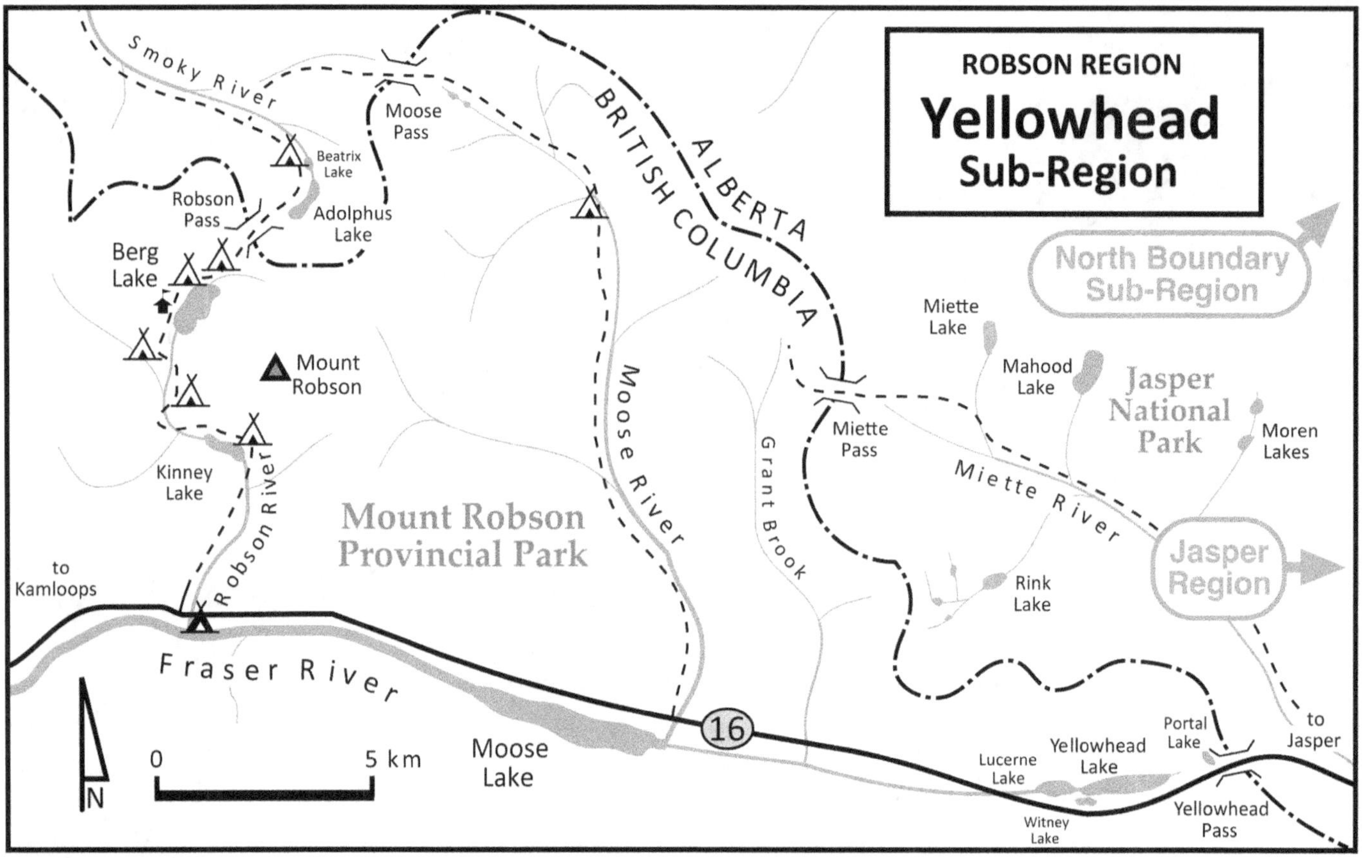

Kinney Lake (BC)
Rainbow trout to 35 cm

Kinney Lake is perpetually silted due to the in and outflow of the Robson River. It is situated 5 km along the Berg Lake trail, and has never been able to sustain a respectable fish population. Small rainbow trout in the 15-20 cm size range inhabit the lake. The outlet area is generally the most productive area, particularly later in the season when the lake's silt levels are lowest.

Berg Lake (BC)
Status: Doubtful

Berg Lake is blessed with one of the most exquisite settings anywhere in the mountain world, and is busy with photographers and sightseers throughout the summer months. The stunning, glacier-clad north face of Mt. Robson towering above the lake is a sight that few people forget. Despite being a strenuous 17 km hike-in from the Yellowhead Highway, the access trail remains one of the most popular backpacking routes in the Rockies. Unfortunately, fishing in ever-silted Berg can be regarded as dismal at best, with rainbow trout supposedly present in small numbers.

Kinney Lake

Berg Lake and Mount Robson

ROBSON REGION: North Boundary Sub-Region

Adolphus Lake (NP)
Rainbow trout to 45 cm
Brook trout to 45 cm
Adolphus Lake is set in open subalpine forest less than 1 km north of Robson Pass in Jasper National Park. Adolphus Lake offers some respite from the crowds at nearby Berg Lake. This headwater of the Smoky River holds good numbers of rainbow and brook trout averaging 23-35 cm in its clear waters. Flies and lures are both effective in Adolphus Lake

Adolphus Lake

Beatrix Lake (NP)
Rainbow trout to 35 cm
Tiny Beatrix Lake is located less than 1 km downstream from Adolphus Lake, and is little more than a widening of the Smoky River. Rainbow trout in the 20-30 cm range are present as well as the odd brook trout, which makes its way from Adolphus Lake from time to time. Heavy brush around the lake will cause problems for those fly casting.

Smoky River (NP)
Bull trout to 70 cm (4.0 kg)
Rainbow trout to 35 cm
Whitefish to 40 cm
The upper Smoky River offers several kilometres of fine stream fishing as it flows north from Adolphus Lake. Meandering quietly back and forth across the broad valley north of Robson Pass, it possesses plenty of fine holes where bull and rainbow trout are present in fair numbers. Progressing downstream, the Smoky begins to accumulate tributaries and increase appreciably in size, and rainbow trout decrease in number, and bull trout and whitefish become predominant. Access is via the North Boundary Trail, which follows the course of the Smoky River to a point approximately 10 km from the northern boundary of Jasper National Park, whereupon the main trail swings east, away from the Smoky River and towards Twintree Lake.

Smoky River

North Boundary Sub-Region

This isolated Sub-Region is located in the remote, rugged northern end of Jasper National Park. The Sub-Region is bounded on the west by Mt. Robson Provincial Park, and on the north by Willmore Wilderness Provincial Park. Jasper's famed North Boundary Trail cuts through the core of the Sub-Region and provides access for horse parties and hardy backpackers. The Snake Indian River parallels the North Boundary Trail from the eastern trailhead at Celestine Lake to the alpine environs of Snake Indian Pass. To the south of this drainage, the Snaring River makes its way east from the heights of the Continental Divide, and like much of the rest of the territory, remains virtually untouched by humans.

Snaring River (NP)
Bull trout to 60 cm (2.5 kg)
Rainbow trout to 40 cm
Whitefish to 45 cm
This major tributary of the Athabasca River joins the Athabasca 17 km east of Jasper and offers fine fishing in its lower reaches for bull and rainbow trout. Whitefish are plentiful in the fall. While its upper sections are located far beyond the reach of the average angler, the lower Snaring is easily accessed from the Celestine Lake Road.

Mile 9 Lake (NP)
Northern pike to 70 (4.0 kg)
Rainbow trout to 40 cm
Brook trout to 40 cm
Mile 9 Lake is situated alongside the Celestine Lake Road, and always attracts a few anglers from the nearby Snaring River campground. The lake's shallow waters hold northern pike, as well as a few rainbow and brook trout.

Harvey Lake (NP)
Status: Unknown
Harvey Lake lies hidden deep within the Snaring River drainage, and remains a mystery to most anglers. It was stocked in the past with rainbow trout, but it has never been determined whether fish are still present. Due to difficult access, Harvey Lake will likely keep its secrets for many years to come.

Vine Creek (NP)
Rainbow trout to 30 cm
Brook trout to 30 cm
Vine Creek is a very minor tributary of the Athabasca River, and joins just west of Jasper Lake. Vine Creek holds small rainbow and brook trout.

Vine Creek beaver dams (NP)
Rainbow trout to 30 cm
Brook trout to 30 cm
There are a series of beaver dams on Vine Creek, within easy walking distance of the Celestine Lake Road. These dams have been stocked in the past with both rainbow and brook trout. However, reproductive success among the trout planted has been limited at best, and fish are present in small numbers.

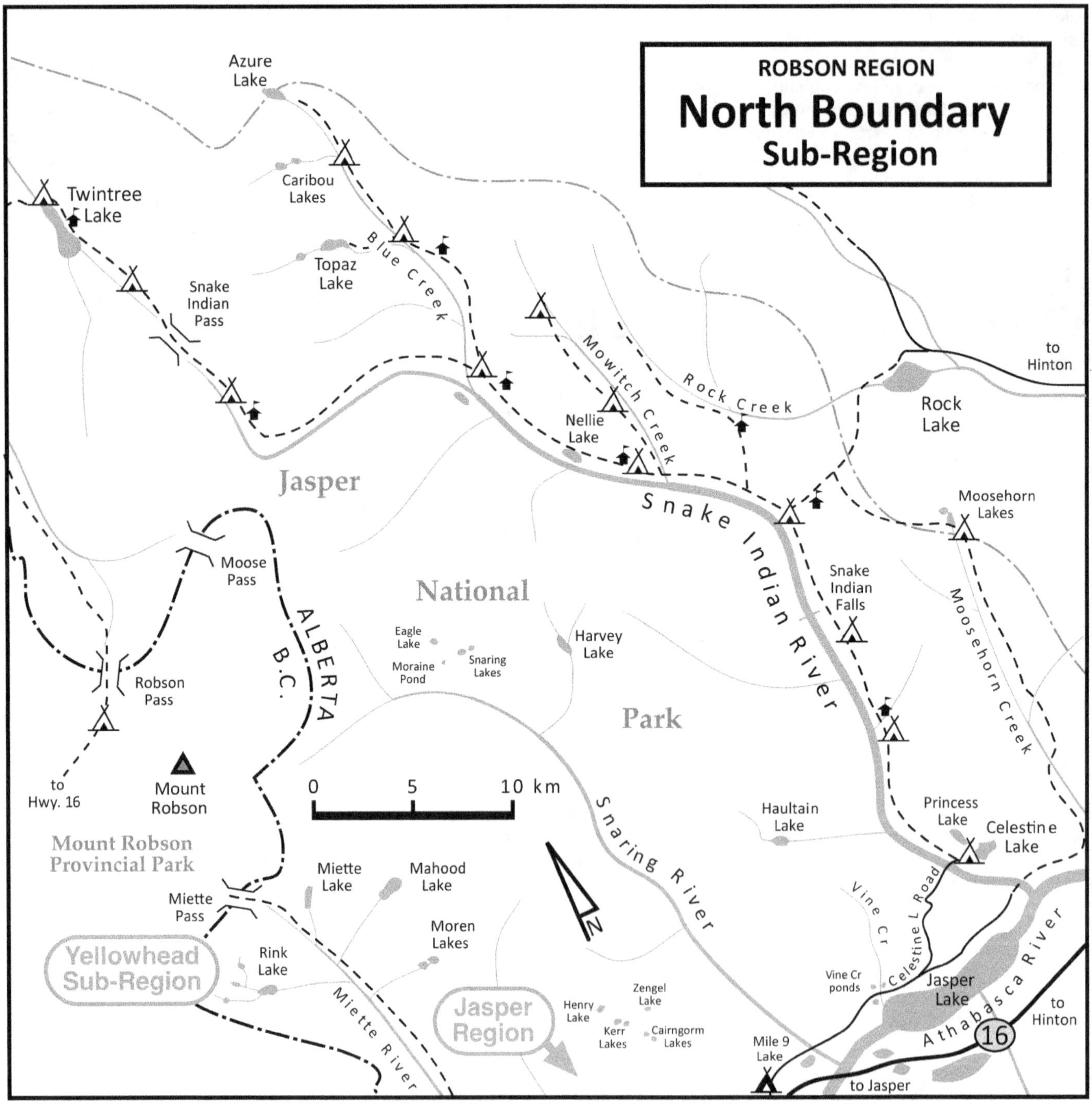

ROBSON REGION: North Boundary Sub-Region

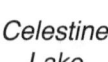

Note: To reach the Celestine and Princess Lakes and North Boundary Trail trailheads, the upper portion of Celestine Lake Road must be negotiated. The final 5 km of the road is currently inaccessible, and must be hiked or biked. Check with the Parks Canada Information Centre in Jasper for updated information.

Celestine Lake (NP)
Rainbow trout to 65 cm (3.0 kg)
Celestine Lake is a 7 km hike from the end of the drivable portion of the Celestine Lake Road. The lake attracts anglers and sightseers alike each summer. The lake's appealing green waters hold rainbow trout averaging 25-40 cm in length, but due to extended shallows around much of the lake and heavy forest cover, those fly fishing will encounter problems. Boats are available for rent through prior arrangement with one of Jasper's sporting goods stores.

Celestine Lake

ROBSON REGION: North Boundary Sub-Region

Princess Lake (NP)
Brook trout to 50 cm (1.5 kg)

The long, narrow form of Princess Lake is located alongside the Celestine Lake trail. Most anglers bypass Princess Lake on their way to Celestine Lake. However, Princess Lake offers decent fishing, and holds fair numbers of brook trout ranging from 20-35 cm in length. Ringed by reeds, Princess will cause troubles for those who are fly casting. Early morning and late evening is when the fish tend to enter the shallows to feed, and will be the most successful time of day for fly fishing.

Princess Lake

Snake Indian River (NP)
Bull trout to 55 cm (2.0 kg)
Rainbow trout to 40 cm
Whitefish to 45 cm

The Snake Indian River is a constant companion to the eastern half of the North Boundary Trail. The Snake Indian River runs muddy much of the summer, and offers little in the way of fishing until early August. At that time, rainbows, bull trout and whitefish can be taken along the entire length of the river. The areas at the confluence with tributaries usually offer the best fishing. Many of the river's overflow lakes hold trout, although marsh generally accompanies these areas. Only a small number of foot or horse parties regularly make their way beyond thunderous Snake Indian Falls, located 21 km from the eastern trailhead at Celestine Lake. The distance from Celestine Lake to the Berg Lake trailhead via the North Boundary Trail is a staggering 175 km.

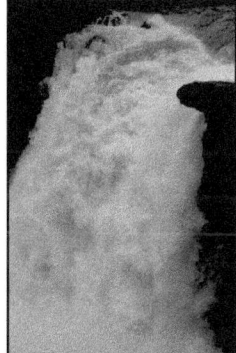
Snake Indian Falls

Snake Indian River

Haultain Lake (NP)
Status: Unknown

Secluded Haultain Lake is set in a valley to the southwest of the Snake Indian River, and remains virtually untouched by civilization. Although the lake was stocked in the past with both cutthroat and rainbow trout, unconfirmed reports indicate that only a few rainbow are still present.

Nellie Lake (NP)
Bull trout to 50 cm (1.5 kg)
Rainbow trout to 35 cm

This large, shallow lake is located 50 km from the Celestine Lake trailhead. It offers only limited opportunities for anglers. The marshy shoreline, complete with reeds, makes access very difficult. Bull and rainbow trout along with the odd whitefish tend to make their way to and from the nearby Snake Indian River, but never seem to be present in large numbers in the lake.

Nellie Lake

Topaz Lake (NP)
Rainbow trout to 55 cm (2.0 kg)
Bull trout to 70 cm (4.0 kg)

Topaz Lake is set in the Blue Creek drainage, the most scenically impressive corner of the entire North Boundary Sub-Region. Topaz Lake attracts only a limited number of visitors due to the extremely long access of over 60 km from the Celestine Lake trailhead. Topaz Lake holds rainbow and bull trout in the 30-45 cm range in good numbers, ample reward for the few anglers who do make it in each year.

Caribou Lakes (NP)
Rainbow trout to 50 cm (1.5 kg)
Bull trout to 70 cm (4.0 kg)

The Caribou Lakes are another link in the chain of sparkling lakes to the west of Blue Creek. The Caribou Lakes contain plenty of good-sized rainbow and bull trout. Angling quality should remain high in these lakes for many years to come, as fishing pressure will undoubtedly be light.

Azure (Indigo) Lake (NP)
Rainbow trout to 50 cm (1.5 kg)
Bull trout to 70 cm (4.0 kg)

Beautifully coloured Azure Lake is much like Topaz and Caribou Lakes to the south, and offers much to those who put forth the extra effort to reach its shore. Outstanding scenery and excellent fishing for rainbow and bull trout averaging 30-40 cm are all wrapped up in this package. Fortunately, distances are great enough to ensure that Azure should remain unspoiled.

ROBSON REGION: North Boundary Sub-Region

Twintree Lake (NP)
Rainbow trout to 70 cm (4.0 kg)
Twintree Lake is located in the most remote corner of Jasper National Park, and is reached via the North Boundary Trail. Twintree Lake is a distant 65 km hike from the Berg Lake trailhead, and an even more distant 105 km hike from the Celestine Lake Road trailhead. Suffice to say that Twintree Lake receives very little fishing pressure each year. Twintree is a large lake, and is normally silted for much of the summer. The fishing picks up only as the lake begins to clear in August. Large rainbow trout, many in the 40-50 cm range, are present in Twintree Lake, although their numbers are not overwhelming. Due to the size of the lake, anglers are advised to work the waters around any inlet creeks where the water is liable to be clearer.

Twintree Lake

Kerr Lakes, Cairngorm Lakes, Zengel Lake, Henry Lake (NP)
Status: Devoid of fish
This cluster of lakes is located in the remote backcountry northwest of Jasper. Access is very difficult, and the area is for explorers only. None of the lakes have ever been stocked, and it is unlikely that any contain fish.

Eagle Lake, Moraine Pond, Snaring Lakes (NP)
Status: Devoid of fish
These lakes are found in the upper Snaring River drainage. They are very isolated and access is extremely arduous. They have not been stocked and contain no fish.

Rink Lake (NP)
Status: Devoid of fish
Rink Lake is located in a side valley to the west of the upper Miette River, beneath the peaks that form the B.C.-Alberta boundary. It has never been stocked and contains no fish.

Moren Lakes (NP)
Status: Devoid of fish
The two small Moren Lakes are set in an isolated valley to the east of the upper Miette Valley. The lakes have never been stocked, and reportedly contain no fish.

Mahood Lake (NP)
Status: Unknown
This large lake is set in a side valley west of the Miette River headwaters, and has never been stocked. Due to its isolated position, few anglers ever make their way into Mahood Lake. It is possible that bull trout have made their way into the lake from the Miette River.

Miette Lake (NP)
Bull trout to 50 cm (1.5 kg)
Miette Lake is at the headwaters of the Miette River, an arduous 25 km hike from the Yellowhead Highway. The lake is west of Miette Pass, and is reached by only a few hikers and outfitters each summer. Miette Lake holds a limited number of bull trout averaging 30-40 cm in length.

Miette (Centre) Pass

Blue Creek, Mowitch Creek (NP)
Bull trout to 60 cm (2.5 kg)
These major tributaries to the Snake Indian River hold limited numbers of bull trout. Access is from the North Boundary Trail, and distances involved are very long. These destinations are for backpacking expeditions only.

Rock Lake (AB)
Lake trout to 90 cm (10.0 kg)
Bull trout to 65 cm (3.0 kg)
Whitefish to 50 cm (1.5 kg)
Rainbow trout to 40 cm
Rock Lake is situated in a heavily wooded valley just west of the Wildhay River. It is accessed from Highway 40 on the Rock Lake Road. Rock Lake attracts many anglers each season. The lake's deep waters hold some lake trout of immense proportions as well as whitefish, bull trout, rainbow trout and the odd pike. Although it is possible to fish from shore from a number of locations, a boat is strongly recommended since trolling deep can be very effective. The campground at Rock Lake is very popular and is usually filled to capacity each weekend during the summer.

Moosehorn Lakes (AB)
Cutthroat trout to 50 cm (1.5 kg)
The Moosehorn Lakes are located just outside the north boundary of Jasper National Park. The lakes are accessed by two main trails, one from the Celestine Lake Road and the other from Rock Lake. Both access trails are over 30 km in length. The Moosehorn Lakes are reported to contain cutthroat trout in good numbers, averaging 25-35 cm in length.

Index to
Lakes, Rivers and Streams
of the Canadian Rockies

FISHING THE CANADIAN ROCKIES: Index

Regions
Banff 157
Canal Flats 115
Canmore 148
Columbia 133
Crowsnest 67
Elkford 86
Fernie 73
Flathead 36
Foothills 99
Icefields 206
Invermere 128
Jasper 214
Kananaskis 105
Koocanusa 42
Kootenay Park 143
Livingstone 92
Louise 170
North Saskatchewan 197
Palliser 122
Robson 224
Skoki 183
Skookumchuck 80
Waterton 25
West Castle 58
Yoho Park 190

Sub-Regions
Abraham (North Saskatchewan Region) 202
Akamina-Kishinena (Flathead Region) 36
Assiniboine (Palliser Region) 125
Baker (Skoki Region) 183
Barrier (Kananaskis Region) 110
Beaver Mines (West Castle Region) 58
Bellevue (Crowsnest Region) 70
Brazeau (Icefields Region) 209
Brisco (Columbia Region) 133
Cascade (Banff Region) 160
Castle Junction (Louise Region) 170
Chain Lakes (Foothills Region) 99
Coleman (Crowsnest Region) 67
Corbin (Fernie Region) 77
Egypt (Banff Region) 166
Elk Lakes Park (Elkford Region) 88
Elko (Koocanusa Region) 42
Emerald (Yoho Park Region) 192
Fording (Elkford Region) 86
Fort Steele (Koocanusa Region) 52
Front Ranges (Skoki Region) 185
Hector (Louise Region) 176
Height of the Rockies (Palliser Region) 122
Highwood (Livingstone Region) 94
Hosmer (Fernie Region) 73
Jaffray (Koocanusa Region) 46
Kicking Horse (Yoho Park Region) 194
Lougheed Park (Kananaskis Region) 105
Lower Elbow (Foothills Region) 101
Maligne (Jasper Region) 221
Marvel (Canmore Region) 154
Miette (Jasper Region) 214
Minnewanka (Banff Region) 1567
Mistaya (North Saskatchewan Region) 197
Mountain View (Waterton Region) 32
North Boundary (Robson Region) 227
O'Hara (Yoho Park Region) 190
Oldman (Livingstone Region) 92
Parson (Columbia Region) 138
Pincher (West Castle Region) 63
Premier (Skookumchuck Region) 82
Prince of Wales (Waterton Region) 25
Saskatchewan Crossing (N. Sask. Region) 199
Sibbald (Foothills Region) 102
Skyline (Jasper Region) 217
Smith-Dorrien (Canmore Region) 151
Sparwood (Fernie Region) 74
Sunshine (Banff Region) 163
Tamarack (Waterton Region) 28
Temple (Louise Region) 174
Three Sisters (Canmore Region) 148
Tonquin (Icefields Region) 211
Upper Athabasca (Icefields Region) 206
Upper Elbow (Kananaskis Region) 108
Upper Flathead (Flathead Region) 38
Upper Kootenay (Kootenay Park Region) 143
Vermilion (Kootenay Park Region) 146
Wardner (Koocanusa Region) 49
Wasa (Skookumchuck Region) 80
Westside (Invermere Region) 130
Whiteswan (Canal Flats Region) 119
Whitetail (Canal Flats Region) 115
Windermere (Invermere Region) 128
Yellowhead (Robson Region) 224

FISHING THE CANADIAN ROCKIES: Index

Lakes, Rivers and Streams
Abraham Lake 203
Abruzzi Lake 91
Adolphus Lake 227
Agnes Lake 175
Akamina Creek 36
Akamina Lake 30
Albert River 122
Alces Lake 119
Alderson Lake 27
Aldridge Creek 86
Aldridge Lakes 88
Alexander Creek 77
Alexandra Pond 202
Alexandra River 202
Alfred Lake 187
Alice Lake 182
Alkaline Lake 56
Allen Bill Pond 101
Allenby Lake 166
Allison Creek 68
Allison Reservoir 69
Allstones Lake 205
Altrude Creek 171
Altrude Lakes 171
Amber Lakes 219
Amethyst Lakes 211
Amiskwi River 193
Andy Good Creek 77
Andy Good Lake 78
Annette Lake (Jasper/Skyline) 218
Annette Lake (Louise/Temple) 177
Aosta Lakes 89
Arctomys Creek 201
Arnica Lake 171
Arrowhead Lake 213
Ashman Lake 37
Assiniboine Lake 127
Aster Lake 106
Astoria River 213
Astral Lake 151
Athabasca River 205, 217
Avalanche Lake 78
Azote Lake 210
Azure Lake 229

Back Lake 123
Badger Lake 162
Baird Lake 140
Baker Creek 185
Baker Lake 183
Baldy Lake 44
Barbour's Rock 130
Baril Creek 96
Barnaby Lake 62
Barnaby Ridge Lakes 62
Barnes Lake 77
Barren Lake 76
Barrier Lake 110
Bateman Creek Ponds 104
Bathing Lake 65
Baynes Lake 46
Bear Lake (Canal Flats/Whitetail) 118
Bear Lake (Koocanusa/Ft Steele) 53
Bear Paw Lake 82
Bear Pond (Foothills/Chain Lakes) 100
Beatrix Lake 227

Beatty Lake 123
Beau Lake 186
Beauvais Lake 63
Beaver Creek 94
Beaver Lake (Jasper/Maligne) 223
Beaver Lake (Westcastle/Beaver Mines) 58
Beaver Mines Creek 59
Beaver Mines Lake 58
Beaverdam Lake 34
Beaverfoot Ponds 145
Beaverfoot River 145
Beavertail Lake 38
Bednorski Lake 51
Belgium Lake 122
Belly River 32
Ben Able Creek 132
Bench Lake 215
Berg Lake 226
Bertha Lake 27
Beryl Lake (Flathead/U. Flathead) 39
Beryl Lake (Icefields/Tonquin) 213
Big Fish Lake 134
Big Iron Lake 100
Big Lake 76
Bighorn Creek (Koocanusa/Elko) 45
Bighorn Lake 162
Bighorn River (N. Sask/Abraham) 205
Billock Lake 41
Bingay Creek 86
Birdwood Lakes 154
Bittern Lake 141
Black Prince Lakes 152
Black Rock Lake 168
Blairmore Creek 69
Blakiston Creek 31
Blakiston Creek ponds 31
Bleasdell Creek 86
Block Lakes 162
Bloom Creek 52
Blue Creek 230
Blue Lake (Canal Flats/Whitetail) 117
Blue Lake (Elkford/Fording) 87
Blue Lake (Icefields/Brazeau) 210
Blue Lake (Invermere/Windermere) 129
Blue Lake (Koocanusa/Ft Steele) 55
Bluebottom Lake 48
Bluff Lake 130
Bobbie Burns Creek 141
Bogart Lakes 113
Boivin Creek 86
Boom Lake 170
Botts Lake 134
Boulder Lake (Banff/Cascade) 163
Boulder Lake (Elkford/Elk Lakes) 91
Boulton Creek 107
Boundary Creek 32
Bourgeau Lake 165
Bovin Lake 65
Bow Lake 178
Bow River 149, 159, 174, 177, 179
Brachineta Pond 211
Brachiopod Lake 183
Brazeau Lake 209
Brazeau River 209
Brewer Creek 116
Brewster Creek 166
Bridal Lake 138

Bronze Lake 56
Bruin Creek 94
Brule Creek 75
Bryant Creek 155
Buck Lake (Icefields/U. Athabasca) 207
Buck Lake (Koocanusa/Ft Steele) 56
Buffalo Creek ponds 28
Bugaboo Creek 142
Bull River 53
Buller Pond 154
Burks Pond 118
Burl Lakes 41
Burmis Lake 72
Burns Lake 109
Burstall Lakes 152
Burton Lake 44
Butcher Lake 64
Buttress Lake 213

Cabin Creek 39
Cabin Lake (Canmore/Marvel) 155
Cabin Lake (Jasper/Miette) 215
Cadorna Creek 90
Cadorna Lake 91
Cairn Lake 211
Cairn River 211
Cairngorm Lakes 230
Caithness Creek 48
Caldron Lake 197
Caledonia Lake 215
Cameron Creek 30
Cameron Lake 28
Campbell Lake 56
Campbell Meyer Lake 56
Canmore Beaver Ponds 149
Canmore Creek 149
Canmore Mines No. 3 Lake 149
Canuck Lake 83
Canyon Creek 102
Capricorn Lake 198
Carbon Creek 77
Carbondale River 63
Caribou Lakes 229
Carnarvon Creek 96
Carnarvon Lake 97
Carol Lakes 146
Carrot Creek 160
Carthew Lakes 27
Cartwright Lake 136
Cascade River 160
Castilleja Lake 186
Castle River 58
Castleguard River 202
Cat Creek 96
Cat's Eye Lake 82
Catacomb Lake 207
Cataract Brook (Yoho/O'Hara) 192
Cataract Creek (Livingstone/Highwood) 98
Cathedral Lakes 192
Cavell Lake 213
Caven Creek 52
Cavern Lake 219
Celeste Lake 194
Celestine Lake 228
Centaur Lakes 118
Centre Lake 219
Cerulean Lake 126

233

FISHING THE CANADIAN ROCKIES: Index

Regions
Banff 157
Canal Flats 115
Canmore 148
Columbia 133
Crowsnest 67
Elkford 86
Fernie 73
Flathead 36
Foothills 99
Icefields 206
Invermere 128
Jasper 214
Kananaskis 105
Koocanusa 42
Kootenay Park 143
Livingstone 92
Louise 170
North Saskatchewan 197
Palliser 122
Robson 224
Skoki 183
Skookumchuck 80
Waterton 25
West Castle 58
Yoho Park 190

Sub-Regions
Abraham (North Saskatchewan Region) 202
Akamina-Kishinena (Flathead Region) 36
Assiniboine (Palliser Region) 125
Baker (Skoki Region) 183
Barrier (Kananaskis Region) 110
Beaver Mines (West Castle Region) 58
Bellevue (Crowsnest Region) 70
Brazeau (Icefields Region) 209
Brisco (Columbia Region) 133
Cascade (Banff Region) 160
Castle Junction (Louise Region) 170
Chain Lakes (Foothills Region) 99
Coleman (Crowsnest Region) 67
Corbin (Fernie Region) 77
Egypt (Banff Region) 166
Elk Lakes Park (Elkford Region) 88
Elko (Koocanusa Region) 42
Emerald (Yoho Park Region) 192
Fording (Elkford Region) 86
Fort Steele (Koocanusa Region) 52
Front Ranges (Skoki Region) 185
Hector (Louise Region) 176
Height of the Rockies (Palliser Region) 122
Highwood (Livingstone Region) 94
Hosmer (Fernie Region) 73
Jaffray (Koocanusa Region) 46
Kicking Horse (Yoho Park Region) 194
Lougheed Park (Kananaskis Region) 105
Lower Elbow (Foothills Region) 101
Maligne (Jasper Region) 221
Marvel (Canmore Region) 154
Miette (Jasper Region) 214
Minnewanka (Banff Region) 1567
Mistaya (North Saskatchewan Region) 197
Mountain View (Waterton Region) 32
North Boundary (Robson Region) 227
O'Hara (Yoho Park Region) 190
Oldman (Livingstone Region) 92
Parson (Columbia Region) 138
Pincher (West Castle Region) 63
Premier (Skookumchuck Region) 82
Prince of Wales (Waterton Region) 25
Saskatchewan Crossing (N. Sask. Region) 199
Sibbald (Foothills Region) 102
Skyline (Jasper Region) 217
Smith-Dorrien (Canmore Region) 151
Sparwood (Fernie Region) 74
Sunshine (Banff Region) 163
Tamarack (Waterton Region) 28
Temple (Louise Region) 174
Three Sisters (Canmore Region) 148
Tonquin (Icefields Region) 211
Upper Athabasca (Icefields Region) 206
Upper Elbow (Kananaskis Region) 108
Upper Flathead (Flathead Region) 38
Upper Kootenay (Kootenay Park Region) 143
Vermilion (Kootenay Park Region) 146
Wardner (Koocanusa Region) 49
Wasa (Skookumchuck Region) 80
Westside (Invermere Region) 130
Whiteswan (Canal Flats Region) 119
Whitetail (Canal Flats Region) 115
Windermere (Invermere Region) 128
Yellowhead (Robson Region) 224

Lakes, Rivers and Streams

Abraham Lake 203
Abruzzi Lake 91
Adolphus Lake 227
Agnes Lake 175
Akamina Creek 36
Akamina Lake 30
Albert River 122
Alces Lake 119
Alderson Lake 27
Aldridge Creek 86
Aldridge Lakes 88
Alexander Creek 77
Alexandra Pond 202
Alexandra River 202
Alfred Lake 187
Alice Lake 182
Alkaline Lake 56
Allen Bill Pond 101
Allenby Lake 166
Allison Creek 68
Allison Reservoir 69
Allstones Lake 205
Altrude Creek 171
Altrude Lakes 171
Amber Lakes 219
Amethyst Lakes 211
Amiskwi River 193
Andy Good Creek 77
Andy Good Lake 78
Annette Lake (Jasper/Skyline) 218
Annette Lake (Louise/Temple) 177
Aosta Lakes 89
Arctomys Creek 201
Arnica Lake 171
Arrowhead Lake 213
Ashman Lake 37
Assiniboine Lake 127
Aster Lake 106
Astoria River 213
Astral Lake 151
Athabasca River 205, 217
Avalanche Lake 78
Azote Lake 210
Azure Lake 229

Back Lake 123
Badger Lake 162
Baird Lake 140
Baker Creek 185
Baker Lake 183
Baldy Lake 44
Barbour's Rock 130
Baril Creek 96
Barnaby Lake 62
Barnaby Ridge Lakes 62
Barnes Lake 77
Barren Lake 76
Barrier Lake 110
Bateman Creek Ponds 104
Bathing Lake 65
Baynes Lake 46
Bear Lake (Canal Flats/Whitetail) 118
Bear Lake (Koocanusa/Ft Steele) 53
Bear Paw Lake 82
Bear Pond (Foothills/Chain Lakes) 100
Beatrix Lake 227

Beatty Lake 123
Beau Lake 186
Beauvais Lake 63
Beaver Creek 94
Beaver Lake (Jasper/Maligne) 223
Beaver Lake (Westcastle/Beaver Mines) 58
Beaver Mines Creek 59
Beaver Mines Lake 58
Beaverdam Lake 34
Beaverfoot Ponds 145
Beaverfoot River 145
Beavertail Lake 38
Bednorski Lake 51
Belgium Lake 122
Belly River 32
Ben Able Creek 132
Bench Lake 215
Berg Lake 226
Bertha Lake 27
Beryl Lake (Flathead/U. Flathead) 39
Beryl Lake (Icefields/Tonquin) 213
Big Fish Lake 134
Big Iron Lake 100
Big Lake 76
Bighorn Creek (Koocanusa/Elko) 45
Bighorn Lake 162
Bighorn River (N. Sask/Abraham) 205
Billock Lake 41
Bingay Creek 86
Birdwood Lakes 154
Bittern Lake 141
Black Prince Lakes 152
Black Rock Lake 168
Blairmore Creek 69
Blakiston Creek 31
Blakiston Creek ponds 31
Bleasdell Creek 86
Block Lakes 162
Bloom Creek 52
Blue Creek 230
Blue Lake (Canal Flats/Whitetail) 117
Blue Lake (Elkford/Fording) 87
Blue Lake (Icefields/Brazeau) 210
Blue Lake (Invermere/Windermere) 129
Blue Lake (Koocanusa/Ft Steele) 55
Bluebottom Lake 48
Bluff Lake 130
Bobbie Burns Creek 141
Bogart Lakes 113
Boivin Creek 86
Boom Lake 170
Botts Lake 134
Boulder Lake (Banff/Cascade) 163
Boulder Lake (Elkford/Elk Lakes) 91
Boulton Creek 107
Boundary Creek 32
Bourgeau Lake 165
Bovin Lake 65
Bow Lake 178
Bow River 149, 159, 174, 177, 179
Brachineta Pond 211
Brachiopod Lake 183
Brazeau Lake 209
Brazeau River 209
Brewer Creek 116
Brewster Creek 166
Bridal Lake 138

Bronze Lake 56
Bruin Creek 94
Brule Creek 75
Bryant Creek 155
Buck Lake (Icefields/U. Athabasca) 207
Buck Lake (Koocanusa/Ft Steele) 56
Buffalo Creek ponds 28
Bugaboo Creek 142
Bull River 53
Buller Pond 154
Burks Pond 118
Burl Lakes 41
Burmis Lake 72
Burns Lake 109
Burstall Lakes 152
Burton Lake 44
Butcher Lake 64
Buttress Lake 213

Cabin Creek 39
Cabin Lake (Canmore/Marvel) 155
Cabin Lake (Jasper/Miette) 215
Cadorna Creek 90
Cadorna Lake 91
Cairn Lake 211
Cairn River 211
Cairngorm Lakes 230
Caithness Creek 48
Caldron Lake 197
Caledonia Lake 215
Cameron Creek 30
Cameron Lake 28
Campbell Lake 56
Campbell Meyer Lake 56
Canmore Beaver Ponds 149
Canmore Creek 149
Canmore Mines No. 3 Lake 149
Canuck Lake 83
Canyon Creek 102
Capricorn Lake 198
Carbon Creek 77
Carbondale River 63
Caribou Lakes 229
Carnarvon Creek 96
Carnarvon Lake 97
Carol Lakes 146
Carrot Creek 160
Carthew Lakes 27
Cartwright Lake 136
Cascade River 160
Castilleja Lake 186
Castle River 58
Castleguard River 202
Cat Creek 96
Cat's Eye Lake 82
Catacomb Lake 207
Cataract Brook (Yoho/O'Hara) 192
Cataract Creek (Livingstone/Highwood) 98
Cathedral Lakes 192
Cavell Lake 213
Caven Creek 52
Cavern Lake 219
Celeste Lake 194
Celestine Lake 228
Centaur Lakes 118
Centre Lake 219
Cerulean Lake 126

Linda Lake 191
Line Creek 75
Lineham Lake North 30
Lineham Lake South 30
Lineham Lakes 30
Linnet Lake 28
Little Baker Lake 183
Little Beaverdam Lake 34
Little Bull Creek 53
Little Cameron Lake 30
Little Elbow River 102
Little Ha Has Lake 81
Little Herbert Lake 178
Little Honeymoon Lake 207
Little Mitten Lake 141
Little Yoho River 194
Livingstone River 93
Lizard Creek 73
Lizard Lake (Fernie/Hosmer) 74
Lizard Lake (Louise/Castle Junction) 174
Lodgepole Creek 45
Lone Duck Lake 192
Lone Lake 30
Lonesome Lake 28
Loomis Creek 96
Loomis Lake 97
Loon Lake (Columbia/Parson) 140
Loon Lake (Koocanusa/Elko) 45
Lorraine Lake 222
Lost Creek (Livingstone/Highwood) 98
Lost Creek (Westcastle/Beaver Mines) 63
Lost Horse Lake 162
Lost Lake (Canmore/Smith-Dorrien) 153
Lost Lake (Elkford/Fording) 85
Lost Lake (Invermere/Windermere) 129
Lost Lake (Kananaskis/Barrier) 114
Lost Lake (Koocanusa/Wardner) 52
Lost Lake (Louise/Temple) 177
Lost Lake (Waterton/Tamarack) 31
Lost Lake (Westcastle/Beaver Mines) 63
Louise Lake 174
Lower Aosta Lake 89
Lower Elk Lake 88
Lower Kananaskis Lake 105
Lower Southfork Lake 62
Lower Waterton Lake 25
Lowerslate Lake 210
Lucerne Lake 224
Luellen Lake 173
Lund Lake 49
Lunette Lake 127
Lusk Creek 104
Lussier River 85, 121
Lynx Creek 63
Lyons Creek 68
Lys Lake 62
Lyttle Lake 129

Maccarib Creek 2121
Macdonald Creek 63
Magog Lake 125
Mahood Lake 230
Maiyuk Creek 124
Maligne Lake 221
Maligne River 223
Mami Lake 34
Manistee Lake 48

Margaret Lake 179
Marion Lake 145
Marjorie Lake 215
Marl Lake (Flathead/U. Flathead) 39
Marl Lake (Kananaskis/Lougheed) 107
Marna Lake 63
Marpole Lake 194
Marr Lake 35
Martin Lake 187
Marushka Lake 156
Marvel Lake 154
Marvel Pass Lakes 155
Mary Lake (Louise/Hector) 178
Mary Lake (Yoho/O'Hara) 191
Maskinonge Lake 27
Maude Lake 107
McArthur Lake 190
McBaines Lake 49
McGillivray Creek 68
McGillivray Pond 151
McLatchie Creek 39
McLean Pond 102
McNair Lakes (Skookumchuck/Premier) 84
McNair Pond (Louise/Temple) 177
McPhail Creek 96
McPhail Creek ponds 97
McPhail Lake 97
Medicine Lake 223
Medicine Tent Lakes 211
Meinsinger Lake 101
Memorial Lakes 113
Merlin Lake 186
Michel Creek 77
Michel Creek ponds 77
Michele Lakes 205
Middle Waterton Lake 25
Middlepass Creek 39
Middlepass Lakes 41
Miette Lake 230
Miette River 217
Mildred Lake 218
Mile 14 JE Lake 220
Mile 16 1/2 JB Lake 220
Mile 27 1/2 JB Lake 207
Mile 54 JB Lake 207
Mile 9 Lake 227
Mill Creek 59
Mina Lake 215
Minaga Creek 217
Minewakun Lake 175
Minnestimma Lakes 175
Minnewanka Lake 157
Minnow Lake 215
Mirror Lake (Koocanusa/Jaffray) 49
Mirror Lake (Louise/Temple) 174
Mist Creek 96
Mistaya Lake 197
Mistaya River 197
Mitchell Lake 55
Mitchell River 127
Mite Lake 76
Mitten Lake 140
Moab Lake 208
Moat Creek 212
Moat Lake 211
Mona Lake 222
Monroe Lake 120

Monument Lake 90
Moose Bath 126
Moose Lake (Canal Flats/Whiteswan) 119
Moose Lake (Columbia/Parson) 140
Moose Lake (Columbia/Parson) 141
Moose Lake (Jasper/Maligne) 222
Moose Lake (Louise/Hector) 181
Moose Lake (Robson/Yellowhead) 225
Moose River 225
Moosehorn Lakes 230
Moraine Creek 175
Moraine Lake (Louise/Temple) 175
Moraine Pond (Robson/N. Boundary) 230

Moren Lake 230
Morin Creek 71
Morning Glory Lakes 191
Mosquito Lake (Louise/Hector) 181
Mosquito Pond (Louise/Hector) 179
Mount Lorette Ponds 111
Mowitch Creek 230
Mud Lake (Canmore/Smith-Dorrien) 152
Mud Lake (Louise/Temple) 177
Mummy Lake 166
Munn Lake 131
Murray Lake 49
Muskrat Lake 48
Myosotis Lake (Banff/Cascade) 163
Myosotis Lake (Skoki/Baker) 185
Mystery Lake (Elkford/ Elk Lakes) 91
Mystery Lake (Jasper/Skyline) 221
Mystic Lake 163
Narao Lakes 196
Natalko Lake 168
Nellie Lake 229
Nestor Lake 126
Nez Perce Creek 68
Nine Bay Lake 141
Nixon Lake (Columbia/Parson) 140
Nixon Lake (Koot Park/U. Kootenay) 144
Norbury Creek 53
Norbury Lake 55
Nordstrum Creek 75
Norman Lake 201
North Saskatchewan River 199, 203
North Scarpe Lake 62
North Star Lake 48
North White River 120
Northcote Lake 131
Numa Creek 147

O'Brien Lake 170
O'Hara Lake 190
O'Rourke Lake 88
Obstruction Lakes 210
Ochre Creek 147
Odlum Creek 96
Odlum Pond 98
Oesa Lake 190
Og Lake 126
Oldman Reservoir 65
Oldman River 66, 92
Oldman River Campground Pond 65
Olive Lake 143
Opabin Lake 190
Opal Lake 223
Oreamnos Lake 210

Osprey Lake 207
Otterhead River 196
Ottertail Lake 196
Ottertail River 196
Outlet Creek 135
Outpost Lake (Icefields/Tonquin) 213
Outpost Lake (Waterton/Mtn View) 32
Outram Lake 201
Ouzel Lakes 211
Owl Lake 155
Oyster Creek 93

Packhorse Creek 39
Paddy Ryan Lakes 132
Paine Lake 34
Paint Pots 147
Palliser Lake 123
Palliser River 122
Palmer Ranch 35
Panther Lakes 189
Panther River 189
Paradise Creek 177
Pasque Creek 93
Patricia Lake 214
Payne Lake 34
Peckhams Lake 55
Peyto Lake 197
Phalarope Lake 211
Pharaoh Creek 168
Pharaoh Lake 168
Phillipps Lake 68
Pickering Lakes 56
Picklejar Creek 96
Picklejar Lakes 96
Pigeon Creek 150
Pika Lakes 211
Pilot Pond 174
Pincher Creek 64
Pinto Lake 201
Pipestone Lake 181
Pipestone River 178
Pipit Lake 189
Plumbob Creek 52
Poboktan Lake 210
Pocaterra Creek 107
Polar Lake 38
Police Lake 32
Police Outpost Lake 32
Policeman Creek 149
Portal Creek 212
Portal Lake 224
Powder Lake 88
Prairie Bluff Lake 64
Prairie Creek 102
Premier Lake 82
Princess Lake 229
Procter Lake 39
Ptarmigan Lake (Canal Flats/Whiteswan) 120
Ptarmigan Lake (Skoki/Baker) 185
Ptarmigan Lake (Waterton/Tamarack) 30
Pyramid Lake 214

Quarrie Lake (Palliser/HOTR) 124
Quarry Lake (Canmore/Three Sisters) 149
Quartz Lake 82
Queen Mary Lake 123
Quinn Creek 53

Quirk Creek 102

Racehorse Creek 92
Rae Lake 108
Rainbow Lake (Banff/Cascade) 162
Rainbow Ponds (Crowsnest/Bellevue) 72
Rainy Lakes 61
Rainy Ridge Lake 61
Rainy Ridge Lake, Upper 61
Ralph Lake 123
Ram Creek 45
Ranger Creek 102
Ranger Lakes 152
Rathlin Lake 215
Raven Lake 45
Rawson Lake 106
Red Deer Lakes 186
Red Deer River 187
Redcliff Lake 140
Redearth Creek 169
Redoubt Lake 185
Reed Lakes 82
Replica Lake 211
Ribbon Creek 113
Ribbon Lake 113
Rice Creek 99
Ridge Creek 94
Riley Lake 215
Rink Lake 230
Riverside Lake 91
Robson River 225
Rock Creek ponds 72
Rock Isle Lake 165
Rock Lake (Palliser/Assiniboine) 127
Rock Lake (Robson/N. Boundary) 230
Rock Lake (Skookumchuck/Wasa) 79
Rockbluff Lake 82
Rockbound Lake 173
Rockwall Lake 107
Rocky Point Lake 138
Rocky River 221
Rosen Lake 49
Ross Lake 195
Rothwell Lake 49
Rowe Lakes 30
Ruault Lake 53
Ruby Lake (Waterton/Tamarack) 31
Ruby Lake (Westcastle/Beaver Mines) 62
Rummel Lake 152
Running Rain Lake 96
Russell Lake 124

Sage Creek 38
Sam's Folly Lake 131
Sand Creek 48
Sand Lake 49
Saturday Night Lake 216
Saugum Lake 57
Savanna Creek 94
Sawback Lake 162
Scarab Lake 166
Scarpe Creek 59
Schaeffer Lake 191
Screwdriver Creek 59
Scud Lake 87
Serpent Lake 141
Seven Mile Lake 51

Shadow Lake 169
Shallow Lake 118
Shark Lake 156
Sheep Lakes 110
Sheep River 110
Sherbrooke Lake 196
Shotnana Lake 45
Shuswap Creek 129
Sibbald Creek 103
Sibbald Lake 103
Sibbald Meadows Pond 103
Siffleur River 181, 204
Silent Lakes 140
Silent Pass Lakes 140
Silver Spring Lakes 42
Simon's Lake 51
Simpson River 147
Sink Lake 196
Skeleton Lake 187
Skoki Lakes 185
Skookumchuck Creek 84
Slacker Creek 93
Slide Lake 137
Smith Lake 173
Smith-Dorrien Creek 152
Smoky River 227
Smuts Creek 153
Smuts Lakes 154
Snake Indian River 229
Snaring Lakes 230
Snaring River 227
Snow Creek Summit ponds 189
Snowflake Lake 189
Snowshoe Creek 63
Snowshoe Lake 44
Solar Lake 81
Sounding Lake 107
South Castle River 58
South Drywood Creek 65
South Galatea Lake 114
South Ghost Lake 151
South Scarpe Lake 61
Southesk Lake 210
Southesk River 211
Southfork Lakes 62
Sowerby Lake 81
Sparkle Lake 121
Sparrows-Egg Lake 107
Spears Creek 94
Sphinx Lake 168
Spillimacheen River 140
Spillway Lake 107
Spionkop Creek 65
Spray Lakes Reservoir 148
Spray River 156, 160
Spring Lakes 49
Spurr Lake 117
Square Lake 168
Squaw Creek 39
St. Eloi Brook 39
Star Creek 68
Starvation Lake 37
Station Creek 93
Steamboat Lake 133
Steele Brothers Ponds 151
Stenton Lake (Canmore/Three Sisters) 151
Stenton Pond (Banff/Cascade) 160

FISHING THE CANADIAN ROCKIES: Index

Stevens Lake 81
Stewart Creek 150
Stewart Lake 137
Stimson Creek 101
Stink Lake 48
Stoddart Creek 129
Stony Creek (Banff/Cascade) 160
Stony Creek (Foothills/Sibbald) 104
Stony Creek (Livingstone/Highwood) 96
Stony Creek ponds 160
Stony Lake 81
Stony Pothole Lake 81
Storm Creek 96
Storm Lake (Livingstone/Highwood) 96
Storm Lakes (Koot Park/Vermilion) 147
Strawberry Creek 96
Strawberry Lake 35
Suicide Creek 59
Summer Creek 53
Summer Lake 53
Summit Creek 77
Summit Lake (Columbia/Parson) 138
Summit Lake (Fernie/Corbin) 77
Summit Lake (Jasper/Maligne) 223
Summit Lake (Waterton/Tamarack) 30
Summit Lake (Yoho/Kicking Horse) 195
Summit Lakes (Jasper/Maligne) 223
Sunburst Lake 126
Sundance Creek ponds 160
Sunkist Lake 41
Sunset Lake 165
Sunwapta Lake 202
Sunwapta Pass Lake 202
Sunwapta River 206
Surprise Lake 223
Surveyors Lake 47
Suzanne Lake 48
Syncline Brook 59

Ta Ta Lake 82
Talbot Lake 220
Talc Lake 168
Talus Lake 110
Tamarack Lake 84
Tanglefoot Creek 53
Taylor Lake 170
Teardrop Lake 101
Ted's Lake 44
Teepee Creek 52
Tekarra Lake 219
Temple Lake 175
Templeton Lake 137
Templeton River 137
Tent Mountain Lake   68
Terrapin Lake 154
Tershishner Creek 205
Thomas Lake 44
Thomson Lake 37
Three Island Lake (Columbia/Parson) 138
Three Isle Lake (Kananaskis/Lougheed) 107
Three Mile Lake 39
Three Sisters Creek 150
Tie Lake 49
Tilted Lake 183
Timber Creek 99
Tipperary Lake 123
Tobermory Creek 90

Toby Creek 130
Todd Creek 66
Tokumm Creek 146
Tombstone Lakes 109
Topaz Lake (Columbia/Brisco) 136
Topaz Lake (Robson/N. Boundary) 229
Totem Lake 199
Tough Creek 32
Tower Lake (Louise/Castle Junction) 173
Tower Lakes (Canal Flats/Whiteswan) 121
Trefoil Lakes 218
Trident Lake 187
Tryst Lake 153
Turquoise Lake 179
Turtle Lake 83
Twin Lake (Koocanusa/Wardner) 52
Twin Lakes (Columbia/Brisco) 134
Twin Lakes (Invermere/Windermere) 129
Twin Lakes (Koocanusa/Wardner) 51
Twin Lakes (Louise/Castle Junction) 171
Twin Lakes (Skookumchuck/Premier) 83
Twin Lakes (Waterton/Tamarack) 31
Twintree Lake 230
Two Jack Lake 157
Upper Aosta Lake 89
Upper Diorite Lake 85
Upper Elk Lake 88
Upper Kananaskis Lake 105
Upper Little Elbow Lake 110
Upper Rainy Ridge Lake 61
Upper Southfork Lake 62
Upper Waterton Lake 25
Upperslate Lake 210
Utopia Lake 221

Valley of the Five Lakes 218
Vera Lake   192
Verdant Creek 147
Vermilion Lakes (Banff/Minnewanka) 159
Vermilion Pond (Koot Park/Vermilion) 147
Vermilion River 147
Vicary Creek 93
Victoria Lake 190
Vine Creek 227
Vine Creek beaver dams 227
Virl Lake 217
Vista Lake 171

Wabasso Lake 218
Wall Lake   36
Wapiti Lake (Koocanusa/Jaffray) 48
Wapiti Pond (Icefields/Brazeau) 211
Wapta Lake 196
Warden Lake (Koot Park/U. Kootenay) 144
Warden Lakes (N. Sask/Sask Crossing) 201
Wardle Creek 147
Warm Lake 48
Warspite Lake 152
Wasa Lake 79
Watchman Lake 202
Waterfowl Lakes 198
Waterton Lake, Lower 25
Waterton Lake, Middle 25
Waterton Lake, Upper 25
Waterton Reservoir 34
Waterton River 27, 34
Waterton Shell Pond 64

Watridge Lake 156
Weary Creek 90
Weatherhead Lake 56
Webber Lake 41
Wedge Pond 111
Wedgwood Lake 126
Wells Lakes 146
Wendy Lake 137
West Castle River 59
West Galatea Lake 152
West Scarpe Lake 62
West Wind Creek 150
Westcastle River 59
Whary Lake 134
Wheeler Creek 77
Whirlpool River 208
Whiskey Creek ponds 159
Whiskey Lake 98
White Creek 94
White River 120, 124
White River, East 120
White River, North 120
White's Dam 132
Whitegoat Lakes 204
Whiteman Pond 149
Whiteswan Lake 119
Whitetail Lake 117
Whitewater Lake 211
Wigmore Pond 189
Wigwam River 44
Wilbur Lake 138
Wild Horse Creek 52
Wilimena Lake 76
Wilkinson Creek 98
Willow Creek 99
Wilmer Lake 131
Wilson Lake 210
Wind Creek 150
Wind Pond 150
Windermere Creek 128
Windermere Lake 128
Window Mountain Lake 70
Wisht Lake 210
Witney Lake 224
Wolf Creek 81
Wolverine Lake (Elkford/Elk Lakes) 91
Wolverine Pond (Icefields/Brazeau) 210

Yankee Lake 83
Yarrow Creek 65
Yellowhead Lake 224
Yoho Lake 194
Yoho River 194
York Creek 68
Yukness Lake 190

Zengel Lake 230
Zigadenus Lake 185

ABOUT THE AUTHOR

Joey Ambrosi (B.A., M.A., M.Des.) enjoys life in the Canadian Rockies. Fishing and hiking are his particular passions. He has hiked over 16,000 kilometres in the Rockies, and has personally visited and fished the vast majority of the waters in this book. When not fishing or hiking in the Rockies, he loves to spend time with his family. Travel is a favourite activity, and the author has been to Japan, Australia, Fiji, Costa Rica, England, Italy, South Africa, Zimbabwe, as well as numerous locations within Canada and the United States. He has previously authored four books; *Hiking Alberta's Southwest*, *Fly Fishing the Canadian Rockies*, *The Courthouse*, and *Hiking the Southern Rockies*, as well as newspaper and magazine articles on hiking and fishing. The author currently lives in the Crowsnest Pass in southern Alberta with his wife Valerie and son Tyler.

RESEARCH ASSISTANT

Jim "Mr. Kananaskis" Rennels of Calgary provided assistance to the author on current fish status in Southern Alberta, including Banff National Park. In addition to his other credits, Jim organizes backcountry trips for youth groups, who claim that "he knows every rock on the trail".

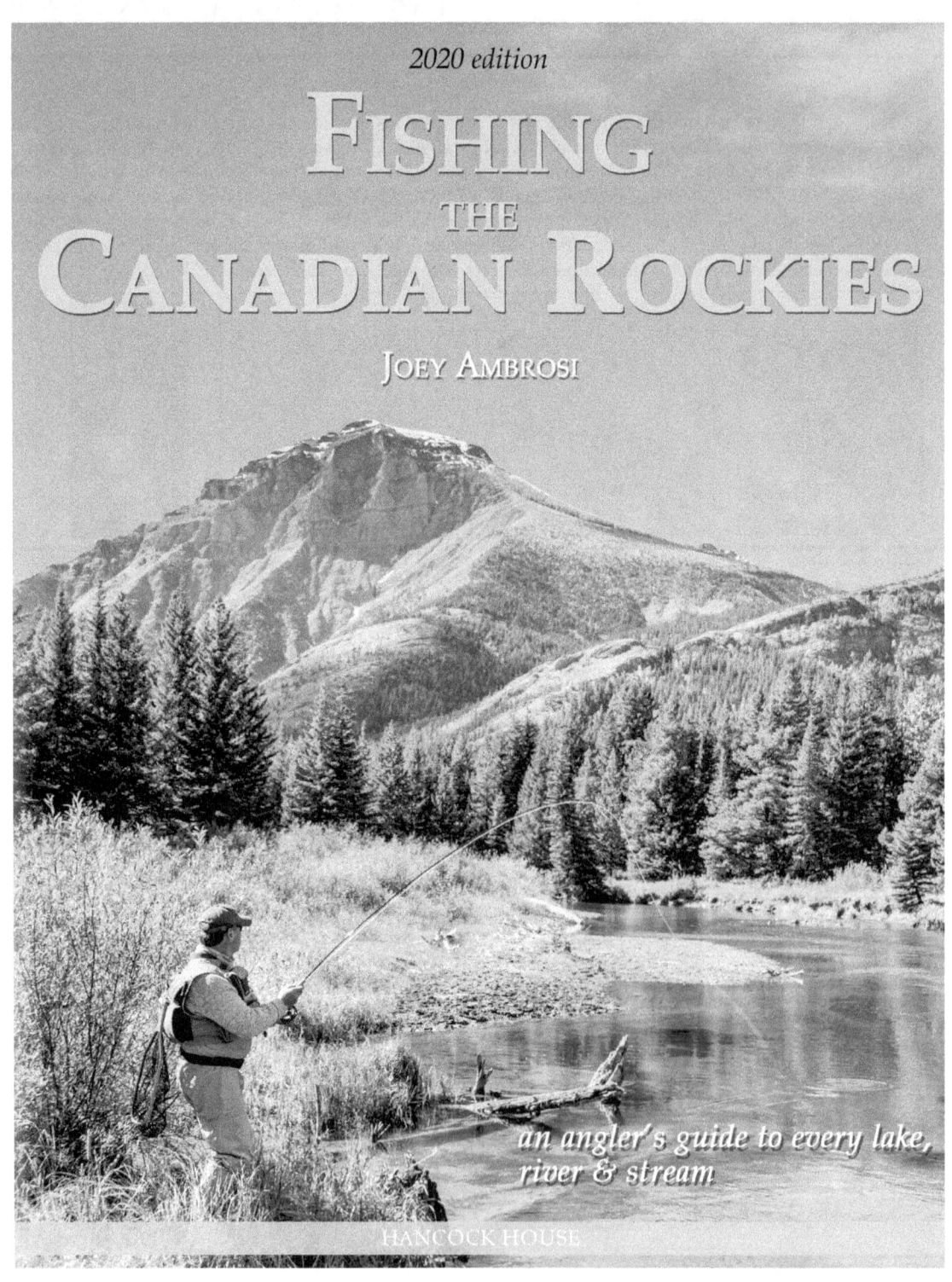

New 2020 Edition Revised and Updated!
- 100+ Maps of the Area ◆ 800+ Full Colour Photos
- Exhaustive Coverage of the Region

Available from HancockHouse.com